VICTORIOUS
LIVING

E. STANLEY JONES

EDITED AND UPDATED BY DEAN MERRILL

Summerside Press™
Minneapolis, MN 55438
www.summersidepress.com

Victorious Living
Original copyright © 1936 by E. Stanley Jones. This edited version copyright © 2010 by Dean Merrill.

ISBN 978-1-60936-136-5

All Scriptures, unless otherwise indicated, are taken from the Holy Bible, New International Version®, NIV®. Copyright © 1973, 1978, 1984 by Biblica, Inc.™ Used by permission of Zondervan. All rights reserved worldwide.

Scripture quotations marked with a cross symbol (†) are taken from The Holy Bible, New Living Translation, copyright © 1996, 2004. Used by permission of Tyndale House Publishers, Inc., Wheaton, Illinois. All rights reserved.

Scripture quotations marked "Moffatt" are taken with permission from The Bible: A New Translation, by James Moffatt, copyright © 1922, 1924, 1925, 1926, 1935 by Harper & Brothers, New York and London.

Scripture quotations marked "Weymouth" are taken from The New Testament in Modern Speech, translated by Richard Francis Weymouth, first published in 1903 by Harper & Brothers, New York and London, now in the public domain.

Scripture quotations marked "kjv" are taken from The Holy Bible, King James Version, now in public domain.

Scripture quotations marked "nkjv" are taken from The New King James Version. Copyright © 1982 by Thomas Nelson Inc. Used by permission.

Scripture quotations marked "asv" are taken from The Holy Bible, American Standard Version of 1901, now in public domain.

Author emphasis within Scripture verses is noted with italics.

Cover and Interior Design by Müllerhaus Publishing Group, www.mullerhaus.net

Photo used with grateful acknowledgment to Asbury College and Asbury Theological Seminary Archives.

Summerside Press™ is an inspirational publisher offering fresh, irresistible books to uplift the heart and engage the mind.

Printed in China.

VICTORIOUS LIVING

E. STANLEY JONES

EDITED AND UPDATED BY DEAN MERRILL

AN **ESJ** DEVOTIONAL

summerside

CONTENTS

A MAN AHEAD OF HIS TIME

E. Stanley Jones (1884-1973) was a Methodist missionary to India during the colonial period. His prolific writing and speaking brought God's truth in fresh ways to audiences both Eastern and Western, often challenging their assumptions and stretching their souls.

Born in Maryland, Jones first arrived in India in 1907 and was assigned to an English-speaking congregation in the city of Lucknow. But he soon showed a gift for connecting with the wider Indian culture, particularly the educated castes. He was a keen student of Hindu and Muslim mindsets, and he carried a deep passion that Christianity not present itself as a Western import. In a sense, he was "seeker-sensitive" at least seventy years before North Americans invented the label.

In 1930 he founded his first "ashram," a place for spiritual retreat that fit the Indian tradition but led many to consider the person of Christ. No doubt the richness of his devotional writing sprang in part from the times he spent there in reflection before God.

A good friend of Mahatma Gandhi (even when they disagreed), Jones spoke out for peace, justice, and racial harmony. He saw clearly that the British rule of this massive nation would have to cease—and said so with enough cogency that the British pulled his visa for six years.

A widely sought speaker in his day, E. Stanley Jones wrote twenty-eight books in all, the best known of which was *The Christ of the Indian Road* (1925). In 1938, *Time* magazine called him "the world's greatest Christian missionary." He was nominated for the Nobel Peace Prize in 1962, and received the Gandhi Peace Award the next year.

> *[Jesus] said to them, "Therefore every teacher of the law who has been instructed about the kingdom of heaven is like the owner of a house who brings out of his storeroom new treasures as well as old."*
>
> *Matthew 13:52*

Yet he never compromised his message. "The straightforward, open proclamation of Jesus is the best method," he wrote with all sincerity. "Jesus appeals to the soul as light appeals to the eye, as truth fits the conscience, as beauty speaks to the aesthetic nature. For Christ and the soul are made for one another.... But the Hindu insists, and rightly so, that it must not be 'an encrusted Christ.' It must not be a Christ bound with the grave clothes of long-buried doctrinal controversy, but a Christ as fresh and living and as untrammeled as the one that greeted Mary at the empty tomb."

In this book, re-edited for the twenty-first century, that Christ becomes real and vibrant again through the insights of a man who was, in more than one way, ahead of his time.

NOT YOUR ORDINARY DEVOTIONAL

When E. Stanley Jones began writing daily readings in the mid-1930s, he had more in mind than just giving a little morning boost, a miscellaneous thought or story to spark up people's day. His goals were substantial.

"In the structure of the book, I have tried to meet three needs," he wrote.

"1. A book of daily devotions for personal, group, and family devotions. Instead of making a book of scattered thoughts, changing from day to day, I have woven the devotions around one theme, victorious living.

"2. I have gathered these daily studies into groups of seven, so that the book can be used as a weekly study book by classes of various kinds.

"3. I have tried to put the subject matter into such a continuous whole that it may be read through as an ordinary book."

What this means is that we don't end each day's reading with a pretty bow tying up the package. We are rather being drawn along a trail, day after day, that takes us deeper and further into spiritual understanding. If we don't sense a "hurrah" or an applause line at the bottom of every page, that is because Jones was not aiming for such a response. He meant instead to make more solid Christians out of us.

Brace yourself to be ruffled occasionally by his convictions on certain topics: war, for example, or cutthroat competition. He does not mean to be either controversial or trendy; he is instead working out a full-orbed faith as he sees it. Listen to the Scriptural basis for his views and decide for yourself if they are valid or not.

The Bible selections printed at the start of each day's reading in this edition are almost always the ones Jones chose himself. When he noted a preference for a certain translation that was popular in his day (for example, "Moffatt" or "Weymouth"), that text is preserved here.

This book "was written during a three-month retreat in the Himalayas," he explained in his introduction, "the mornings being spent in writing and the afternoons and evenings in going through a course of reading—the only vacation (if it can be called one) that I have had for some years. It was the cold season, and these hills were deserted at the time, so that my only companions were an Indian [man who served as my] secretary, and the wild animals that roamed the area—the deer, the panther, the tiger, and the wild pig.

"At noon, after a morning of writing, I would take a walk through these lovely mountain paths to clear my brain, only to return to find that my faithful secretary, who was unused to the mountains, had been spending anxious moments of prayer for me until I got back safely! It was the unknown to him; to me it was the beloved known.

"Perhaps many of my readers across the seas will share that same anxiety as we penetrate from the known personal to the jungle of social relationships, wondering if we should not stick to the beaten paths of personal religion. But this jungle of social relations must be Christianized. For Christ must claim all of life."

Welcome to the upward trail.

VICTORIOUS
LIVING

QUESTIONS THAT INTERRUPT US

Can you fathom the mysteries of God? Can you probe the limits of the Almighty? They are higher than the heavens above—what can you do? They are deeper than the depths of the grave—what can you know? (Job 11:7-8)

Philip said, "Lord, show us the Father, and that will be enough for us." (John 14:8)

In trying to comprehend life, it would be nice if we could all start out the way Genesis 1:1 does ("In the beginning God…"). It would put a solid fact beneath our searching feet.

But many of us cannot begin there. God seems to be vague, unreal. We wish we could believe in Him, get hold of Him—for life without the Great Companion has a certain emptiness to it. However…

The skepticism of many people is not voluntary. To them, the facts of life are too much to swallow—the unemployment, the hunger of little children, the underlying strife in modern society, the exploitation of the weak by the strong, the apparently unmerited suffering all around us, the heartlessness of nature, the discoveries of science that seem to render the God-hypothesis unnecessary. All these things and more seem to shatter our belief in God.

We do not intentionally reject that belief; it simply fades away and becomes unreal. We cannot assert what to us is not real. For amid all the losses of our modern day, we are trying to save one thing amid the wreckage—our desire for reality. We have to hang onto an inner integrity.

That leads us to face the fact that our skepticism has gone deeper than the matter of belief in God; we find ourselves questioning life itself. Does it have any meaning? Any goal? Is the flame of life within us different from the flame that leaps from the logs in the fireplace, or are both of them the result of material forces…and both destined to die down into a final ash?

O God, our Father (if we may call you that), as we begin this quest, we are haunted with many a biting fear and hesitation. Help us to face them all and come out, if possible, on the other side into victorious living. Amen.

LIFE: A MATTER OF NO OR YES?

I looked and saw all the oppression that was taking place under the sun: I saw the tears of the oppressed—and they have no comforter; power was on the side of their oppressors—and they have no comforter. And I declared that the dead, who had already died, are happier than the living, who are still alive. (Eccl. 4:1-2)

[Jesus said:] "The thief comes only to steal and kill and destroy; I have come that they may have life, and have it to the full." (John 10:10)

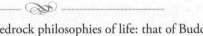

I believe there are just two bedrock philosophies of life: that of Buddha and that of Christ. The rest are compromises between. Christ and Buddha both looked at the same facts of life and came to opposite conclusions. One was a final Yes, the other a final No.

Buddha, pondering under the Bo-tree, concluded that existence and evil are one. The only way to get out of evil is to get out of existence itself.

"Is there any existence in Nirvana?" I asked a Buddhist monk in Ceylon (Sri Lanka). "How could there be?" he replied. "For if there were existence, there would be suffering."

"Then is it an emptiness, a zero?" He nodded yes.

Nirvana is called "bliss," but it is the bliss of the world-weary. In its revolt against life, the soul performs its final self-destruction…clothed, it is true, with an air of sanctity and nobility. Buddha wanted to cheat the sufferings and evils of life by getting rid of life itself.

There is much to be said for Buddha's position. Everything in our world seems to be under the process of decay. The blushing bride becomes the withered old woman shriveling to fit her narrow shroud. We grasp the vivid colors of the sunset and soon find that we have grasped the darkness.

Is this the best life can offer?

O God, our Father, we stand confused and dismayed, not knowing if we will be compelled to adopt the noble pessimism of souls like Buddha. Perhaps there is another way. We hardly dare to believe it. But show us the way—the way to life. Amen.

A BUBBLE OR AN EGG?

We know that if the earthly tent we live in is destroyed, we have a building from God, an eternal house in heaven, not built by human hands. Meanwhile we groan, longing to be clothed with our heavenly dwelling…so that what is mortal may be swallowed up by life. (2 Cor. 5:1-2, 4)

A noble missionary said to me once, with a sigh, "Every new affection brings a new affliction." Buddha would certainly have agreed.

Bertrand Russell, the British philosopher, also took his stand with Buddha when he said gloomily, "All the loneliness of humanity amid hostile forces is concentrated upon the individual soul which must struggle alone." There are many modern followers of Buddha, unconscious, of course, but driven there by the hard facts of life. They worship with a sigh at the shrine of the *stupa*.

Standing in the middle of a Buddhist ruin, I asked the learned Indian curator why the stupa was always oval-shaped. "Because Buddhism believes that life is a bubble; therefore the stupa is shaped like one," he replied. Life as a bubble—*sunnayavada* (in Sanskrit)—nothingness at its heart!

At that moment, I felt darkness close in upon me. But as I looked at the shrine again, light seemed to dawn. "Why, it isn't shaped like a bubble, it's shaped like an egg!" I remarked.

Is life a bubble or an egg? Does it contain nothing inside, or is it filled with infinite possibilities for growth and development and perfection?

Of course I grant that even an egg, if badly handled, can turn rotten. So can life. Nevertheless, I have to vote on one side of that question or the other, and I shall tell you why I choose the egg view.

I follow a Man who saw just as deeply and more deeply than Buddha into the sorrow, the sheer misery of existence…and yet came out at the other end of it all affirming His faith in life. To Him, life was not a bubble, but an egg.

O God, our Father, light gilds our dark horizon as we listen to this Man. But will it be a will-o'-the-wisp that leaves us floundering in the swamp of final despair? Help us, we pray. Amen.

TWO POINTS OF VIEW

If our hope in Christ is only for this life, we are more to be pitied than anyone in the world. But in fact, Christ has been raised from the dead. He is the first of a great harvest of all who have died.... The last enemy to be destroyed is death. (1 Cor. 15:19-20, 26 †)

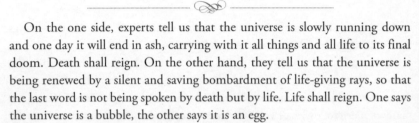

On the one side, experts tell us that the universe is slowly running down and one day it will end in ash, carrying with it all things and all life to its final doom. Death shall reign. On the other hand, they tell us that the universe is being renewed by a silent and saving bombardment of life-giving rays, so that the last word is not being spoken by death but by life. Life shall reign. One says the universe is a bubble, the other says it is an egg.

On the one side, they tell us man is made up of elements that can be purchased in a chemist's shop for a few cents, so that life is only mucus and misery. On the other hand, they tell us man is made in the image of the Divine, that he has infinite possibilities of growth and development before him. One says man is a bundle of futilities; the other says he is a bundle of possibilities.

On the one side, they say man is just a composite of responses to stimuli from environment, mechanically determined and with no real power of choice. On the other hand, they say man has sufficient freedom to determine his destiny, and that the soul shapes its environment as well as being shaped by it.

Some say prayer is an auto-suggesting of oneself into illusory states of mind; that nothing comes back save the echo of one's own voice. Others say that in prayer, actual communication takes place; that one is linked with the resources of God, so that one's powers and faculties are heightened and life is strengthened and purified at its center. One says prayer is futile, the other says it is fertile.

O God, our Father, we want life, but not false life. Show us if there is real life, and if there is, help us to choose it. Amen.

GOD BEYOND THE GAPS

As the deer longs for streams of water, so I long for you, O God. I thirst for God, the living God. When can I go and stand before him? Day and night I have only tears for food, while my enemies continually taunt me, saying, "Where is this God of yours?" (Psalm 42:1-3 †)

On the one side, there are those who tell us that God is an unnecessary hypothesis, that science can explain all, that the crevasses and gaps of the universe into which we used to put the working of God are being slowly but surely filled up by science, so that the universe is self-sufficient, law-abiding, and predictable.

On the other hand, there are those who tell us that God is not to be found in the gaps and crevasses, or in an occasional breaking into the process, but He is in the process itself—the life of its life. They say that the universe is dependable because God is dependable; that it works according to law because God's mind is an orderly mind, not whimsical and notional. In the words of Sir James Hopwood Jeans, the English physicist, "The universe is more like a thought than a machine."

Since the universe seems to work toward purposeful ends, we must either endow matter with intelligent purposes (in which case it would be more than mere matter), or we must put a purposeful, creative Intelligence into (and back of) the process. Since the universe, from the tiniest atom to the farthest star, is mathematical, we must either believe that matter has sufficient intelligence to be mathematical, or else that God is a pure mathematician.

It would seem that the purposeful-matter hypothesis takes more credulity than that there is an infinite Spirit, called God, who is inside the process working toward intelligent moral ends, inviting our limited spirits to work with Him.

O God, our Father, shall I rule You out and vote for a dead universe, assuming its final goal is death? Or shall I vote for a living universe with You as its genesis, its perpetual Creator, its goal and end? Clarify my mind and my heart, that I may not lose myself—and You—amid the maze of things. Amen.

TWO VIEWS OF CHRIST

It is no weak Christ you have to do with, but a Christ of power.
(1 Cor. 13:3 MOFFATT)

Long ago God spoke many times and in many ways to our ancestors through the prophets. And now in these final days, he has spoken to us through his Son. (Heb. 1:1-2†)

There are those who tell us that Christ is a spent force in humanity; that Thomas Carlyle, the Scottish satirist, was right when he stood at the Italian wayside crucifix and slowly shook his head, saying, "Poor Fellow, you have had your day." They say His day is over because He spoke to a simple age, but now we face a complicated, scientific time; that He was good, but not good enough—for us.

On the other hand, there are those who feel (with the Carlyle of later years) that Christ's day is just beginning. They affirm that what has failed has been a miserable caricature and not the real thing. They point out that even the partial application of His teaching and spirit has been one thing that has kept the soul of humanity alive. This viewpoint says that when we expose ourselves to Him in simplicity and obedience, life is changed, lifted, renewed. It sees Him as the one truly unspent force, facing this age as the Great Contemporary and its Judge.

Some people say conversion is an adolescent phenomenon that coincides with and is caused by the awakening of the sexual instinct. Others say it is the result of mob-suggestion, easily induced and quickly fading. On the other hand, many affirm that this change called conversion helps them control and redirect the powers of the sexual instinct and that, far from being mob-suggestion, it helps them to cut across the purposes of both the mob and the self when they are wrong. To one, conversion is a worthless bubble; to the other, an egg of great value.

O God, our Father, hold us steady as we face the issues. May there be no dodging, no turning to irrelevancies, and no excuses. Save us to the real. Amen.

MAKING OUR CHOICE

*[Joshua said:] If serving the L*ORD *seems undesirable to you, then choose for yourselves this day whom you will serve.… But as for me and my household, we will serve the L*ORD*. (Josh. 24:15)*

The issues of life are before me. I must vote for or against a view of life that has worth, purpose, and goal.

If I vote that the universe has no meaning, then I vote that my own life has none. But if my life has no meaning and hence no purpose, it will go to pieces, for psychology tells us that without a strong controlling purpose to coordinate life, the personality disintegrates through its own inner clashes.

But that purpose must be high enough to lift me out of myself. If my purposes end with myself, again I disintegrate. They must include God, who gives basis and lasting meaning to my purpose. If I lose God, I lose myself, my universe, everything. I see that Voltaire, the French critic, was right when he said, "If there is no God, we will have to invent one to keep sane."

If I let go of Christ, then God becomes the Distant, the Vague, the Unreal. In Christ I find "the near side of God." In Him, God speaks to me a language I can understand, a human language. And as I listen to that language, my universe seems to become a Face—tender, strong, forgiving, redemptive.

If I do not sincerely get into touch with God through the written Word, I neglect the greatest and most redemptive fact of history, paying the penalty of being unfed at the place of my deepest need. If I do not pray, I shall probably become cynical and shallow. If I do pray, I shall probably get courage, a sense of adequacy, power over wayward desires and passions. If I undergo a moral and spiritual change called conversion, I shall probably be unified, morally straight, and spiritually adjusted. If I do not, I shall probably become a stunted human soul.

So I must vote. I vote for life.

O God, our Father, I make the choice, I do choose life with all its fullest, deepest implications. Help me to find life and live it—victoriously. Amen.

WHY ARE WE RELIGIOUS?

All creation is yearning, longing to see the manifestation of the sons of God. For the Creation was made subject to futility, not of its own choice, but by the will of Him who so subjected it; yet with the hope that at last the Creation itself would be set free from the thralldom of decay to enjoy the liberty that comes with the glory of the children of God. (Rom. 8:19-21 WEYMOUTH)

There are a hundred and fifty or more definitions of religion. One says it is "what we do with our solitariness"; another that it is "how we integrate ourselves socially"; another that "the root of religion is fear," and so on.

The reason it is so difficult to define is that life itself is difficult to define. When we define religion in terms of its various manifestations, we get partial, sometimes contradictory definitions. But religion, having many forms, has only one root. That root is the urge after life, fuller life. In everything, from the lowest cell clear up to the highest person, there is an urge toward completion.

Religion is the urge for life turned qualitative. It is not satisfied with life apart from quality. The urge for quantitative life reached its crest in the dinosaurs. That failed—it was a road with a dead end. The huge animals died. In human beings, the life urge turns from being merely big to being better.

We are religious, then, because we cannot help it. We want to live in the highest, fullest sense, and that qualitative expression of life is called religion. So religion is not a cloak we can put on or off; it is identified with life itself. We are all incurably religious. Even the Communists[1], though repudiating religion, are deeply religious. They want a better social order. They may be right or wrong in their method of getting it, but the very desire for a better social order is religious. For religion is a cry for life.

O God, our Father, who planted this urge for completion within us? Did You? Then, O my God, this urge is not in vain. You have inspired it. You will satisfy it with Yourself. Amen.

---

1. When Jones wrote this in 1936, Stalin was in power and Soviet Communism was still in its adolescence.

THE DIVINE INITIATIVE

In the beginning the Word already existed. The Word was with God, and the Word was God.... The one who is the true light, who gives light to everyone, was coming into the world.... To all who believed him and accepted him, he gave the right to become children of God. They are reborn—not with a physical birth resulting from human passion or plan, but a birth that comes from God. (John 1:1, 9, 12-13†)

The other side of the truth about religion is that we seem to be pressed upon from above. We do not merely aspire, we are inspired. We feel we are being invaded by the Higher. This pressure from above awakens us, makes us discontent, makes us pray—sometimes with unwordable longings.

This is the divine initiative—the cosmic Lover wooing His creation to Himself and therefore to its own perfection.

Friedrich von Hügel, the Catholic theologian, speaks of this double movement in religion as the going up of one elevator and the coming down of another; we move toward God, and God moves toward us. The Old Testament is humanity's search for God, the New Testament is God's search for us. This is true in general but not entirely true, for there would have been no search for God in the Old Testament (and in the various religions) had God not inspired and initiated that search. So when men and women began to seek, they had in a sense found Him. But God was in the very search for Himself—its author and hence its finisher.

Impossible? Too good to be true? Not if we study the nature of life. Life not only wants more life, but it wants to impart life. The creative urge is within it. God, being the perfect life, would of the very necessities of His being desire to impart, to share, to create.

Hence the divine Initiative. We are religious because we long and because He loves. He creates, we crave.

My Father, if this is true, I am not far from You, for You are not far from me. Perhaps this very longing within me is a scent of Your being. There my heart grows eager, because I want to find You. Amen.

MEETING IN THE MIDDLE

The Word became flesh and made his dwelling among us. We have seen his glory, the glory of the One and Only, who came from the Father, full of grace and truth. (John 1:14)

Yesterday we said that religion resulted from the double movement of our aspirations and God's inspirations. His life impinges upon ours at every point.

The meeting place of this upward movement and this downward movement is Christ. He is man ascending and God descending—the Son of man, the Son of God. Since He is the meeting place of the two sides of religion, He becomes its definition. To the dozens of other definitions we add one more: Christ.

This is not a spelled-out but a lived-out definition. Some things cannot be said; they have to be shown. So it has been shown to us what constitutes religion: Christ's spirit of life. His relationships with God and humanity. His purity, His love, His mastery over the environment of people and things. His care for the sinful and the underprivileged. His redemptive purposes for individuals and society. His overleaping sympathy that wiped out all race and class and bound us into a brotherhood. His final willingness to take all pain, all defeat, all sin into His own heart and die for us. His offer of a new way and program of life—the kingdom of God on earth. All this, and His sheer victory of spirit amid it all, constitutes religion.

Never was there such a definition as Christ gives in His own person. It cleanses away all irrelevancies, all magic, all superstition, all controversies about rite and ceremony and superiorities. It turns us to the serious business of learning how to live and to live victoriously. When people ask me about this rite and that ceremony, this order, that church polity—all marginal—I simply say, I am not interested, for I have seen the Center. This is what grips me.

O God, we have seen what we ought to be, what we must be if we are to live. Help us from this day to give ourselves to it with a whole-being devotion until it becomes actual within us. In Jesus' name. Amen.

EMBEDDED INTO OUR FOUNDATIONS

Once, having been asked by the Pharisees when the kingdom of God would come, Jesus replied, "The kingdom of God does not come with your careful observation, nor will people say, 'Here it is,' or 'There it is,' because the kingdom of God is within you." (Luke 17:20-21)

From that time on Jesus began to preach, "Repent, for the kingdom of heaven is near." (Matt. 4:17)

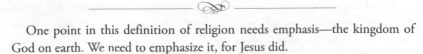

One point in this definition of religion needs emphasis—the kingdom of God on earth. We need to emphasize it, for Jesus did.

In another book, I said the kingdom of God is a new order founded on the fatherly love of God, redemption, justice, brotherhood, and it stands at the door of the lower order founded on greed, selfishness, exploitation, unbrotherliness. This higher order breaks into, cleanses, renews, and redeems it.

This is true, but not the full truth. It is an offer from outside. Jesus said it was "near." And yet it is also inside us—"The kingdom of heaven is within you." This kingdom has been "prepared for you from the foundation of the world" (Matt. 25:34 NKJV). Did He mean that this kingdom has been built into the very foundations of the world and into the very structure of our own mental and moral make-up? Yes, I believe He meant just that.

I grant that there is something beyond—it is "near," and we shall see what that means later. But the Scripture also means that the kingdom is written not merely in sacred books. When we study the laws deeply embedded in the universe, in our own mental and moral and physical being, the laws that constitute true sociological living, we discover the laws of the kingdom of God. Not fully, mind you, but nevertheless really and actually.

This is important, for when we start with this business of victorious living, we are starting with the solid facts of the laws written within our own being, within the structure of society and the universe around us.

Our Father, we are enveloped with You. Your laws are the laws of our being. Your will has been woven into the texture of things. Help us to discover Your kingdom and obey it. Amen.

E. STANLEY JONES | 11

LAWS THAT BREAK US

When Gentiles, who do not have the law, do by nature things required by the law, they are a law for themselves, even though they do not have the law, since they show that the requirements of the law are written on their hearts, their consciences also bearing witness, and their thoughts now accusing, now even defending them. (Rom. 2:14-15)

Moral laws are deeply embedded in the constitution of things. We do not break them, we break ourselves upon them. For instance, many after [World War I] demanded freedom to do as they liked; they revolted against morality as man-made; they said they would express themselves as they desired. The result? That generation is now sad and disillusioned. It stands abashed and dismayed. At what? At the fact that the thing will not work.

Said one disillusioned young woman who had revolted, "I thought that faithful marriage was hell, but what have I been living in?" She found her revolt had been not merely against moral codes, but against herself and her own happiness. She was breaking herself upon the laws of the kingdom.

What does the psychologist mean when he says, "To be frank and honest in all relations, but especially in relations with oneself, is the first law of mental health"? Isn't he saying that the universe and you and I are built for truth, that the universe won't back a lie, that all lies sooner or later break themselves upon the facts of things? Since the kingdom stands for absolute truth, and our own mental make-up demands the same thing, then are not the laws of the kingdom of God written inside us?

The right thing is always the healthy thing. The wrong thing is always the unhealthy thing. We cannot be healthy and functioning at our best unless we discover the right and obey it. Sin is not only bad but also unhealthy and crippling. The sinful are diseased as well as guilty. This sobers us.

O God, our Father, the moral law written within makes us tremble like an aspen leaf. But are these laws redemptive? Are You saving us through hard refusals? Teach us. We listen. Amen.

THE KINGDOM EQUALS LIFE

Jesus answered, "I am the way and the truth and the life. No one comes to the Father except through me." (John 14:6)

The Word gave life to everything that was created, and his life brought light to everyone. (John 1:4†)

Jesus made the kingdom and life synonymous. In a stern warning about causing harm to children, He said, "If your hand causes you to sin, cut it off. It is better for you to enter life maimed.... And if your eye causes you to sin, pluck it out. It is better for you to enter the kingdom of God with one eye..." (Mark 9:43, 47). Here He used the terms "life" and "the kingdom of God" interchangeably. To Him they were one.

But this kind of life ought to be spelled with a capital "L" to express what Jesus meant. He meant more than just this life and its laws within ourselves and the universe. If that had been all, it would have been a naturalism. Not that we thereby condemn it, for nature (human and non-human) is God's handiwork. But while God wrote the elemental laws of the kingdom within us, He did not stop there.

The kingdom is "within us," but it is also "near." Something from the outside is prepared to invade us, to change us, to complete us. When that happens, we too shall have to spell life with a capital "L." Every fiber of our being will know that this is Life. The two charged electrodes of life, natural and supernatural, will meet, and when they touch, the white light of Life will result.

The kingdom, then, is life-plus. It is the grafting of a higher Life upon the stock of the lower. The stock will still be there, its roots deeply in the soil of the natural, but we will bud and bloom with new possibilities. The kingdom is the Ought-to-be standing over against the Is, challenging it, judging it, changing it and offering it Life itself.

O God, our Father, we talk of the kingdom—but You are the kingdom. You are at our doors. We put our trembling fingers to the latch and let You in. And when You are in, we know we have let in Life. Amen.

ARE RELIGIOUS PEOPLE STRANGE?

Think of what you were when you were called. Not many of you were wise by human standards; not many were influential; not many were of noble birth. But God chose the foolish things of the world to shame the wise; God chose the weak things of the world to shame the strong…so that no one may boast before him. (1 Cor. 1:26-29)

Are religious people strange? They sometimes are, and this makes many honest souls hesitant, for they do not want to be odd or impossible. Many people feel that religion tries to give human nature a bent that it won't take, that is an imposition on life, something that makes us unnatural and out-of-joint.

A medical student expressed this fear to me when he asked, "Is religion natural?" He feared the unnatural. On the other hand, Tertullian said back in the third century that "the soul is naturally Christian." He was right.

When I obey Christ, I feel naturalized, at home, universalized, adjusted. When I disobey Him, I feel orphaned, estranged, out-of-joint with myself and the universe. I seem to be made for this Man and His kingdom.

It is true that when we obey Him, we have to break with society in many things. That makes us seem odd and impossible. But may it not be that society, at those points, is the odd one? We call a person odd when they are eccentric— "off the center." Isn't society, insanely bent on its own destruction through its selfishness, clashes, and lusts, eccentric? A great flywheel off its center shakes itself and the building to pieces. But if it is on the center, it is a thing of construction and production.

The center of life is Christ; when we are adjusted to Him, life catches its rhythm, its harmony. When life revolves around something else, it is eccentric, and therefore self-destructive as well as society-destructive.

O God, our Father, we have become so used to the insanities of life around us that we look on the sane as the insane. Give us a clarity of mind and heart, that we may turn from selfishness and greed to the sanities of Your way. For we know that life will not work in any way but Yours. In Jesus' name. Amen.

ROWING IN THE DARK

When evening came, his disciples went down to the lake, where they got into a boat and set off across the lake for Capernaum. By now it was dark, and Jesus had not yet joined them. A strong wind was blowing and the waters grew rough…. They saw Jesus approaching the boat, walking on the water; and they were terrified. But he said to them, "It is I; don't be afraid." Then they were willing to take him into the boat, and immediately the boat reached the shore where they were heading. (John 6:16-21)

We must get clear this whole matter of whether the Christian way will work before we can go on to "victorious living." For as long as we have the suspicion lurking in our minds that we are trying something that cannot be done, that the universe won't back it, there is a paralysis at the center. On the other hand, if we are sure that the sum total of things is behind what we are attempting, then our wills are steeled to do the hitherto impossible.

The disciples were rowing in the dark and getting nowhere. The wind and waves were against them, and the whole thing was ending in futility. Then Jesus came. They cried out, fearing that He was a ghost. But finally they took Him in, and "immediately the boat reached the shore where they were heading."

Is that the history of our lives? We strive for goals we cannot reach. The whole thing ends in futility. We are rowing and getting nowhere. We are up against it. Everything is very dark. Life is too much for us.

Then Jesus comes—and we are afraid of Him. He is ghostly, unnatural. This is our first reaction. But finally we let Him in—and suddenly we are at the very place we were striving to reach! This is the way it works.

But there is no doubt that we are initially afraid of Jesus. It was said that when Jesus came to earth, King Herod "was disturbed, and all Jerusalem with him" (Matt. 2:3). Disturbed at the coming of the Deliverer! They were naturalized in their own lostness.

O gentle, redeeming, impinging God, help me not to keep You at a distance through fear. Help me to take You into my troubled little boat. Amen.

HOW DO WE EXPRESS OURSELVES?

May I never boast except in the cross of our Lord Jesus Christ, through which the world has been crucified to me, and I to the world. (Gal. 6:14)

Take the natural things within us, things which are a part of our very make-up—can these instincts be fulfilled and reach their goal apart from Jesus?

For example, the instinct of self-expression, which noted psychologist Alfred Adler says is the strongest of the three major instincts—self, sex, and the group. It is natural and normal and right. We strive to express ourselves; we all do. I remember the smallest member of one of our ashrams [retreats], a three-year-old, who sang the table grace at the top of her voice and then announced triumphantly at the conclusion, "I sang!" At which we all laughed.

In polite adult society, however, we do not laugh at such self-promotion—we get irritated. Place a dozen people in one situation, all of whom want to express themselves, and you have the stage set for clash and jealousy. The result is refined strife.

Then across the troubled waters, Jesus comes to us. We cry out in fear against Him, for we suspect what He will ask of us. He will ask that we cease all this and lose ourselves. And that is exactly what we do not want to do—we want to express ourselves. It is unnatural, ghostly, impossible.

But as we strain further into our futilities, He keeps coming, till at last we let Him in. Then we lose ourselves in His will and purposes. We forget about our self-expression. And suddenly, we are at the land where we were going!

We are never so much ourselves as when we are most His. We have found ourselves. We have arrived. We have obeyed the deepest law of the universe: "If you cling to your life, you will lose it, and if you let your life go, you will save it" (Luke 17:33 †). It works.

O Christ, we feared You. We, who were drowning, feared the lifeline. Forgive us. But Your very coming to us is Your forgiveness. We thank You. Amen.

HOW DO WE GET RID OF ENEMIES?

Jesus: *"You have heard the law that says, 'Love your neighbor' and hate your enemy. But I say, love your enemies! Pray for those who persecute you! In that way, you will be acting as true children of your Father in heaven. For he gives his sunlight to both the evil and the good, and he sends rain on the just and the unjust alike." (Matt. 5:43-45 †)*

Take another natural instinct—our desire to get rid of those who thwart us, who hurt our feelings, who do us harm. Sometimes we try the crude method of fists; sometimes, if we are more refined, we strive to behead them by the sharpness of our tongues, or socially we cut them off.

Or we go to court and hope in this way to make them bend the knee. Or collectively we go to war with waving banners, lying propaganda, and belching cannon. In all these ways and many others, we strive to get rid of our enemies.

But we are soon straining at the oars and getting nowhere. We are not eliminating our enemies, we are multiplying them. We soon find that harsh words produce harsh words. Sharp tongues have a way of sharpening other tongues. Cutting off other people results in isolating ourselves. Court cases produce more court cases. We get nowhere. Blank futility.

Then Jesus comes to us across our troubled waters. We are afraid, for we suspect He will ask us to love our enemies. And we do not want to love them. We want to get rid of them.

But He keeps coming, until finally we let Him in. And then something strange happens. As we catch His way, we find a positive desire, even a craving, to do good to people, even to our enemies. And suddenly, we are at the land where we were heading. Our enemies are gone. We have gotten rid of them in the only possible way—we have turned them into friends.

Even if they do not respond, our enmity has gone, and hence our enemies. We have arrived.

O Christ, help us today to take Your way, even toward our enemies. And it may be that at nightfall we shall have no enemies. We too shall arrive. Amen.

HOW DO WE ARRIVE AT GREATNESS?

James and John, the sons of Zebedee, came to him. "Teacher," they said, "we want you to do for us whatever we ask."

"What do you want me to do for you?" he asked.

They replied, "Let one of us sit at your right and the other at your left in your glory."

"You don't know what you are asking," Jesus said. (Mark 10:35-38)

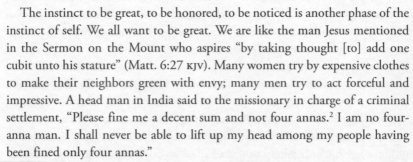

The instinct to be great, to be honored, to be noticed is another phase of the instinct of self. We all want to be great. We are like the man Jesus mentioned in the Sermon on the Mount who aspires "by taking thought [to] add one cubit unto his stature" (Matt. 6:27 KJV). Many women try by expensive clothes to make their neighbors green with envy; many men try to act forceful and impressive. A head man in India said to the missionary in charge of a criminal settlement, "Please fine me a decent sum and not four annas.[2] I am no four-anna man. I shall never be able to lift up my head among my people having been fined only four annas."

But what difference is there in this case and in the person who fines himself the price of a new car each year when he does not need it? He too must keep up appearances; he must seem to be great. Or the student who swaggers because she thinks it will raise her standing in the eyes of her peers?

It doesn't work. It ends in futility. We grow small trying to be great. We strain in rowing, trying to get to the land of greatness, and end nowhere.

Then Jesus comes. Again we fear Him, for we fear what He will say to us.

But we let Him in. We forget greatness as we bend with Him to serve the rest. And, to our surprise, as we bend we rise. The servant of all becomes the greatest of all. We have arrived.

O Christ, the Man who came not to be served but to serve, help me to be like You this day. Amen.

---

2. During the colonial period in India, it took 16 annas to equal just one rupee; thus, four annas would have been a very small amount.

HOW DO WE GET TO HAPPINESS?

By all the stimulus of Christ, by every incentive of love, by all your participation in the Spirit, by all your affectionate tenderness, I pray you to give me the utter joy of knowing you are living in harmony, with the same feelings of love, with one heart and soul, never acting for private ends or from vanity, but humbly considering each other the better man, and each with an eye to the interest of others as well as to his own. (Phil. 2:1-4 MOFFATT)

We all want to be happy. And rightly so. This is a deep-rooted instinct. God must have planted it there. The God who made sunsets, painted the rose, and put play into the kitten is surely not happy when we are unhappy.

So we start out to get to the land of happiness. We declare that the world must show us a good time. But somehow it eludes us. It slips through our fingers before we can grasp it. The most miserable and fed-up people I know are the people most bent on being happy.

They are saying to their souls what the old lady said to the frightened young child whom she had taken to the circus, as she shook him till his teeth rattled, "Now, enjoy yourself! Do you understand, I brought you here to enjoy yourself—*now do it.*"

But the soul weeps within and doesn't know how to enjoy itself. It has missed the way. It is straining at the oars and getting nowhere. Then comes a Figure across the waters! We are afraid. Is not this A. C. Swinburne's "pale Galilean" whose breath has turned the world grey? We cry out in fear.

But this patient insistence overcomes us, and we let Him in. We now forget our happiness as we begin to think about the happiness of others. We walk with Him into saddened homes and strive to lift that sadness. As we do, our hearts sing with a strange new joy that is deep, fundamental, and abiding. We have arrived.

We have misunderstood You, O Christ. We thought because Your symbol was a cross that You were, therefore, Christ the Sad. Forgive us. We now see that You are Christ the Glad. One touch of Your gladness, and our hearts forever sing. Amen.

HOW DO WE FIND SEXUAL FULFILLMENT?

"Haven't you read," [Jesus] replied, "that at the beginning the Creator 'made them male and female,' and said, 'For this reason a man will leave his father and mother and be united to his wife, and the two will become one flesh'? So they are no longer two, but one." (Matt. 19:4-6)

Sex is an integral part of human nature and is therefore God-given. In itself, sex is not unclean. It is as natural as the appetite for food. God has given us this strange power through which we share His creatorship. It is, therefore, not something to be whispered about in dark corners or brooded over furtively in the mind. It must be treated openly and frankly.

Through this strange power, mere femaleness turns to motherhood, and mere maleness turns to fatherhood. A home is set up—a child is "in the midst of them" (Matt. 18:2 NKJV). Love binds all three. Nothing is more beautiful on earth.

But while sex, under the guidance and restraint of pure love, can be a heavenly thing, it can also turn earth into hell if used in the wrong way. Sex has produced more happiness and more unhappiness than any single thing in life. It all depends on what you do with it.

Many try to find sexual fulfillment through unrestrained freedom. They say they have a right to taste all experience, including sexual experience, apart from morality. So they try. They are soon rowing hard. It is getting dark. The promised heaven turns to a present hell. They are getting nowhere except into deeper self-loathing.

Then Jesus comes. Men and women are afraid of Him. He is unnatural and strict. But since we get nowhere without Him, we let Him in. And we find we are at the land we wanted all along.

O Christ, You are shutting the gates to lesser life in order that You might open them to larger life. Help us not to complain when You will not let us be swine. For You want to make us after Your own image. Help us to arise and follow. Amen.

HOW DO WE PULL OURSELVES TOGETHER?

As a prisoner for the Lord, then, I urge you to live a life worthy of the calling you have received. Be completely humble and gentle; be patient, bearing with one another in love. Make every effort to keep the unity of the Spirit through the bond of peace. (Eph. 4:1-3)

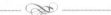

If there is one thing that both modern psychology and the way of Christ agree on, it is this: Apart from inward unity there can be no personal happiness and no effective living.

Jesus said, "Every kingdom divided against itself will be ruined" (Matt. 12:25). That simple statement has within it all the depths of wisdom that modern psychology has discovered. Divided personality, inward clash—these are the things that bring desolation to human personality.

Many say to a distracted soul, "Pull yourself together." But this is futile advice when there are mutually exclusive things within us.

"Exert your will," counsels another. But suppose the will, which expresses the personality in action, is itself divided? Again, futility results.

The psychoanalyst, after getting hold of the distracting place in a disordered life, and after relating it to the rest of life, says that to be held together, there must be something upon which you can fasten your affections. This will lift you out of yourself and keep you unified. But often he has nothing to offer.

So we strain in rowing, trying to get to the land of inward unity. We are tossed by many a wind and many a wave. And it gets very dark. Then Jesus quietly comes. We more easily let Him in this time, for there seems no other alternative. The soul seems instinctively to feel that, as Martha announced to her sister, "the Master is come, and calleth for thee" (John 11:28 kjv). This Master gathers up our inward distinctions, cleanses away the points of conflict, and unifies life around Himself. We have arrived.

O Christ, we need a master, someone to command us. You are that law. Your commandments are our freedom. Help us to accept Your way, that we may find our own. Amen.

HOW CAN I FIND GOD?

The God who made the world and everything in it...gives life and breath to everything, and he satisfies every need.... His purpose was for the nations to seek after God and perhaps feel their way toward him and find him—though he is not far from any one of us. (Acts 17:24-25, 27 †)

We have seen that life will work only in one way—God's way. The statement of Augustine is often repeated because it is often corroborated: "You have made us for Yourself, and we are restless until we rest in You." Let that fact be burned into our minds. Let it save us from all trifling, all dodging, and bend us to the one business of finding God and His way.

Hold in mind that the purpose of your very being, the very end of your creation, is to find and live in God. As the eye is fashioned for light, so you are fashioned for God.

But many question this. A Hindu student once asked me this question, "If there is a God, what motive of His is seen in the creation of this universe, where to think is to be full of sorrow?" At one morning interview time, five students wrote separately, in one form or another, "Why was I created?"

I could only answer: Of course we cannot see the whole motive of creation, for we are finite. But why do parents create? Simply to satisfy physical lust? Not if they have attained the higher reaches of parenthood. Do not parents create because of the impulse of love, to have an object upon which they can lavish their love and to whom they can impart themselves in the development and growth of the child? It is the same with God. Could God, being love, have done anything other than to create objects of that love? And having created us, will He not give Himself to us? If not, then His whole apparent good is stultified.

With that thought in mind, to think is not "to be full of sorrow," but to be full of hope and expectancy. The creative Lover is at the door.

Father God, You have come a long way through creation to the very door of my heart. I hear Your footsteps there. Now I let You in. Welcome, Lover of my soul. Amen.

THE RISK GOD TOOK

Jesus continued: "There was a man who had two sons. The younger one said to his father, 'Father, give me my share of the estate.' So he divided his property between them.

"Not long after that, the younger son got together all he had, set off for a distant country and there squandered his wealth in wild living." (Luke 15:11-13)

Here is a question: Was it not risky for God to create us with the awful power of choice, with the possibility that we might stray, breaking our hearts and His? Yes, very risky indeed. He might have made us without the power of choice, or with the power to choose only the good. But this would not be choice, for to be able to choose you must be able to choose between two directions, not just one.

Besides, if we are able to choose only the good, then it isn't the good for us. We would be predetermined. The very possibility of goodness lies in freedom. The German philosopher Immanuel Kant said in the eighteenth century, "There is nothing in the world, or even out of it, that can be called good, except a good will." So where there is no will there is no goodness, no badness—in fact, no personality. There was no other way to create personalities except to give them freedom. Risky? Yes.

But parents take that same risk when they bring a child into the world. That child may go astray, crushing their lives and his own. Still, parents assume that awful risk. Why? Because they determine that, whatever happens, they will do their best for the child—they will enter into his or her very life.

This will mean a cross, to be sure. But parenthood accepts that cross because it cannot do otherwise. So with God. Our creation meant that He would enter into our very lives—our troubles His troubles, our sins His sins, our joy His joy. Creation indeed became a cross for God. But He took it. Love could not do otherwise.

God, we stand astounded at Your courage. But You did create us—it may be, to recreate us. That is our hope. We clasp it to our souls. Amen.

GOD'S SEARCH FOR ME

"Suppose a woman has ten silver coins and loses one. Does she not light a lamp, sweep the house and search carefully until she finds it? And when she finds it, she calls her friends and neighbors together and says, 'Rejoice with me; I have found my lost coin.' In the same way, I tell you, there is rejoicing in the presence of the angels of God over one sinner who repents." (Luke 15:8-10)

If what we learned yesterday is true, then we must accept the thought that God is in a persistent, redemptive search for us. It seems too good to be true.

My answer is that it is too good not to be true. Many others are not convinced, of course. Said Plato: "The author of the universe is hard to find."

An austere Hindu sage was rebuked in this way: "Why do you trouble God with your austerities so that He cannot sleep?"

Mahatma Gandhi said once to me, "In finding God you must have as much patience as a man who sits by the seaside and undertakes to empty the ocean, lifting up one drop of water with a straw."

But in Luke 15, Jesus flings back the curtains and lets us see the God of the shepherd-heart who seeks and seeks the lost sheep until He finds it. And then the woman who sweeps the house for the lost coin. So, says Jesus, God will sweep the universe with the broom of His redeeming grace until He finds that lost soul. For as the king's image is stamped upon the coin, so is the divine image stamped upon the human soul, lost though it may be amid the dust of degradation.

It is true that the father of the prodigal did not go into the far country after the son. But wasn't his love there with him? And wasn't that love the line along which the son felt his way back to his father's house? Once I saw blind children running a race with a cord in their hands attached to a ring upon a wire that led them to the finish line. So this young man got hold of his father's outreaching love, and it led him back to the father's embrace.

O God, I dare not close my heart to You. You conquer me with Your persistence. How glad I am to be found! Thank You. Amen.

THE GENTLE SUITOR

We know how much God loves us, and we have put our trust in his love.

God is love, and all who live in love live in God, and God lives in them. And as we live in God, our love grows more perfect. So we will not be afraid on the day of judgment, but we can face him with confidence because we live like Jesus here in this world.

Such love has no fear, because perfect love expels all fear. If we are afraid, it is for fear of punishment, and this shows that we have not fully experienced his perfect love. We love each other because he loved us first. (1 John 4:16-19†)

There is the persistent question in many minds: "Very well, but aren't some souls incapable of finding God by their very mental and spiritual make-up? Some are more mystically inclined—those may find God, but some of us cannot. We are not mystics."

But God does not come to us only by the way of the emotions. He comes by the way of the mind and the will as well. He makes a full-life approach to us, and this includes all three. So if you are a person whose active side is more developed than the emotional, you can receive Him at the door of the will. If you lean toward the intellectual, then you have the privilege of accepting Him at the door of the mind. But if He comes in at any of these doors, He possesses the whole person, by whatever door He enters.

Are you sufficiently mystical to love? Everybody is! A man who was very intellectually inclined said he couldn't find God because he wasn't a mystic. But he loved his wife very tenderly. He was mystical enough to love his wife, but not mystical enough to love God! He was wrong and soon found his mistake.

Everyone has a capacity to love God. Everyone who is willing to pay the price of finding can find God. Remember this: No one is constitutionally incapable of finding God. If we do not find God, the cause is not in our constitution, but in our consent.

O God who fashioned us, You fashioned us for Your own entrance. Our doors may be lowly, but Your cross has bent You so low that You can get into the very lowest of doors. Come, Gentle Suitor, come. Amen.

AVAILABLE TO ALL

Keep on asking, and you will receive what you ask for. Keep on seeking, and you will find. Keep on knocking, and the door will be opened to you. For everyone who asks, receives. Everyone who seeks, finds. And to everyone who knocks, the door will be opened. You fathers—if your children ask for a fish, do you give them a snake instead? Or if they ask for an egg, do you give them a scorpion? Of course not! So if you sinful people know how to give good gifts to your children, how much more will your heavenly Father give the Holy Spirit to those who ask him. (Luke 11:9-13†)

Many feel that, since Jesus called His disciples away from their ordinary occupations, we must now leave the ordinary "secular life" to find God. This is a mistake.

Jesus did ask His twelve disciples to leave their occupations and follow Him—but did He not also, in the very act of calling Peter and his friends, approve their occupation by filling their boats with fish? (See Luke 5:1-11). And did not 120 disciples wait in the Upper Room for the Holy Spirit, perhaps only 12 of whom had left their occupations?

A Hindu youth asked me one day, "Shall I be a student, or shall I be a religious man?" I could only reply that I saw no conflict; that if he found God, he would be a better student. Before Christ came into my life, I was at the bottom of my class. Afterward I felt that the bottom of the class was no place for a Christian—and left it. I studied my lessons on bended knees, praying my way through.

There are those, especially in India, who feel that one has to be mature, even old, to find God. But the Christian way is different. To find the kingdom of God, Jesus said we must catch the childlike attitude of open frankness and willingness to follow.

O Christ, You hallowed every worthy occupation. In your Father's house there is the sound of the hammer and the laughter of little children as well as the quiet oratory for prayer. We thank You. Amen.

GETTING DOWN TO THE REAL ISSUES

Your eye is the lamp of your body. When your eyes are good, your whole body also is full of light. But when they are bad, your body also is full of darkness. See to it, then, that the light within you is not darkness. (Luke 11:34-35)

The barriers to finding God are not on God's side, but on ours. Since God is seeking us, the problem is not our finding God, but our letting Him find us. We must put ourselves in the way of being found by God. Some of us are not there. There are definite barriers on our side.

Some of them are intellectual. People do have honest doubts, and I have spent many years in meeting those—perhaps too many years, for I now see that the problem is usually deeper. Not always, but usually.

For example: A young man came to me puzzled about the Trinity. I replied that the emphasis in Christianity was not upon the Trinity but upon the Incarnation. I said that the doctrine of the Trinity was rather overheard than heard in the New Testament. But still, I continued, I could see reasons why the Trinity is reasonable. The lowest life is the simplest life; the amoeba is a single cell. But as we come up the scale of existence we find complexity emerging, so that when we come to human beings we find something highly complex made up of body, mind, and spirit. In other words, we are a trinity.

When we get to the highest life of all, God, we should expect not simplicity but complexity—the Trinity is the natural culmination. In God there is a richer unity in the richer Trinity.

I waited to see if my answer had any effect on the young man. It had none. By a swift insight I saw his problem was not intellectual, but moral.

I put my hand on his and quietly asked if he was living a pure lifestyle. His eyes dropped. He was not. His trouble was not honest doubt, but dishonest sin.

O God, hold us steady at this point. Help us to be absolutely honest, and it may be that as the barriers go down, Your presence will strangely warm our hearts. In Jesus' name. Amen.

FIVE PIERCING QUESTIONS

Examine yourselves to see whether you are in the faith; test yourselves. Do you not realize that Christ Jesus is in you—unless, of course, you fail the test? And I trust that you will discover that we have not failed the test. (2 Cor. 13:5-6)

In a moral world, the deepest organ of knowledge is moral response. Without that, we are blind, however much we may think.

I have a friend whose moral and spiritual influence is potent and penetrating. I discovered the secret of it in his relentlessness toward himself. Once a week he goes aside and examines his life in the light of five pointed questions. In quietness before God, in an air of absolute realism in which there is no equivocation, he asks himself:

1. *Am I truthful?* Are there any conditions under which I will or do tell a lie? Can I be depended on to tell the truth, no matter the cost?

2. *Am I honest?* Can I be absolutely trusted in money matters? In my work? With other people's reputations?

3. *Am I pure?* In my relationships with those of the opposite gender? In my habits? In my thought life?

4. *Am I loving, or am I easily offended?* Do I lose my temper? Am I quick to notice slights? Or am I taking the attitude of love, which refuses to be offended?

5. *Am I consecrated to higher purposes, or am I selfish?* What am I living for—myself, my own position, money, place, power? Or are my powers at the disposal of human need? At the disposal of the kingdom of God? Where is my focus—myself or others?

As we are about to go on in our quest for victorious living, let us put ourselves before ourselves and look at ourselves. The bravest moment of a person's life is the moment when we look at ourselves objectively without wincing, without explaining away.

O Christ, it was said that You know what is in every person. We do not even know what is in ourselves, for we have never looked at ourselves with honest eyes. Help us to do it this day. Amen.

AM I TRUTHFUL?

A man named Ananias, together with his wife Sapphira, also sold a piece of property. With his wife's full knowledge he kept back part of the money for himself, but brought the rest and put it at the apostles' feet.

Then Peter said, "Ananias, how is it that Satan has so filled your heart that you have lied to the Holy Spirit and have kept for yourself some of the money you received for the land?" (Acts 5:1-3)

One test of a person's character is this: Will you lie? And yet how easy it is to lie—even for religious people. The willingness to twist a meaning to gain a point…to misquote if the misquotation gains a desired end…exaggerations to make impressions…a lack of complete truth in making appeals for funds… misrepresentations in presenting goods for sale.

What is at the basis of this looseness with the truth? Is it not often in the fact that we think a lie is sometimes justifiable?

I once asked some students whether a lie is ever justifiable and got these answers: (1) Yes, in business. (2) In politics. (3) To save a life. (4) In war. One argued that it is all right to tell "a little one" in behalf of a great cause. (She wasn't sure of a big one!) These students thought to be able to lie well was an asset. They did not see that lying is a liability.

Get hold of two principles that Presbyterian mission leader Robert Elliott Speer lays down: First, *God cannot lie.* Second, *He cannot delegate to you the privilege of lying for Him.* Truth is inviolable. The early Christians, while standing before Roman tribunals with their lives in the balance, could tell the slightest lie and save themselves. They refused. They could die, but not lie.

If we lie, we are not Christian. The Scripture is unequivocal at this point. "Do not lie to each other, since you have taken off your old self with its practices" (Col. 3:9). If lies are still within us, no matter how religious we may be, we are still in the old self.

O crystal Christ, make me from this moment transparent with nothing covered, nothing I must conceal from myself or others. I ask, as David did, for "truth in the inward parts." I will do my share. Amen.

AM I HONEST?

Paul: *We are traveling together to guard against any criticism for the way we are handling this generous gift. We are careful to be honorable before the Lord, but we also want everyone else to see that we are honorable. (2 Cor. 8:20-21†)*

The second question is this: Am I honest?

It is not easy to be absolutely honest with ourselves, because of the tendency toward rationalization. This means that we are seldom objective in our attitudes toward ourselves. We set our minds to work not upon the facts as they are, but upon the business of inventing reasons for our courses of conduct.

The man in Jesus' parable who was negligent with his talent (Matt. 25:14-30) laid the blame on the hardness of the master. That was rationalization. A man today allows himself to fall in love with another man's wife, and then he proceeds to rationalize the whole thing by talking to himself about the sacredness of this feeling of love, until black looks white. The mind has played a trick on him. He is self-deceived.

We need the objectivity and honesty of the youth who said to me: "I cannot keep my degree. It is the badge of my shame. I got help during my examination. I am going to send it back to the university." He did.

The vice-chancellor replied: "The end of education is to produce honest character. You now seem to be an honest man. We hope you will keep the degree."

But will God forgive the sin of dishonesty without such restitution? How can He? He can forgive the sin of the act only as we are willing to restore. We may not be able to restore all at once, but we must be willing. God sometimes has to take us on faith.

Am I willing to cut out of my life—ruthlessly—every dishonest thing, no matter how deep the humiliation may be?

O relentless Pursuer of our souls, You are not content to leave us half-sick. You have Your finger on our cancers. Help us not to beg off from the surgeon's knife. Cut, O Christ, deeply if need be. But make us well. Amen.

AM I PURE?

Run from sexual sin! No other sin so clearly affects the body as this one does. For sexual immorality is a sin against your own body. Don't you realize that your body is the temple of the Holy Spirit, who lives in you and was given to you by God? You do not belong to yourself, for God bought you with a high price. So you must honor God with your body. (1 Cor. 6:18-20†)

This question of purity is fundamental. The battle of life will probably not rise above the sexual battle. If life sags at that place, it will probably sag all down the line.

Obviously, the first thing to do in this matter of purity is to acknowledge the fact of sex. To act as though there are no such things as sexual desires is to repress them, which sets up a complex in the subconscious. Every normal person has sexual desire.

But does sexual desire have us? As a servant of the higher purposes of life, it is wonderful, giving drive and beauty to the rest of life. As a master—it is hell.

A young man threw himself into a chair in front of me and said bluntly: "Give me a prescription. I'm desperately sick. Everything is wrong with me morally." This seemed encouraging, for he was apparently ready to face the facts of his life. But when I got down to the details, he wasn't honest. He dodged. When I came to the question of purity, he said, "Well, I do go to women, but I would not consider myself a fallen man. I am not in the gutter." Not in the gutter, though the gutter was in him!

Because he was a non-Christian, I could excuse him in a way. But there is no excuse for myself or you who have come under the influence of a Master who set the place of guilt not merely in the outer act, but in the inward thought (see Matt. 5:28). Am I committing adultery in act or in thought? If so, will I surrender it? Now? Or will I pray the prayer of the unregenerate Augustine in the fourth century, "Make me pure, but not yet"?

O Man of the pure mind, the pure habit, the pure act, cleanse the festering places of my heart and make me from this hour a person of purity. Amen.

AM I LOVING?

Therefore, as God's chosen people, holy and dearly loved, clothe yourselves with
compassion, kindness, humility, gentleness and patience. Bear with each other
and forgive whatever grievances you may have against one another. Forgive as
the Lord forgave you. And over all these virtues put on love, which binds them
all together in perfect unity. (Col. 3:12-14)

Yesterday we tested our lives at the place of the sins of the flesh. Today we must test them at the place of the sins of the disposition. Henry Drummond has called our attention, in the parable of the prodigal, to the two manifestations of sin in the younger brother and the elder brother. The younger son sinned low down in his flesh, in his lusts and appetites. The elder brother sinned high up in his disposition, in his bad temper and lack of love, in his smallness of soul, in his unwillingness to cooperate and forgive.

Now the sins of the flesh are despised by us. They are not respectable. But the sins of the disposition are sometimes highly respectable. If a man commits adultery, we have a church council and put him out. But if he sins in his disposition—if he is bad-tempered and selfish—we have a church council and make him a member!

And yet it is quite probable that the sins of the disposition do as much harm to the kingdom of God as the sins of the flesh—perhaps more. Bad-tempered, touchy and quarrelsome religious people do as much harm to the kingdom of God as drunkards or adulterers. Suppose the younger brother had met the elder brother on the road to their father's house? One look, and he would have turned back to the far country, driven back by a wrong spirit.

Am I prepared to face the fact of my irritability and bad temper, and to consent to have the whole thing taken out—even if it involves a major operation?

O Christ of the quiet, disciplined heart, You who stood poised and unruffled
amid the grossest insults and provocations, give to me that loving, disciplined
spirit, that I may go through life with healing good will. In Your name. Amen.

AM I CONSECRATED TO HIGHER PURPOSES?

Do nothing out of selfish ambition or vain conceit, but in humility consider others better than yourselves. Each of you should look not only to your own interests, but also to the interests of others. Your attitude should be the same as that of Christ Jesus. (Phil. 2:3-5)

Do your best to come to me quickly, for Demas, because he loved this world, has deserted me and has gone to Thessalonica. (2 Tim. 4:9-10)

In the final analysis, what controls my actions—self-interest or Christ-interest? In the deepest citadel of my spirit, who gives the final word? Do I or Christ?

Sat Tal, the ashram (retreat) center in northern India where I am writing, means "Seven Lakes." The legend says that during a drought, a very holy man was dying of thirst by the wayside. A poor village woman, seeing his distress, ran off and at great trouble brought him seven handfuls of water. These seven handfuls became the seven beautiful lakes.

On the other side of the ridge is a lake, really a swamp, the place where the dead are cremated. This was the seat of a great kingdom. But the *rani* (the queen) thought only of herself when the drought came and cried to the gods for water. They gave her so much that she and her palace were drowned and are now beneath the swamp.

The legend teaches what life teaches: If my desires dominate me, I shall be drowned in my own desires. I shall have my way and then I shall loathe my way. If self is on the throne, its inner subjects are unhappy, discordant.

That self may be a very refined self. It may be a very religious self, even an apparently serving self. But if it is on the throne and makes the final decisions, then I shall lose my life. My life needs a master, but self is not the master it needs.

Hush your heart and ask yourself this question: "Who has the ultimate say in my life—self or Christ? Am I self-directed or Christ-directed?"

O Christ, I know in my heart of hearts that when my hand is on the helm, my life drifts toward the rocks. I cannot manage my boat. Take the helm. Amen.

DO I HAVE TO CONFESS?

There is nothing concealed that will not be disclosed, or hidden that will not be made known. What you have said in the dark will be heard in the daylight, and what you have whispered in the ear in the inner rooms will be proclaimed from the roofs. (Luke 12:2-3)

Confess your sins to each other and pray for each other so that you may be healed. The earnest prayer of a righteous person has great power and produces wonderful results. (James 5:16 †)

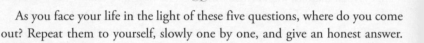

As you face your life in the light of these five questions, where do you come out? Repeat them to yourself, slowly one by one, and give an honest answer. Your self will want to excuse, to rationalize, to go off to the irrelevant—don't let it.

Hold it to the issues. If you fall down at any or at all of these five places, confess it honestly and straightforwardly. *Confess it?* Yes. Both modern psychology and the teaching of Jesus agree at this point. Dr. Clifford E. Barbour writes in his book *Sin and the New Psychology*, "When the conscience…condemns the ego for wrong actions, and the feeling of guilt results, there are three possible modes of conduct. The consciousness may do nothing whatever about it, allowing the emotion full play; it may repress the feeling; or it may rid itself of the depressing sensation by means of spiritual catharsis, through confession" (p. 215).

The first two methods are obviously unsatisfactory, and more—they are disastrous. To find oneself wrong and to do nothing about it is to condemn oneself to live with oneself when one cannot respect that self. That is incipient hell.

To repress it is worse. The new psychology, of all the schools of Freud, Adler, Jung, and MacDougall, unite on this. All the schools of modern psychology and all the teachings of Jesus agree that repression must be found, brought up, exposed to the light, and resolved through confession. There is no other way out.

O Christ, we here take a deep breath, for this confession means humiliation to our inmost selves. We want to hide our wounds. But we dare not. We open them to You. We dare to do it now. Amen.

CONFESS TO WHOM?

Many also of those who believed came confessing without reserve their practices, and not a few of those who had practised magical arts brought their books together and burnt them in the presence of all…. Thus mightily did the Lord's word spread and triumph. (Acts 19:18-20 WEYMOUTH)

If we confess our sins, he is faithful and just and will forgive us our sins and purify us from all unrighteousness. If we claim we have not sinned, we make him out to be a liar and his word has no place in our lives. (1 John 1:9-10)

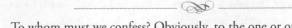

To whom must we confess? Obviously, to the one or ones against whom we have done the wrong. That brings in at least three individuals. When we do wrong, we sin against ourselves, against God, and against society, or, to be more personal, against our brother or sister.

First, we sin against ourselves. We have been false to our highest interest, we have betrayed our ideals, we have sinned against our higher nature. We must then acknowledge it to ourselves.

Second, we must confess it to God. We have not merely broken a law, we have broken a Heart. You must tell Him so. The approach to God has now been made easy through Jesus. His awful purity condemned sinners yet invited them. For they saw that His purity was not forbidding, but forgiving. You dare to expose your heart to that Heart. You must—to get relief. But, again, it must be wholehearted and without anything held back, for one thing held back spoils it all, canceling the rest.

Third, we must confess it to those whom we have wronged. We do not need to broadcast our sins to everybody. Promiscuous confession to promiscuous gatherings is not healthy. There are some things God deals with in His private office. But when we have wronged others or others have wronged us, we must both ask forgiveness and offer it.

O Christ, your knife is going deep. We wince, and yet we consent that the whole thing be taken out by the root. Leave no lingering roots behind. For we do not want only to be better—we want to be well. Amen.

UNTANGLING OUR LIVES

If you are presenting a sacrifice at the altar in the Temple and you suddenly remember that someone has something against you, leave your sacrifice there at the altar. Go and be reconciled to that person. Then come and offer your sacrifice to God. (Matt. 5:23-24†)

Suppose we have been dishonest. No matter what it does to us or to our positions, we must confess it and restore it. I knew of a Christian minister who laid down 450 rupees on the table—the weight that had lain upon his soul for twenty years and the cause of his barrenness. Hard to do, but it opened a door.

Whether you have wronged your brother (as described above in Matthew 5) or whether your brother has sinned against you (as Jesus mentioned later in Matthew 18), in either case you are to go and be reconciled. Whether sinned against or sinning, the Christian is under obligation to take the initiative in settling the dispute.

But you say, "I can't forgive." Then may I say it very quietly, but very solemnly: *You can never, never be forgiven.* That is what Christ clearly stated: "If you refuse to forgive others, your Father will not forgive your sins" (Matt. 6:15†). Do you not remember that in the Lord's Prayer we pray, "Forgive us our trespasses, as we forgive those who trespass against us"?

So if you do not forgive, you ask not to be forgiven. In refusing forgiveness to others, you have broken down the bridge over which you yourself must pass.

As I sit in this ashram, I am reminded of one of our group, a government official, who harbored resentment against a subordinate. A wrong had been done, and the resentment was deep. It was not easy to confess that resentment to a subordinate—not in India, where rank counts for much.

But it was done. Release was found, and now that man's life is radiant and spiritually contagious. You can do the same. By His grace, you will, won't you?

O Christ, who hung on the cross, tortured in every nerve, yet prayed for Your enemies, "Father, forgive them," help me this day, now, to forgive those who have wronged me in a lesser way. In Your name. Amen.

DIGGING OUT THE ROOT

The kingdom of heaven is like a king who wanted to settle accounts with his servants. As he began the settlement, a man who owed him ten thousand talents was brought to him. Since he was not able to pay, the master ordered that he and his wife and his children and all that he had be sold to repay the debt.

The servant fell on his knees before him. "Be patient with me," he begged, "and I will pay back everything." The servant's master took pity on him, canceled the debt and let him go.

But when that servant went out, he found one of his fellow servants who owed him a hundred denarii. He grabbed him and began to choke him. "Pay back what you owe me!" he demanded. (Matt: 18:23-28)

You say, "Well, I'll forgive, but I cannot forget." You don't really mean that, do you? See how it looks as you pray that prayer again, "Father, forgive me as I forgive others: Forgive me, but don't forget my sins, and when I do something wrong bring the whole thing up again."

God cannot and does not forgive that way. He blots it out of the book of His remembrance. So must you.

Or again you say: "Well, I'll forgive, but I'll have nothing more to do with that person." Now pray that prayer again, "Father, forgive me as I forgive others. Forgive me, but have nothing more to do with me. I'll get along without you." You see its absurdity, don't you?

A village woman begged the doctor for a poultice to put over an abscess. The doctor said no, for that would heal it over and drive the poison in; it must instead be lanced. The woman begged for her poultice, pleading that the knife would hurt. When the doctor refused, she went away. In a few days the poison had spread through her whole system and had killed her.

Don't ask for the poultice of a half-way measure. Resentment is physical, mental, and spiritual poison. Get it out!

O Christ who forgave those who spat in Your face, help me now to open my heart to the healing of Your forgiveness. Help me to give it as You have given it to me. Amen.

THE CENTRAL LOG IN THE JAM

Herod himself had sent and laid hold of John, and bound him in prison for the sake of Herodias, his brother Philip's wife; for he had married her. Because John had said to Herod, "It is not lawful for you to have your brother's wife."

Therefore Herodias held it against him and wanted to kill him, but she could not; for Herod feared John, knowing that he was a just and holy man, and he protected him. And when he heard him, he did many things, and heard him gladly.

Then an opportune day came. (Mark 6:17-21 NKJV)

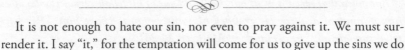

It is not enough to hate our sin, nor even to pray against it. We must surrender it. I say "it," for the temptation will come for us to give up the sins we do not mind in lieu of the central master-sin. For there is usually a master-sin—a central log in the jam. Unless that is pulled out, there is no release.

King Herod was probably earnest in his quest after a new life. He was fascinated by the good. But John one day put his finger on the master-sin in Herod's life. Herod turned pale. A life struggle was on.

The outcome? *He did many things*—yes, everything except the one thing, which was to give up Herodias. He was willing to give up this thing, that thing, the other thing, but not the woman. Herod was willing to have any other log pulled out, but not this one. There was no release.

The little daughter of a missionary went into a guest's room, took some candy, and told her first lie. The broken-hearted mother put her on her lap and told her what it all meant. The little girl wept bitterly, seemed penitent, so the mother said: "I am glad you are penitent. Now take the candy out of your mouth."

The little girl looked at her mother through her tears, clamped her teeth shut tight, and said, "No." She hated the sin, she wept over it, she did everything except one thing—give it up!

O Christ, You drive me into a corner. I want to escape, but You will not let me. Nor do I really want to, for I know if I escaped, I would escape from life. Take from my heart these things that keep me from You and from full life. Amen.

I SURRENDER

The kingdom of heaven is like treasure hidden in a field. When a man found it, he hid it again, and then in his joy went and sold all he had and bought that field.

Again, the kingdom of heaven is like a merchant looking for fine pearls. When he found one of great value, he went away and sold everything he had and bought it. (Matt. 13:44-46)

I have now come to the place in my quest for victorious living where I see I cannot go on until I make the great decision. I must break down every barrier that stands between me and God. I must withhold no part of the price.

But I see I must go further. Beyond giving up every barrier, I must give up myself. I know that something or other will certainly master me. In the shrine of my heart, I am bound to bend the knee to something. I may bow before myself and take orders from myself. Or I may let sexual passion or money have the final say. Or I may bow before the fear of society.

Or—and this seems to me my best alternative—I can let Christ master me. I have the decision as to who shall have the final say in my life. I deliberately make that decision. There is nothing to be weighed out or measured, nothing the eye can see. But will has been given to Will. It is done.

In Copenhagen, as I walked up the cathedral aisle to see the wonderful statue of Thorvaldsen's "Christ," I was almost overcome with awe. I saw the Figure with the soft light upon it dominating the whole cathedral. But as I walked along, a Danish friend whispered: "You will not be able to see His face unless you kneel at His feet."

It was true, for Christ was standing with outstretched arms but looking down. I knelt at His feet, and only then was His face looking into mine.

You cannot really see Christ till you surrender to Him. Those who stand afar off, surveying Him, never really see His face. So bend the knee. Be conquered by Him.

O Christ, at last my heart has said the word. I hold within my trembling palm this will of mine. It is not much, but when You have it, You have my all. And I am glad. Amen.

THRONGING OR TOUCHING?

A great multitude followed Him and thronged Him.

Now a certain woman had a flow of blood for twelve years, and had suffered many things from many physicians. She had spent all that she had and was no better, but rather grew worse. When she heard about Jesus, she came behind Him in the crowd and touched His garment. For she said, "If only I may touch His clothes, I shall be made well."

Immediately the fountain of her blood was dried up. (Mark 5:24-29 NKJV)

The woman in deep need who came timidly through the throng was determined to touch Jesus' cloak. "Who touched me?" He immediately asked.

Understandably, His disciples said to Him, "You see the multitude thronging You, and You say, 'Who touched Me?'" (Mark 5:31 NKJV).

There is a difference between thronging Jesus and touching Jesus. These who throng Jesus get little. Those who touch Jesus get everything.

Never has the world's thinking so thronged Jesus as now. There is more interest in Him than at any time in human history. Other ways of life are breaking down, and we turn wistfully to Him. I see this both in the East and West. And yet I have the feeling it is more of a thronging of Him than a touching of Him. Inspiration? Yes, but not life.

Sunday after Sunday the multitudes go to church and listen. Their thoughts throng Jesus. But how many of the thronging multitudes really touch Him—set up a connection with Him, and live by Him? How many touch Him so that they go away not merely better, but well?

Yesterday you said you would surrender to Christ. Good; nothing better. But now, go ahead and touch Him. Touch Him for forgiveness, for power over temptation, over fears, over anxieties, over everything that stands in the way of victorious living.

O Christ, as You pass by, I cease my tentative attitudes. I move up from those who throng to those who boldly touch. By the touch of faith I receive Your healing and Your health into the core of my being. Amen.

WHAT DOES "FAITH" REALLY MEAN?

Then the woman, knowing what had happened to her, came and fell at his feet and, trembling with fear, told him the whole truth. He said to her, "Daughter, your faith has healed you. Go in peace and be freed from your suffering." (Mark 5:33-34)

He could not do any miracles there [in Nazareth], except lay his hands on a few sick people and heal them. And he was amazed at their lack of faith. (Mark 6:5-6)

This woman's faith had a touch of the superstitious in it, for she thought that virtue resided in His clothing, and that by a touch she would be made whole. Jesus corrected that misunderstanding by His statement (above). What did He mean by "your faith"?

Certainly, faith is not an intellectual assent to a fixed creed. I do not decry creeds, for anyone who thinks has to have something they believe, that is, a creed. But a person may have an intellectual belief in everything in the creed of the churches and still not have faith.

Faith is an adventure of the spirit, the whole inner life responding to something we believe to be supremely worthwhile. It is the wagering of the life and not merely the nodding of the head. It is not discussion, it is decision.

Jesus forged something amazing when He made faith the conditioning instrument, for faith is trust in another, and yet it is also an adventure and an attitude of our own. It therefore develops self-reliance and Other-reliance at the same time. If it were mere passivity, it would not develop self-reliance; if it were mere activity, it would not develop Other-reliance. It is both activity and receptivity.

Jesus said to two blind men who pursued Him, "According to your faith will it be done to you" (Matt. 9:29). You do it, and He does it. You are not stifled, and He is Savior.

O amazing Christ, as You save us from ourselves, You save ourselves. You ask for faith, and that very faith makes us well—and makes us. We fling away ourselves to follow You and we find You—as well as ourselves. We thank You. Amen.

MUST I UNDERSTAND FIRST, THEN FOLLOW?

As he was going into a village, ten men who had leprosy met him. They stood at a distance and called out in a loud voice, "Jesus, Master, have pity on us!"

When he saw them, he said, "Go, show yourselves to the priests." And as they went, they were cleansed. (Luke 17:12-14)

Another time Jesus went into the synagogue, and a man with a shriveled hand was there…. He…said to the man, "Stretch out your hand." He stretched it out, and his hand was completely restored. (Mark 3:1, 5)

Faith is an adventure. Very little faith is enough to start on, for as we act, it grows. The ten lepers had the word of Christ to show themselves to the priests. They had that, and their leprosy. Then that word grew until it possessed them.

Don't wait to follow Christ until you understand all about Him. None of us really understand electricity. But I am not going to sit in the dark until I do. I don't know all about digestion, how food turns into blood and bone and tissue, but I'm not going to sit and starve until I do. There are a thousand and one things I don't understand about Christ, but I know this: When I expose my soul to Him in trust and obedience, He meets my deepest need. That is enough, at least to begin on.

Jesus asked the man with the withered arm to stretch it out—the one thing he couldn't do. He must have looked at Jesus with helpless astonishment at such a demand. And yet, he responded with the little grain of faith he had. He threw his will into raising that arm—and in the very process of obedience, the strength came. His arm was well!

As you launch out to follow Christ, you will think you are stepping out into a void, but that void will turn to rock beneath your feet. You step out, and He steps in—into your battles, your temptations, your tasks. You begin living on a cooperative plan. Faith seals the bond.

O Christ, I do not see all, but I see You. Let that be enough for me. I will take the first steps. I will supply the willingness. You will have to supply the power. Amen.

TAKE THE FIRST STEP

Two disciples [of John] followed Jesus. Turning around, Jesus saw them following and asked, "What do you want?"
They said, "Rabbi" (which means "Teacher"), "where are you staying?"
"Come," he replied, "and you will see." (John 1:35-39)

A Chinese engineer sat down with me and abruptly said: "What are you going to do with me? I am a man without any religion. The old is dead, and I have nothing new to take its place. In America no church would take me, for I cannot believe in the divinity of Christ." I could almost see him inwardly stiffen to meet my arguments.

So I used none. Instead I asked: "What do you believe? How far along are you?"

"Well," he said, "I believe that Christ was the best of men."

"Then let us begin where you can. If He is the best of men, then He is your ideal. Are you prepared to act according to that ideal? To cut out of your life everything that Christ would not approve?"

He was startled and said, "But that is not easy."

"I never said the way of Christ is easy. Are you prepared to let go of everything He will not approve?"

"If I am honest, I must," he quietly replied, "and I will."

"Then, whoever Christ turns out to be—a man or more than man—wouldn't you be stronger and better if He were living with you, in you, all the time?"

"Of course, I would be different." I soon led him in a prayer of reconciliation. "This is different," he said as we arose, "for they always told me I had to believe first. Now at least here is something for me to begin on."

The next day he came again, his face radiant. "I didn't know a person could be as happy as I am today. I have been talking to my wife, and she wants it too."

Christ had verified Himself. He does, when we give Him a chance.

O soul of mine, full of doubts and fears, arise and take the first steps. Here and now, I consent to cut from my life everything You cannot approve, O Christ. Amen.

E. STANLEY JONES | 43

WHAT IS "CONVERSION"?

Teach me your way, O LORD, and I will walk in your truth; give me an undivided heart, that I may fear your name. (Psalm 86:11)

This young engineer had undergone the change called "conversion." What do we mean by it?

Just as the modern church has been allowing conversion to slip into the background, modern psychology has stepped in and re-emphasized it. Not in the same language, and often not with the same belief in God. But they tell us that the subconscious mind is the place of driving instincts, which think only of the pleasure of their own fulfillment, apart from any moral considerations.

Meanwhile, in the conscious mind is built up what Freud calls "the reality principle," or ego ideal, a conscious life-purpose. A conflict starts up between the conscious and the subconscious minds. This split at the very center of life brings disturbance, unhappiness.

This conflict can be resolved in one of two ways: Either the ideal side can be brought down and forgotten, giving the instinctive side full play, or else the instinctive side can be subordinated to and made to contribute to the ideal side of life.

The first alternative is unthinkable for us, for if we take it, we return to the level of beasts. Besides, we can never fully forget the ego ideal. The conflict will continue. The second is the only way out.

The process by which this is done is called by Freud "re-education;" by Adler, "re-orientation to reality;" by Jung, "re-adaptation;" by McDougall, "reintegration." When Christianity puts within it the content of the moral and spiritual as well as the psychological, we call it "conversion." All of these are driving toward the same goal, namely, unifying the personality and bringing harmony into the center of life. All life says we must undergo a change.

O Christ, You have put Your finger on our need. We must be born again and born different. Help us, we pray, to know this change through a living experience of it. Amen.

BORN FROM ABOVE

There was a man named Nicodemus, a Jewish religious leader who was a Pharisee. After dark one evening, he came to speak with Jesus. "Rabbi," he said, "we all know that God has sent you to teach us. Your miraculous signs are evidence that God is with you."

Jesus replied, "I tell you the truth, unless you are born again [born from above], you cannot see the Kingdom of God." (John 3:1-3†)

The alternate translation of this important statement by Jesus is significant. What did He mean by being "born from above"?

According to modern psychology, life can be "born from below." The instincts and drives that reside in the unconscious can control the conscious mind. These instincts can be warped and twisted by what we might call a "sin-bias"—the nesting place of fears, inhibitions, a sense of guilt.

Opposite this stands what Sir Arthur Tansley calls "the ethical self." The Christian would say that this "ethical self" is the beginning of operating in a higher environment, namely, the kingdom of God. It is a place where higher ideals and motives reside.

Now, life depends upon corresponding to an environment. But to which environment? Shall we make life correspond to the environment that arises from below? In that case we shall have to sacrifice and slay the ethical self at the shrine of the beast. Or shall we make life correspond to the higher environment, the ultimate order for human living, the kingdom of God? In which case we shall have to slay our sins and offer our instincts as a living sacrifice.

The choice is in your hands. In the quietness of your heart, you must decide between the high and the low. I said that once to a student, and he replied, "I have no quietness of heart." Neither he nor you will ever have quietness of heart in the deepest, fullest sense until you choose that your life shall be born from above.

O Christ of the gently pressing kingdom, we open our hearts to it and to You. We cannot go back to the beast; we must go forward to the new person. Amen.

EMPTY

Jesus: *"When an evil spirit leaves a person, it goes into the desert, seeking rest but finding none. Then it says, 'I will return to the person I came from.' So it returns and finds its former home empty, swept, and in order. Then the spirit finds seven other spirits more evil than itself, and they all enter the person and live there. And so that person is worse off than before. That will be the experience of this evil generation."* (Matt. 12:43-45[†])

It may be that for some of you, life is not the Great Struggle, but the Great Emptiness. Your difficulty is not the innate but the inane.

Jesus had a description for that type of individual. He told of an empty house that was "swept and garnished" (KJV). Modern civilization is "swept." It has banished superstitions that its forefathers held; now it doesn't believe in this, that, and the other. It is freed from magic and superstition.

It is also "garnished"—garnished with intellectual facts and mechanical toys. Look at our achievements in science and culture and comfort! Our stores are crammed with the mechanical, and we are urged to buy the latest toy, which will be sure to bring us final happiness.

But—and this is the point—it is empty, empty of any constructive philosophy of life. We are all dressed up and don't know where to go! We look with disdain on the barbarous, superstitious ages gone by, we point with pride to our garnished, not to say garish, civilization and its achievements, and yet modern civilization is empty.

Closer to home, perhaps you are empty. You need to be reborn just to know what life is. Moreover, I will tell you that this emptiness will not last long. Modern civilization is drawing to itself the seven devils of unrest, pleasure, exploitation, materialism, selfishness, war, and crime to fill the emptiness.

So will you. Nature and the soul both abhor a vacuum. To fill the emptiness, you must choose between these devils (or some others), and Christ.

O Christ, my house, my soul is empty. I cannot fill it with anything other than You. I despise emptiness, and I fear devils—but I can trust You. Amen.

CONVERSION AND SEX

Live by the Spirit, and you will not gratify the desires of the sinful nature. For the sinful nature desires what is contrary to the Spirit, and the Spirit what is contrary to the sinful nature. They are in conflict with each other, so that you do not do what you want. But if you are led by the Spirit, you are not under law. (Gal. 5:16-18)

Some psychologists trace almost everything to the sex instinct, including the phenomenon called conversion. They point out that most conversions take place in adolescence, and since this is the period when sex awakens, they theorize that religious conversions are caused by it and are founded on it.

The rebuttal is obvious. Adolescence is not only the period when sexual interest awakens, but the total personality as well. The self-instinct, with its restlessness, its revolt against authority, and the group-instinct, with its tendency to form gangs, are also awakened during this time. It is the period when the whole of life awakens.

Now, religion, as we saw several weeks ago, is a cry for life—for complete, fuller, more qualitative life. It is therefore not strange that young people, feeling the awakening of life, should turn to religion to guide and complete that life-urge. Turning to religion often means conversion. It does not come out of the sexual urge but out of the life-urge. The sexual urge, redirected by conversion, pushes life into higher creative channels.

Moreover, religion holds the sexual urge in restraint. How, then, could it be identified with it? If religion were a manifestation of the sexual urge, then when life ripens into old age and the sexual urge dims, we should expect the religious side of life to dim with it. But does it?

Just the opposite. Youth and old age are the most religious periods of life. Why? In youth we want fuller life, in old age we want lasting life. In each, our faith is the cry for life.

O Christ, You are creative Life moving upon lesser life and awakening it. Make me into a new person, with a new goal and a new power to move forward. Amen.

ARE ALL CONVERSIONS ALIKE?

He called a little child and had him stand among them. And he said: "I tell you the truth, unless you change and become like little children, you will never enter the kingdom of heaven. Therefore, whoever humbles himself like this child is the greatest in the kingdom of heaven." (Matt. 18:2-4)

This title question has bothered many souls, for they have seen a type of conversion that greatly moves them, and they are dissatisfied because they cannot reproduce that pattern.

This is a mistake. No two conversions are exactly alike, for no two persons are exactly alike, and no two persons come up under exactly the same act of circumstance. After God made you He broke the pattern. You are unique.

It may be said, nevertheless, that conversions do fall into two great categories—the gradual and the sudden, with shades between. After questioning groups of Christian workers in many lands, I find the usual proportion is about 60 percent gradual and 40 percent sudden.

The gradual types usually come out of a home where from childhood they are taught to know and love Christ. They cannot tell where they crossed the line, for they have seen no line. It has always been so. They have opened like a flower to the sun. They are sure *that* they do belong to Christ, even though they are not sure *when* they began to belong to Him.

Then there are others—and I am among them—to whom conversion came all of a sudden. I had come up through a religious childhood with constant attendance at Sunday school and church, but like some vaccinations, it didn't "take." Then came the Great Change. Nothing after that was the same.

Which of these is the valid type? Either one may be. Not the phenomena that surround conversion, but the facts that underlie it and the fruits that come from it make it valid.

O Christ, who calls the child in its innocence and the older ones in their iniquities, we both come to You. As Peter said, to whom else can we go, for You have the words of eternal life? We find You satisfying because You are saving. Amen.

CONVERSION AT ITS CORE

"Take my yoke upon you and learn from me, for I am gentle and humble in heart, and you will find rest for your souls. For my yoke is easy and my burden is light." (Matt. 11:29-30)

"You call me 'Teacher' and 'Lord,' and rightly so, for that is what I am. Now that I, your Lord and Teacher, have washed your feet, you also should wash one another's feet." (John 13:13-14)

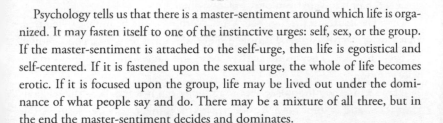

Psychology tells us that there is a master-sentiment around which life is organized. It may fasten itself to one of the instinctive urges: self, sex, or the group. If the master-sentiment is attached to the self-urge, then life is egotistical and self-centered. If it is fastened upon the sexual urge, the whole of life becomes erotic. If it is focused upon the group, life may be lived out under the dominance of what people say and do. There may be a mixture of all three, but in the end the master-sentiment decides and dominates.

Modern psychology tells us that in curing a patient of inward conflict or complex, it is necessary to have the patient transfer his or her sentiment from self to someone outside (usually to the psychoanalyst himself). This is called Transference. The patient is loosed in this way from the problem by the expulsive power of a new affection.

Now, the central thing in conversion is just that transference. While conversion involves breaking from this sin, that habit, this relationship, that attitude, yet all these things are the negative side. The real thing that happens is the transference of the master-sentiment from self to Christ.

Jesus quietly said to individuals long ago, "Follow Me"—not follow a set of doctrines, however true; nor a rite or ceremony, however helpful; nor an organization, however beneficial; but "Follow Me." They did. The transference was made.

The conversion of the master-sentiment became a fact.

O Christ, You have our master-sentiment—and therefore us. We dare not give our love wholly to anyone save the Divine. Take it and us. Amen.

HOW DO I KNOW?

Paul: *We know, dear brothers and sisters, that God loves you and has chosen you to be his own people. For when we brought you the Good News, it was not only with words but also with power, for the Holy Spirit gave you full assurance that what we said was true. (1 Thess. 1:4-5†)*

You may ask what is the basis of assurance by which you will know you are accepted. God assures us from a number of directions, which makes it far stronger than if it were from one direction alone.

First, He assures us through the Word. Nothing could be more explicit than that Christ received sinners. People did not wait until they were good enough to come to Him. They came as they were, and they were made good in the very coming.

That seems a commonplace idea to us today, but it scandalized the religious class then, and it does now. A modern Jewish thinker criticizes Jesus at this point: "Jesus was too familiar with God and too familiar with sinners."

Celsus, debating in the second century with Origen, said: "Those who invite people to other solemnities make the following proclamation: 'He that hath clean hands and sensible speech may come near….' But hear what persons these Christians invite: 'Anyone who is a sinner,' they say, 'or foolish, or simple-minded'—in short, any unfortunate, will be accepted by the kingdom of God! And what do they mean by 'a sinner'?… An unjust person, a thief, a burglar, a sacrilegious person, a poisoner, a robber of corpses. Why, if you wanted a band of robbers, these are the very people you would invite."

Origen's answer was explicit: "Though we call those whom a robber chieftain would call, we call them for a different purpose. We call them to bind up their wounds with our doctrines, to heal the festering wounds of their souls with the wholesome medicine of faith…" (Origen, *Contra Celsus*, iii, LIX).

We glory in what Celsus conceived to be our shame.

O Christ, You received sinners then, and You will not reject me now. I may have dragged my soul through hell, but You will wash it. I thank You. Amen.

ASSURED BY THE WORD

You have been born again, but not to a life that will quickly end. Your new life will last forever because it comes from the eternal, living word of God. As the Scriptures say, "People are like grass; their beauty is like a flower in the field. The grass withers and the flower fades. But the word of the Lord remains forever." And that word is the Good News that was preached to you. (1 Peter 1:23-25†)

The promises of the Word could not be more explicit: "Come to me...and I will give you rest" (Matt. 11:28). "If we confess our sins, he is faithful and just and will forgive us our sins" (1 John 1:9).

Does it seem out of date to quote passages from Scripture to heal present need? Some may think so. But those of us who have been up against raw human need for years know that people need nothing, absolutely nothing, as much as they need the simple assurance that they are reconciled to God. If unhealed at that place, they wear a mortal hurt.

"Please leave India," said a Hindu holy man who listened to a missionary describe how Christ died for us on the cross, "for we have no such story in our books. The heart of India is very tender, and if it hears that story, it will leave our temples to follow." But we cannot leave India, nor can we leave the world. This fact of grace is what the world, and India, and you, and I desperately need.

Jesus also assures us through the revelation of His acts. He says to an adulterous woman, "Neither do I condemn you.... Go now and leave your life of sin" (John 8:11). He says to a hard, money-loving publican, "Today salvation has come to this house" (Luke 19:9). This is the eternal Word speaking through the language of action. It is the Spacious speaking through the specific.

Then grasp this thought: The love of God shining through those specific acts will not deal differently with me. He forgave and restored them; He forgives and restores me.

O You whose very healing was a revealing, You who made timeless truth speak through the facts of time, who speaks to my heart, "Your sins are forgiven"—I receive it. For Your very character is behind those words, and You are changeless. Amen.

E. STANLEY JONES | 51

ASSURED BY MANY WITNESSES

Therefore, since we are surrounded by such a great cloud of witnesses, let us throw off everything that hinders and the sin that so easily entangles, and let us run with perseverance the race marked out for us. (Heb. 12:1)

God assures us through the Word. But that Word, speaking specifically and fully through words and deeds in the New Testament, keeps on speaking. The Acts of the Apostles was not completed. It is still going on.

A Chinese cook, hearing that it was the twenty-fifth anniversary of my sailing to India, brought in a cake decorated wtih the words: "Through the ages, one word." It was a quotation from a Confucian classic, but applied to the fact that through the years I had centered my work on just one word—*Christ.* Through the ages, the timeless Word speaks the language of time.

When I was only a teenager, as I knelt seeking restoration to God, someone knelt beside me and quietly said, "God so loved Stanley Jones that He gave His only begotten Son, that if Stanley Jones will believe in Him, he shall not perish but have everlasting life." Did that Christian have a right to assure me in this way? He did. At this altar it was the church whispering its collective witness into my ear.

Sometimes assurance is given through the absolution of a duly appointed priest. I will not quarrel with those who can get assurance in this way, though I must confess I shrink from the idea of the grace of God being almost mechanically dispensed. But, nevertheless, even this may be a phase of that collective witness where men and women and children have arisen from every tribe and tongue and people, in every walk of life, from the peasant to the professor, from every stage of human development, from the ripened sage to the ransomed sinner, and have whispered into the ear of the seeker, "Go on, brother, we give you our collective assurance. We have tried it, and it works."

O Christ of the emerging new humanity, we thank You that there are millions whose hearts You have touched and enlightened, who now lay their grateful tribute at Your feet, and ours. We joyfully join their ranks. Amen.

ASSURED BY NEW MORAL POWER

Oh, what joy for those whose disobedience is forgiven, whose sin is put out of sight! Yes, what joy for those whose record the LORD has cleared of guilt, whose lives are lived in complete honesty! (Psalm 32:1-2†)

Every child of God defeats this evil world, and we achieve this victory through our faith. (1 John 5:4†)

------------------------------ ✦ ------------------------------

In addition to the Word and the collective witness, there is another assurance—the fact of new moral power over sin. God shows Himself within you in your heightened ability to do the right thing.

A man came to me one day and said: "I went out of the meeting last night determined to do just what you asked us to do, namely, to take Christ into our lives. I took Him as you asked us to take Him—by faith. I felt no change at the time. But the next day when I went out into the old surroundings, amid the old temptations, I found to my astonishment that the old temptations had lost their hold on me. I simply didn't want them. Then I woke up to the fact that there was a new power in my life. Christ was there."

Another man did much the same thing—took what I said on faith without any consciousness of change. But he said afterward: "I was a bad-tempered man. If anyone crossed me, I easily flew into a temper. But the next day when someone did me a wrong, instead of anger I felt only pity. I was astonished beyond words at myself."

When we begin to show the fruit of Galatians 5:22-23—"love, joy, peace, patience, kindness, goodness, faithfulness, gentleness and self-control"—then we know we are connected with the root, Christ. The new life is at work within us. I do not mean that these things will be present in full maturity, nor perhaps even in purity, but I do say they will be there in the beginnings. Let that fact assure you. The bud is the prophecy of the flower.

O Christ, I thank You that already I feel within me the stirrings of a new life. I am making the first unsure steps. And as I walk, my legs will grow stronger, and the moral power now begun within me shall ripen into perfect strength. I thank You. Amen.

ASSURED BY THE IMPULSE TO SHARE

Restore to me the joy of your salvation and grant me a willing spirit, to sustain me. Then I will teach transgressors your ways, and sinners will turn back to you. (Psalm 51:12-13)

Because we understand our fearful responsibility to the Lord, we work hard to persuade others…. Christ's love controls us. (2 Cor. 5:11, 14†)

--------------------------------- ⤳ ---------------------------------

There is another source of assurance that the new Life is within us. We will be conscious of the impulse to share something—yes, to share Christ.

Life manifests itself not merely in a desire for more life for itself, but also for more life for others. The two sides of religion are love to God and love to people, and the moment we touch God we will have an impulse to touch people. If, therefore, we are not sure of our love to God, we may be assured of it if we find our love toward people increasing.

If nothing else had assured me that the new life was working within the Chinese engineer, this fact would have assured me: "And, I have been talking to my wife, and she is wanting it too." Now, the wife had been a nominal Christian and he a Confucianist. But the moment the new life came, he wanted to share it, apart from the question of labels.

The moment I arose from my knees after surrendering myself to Christ, I wanted to put my arms around the world. There was an almost irresistible impulse to give this precious fact. I feel that way still.

It may be that you have no such overwhelming impulse; it may be very feeble; it may be just the timid peeping of the bud through the yet partly frozen ground of your reserves, and yet it is there. Act on it today.

You may be rebuffed as I was, when the next day I spoke to my library companion of what had happened. His response: "What? I'll knock that out of you in two weeks." He didn't—he only knocked it deeper.

O Christ, Your love is conquering me, and I want to conquer others for You. Let this feeble love come into flame so that I shall not rest until I have found my brother. Amen

ASSURED BY THE HOLY SPIRIT

Those who obey his commands live in him, and he in them. And this is how we know that he lives in us: We know it by the Spirit he gave us. (1 John 3:24)

But, you say, although these assurances are good and precious beyond words, shall I not see Him face to face? You shall.

I cannot feel that God would give the intimations of His presence by giving His gifts, but would withhold Himself. Would you as a father, a mother, do that to your child? Then, as Jesus put it, "If you then, though you are evil, know how to give good gifts to your children, how much more will your Father in heaven give the Holy Spirit to those who ask him!" (Luke 11:13).

Listen to these words: "The Spirit himself testifies with our spirit that we are God's children" (Rom. 8:16). The Spirit—our spirit. They come together. Now, there is nothing between.

Listen! He speaks, so gently, so intimately. "Child of mine, you will never know how far I have come to find you. I came seeking you through a cross. Now I have found you. You have thrown down the barriers. That is what I've waited for. Now throw away that lingering doubt and fear. It is I. Be not afraid.

"When that last fear is gone, then we will talk together. All you have is Mine—you said it. And now all I have is yours—I say it. Draw on Me for what you need. My resources are adequate, inexhaustible. Tell Me all your troubles, even the little ones, and I will tell you some of Mine. After all, it costs to be God. We shall share together.

"And as we share together, you shall grow, and some day, My son, I want you to be like My other Son. I can think of nothing better for you. You know by My coming that all your sins are forgiven. I blot them out of the book of My remembrance forever. I will not remember them, and you must not."

O God, my Father, I bow in speechless adoration. I, though once vile, am now fully accepted. Amazing grace! I bow at Your feet. And as I do, I feel Your love enfolding me to Your heart. I thank you. Amen.

BEYOND FEELINGS

Just as you received Christ Jesus as Lord, continue to live in him, rooted and built up in him, strengthened in the faith as you were taught, and overflowing with thankfulness. (Col. 2:6-7)

We now have the fivefold strands of assurance binding themselves about our hearts: the Word, the collective witness, our new moral power, our impulse to share, and the direct witness of the Spirit to our spirits. Surely, this should give the strongest assurance that can be given to any mortal.

These lines of assurance all converging give not only a spiritual but an intellectual certainty as well. For the mind, gathering up the facts in experience and the universe results in a sense of wholeness that comes to a mental satisfaction.

But is all this dependent on how I feel about the matter? What if my feelings change?

Our assurance of conversion depends partly on feeling, but only partly. We should not be afraid of emotions, for they are a part of us—an integral part. They give driving force to the soul. But they are liable to fluctuation, according to the state of physical health and many other things. The spiritual life must use them, but it must not be founded on them. It must be centered in the will.

You have made what is called in psychology "a permanent choice." It is one of those choices that does not have to be made over again every day. The lesser choices of life fit into this central permanent choice, not it into them. It remains the permanent abiding fact amid the flow and flux of feeling.

But the decision of the will is not a bare, hard, unfeeling thing. It has its emotional tone, and the more decisive the choice, the deeper the emotional tone. But whether the Ganges is made rough by storms or smooth by calm, it flows on its way. So with you. Yours is a permanent life-choice. Don't raise the issue again every time your feelings change.

O Christ, You do not change, no matter how my feelings fluctuate. You will stay in my heart whether I feel You there or not. I thank You that, as I make the permanent choice, You take up Your permanent residence. Amen.

THE TAKE-OFF

I always pray with joy because of your partnership in the gospel from the first day until now, being confident of this, that he who began a good work in you will carry it on to completion until the day of Christ Jesus. (Phil. 1:4-6)

The first days of adjustment after one makes a life decision are the most difficult. Infant mortality in the kingdom of God is as devastating as infant mortality in India. But most of this in India is preventable. So too, if there are casualties in the new Christian life, they are preventable.

But there is no dodging the fact that the first few days and weeks are the crucial days. An expert in airplanes told me that it takes twice the power for the machine to rise from the ground (or the water surface) as it does to fly. Similarly, it takes twice the power to break with one's old life as it does to live the new life after new habits have been formed.

That need not appall you. This morning in my quiet time I came across this verse: " 'Who will roll the stone away from the entrance of the tomb?' But when they looked up, they saw that the stone, which was very large, had been rolled away" (Mark 16:3-4). We see the difficulties of Christian living like huge stones before us, but as we get to them one by one, they are rolled back. Remember the Silent Partner is also at work, and He is experienced at rolling back stones.

Certain laws of the spiritual life are as definite as the laws that underlie our physical life. Granted, the Christian life is not mechanically and minutely obeying a set of rules. It is a love affair. And lovers don't sit down and look at the rules to see what is to be done next.

Nevertheless, even in love there are underlying laws of friendship that have to be obeyed or else there will be shipwreck. One of the reasons for so many casualties is that we are haphazard. And if we are haphazard, we shall not be happy.

O Christ of the disciplined will, teach me to live the life according to Your way. I come stumblingly, but I come. I am set to obey; teach me. Amen.

COMMIT YOURSELF

Elijah went before the people and said, "How long will you waver between two opinions? If the LORD is God, follow him; but if Baal is God, follow him." (1 Kings 18:21)

The man who had been blind...replied, "Whether he is a sinner or not, I don't know. One thing I do know. I was blind but now I see!" (John 9:24-25)

The Christian life is the beginning of a life as different from the ordinary person as the ordinary person is different from an animal. You are different, and therefore you will act differently. The temptation will be for you to raise no issues, to upset no life-habits, to take on protective resemblance to your environment, and to settle down, hoping that the inward life will somehow or other manifest itself. It won't. You must decide that it shall.

Professor William James, speaking from the standpoint of sound psychology, says in regard to any decision: "When once the judgment is decided, let a man commit himself irretrievably. Let him put himself in a position where it will lay on him the necessity of doing more, the necessity of doing all."

Note that word "irretrievably." Leave no open door behind you. The mind in a fearful moment may be tempted to take that way of escape. You are no longer a person of an escape mentality.

I was recently called out at night by an aide who told me a man was waiting to see me in the garden. As I approached this figure in the dark, I thought I was being held up, for he had a handkerchief over his face, and his hands in his pockets. But he said he wanted to find power over habits and to find a new life.

I did my best in talking with him. But I went away with little hope in my heart. He was afraid that I and others might recognize him.

Off with the handkerchief! Come out of dark gardens where the timid hide behind bushes. Stand before the world, open and decisive. Be ashamed of nothing but sin. Commit yourself.

O Christ, I offer You my resolves. May I take the first bold steps. And help me to take them today. Amen.

DISCIPLINE YOURSELF

Train yourself to be godly. For physical training is of some value, but godliness has value for all things, holding promise for both the present life and the life to come.... Watch your life and doctrine closely. Persevere in them, because if you do, you will save both yourself and your hearers. (1 Tim. 4:7-8, 16)

The word *discipline* and the word *disciple* have a close kinship. The fact is they are one—no discipline, no disciple.

One need of the present day is to put discipline back into life. We have reacted so strongly against the imposed authority and taboos of the Victorian age that we have swung into license, which we thought was liberty. We are now finding out that it isn't.

Teachers today have said the child must be left to guide itself, which meant, in large measure, that the teacher did not want to take on the work of discipline. He was afraid of youth, so he rationalized his fear. But both teacher and youth need discipline.

Otherwise we shall arrive where the Swiss philosopher Henri-Frédéric Amiel, who spent his life dissecting and debunking his own moods, arrived, when he cried out in his *Journal Intime:* "What a strange creature I am! If I were charged with the education of someone, I should seek what is best everywhere and in everything. But for myself I no longer have the taste to reprimand and direct myself. I merely examine myself and state my preference.... I no longer know courage except by name, and hope except by hearsay."

I do not mean that you will have a discipline imposed on you arbitrarily. Instead, you will accept a discipline of your own choosing, under the guidance of God. It will therefore be both yours and God's. In our ashram, we accept a discipline that we arrive at after corporate prayer and consultation. It is not handed to us. We accept it from within.

Sit down in thought and prayer, asking for guidance as you take on yourself a spiritual discipline. When you accept a discipline, then you are a disciple.

O Christ, help me this day to find Your yoke and take it upon me. For Your discipline is my desire. Amen.

ESTABLISH THE PRAYER HABIT

In the morning, O LORD, you hear my voice; in the morning I lay my requests before you and wait in expectation. (Psalm 5:3)

Devote yourselves to prayer, being watchful and thankful. (Col. 4:2)

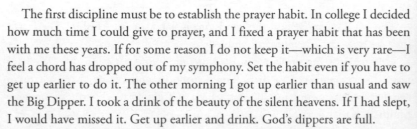

The first discipline must be to establish the prayer habit. In college I decided how much time I could give to prayer, and I fixed a prayer habit that has been with me these years. If for some reason I do not keep it—which is very rare—I feel a chord has dropped out of my symphony. Set the habit even if you have to get up earlier to do it. The other morning I got up earlier than usual and saw the Big Dipper. I took a drink of the beauty of the silent heavens. If I had slept, I would have missed it. Get up earlier and drink. God's dippers are full.

A great Christian in England was very sleepy-headed as a youth, and no matter how much he resolved, he slept past his prayer time. He decided on desperate measures—a penalty that he would throw a guinea into the river every time he missed his prayer time. He did this for several mornings and sadly paid the penalty, which was heavy for a poor student. But at last the mind responded, the prayer habit was fixed, and he became one of the outstanding spiritual men of his generation.

Don't fool yourself into saying you don't need the particular time and place because you will find God all the time and everywhere. If you are to find God all the time, you must find Him sometime; and if you are to find Him everywhere, you will have to find Him somewhere. That sometime and someplace will be the special prayer time and the special prayer place. Establish them.

And as you do, you put your feet upon the road that leads to victory. For spiritual prayer and spiritual fare sound alike and are alike—they are one.

O Christ of the silent midnight hour, teach me to fix the habit of prayer, that I may find the habit of victory. Help me to begin this day in unhurried talk with You. Amen.

INGEST THE LIVING WORD

People do not live by bread alone; rather, we live by every word that comes from the mouth of the LORD. (Deut. 8:3 †)

I have hidden your word in my heart that I might not sin against you. (Psalm 119:11)

Into the prayer hour, take your Testament and a pen. Had I not written down what came to me through the years in the quiet hour, I should have done myself a wrong. For those notes now seem to have been written by someone else. They seem so fresh and new.

A British government official told how he came out to India with no basis for life. His mother gave him a New Testament, which he put in his trunk—at the bottom. But one day out in camp, sick and discouraged, he remembered the Book, fished it out of his trunk…and the first thing his eye fell on was the word "redeemed." That one word was the pivot around which life swung from moral defeat and discouragement to victory and a new life.

You will find such words in the Book, and they will meet your need just when you need them. God has gone into these words, so He comes out of them and meets you there. Sometimes in the rhapsodies of my early Christian life, I would find myself pressing my lips to some verse on the page that seemed so living and saving. I do so still. And why not? For through that verse I kiss my Father's cheek. Does His face not shine through those words? In this way I tell Him I am so grateful that I cannot use the language of words.

And sometimes the word seems so personal—almost as if your own name were called through it, as when my Chinese friend, Doctor Lo, homesick and discouraged in America, turned to his New Testament for light and comfort. The first verse his eye fell on was "Lo, I am with you always" (Matt. 28:20 KJV). It is often just as personal as that!

O Christ, in Your Word we find the Bread of Your life, and we ingest it. We thank You for this food. Amen.

THE HABIT OF SHARING

Now bands from Aram had gone out and had taken captive a young girl from Israel, and she served Naaman's wife. She said to her mistress, "If only my master would see the prophet who is in Samaria! He would cure him of his leprosy." (2 Kings 5:2-3)

Freely you have received, freely give. (Matt. 10:8)

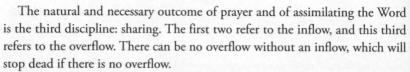

The natural and necessary outcome of prayer and of assimilating the Word is the third discipline: sharing. The first two refer to the inflow, and this third refers to the overflow. There can be no overflow without an inflow, which will stop dead if there is no overflow.

We should discipline ourselves as definitely to share by action and word what we have found, as to pray and read the Word. Many do not do this. They are earnest and regular in their quiet time, but have never disciplined themselves to share. If a happening or a conversation bumps against them and jolts it out of them, well and good. But sharing seems to depend on accident instead of choice—it seems to be in the whim instead of the will. Rather, it should be the natural flowering of communion with God.

A doctor found a little dog by the roadside with a broken leg, took it to his house, and attended to it till it was well. It began to run around the house. And then it disappeared. The doctor felt let down. But the next day there was a scratching at the door. His little dog was back, another little dog was with him—and the other little dog was lame!

The impulse in that dog's heart was natural and right. Has not Christ healed you? And if so, is not the natural, normal thing for you to find somebody else who needs that healing too?

O Christ, Your healing is upon our hearts. Help us to bear Your healing help within our hands. Help us this day to find some crippled human spirit whom we can lead to You. Amen.

THE NEW LIFE AND ENTERTAINMENT

Whether you eat or drink or whatever you do, do it all for the glory of God. (1 Cor. 10:31)

Do your best to present yourself to God as one approved, a workman who does not need to be ashamed and who correctly handles the word of truth. (2 Tim. 2:15)

You must now relate your new life to your recreations and entertainments. Or, rather, you must relate those things to the new life. For recreation must not be the center, and the new life fitted into it. If you try that, the new life will die. You must now go over your recreations and see whether they contribute to or dim the new life. They should stay only as they minister to your total fitness.

Some recreations do not re-create—they exhaust one. They leave one morally and spiritually flabby and unfit. They should therefore go, or be so controlled that they really do re-create. I find after seeing some films that I have been inspired and lifted. But often a film leaves one with the sense of having been inwardly ravished. The delicacies of life seem to have been invaded, the finest flowers of the spirit trampled upon. You come out drooping. We should never expose ourselves to such a film—not if we value the higher values.

The same can be said of many books. The idea that you must read everything that comes along in order to understand life is a false notion. Does the doctor have to take typhoid germs into his body before he can understand typhoid? Does one have to wallow in a mud hole in order to understand the meaning of filth? Only cleanliness can understand the meaning of filth.

To spend long and exhausting hours over bridge tables with emotions aroused that have no constructive outlet is to leave one spiritually weaker. Ask yourself, therefore, whether your "bridge" is a bridge toward finer and more victorious living, or whether it is a bridge that leads to spiritual anemia.

Go over your whole life and ask whether your recreations really re-create.

O Christ of the fit body and soul, make me fit in every part of my being. And may my recreations contribute to that end. Amen.

WHO NEEDS CHURCH?

How good and pleasant it is when brothers live together in unity! (Psalm 133:1)

Let us consider how we may spur one another on toward love and good deeds. Let us not give up meeting together, as some are in the habit of doing, but let us encourage one another—and all the more as you see the Day approaching. (Heb. 10:24-25)

The spiritual life cannot be lived in isolation. Life is intensely personal; it is also intensely corporate, and you cannot separate them. If you should wipe out the church today, you would have to put something like it in its place tomorrow, for there must be a corporate expression of the spiritual life as well as an individual.

The idea that it is your duty to support the church seems to me to be all wrong. The church is not founded upon a duty imposed on you from outside. It is founded on the facts of life. Your very inner nature demands it. American evangelist D. L. Moody, in answer to a man who said he did not need the church, quietly pulled a coal from the hearth and separated it, and together they watched it die. It was a legitimate answer.

I am quite sure I would not have survived as a young Christian had I not had the corporate life of the church to hold me up. When I rejoiced, they rejoiced with me. When I was weak, they strengthened me. And once when I fell—a rather bad fall—they gathered around me by prayer and love, and without blame or censure they lovingly lifted me back to my feet again.

The church's stupidities and inanities and irrelevancies and formalities—yes, I know them all. But nevertheless, the church is the mother of my spirit, and one loves his mother in spite of weakness and wrinkles. My word, then, to you is that, as you begin this new life, you begin it as a member of the Family.

Christ, who read our deepest need and who gathered us together into a Family in which You are the Elder Brother and God is our Father, we thank You that You invite us to take our place in the Family circle. We do. Amen.

AN HONEST LOOK AT CHRISTENDOM

Dear brothers and sisters, when I was with you I couldn't talk to you as I would to spiritual people. I had to talk as though you belonged to this world or as though you were infants in the Christian life. I had to feed you with milk, not with solid food, because you weren't ready for anything stronger. And you still aren't ready, for you are still controlled by your sinful nature. You are jealous of one another and quarrel with each other. (1 Cor. 3:1-3†)

It would seem that we might now go straight from the beginning of the new life and talk about our relationships to the social order. But we cannot—not yet.

For to do that would mean to bypass the question of victorious living within the ranks of Christians themselves, within the ranks of the converted and the semiconverted and—shall I add?— the unconverted inside the church. For we have all three. Even the most enthusiastic would scarcely claim that victorious living characterizes the church's rank and file. Here and there one sees it, but the chief thing that strikes me in looking at Christendom is the lack of it.

I had asked a congregation in India to express this desire for a new life, and many had done so. The pastor was translating my prayer, in which I said, "O God, we do not know what these people need, but you know." He translated, "O God, you know what these people need, and so do we"! He could not let my statement pass!

Spiritually we seem to have turned gray. The vivacity, the sparkle, the spontaneity, the joy, the radiance that should characterize people called Christians seems to have faded out. Moreover, there seems a lack of moral dynamic, a paralysis that makes us limp and helpless in the face of rampant wrong. We protest, but seem to have little power to change.

There is nothing, absolutely nothing needed so much among Christians today as the discovery of the secret of victorious living. If we can find that, anything can happen. Without that, nothing will happen, except staleness, tastelessness, and bitter disappointment with religion.

O Christ, are You putting Your finger on our need? Then help us not to rest till we know this secret, and use it in our living. Amen.

E. STANLEY JONES | 65

EXPECTING NOTHING

He said to his disciples, "Why are you so afraid? Do you still have no faith?"
(Mark 4:40)

"When the Son of Man comes, will he find faith on the earth?" (Luke 18:8)

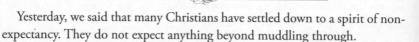

Yesterday, we said that many Christians have settled down to a spirit of non-expectancy. They do not expect anything beyond muddling through.

I have watched what the awful power of fatalism can do when it falls upon a civilization. I have seen the lovely people of the East paralyzed at the center by a strange resignation that makes them throw up their hands. Across the world, that danger is at our doors. It has slowly crept into many a heart, and we are resigned to moral and spiritual defeat.

Dr. Elwood Worcester of Boston, who has labored for years in clinics for people troubled in body and soul, can say these astonishing words: "Most Christians do not expect their religion to do them any great or immediate good." When one tells them that this condition of moral and spiritual defeat need not last for a single hour, that we can find victory and adequacy and buoyancy in living, they look at you as one who announces strange doctrine. For they have become naturalized in defeat.

In his book, *Reason and Emotion* (p. 86), John Macmurray quotes Mathias Alexander, who tells the story of a little girl who was permanently lopsided and who was brought to him for treatment. After working with her for some time, he managed to get her to stand quite straight. Then he asked her to walk across to her mother. She walked perfectly straight for the first time in her life and then, bursting into tears, threw herself into her mother's arms, crying, "Oh, Mummy, I'm all crooked."

We, too, think of being spiritually straight and upstanding and adequate as something strange and unnatural.

O Christ, speak to our dead desires and tell them to rise. We know we cannot live unless, first of all, we desire it. We do desire to live, fully and adequately. Your pressure awakens us. Our eyes are coming open. Amen.

IS FORGIVENESS THE BEST WE CAN EXPECT?

What shall we say, then? Shall we go on sinning so that grace may increase? By no means! We died to sin; how can we live in it any longer? Or don't you know that all of us who were baptized into Christ Jesus were baptized into his death? (Rom. 6:1-3)

Many Christians do not expect anything beyond repeated forgiveness for constantly repeated sins. They do not expect victory over sins. Therefore, in Christianity the most beautiful thing, namely the forgiving grace of God, is often turned into the most baneful, for it actually turns out to be something that encourages evil. What a cross that must be on the heart of God! And what a travesty it is on our Christian faith!

The Hindu believes he will have to suffer for his sins; the law of karma will exact the last jot of retribution. There is no forgiveness. Samuel Evans Stokes Jr., a famous American missionary who turned Hindu, told me that one reason he did so was that he wanted his "children to be brought up under karma, rather than under redemption." I could see his point if redemption meant constant forgiveness for constantly repeated sins. And if I had to choose between a cheap, easy forgiveness on the one hand and the law of karma on the other hand, I would choose the law of karma.

But I do not have to make that choice. The gospel does offer forgiveness for sins, but along with it, and as a part of it, offers power over the sins forgiven. Forgiveness and power are the indissoluble parts of the grace of God. We cannot take one without the other.

If we try to take the forgiveness without the power, it means that moral weakness remains. And if we try to take the power without the forgiveness, it means that moral guilt remains. God does not give one without the other. We must take both or neither.

O Christ, we thank You for redemption, which comes out of the cross. But we have twisted it and made it into a further cross for You. Forgive us—and give us power to do so no more. Power—we need power. Amen.

THE GOSPEL'S AMAZING OFFER

Therefore, there is now no condemnation for those who are in Christ Jesus, because through Christ Jesus the law of the Spirit of life set me free from the law of sin and death. (Rom. 8:1-2)

There are two dangers at this point. One is to make the standard of godliness too low, and the other is to make it too high. In either case, it paralyzes us—one because it demands no change, and the other because it demands such a change that we simply feel helpless and give up the struggle. We must avoid this double danger.

It is interesting that both modern psychology and the gospel unite in being pessimistic about humanity. They both say we are less perfect than we might be; that there are great possibilities for idealistic progress that we universally reject. One author quotes Freud as saying, "Psychoanalysis here confirms what the pious were wont to say—that we are miserable sinners."

But while they are both pessimistic about humanity, they are both amazingly optimistic. Both modern psychology and the teaching of the gospel unite in saying that this divided state must not continue, that people and their ideals must come together if human happiness is to result. Sin is no necessary part of our make-up. It is no more necessary to give spice to life than sand in the eye is necessary for sight.

The first thing, then, is to get hold of this: The gospel offers freedom and release from every single sin. There is no compromise at that point, for compromise would be deadly! It sweeps the horizon and says, "Sin shall not be your master" (Rom. 6:14).

We have repeated these words until they are, to many of us, threadbare. But, in truth, they are the astonishing offer of God to give us release from the tyranny of evil.

O Christ, we thank You for what this opens up to us. It is the open door out of our inner divisions, strife, and confusions. It leads to harmony, to just what we want. We thank You. Amen.

WHAT THE VICTORIOUS LIFE IS NOT (PART 1)

Because he himself [Christ] suffered when he was tempted, he is able to help those who are being tempted. (Heb. 2:18)

The temptations in your life are no different from what others experience. And God is faithful. He will not allow the temptation to be more than you can stand. When you are tempted, he will show you a way out so that you can endure. (1 Cor. 10:13†)

In order to see what the victorious life is, we must first see what it is not.

It is not freedom from temptation. Sin results from using a good thing in a wrong way. Just as dirt is misplaced matter, so sin is misplaced good. Sex is natural and right; adultery is sin. Self-respect, if pushed too far, becomes pride, hence sin. Self-love is normal; if pushed beyond limits, it becomes selfishness. The group instinct is right, but when it goes against our ideals and we make the group the final arbiter, it is sin.

James says, "When you are being tempted, do not say, 'God is tempting me.'… Temptation comes from our own desires, which entice us and drag us away." (James 1:13-14†). Note the phrase "drag us away." The natural is coaxed too far into the sinful.

Now, the natural is always with us. Every moment it presses upon the boundaries we set up. Every moment, therefore, we shall be tempted. But temptation is not sin. Only when we yield does it become sin. As the old saying puts it, "You cannot stop the birds flying over your head, but you can stop them from building nests in your hair." You cannot stop the suggestion of evil, but you can stop holding it, harboring it, and allowing it to rest in your mind till it hatches its brood. If dismissed at once, it leaves no stain. Thoughts of evil only become evil thoughts when we invite them in and offer them a chair.

It is safe to say: Constant temptation may be consistent with victorious living.

O Christ of the wilderness struggle, we thank You that You are in our struggles, lifting, saving, and turning the tide of battle. Go with me today as I turn temptation into character. Amen.

E. STANLEY JONES | 69

WHAT THE VICTORIOUS LIFE IS NOT (PART 2)

Paul: *I don't mean to say that I have already achieved these things or that I have already reached perfection. But...I focus on this one thing: Forgetting the past and looking forward to what lies ahead, I press on to reach the end of the race and receive the heavenly prize for which God, through Christ Jesus, is calling us. (Phil. 3:12-14†)*

Nor does victorious living mean freedom from mistakes. We are personalities in the making, limited and grappling with things too high for us. Obviously, we, at very best, will make many mistakes. But these mistakes need not be sins.

Our actions are the result of our intentions and our intelligence. Our intentions may be very good, but because the intelligence is limited, our action may turn out to be a mistake. That is not the same thing as a sin, for sin comes out of a wrong intention. The misguided action carries a sense of incompleteness and frustration, but not of guilt.

Nor does it mean maturity. It does mean a cleansing away of things that hinder growth, but it is not full growth. In addition to many mistakes in our lives, there will be many immaturities. Purity is not maturity. This gospel of ours is called the Way. Our feet are on that Way, but we have not arrived at the goal.

Nor does it mean that we may not occasionally lapse into a wrong act, which may be called a sin. At that point we may have lost a skirmish, but it doesn't mean we cannot still win the battle. We may even lose a battle and still win the war. One of the differences between a sheep and a pig is that when a sheep falls into a mud hole, it bleats to get out, while the pig loves it and wallows in it.

In saying that an occasional lapse is consistent with victorious living, I am possibly opening the door to rationalization. There must be no such provision in the mind. But victorious living can exist with occasional failure.

O Christ, we thank You for the truth of what the Psalmist said: "He knows our frame; He remembers that we are dust" (Psalm 103:14 NKJV). And yet we know that You can remake that frame in Your likeness. We gladly put ourselves under Your processes. Amen.

WHAT THE VICTORIOUS LIFE IS NOT (PART 3)

After some time Paul said to Barnabas, "Let's go back and visit each city where we previously preached the word of the Lord, to see how the new believers are doing." Barnabas agreed and wanted to take along John Mark. But Paul disagreed strongly, since John Mark had deserted them in Pamphylia and had not continued with them in their work. Their disagreement was so sharp that they separated. (Acts 15:36-39†)

Victorious living does not mean the ability to get along with everybody. There are certain people whose outlook and interests are so different from ours that, when we are thrown into close contact, we find it practically impossible to get along with them. And they may be very good people. Nevertheless, we find ourselves incompatible.

John Wesley was married to one such person. Others are. But who would say that John Wesley was not a victorious soul? He used that situation to make him a better, more patient, victorious man.

If two of you are in Christian work and find you are incompatible, the best thing to do is to talk the matter over frankly and honestly. If there is no other way out, get a transfer. But—and this is the point—as you talk the matter over calmly and honestly, you will probably find that what you thought were incompatibilities are misunderstandings. You will see the other person's point of view, and seeing it, you will probably sympathize with it. It is not at all necessary to agree with another person to get along with them.

In our ashram, we bring together people of differing outlooks, temperaments, races, and theological beliefs. We undertake to make a community out of these differences. We see very often that the difficulties are not rooted in our real nature, but in complexes, in hidden sin, in wrong attitudes, which when brought out and corrected lead to an amazing depth of fellowship. There are some incompatibles—but they are very, very few.

O Christ of the patient heart, we thank You for the possibility of bridging gulfs through love. Teach us to love even those whom we find hardest to love. Amen.

THE VICTORIOUS LIFE DEFINED (PART 1)

May God himself, the God of peace, sanctify you through and through. May your whole spirit, soul and body be kept blameless at the coming of our Lord Jesus Christ. The one who calls you is faithful and he will do it. (1 Thess. 5:23-24)

<hr>

We have seen what the victorious life is not. We must now see what it is: *It is the life of Christ reigning victoriously in every portion of our being and in every one of our relationships.* Many Christians have certain areas of their lives in which Christ functions, feebly perhaps, but there is a functioning. But there are areas withheld. There are "reserved subjects" in the government of the soul. Over these reserved areas we rule; we make the decisions there.

When the British reserved certain subjects after turning over other subjects to Indians, that kind of government was called "dyarchy." It was a failure. The attempt to have a spiritual dyarchy within our souls is also bound to fail. Yet millions of Christians attempt it and wonder why the spiritual life is so unsatisfactory.

We cannot be happy and effective with an inner division. We must be unified. You must make your choice: Either you must dismiss Christ entirely from your life and forget Him, taking over the entire control into your own hands, in which case you will be unified under the control of self; or you must make a complete surrender of every withheld area into the control of Christ, in which case the life will be Christ-controlled and therefore unified.

There is no intermediate way. And yet millions are trying the way of compromise between. It won't work. We have just enough of the love of Christ in our hearts to make us miserable. A war is set up between opposing ideas of life, and we live in that war and call it being Christian.

As pure unadulterated pagans we might be happy. "Might be," I say, for the attempt has so far not succeeded. But as compromised Christians we can never be happy.

O Christ, forgive us that we have thought to make You a half-king, leaving other half-gods in our hearts. We cannot bow at a double shrine. Forgive us. Amen.

THE VICTORIOUS LIFE DEFINED (Part 2)

Though you bring choice fellowship offerings, I will have no regard for them. Away with the noise of your songs! I will not listen to the music of your harps. But let justice roll on like a river, righteousness like a never-failing stream! (Amos 5:22-24)

No one can serve two masters; for either he will hate the one and love the other, or else he will be loyal to the one and despise the other. You cannot serve God and mammon. (Matt. 6:24 NKJV)

Duality cannot be introduced within the soul without disaster. But there is another point of duality that is just as disastrous—it is the point between the individual and the social. If duality is introduced at that point, there will also be defeat. The life of Christ must rule in every one of our relationships.

Now, many try to decide that Christ shall function in their personal lives, but the social and economic life is something else. There, other ideas and ideals must be applied.

Of these two dualities I am not certain which is the more disastrous. Possibly the latter. For if an amazing amount of unhappiness is born of inner division, then a greater amount of unhappiness comes out of this division which applies one rulership on the inside (Christ) and another rulership on the outside (mammon). This is the point where the house of present-day civilization is divided against itself, and it cannot stand. With this duality at its heart, our present-day life is unhappy and paralyzed.

My relationships with others are just as much a part of my personal life as my so-called inner life. Think of how much of your personal life is made up with relationships with others, and how much is made up of relationships with yourself alone, and you will see at once that they cannot be divided.

Victorious living must include both, for it takes in life, and life takes in both.

O Christ, You are claiming the whole of life. We can no longer tolerate these paralyzing divisions. Help us to end them by bringing everything under Your sway. Amen.

DOES CONVERSION GIVE US VICTORY?

Live by the Spirit, and you will not gratify the desires of the sinful nature. For the sinful nature desires what is contrary to the Spirit, and the Spirit what is contrary to the sinful nature. They are in conflict with each other, so that you are not to do what you want. But if you are led by the Spirit, you are not under law. (Gal. 5:16-18)

Now let us step back a bit. Does the victorious life take place in what we call conversion? Or is a further crisis, or a number of crises, necessary to bring about this complete sway of the life of Christ?

Conversion is certainly the beginning of victorious living. Here life is lifted to a permanently higher level. Things are changed. "Do you know me?" eagerly asked a Hindu youth. "I am sure you don't, for I am not the same person who saw you yesterday. Last evening as I sat on the hilltop looking at the sunset, Christ came into my life. I am strangely new today." Indeed he was; we all are, when the new life is introduced within us.

Most of us experience a rapid climb to a new height in conversion. But afterward there unfolds a tableland of alternate defeat and victory. It is up and down. A very radiant soul in one of our Round Table Conferences said religion meant three things to him: victory, victory, victory. But to some of us it means no such thing. On the lowest scale, it means defeat, defeat, defeat. A little higher, it means an alternation of defeat, victory, defeat. Or, better still, it may mean victory, defeat, victory. Often we feel disappointed and aggrieved. We expected more.

Conversion introduced new life, but not full life. As the first flush of the new life ebbs a bit, we find things within us we did not dream could survive the inrush of the new. But they have. The rank growth of weeds has been cut down, but roots have remained. We cry out for full deliverance.

O Christ, having begun a new work within us, will You not complete it? Our very uneasiness is a sign of Your redemptive love at work, gently pointing out that we ail here and ail there. Heal us where we ail, and heal us completely. Amen.

THE INNER CONFLICT

We know that the law is spiritual; but I am unspiritual, sold as a slave to sin. I do not understand what I do. For what I want to do I do not do, but what I hate I do…. I have the desire to do what is good, but I cannot carry it out. (Rom. 7:14-15, 18)

I found after my conversion a strange conflict ensuing. For weeks I did not think there could be any conflict; life was one glad and unified day. But I soon found something rather strange for me—I began to be bad-tempered and morose. I had usually been sunny-tempered, so the tendency to get out of patience startled me.

I could not account for it, for I was never more earnest and Christ was never more precious. I found myself divided.

Modern psychology tells us that down in the subconscious lie the instincts, holding within them the basic habits and tendencies of humanity. They reflect experience running back through a long history. They have certain leanings, certain drives that if unrestrained tend toward evil. This all sounds strangely like the almost forgotten doctrine of original sin. But there it is.

Conversion sweeps out of the *conscious* mind all that conflicts with the love of Christ and the establishing of His reign there. For weeks perhaps, no conflict ensues; the new life reigns supreme. These instincts in the subconscious are cowed—but hardly converted. They soon demand recognition and expression. They knock at the door of the conscious. We are startled that there are voices in the cellar.

To change the metaphor: These suppressed instincts are like pirates who hide in the hold of the vessel, then rise up while the ship is on her voyage and try to capture the bridge. A fight breaks out.

With the introduction of new life within me by conversion, a conflict began between this new life and the old life found in the instincts. I was divided.

O Christ, You know what is in every human being. I open all of myself to You. Cleanse me in the secret places, the hidden depths. I want to be unified. Amen.

CAN THE SUBCONSCIOUS BE CONVERTED?

Since we have these promises, dear friends, let us purify ourselves from everything that contaminates body and spirit, perfecting holiness out of reverence for God. (2 Cor. 7:1)

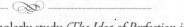

Dr. R. Newton Flew ends his scholarly study *(The Idea of Perfection in Christian Theology)* with this rather startling question: "Is salvation possible for the subconscious? This is the real question for the seeker after holiness in our time." He has raised a most important issue.

These instincts cannot be eradicated, though India has certainly tried. Her holy men try by every possible device to root them out. But, expelled through the door, they come back by the window. I have seen naked sadhus, who had renounced not only the world but even themselves, become entirely touchy about getting the proper place and prestige in processions going to bathe in the sacred Ganges. These instincts still showed through the ashes! You cannot eradicate them.

Nor must you repress them. If they are repressed, then they are driven below and form what is called a complex, "a system of emotionally toned ideas arranged around one central idea." They are festering places in the subconscious mind. To repress them is dangerous.

Then, if they cannot be eradicated, and they must not be repressed, and in the interests of the new life we cannot tolerate them, is there no way out?

Psychology says they can be redirected—that is, turned into expression in a higher form. In the language of religion, we say they can be converted. We cannot put them out, nor put them under, but we can put them *behind* the central purposes of our lives, where they can become the driving force. Our former enemies now become the allies of the new life. The wild horses are now tamed and harnessed to the tasks of the kingdom.

O Christ, we thank You that in Your life every power, conscious and subconscious, was dedicated to the kingdom. We want that oneness within us. Amen.

A FURTHER STEP

Jesus to His disciples: *"You are witnesses of these things. I am going to send you what my Father has promised; but stay in the city until you have been clothed with power from on high." (Luke 24:48-49)*

All of them were filled with the Holy Spirit and began to speak in other tongues as the Spirit enabled them. (Acts 2:4)

Of course we all face many spiritual crises along the spiritual way. But what about another decisive event like conversion? Yes, I think that usually we must have it. For we cannot go on changed in our conscious mind while we are unchanged (or only partially changed) in the subconscious. The instincts must be brought into line. We must be inwardly unanimous, or we shall be outwardly defeated. We cannot carry on a civil war and a foreign war at the same time.

It is instructive to find many different types of movements—the Holiness movement, the Pentecostal, the Wesleyan, the Keswick, the Oxford Group, and many others—all converging on this one fact, namely, that we need to bring the whole of life into line with the will of God. And they all say that while conversion began this process, a further crisis in some form or other is necessary.

Are they all wrong about this? I grant that they are wrong in many things, for many stupidities have been built up around these movements. But in the central thing I believe they are profoundly right. At least I have found it so in my own experience and in the lives of thousands of others with whom I have dealt.

I have seen hundreds of missionaries come out to India, and their dedication to mission work carries them through for a year, perhaps longer. But the environment sooner or later strips them bare. India finds them. They are then driven to a deeper and more complete self-giving and thus go into victory—or they sink back into being very mediocre Christians, serving Christ but not living like Him. They develop bad tempers and superiority complexes and attitudes of patronage. The result is not a clear-cut Christian impression, but a spiritual blur.

O Christ of the united will, we bring ours to You. Our wills are not united, but we want them to be. We consent for them to be. Amen.

THE OLD AND THE NEW SIDE BY SIDE

Once when Jesus was praying in private and his disciples were with him, he asked them, "Who do the crowds say I am?"

They replied, "Some say John the Baptist; others say Elijah; and still others, that one of the prophets of long ago has come back to life."

"But what about you?" he asked. "Who do you say I am?"

Peter answered, "The Christ of God." (Luke 9:18-20)

This fact of the old and the new side by side and unrelated to each other can be seen in the case of the disciples. Read carefully Luke 9:18-62.

Jesus took them to Caesarea Philippi, where there was a white rock with a grotto and temple in which the image of Caesar was worshiped as God in the flesh. Here the great battle was joined: Is Caesar God manifest in the flesh? In other words, is force the final word? Or is Jesus God manifest in the flesh? Is love the final word?

Peter gave the great confession. We would have thought that from this moment on, everything in their lives would have adjusted itself to that fact and their spiritual lives would have taken on harmony and power.

On the contrary, nothing goes right in the rest of Luke 9. Peter talks out of turn at the Transfiguration. The nine disciples fail at casting out a demon. The group argues about their relative status. John shows a sectarian streak. Then he and his brother, James, wish to call down fire on a Samaritan village.

Jesus does nothing to the end of the chapter but correct their mistakes. What is wrong? Had they not seen this glorious fact of Christ, the Son of the living God? Yes, the conscious mind had accepted that fact, but the subconscious mind had not. They had been converted, but their instincts had not.

Jesus immediately said to them, "If anyone would come after me, he must deny himself" (v. 23). He launched a dart straight at the self.

O Christ, we come to You. You have Your finger upon our problem—it is this inmost self. If You heal us there, we will be healed everywhere. So heal us there, we pray. Amen.

THE CENTRAL DIFFICULTY

He took Peter, John and James with him and went up onto a mountain to pray. As he was praying, the appearance of his face changed, and his clothes became as bright as a flash of lightning. Two men, Moses and Elijah, appeared in glorious splendor, talking with Jesus. They spoke about his departure [in Greek: exodus*], which he was about to bring to fulfillment at Jerusalem. (Luke 9:28-31)*

Jesus undertook to show His disciples that He Himself was going to the cross to lay down Himself, and they too must do the same—they must go through spiritually what He was going through physically. The central thing in their being sons of God must be a self-losing. But in losing themselves, they would find themselves.

They did not catch this profoundest of spiritual lessons. So He took three of them to the mountain to show them the same thing in a kindergarten way. As He talked with Moses and Elijah about His death, His face began to shine. The lesson? Life only shines as it faces its cross.

They did not get the meaning. At the foot of the mountain the other disciples were fumbling. Divided in inner allegiance, they were defeated in outer attempts. So Jesus cast out the evil spirit with a word. "They were all amazed at the majesty of God" (v. 43 NKJV). But as they marveled, Jesus said to His disciples, "Listen to me and remember what I say. The Son of Man is going to be betrayed into the hands of his enemies." (v. 44†). In other words, You think My "majesty" is in performing miracles of deliverance, but My "majesty" lies in the miracle of self-losing. That is the central thing I have come to do in Myself—and you.

"But they understood not this saying" (v. 45 KJV). They understood not this saying because they understood not this attitude. We really think more with our emotions than with our minds, and their emotions were still fastened on the self. They were not surrendered.

O Christ, You have blazed the way for us. We see Your amazing example of self-losing that turned into an amazing self-finding. We want to follow You. Amen.

SELF-INSTINCT ON DISPLAY

His disciples began arguing about which of them was the greatest. But Jesus knew their thoughts, so he brought a little child to his side. Then he said to them, "Anyone who welcomes a little child like this on my behalf welcomes me, and anyone who welcomes me also welcomes my Father who sent me. Whoever is the least among you is the greatest." (Luke 9:46-48†)

This attitude of the unchanged self-instinct began to show itself in social consequences. The clashes began. Wherever there is a group of people who have unsurrendered (and therefore unsocialized) selves, the stage is set for clash and strife. If the self is supreme on the inside, it will try to be supreme on the outside.

Here was Christian disciple clashing with Christian disciple, and all were clashing with the whole outlook of the Master. Of course they all fought for principle! For the self soon learns that it cannot get its way in the presence of religious scruples unless its assertions are clothed with religious principles. Each convinced himself that the interests of the kingdom demanded that he be first. "I am the oldest," we can imagine Peter saying, "and, besides, I made the great confession of His Messiahship. The interests of the kingdom demand that age and insight be first."

"But who brought you here?" demanded Andrew. "First here, first in authority."

"But I have connections to the high priest," replied John. "After all, if we are to influence these big people for the kingdom, I must lead."

"But the kingdom depends on solid financial sense. I am treasurer and therefore first," said Judas with an air of finality. And so probably it went.

Nine-tenths of the difficulties in Christian service come out of clashes between Christian workers. And nine-tenths of these clashes come out of the unregenerate self-instinct of otherwise converted people.

O Christ, who showed the nature of the kingdom through a little child, make me a child again. I must be reborn deeper this time. Amen.

GROUP RIPPLES

"Master," said John, "we saw a man driving out demons in your name and we tried to stop him, because he is not one of us."

"Do not stop him," Jesus said, "for whoever is not against you is for you." (Luke 9:49-50)

When the unregenerate self-instinct is dropped into human relationships, it sends out waves of clash to the far shores of society.

As Jesus was dealing with His disciples over the matter of their comparative greatness, John felt the sting of it and brought up what had been said to the uncertified exorcist. Here was a second clash—one group of workers with another group of workers. While the unregenerate self-instinct may readily fight with individual members of its own group for place and power, it is quite ready to combine with them against the encroachments of another group. The self sees in any threat to the group a threat to its own self. It is ready to stand up and fight—for principle, of course! "Who are these unauthorized people? They are dangerous. They are not from the proper line. Besides, did they say the formula for casting out devils properly as we do? It must be stopped."

The unregenerate self-instinct is behind the religious party spirit, and it is the basis of a great deal of denominational refusal to unite with other Christians.

1 was trying to heal a breach within a church that had resulted in spending the equivalent of $200,000 in court for the right to manage an endowment of $4,000. Said a high ecclesiastic, one of the party leaders concerned, "We must defend the faith."

I think he really thought he was defending the faith, for the self often stands concealed in the shadows of the unconscious. But anyone could see that "the defense of the faith" meant only that the self was defending and asserting itself through group supremacy. The faith was really in the mud.

O Christ, how our narrowness and bigotry must re-crucify You, for Your heart is kingdom-wide, and beyond! Make us like that. Amen.

RACIAL RIPPLES

As they went, they entered a village of the Samaritans, to prepare for Him. But they did not receive Him, because His face was set for the journey to Jerusalem. And when His disciples James and John saw this, they said, "Lord, do You want us to command fire to come down from heaven and consume them, just as Elijah did?"

But He turned and rebuked them, and said, "You do not know what manner of spirit you are of." (Luke 9:52-55 NKJV)

Jesus sent His disciples to a Samaritan village to prepare for Him. The Samaritans refused to accept them because He was heading for Jerusalem, the Jewish capital. The two disciples were furious, suggesting a mass immolation.

The self is ready to assert itself through one race against another race. Again, it does so religiously: "Lord…from heaven…just as Elijah did." But underneath all this religious verbiage was the stark fact that the inner Jewish self hated Samaritans, for they were in a struggle for position and power. We dress up our prejudices in religious garments in order to conceal the naked selfishness beneath.

But such racial prejudices are not inborn. The self learns them from the social heredity. Missionary children born in other lands grow up among children of another race and know no such bias. Deep and abiding friendships are born. If they later absorb racial prejudice, it is from surroundings, not inherited.

With all of us, these prejudices are dropped into the subconscious, and the self-instinct absorbs them there. We wonder why we are critical about other races, easily finding their faults, even glorying in their weaknesses. The reason is that the subconscious mind has absorbed the prejudices, and the subconscious mind is still unregenerate. The self-instinct has not yet bowed to the yoke of the kingdom of God.

O Father, who made every person of every race, forgive me for not loving all You made. But I cannot do it unless this inner self bends its head and accepts Your yoke. Help me to do it. Amen.

STARK CONTRAST

For he himself is our peace, who has made the two one and has destroyed the barrier, the dividing wall of hostility. (Eph. 2:14)

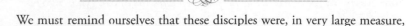

We must remind ourselves that these disciples were, in very large measure, changed men. Most of their conscious mind was under the sway of Christ; however, most of the unconscious was not.

Take note of these contrasts. We saw in Luke 9 that recognizing Christ as the Son of God solved very few of their spiritual problems. It left untouched the problems of inner adjustment, adjustment between individuals, between groups, and between races. But those four problems were later solved so easily and majestically that we scarcely notice. Now look:

Acts 2:46 (KJV) speaks about the disciples' "gladness and singleness of heart." Problem number one was gone; they were no longer at war with themselves in the inner life. They were single-hearted, no longer double-hearted.

Acts 2:14 tells how "Peter stood up with the Eleven." They willingly stood together. Problem number two had evaporated; they were no longer competitive, but cooperative.

Acts 2:44 plainly states, "All the believers were together." This made them into a living brotherhood, where they rejoiced in each other's successes. That solved problem number three: There was no longer suspicion among groups.

Acts 8:14-17 relates, "When the apostles in Jerusalem heard that Samaria had accepted the word of God, they sent Peter and John to them. When they arrived, they…placed their hands on them, and they received the Holy Spirit." Instead of calling down fire from heaven to consume the Samaritans, they tenderly laid hands on their heads, that they might receive the Holy Spirit. That solved problem number four: Their racial prejudices disappeared.

All four of their problems had vanished. How? It can be answered in one phrase: The Holy Spirit!

O God, our Father, we thank You that You have provided for the depths. You are not leaving us unhealed there. We thank You. Amen.

AN ARTESIAN WELL, NOT A PUMP

If you live according to the sinful nature, you will die; but if by the Spirit you put to death the misdeeds of the body, you will live. (Rom. 8:13)

Since we live by the Spirit, let us keep in step with the Spirit. (Gal. 5:25)

Most of Christendom stands with the disciples and declares that Jesus Christ is the Son of God, but is appalled and dismayed that this does not solve their spiritual problems. It leaves practically all their great problems intact.

To recognize Christ as the Son of God is more or less an outer thing, a matter of the perceptive intelligence, a matter of our conscious mind. This may not touch the subconscious at all. But the Holy Spirit does.

For the area of the work of the Spirit is in the subconscious as well as the conscious. The subconscious can be cleansed, converted, controlled, and united with the purposes of the conscious mind by (and only by) the Holy Spirit. Following Christ as an example will not do it, for this is more or less outer. What we need has to be deeply and permanently inward.

Even seeing the Holy Spirit as an influence that comes now and again will not do it. The Holy Spirit as a living Person must permanently abide in the depths of our being, assuming full control, cleansing, directing, and coordinating the powers of the instincts to the purposes of the kingdom of God.

The disciples after Pentecost were not mechanically trying to copy Christ in their actions. They were joyously expressing a new life that welled up from within. The Christian life was not a force pump, but an artesian well.

Therefore their lives were not mechanically and jerkily trying to copy an Example. They were rhythmically and harmoniously giving vent to an inner Life. They were no longer double-minded, with the conscious domain warring against the subconscious. They were single-minded because they were single-controlled. They were Spirit-filled people.

O God our Father, we thank You that we need not go through life with an inner contradiction. You can bring everything under Your way. Then there will be no part that is dark. Amen.

STUNTED LIVES

We have much to say about this, but it is hard to explain because you are slow to learn. In fact, though by this time you ought to be teachers, you need someone to teach you the elementary truths of God's word all over again. You need milk, not solid food!... Therefore let us leave the elementary teachings about Christ and go on to maturity. (Heb. 5:11-12; 6:1)

Spiritual freedom is not a characteristic of present-day Christianity. We are stiff, stilted, inwardly tied-up Christians. Said one horrified English lady, "People in this place will insist on talking about God outside of church." God as the thought of our thought, the joy of our joy, and the life of our life—well, that isn't our common experience. Yes, but it is normal Christianity.

"I came to India as a medical missionary so I would not have to speak about God," said one woman describing her tied-up condition. She was free in her hands, but not in her heart. She could minister to the body, but beyond that she was out of her depth. Later, when she was inwardly released, she joyously said, "I do believe I am getting vocal about God."

The Japanese have a way of stunting forest trees so that they never grow higher than a couple of feet. They become potted plants instead of forest giants. This is done by tying up the taproot, so that the tree lives off the surface roots. It remains a stunted thing.

Many of our lives are like that. We live off the surface roots, not from the depths. The surface roots go out into the cultural, educational, economic, social, political, perhaps also the thin religious life of our churches, and they draw sustenance from these. But it leaves the life stunted, for the taproot has not gone deep into God.

Only as the taproot goes into the depths of the Divine and draws its sustenance from those depths every moment do we fully and truly live.

Are you spiritually stunted?

O Christ, who came to give us life and to give it abundantly, we ask You to help us put our taproot into Your resources, drawing power and life and victory from You. Amen.

POSSESSED BY POSSESSIONS

Let there be no…greed among you. Such sins have no place among God's people.… You can be sure that no…greedy person will inherit the Kingdom of Christ and of God. For a greedy person is an idolater, worshiping the things of this world. (Eph. 5:3, 5[†])

Is there anything more pitiful than a child who never grows up? The body is that of a man or a woman, the mind that of a child. We are deeply troubled by that tragedy. But are we as deeply moved by the sight of adults who remain absolutely undeveloped in soul? Moral and spiritual dwarfs.

What are some of the things that inwardly tie up the taproot and arrest our growth as spiritual beings? I will name, first of all, *possessiveness*. In a competitive world, the mark of success is the amount of possessions we can accumulate.

One Hindu said the sequence of life is this: "Get on, get honor, get honest." He was speaking from the outlook of many. To "get on" means to get possessions. In an acquisitive society, "honor" then comes as a result of this getting on. To "get honest" is often left as an afterthought, when we are compelled to make peace with God and our souls—souls now so stunted we can hardly find them amid the accumulation of things.

We have become so intent on putting our surface roots into the economy around us that we forget they are only surface roots. True, they are necessary roots and are quite legitimate if the taproot goes deeper. But life that feeds upon them alone becomes very shallow. Jesus said, "Beware! Guard against every kind of greed. Life is not measured by how much you own" (Luke 12:15[†]). He was not moralizing, but announcing simple fact.

Many a person finds that in gaining the outer world they have tied up the inner world. They have gained all, and lost a greater all. Often possessiveness turns into inner powerlessness. The taproot is tied up.

O God our Father, You know we need these things, and yet we allow them to be first things. Save us from the secondary. Unloose our spiritual lives. Amen.

TIED UP BY FEAR

The man who had received the one talent came. "Master," he said, "I knew that you are a hard man, harvesting where you have not sown and gathering where you have not scattered seed. So I was afraid and went out and hid your talent in the ground. See, here is what belongs to you." (Matt. 25:24-25)

Since the children have flesh and blood, he [Jesus] too shared in their humanity so that by his death he might destroy him who holds the power of death—that is, the devil— and free those who all their lives were held in slavery by their fear of death. (Heb. 2:14-15)

Is anything in human life quite as prevalently paralyzing as fear?

Of course there is a fear that is biological, which tends to efficiency. As I came up the operating room steps, the famous surgeon asked me, "Are you afraid?" The question might have been turned back toward him, for if he was not afraid of cutting into wrong places, I should hardly let him operate.

I have a fear of hurting my inner spiritual life; otherwise, I would be careless. One must also be afraid of letting other people down spiritually. When a temptation is presented, it is right to say: "I am afraid to do that—I would let other people down. Besides, what would happen to my work?"

But there are other fears that paralyze. Someone told me about seeing a wild Himalayan chicken crouching in fear before a cobra. It could not move half an inch. Some of our fears may be outer things that seem to stand over us like a cobra's hood and make us afraid. Or they may be vague inward fears of poverty, sickness, death, failure, of what people will say, of attempting anything new, of certain people, of being laughed at—all these, and many more, tie up the inner life.

How to deal with these fears will come later. But now we simply note that unless we can unbind the cords of fear from the taproot of our lives, we shall remain stunted beings.

O God, our Father, these fears infest the inner life and keep us little. Release us from them. And help us to stand up unafraid because Your hand is upon the center of our lives. Amen.

E. STANLEY JONES | 87

TIED UP BY MENTAL PRIDE

Pride goes before destruction, a haughty spirit before a fall. (Prov. 16:18)

Then you will know the truth, and the truth will set you free. (John 8:32)

------------------------------- ❧ -------------------------------

The outer motions of life leave their influence upon our inner life. The scientific movement has captured the minds of many and has left the inner life tied up. We have come to terms with the natural world and natural law to such an extent that we have become naturalized in nature. We are afraid that there are no other roots of life besides these surface roots that go into the natural order. Is there a taproot, and is there a Deeper Soil?

We are afraid to unbind the taproot completely and let it go into God, lest we seem to be unscientific. And we fear that. We cannot be mentally out of fashion.

But surely it is scientific to live and to live abundantly. When Charles Steinmetz, the wizard of electricity, was asked what he thought would be the greatest discovery of the future, he unhesitatingly replied, "In the realm of the moral and social and spiritual," rather than the scientific. He was right, for having turned to the outer laws, we must now return to the inner.

Modern religious liberal thought has gained its altitudes; it must now find its depths. Much of it is shallow, feeding on the surface roots of modern culture. It cannot go further till it goes deeper.

It will be wrenching for some of us to lay down our mental pride and confess to needs deeper than the mind, but we must do it if the inner life is to be freed. Laying down the pride of the mind will be the symbol of laying down the self. There must be a crucifixion of mental pride in order to attain to a resurrection of the spiritual life. You must become a little child—and that is scientific as well as Christian.

In doing so you will find an inner release that will astonish you. You will then know you are truly alive—alive at the center.

O Christ, help us to lay down our mental pride, that we may gain life. Amen.

TIED UP BY MORAL DEFEAT

How can I know all the sins lurking in my heart? Cleanse me from these hidden faults. (Psalm 19:12†)

You have been called to live in freedom, my brothers and sisters. But don't use your freedom to satisfy your sinful nature. Instead, use your freedom to serve one another in love.... Those who belong to Christ Jesus have nailed the passions and desires of their sinful nature to his cross and crucified them there. (Gal. 5:13, 24†)

It would be nice, more respectable, to say we are inwardly tied up by "mental difficulties" rather than by "moral defeats." But respectable or not, this is where many of us will have to hold our attention if we want to get release. The problem is just plain sin.

It is not easy to confess that to ourselves, especially if we are religious persons. It is easier to keep up pretenses. Easier—and more deadly. Suppose we gossip about others, tearing their reputations to pieces (doing it, of course, in the interests of the kingdom)...or suppose we are jealous and make light of a rival's ability and work...or we hold resentments in the heart...or impure thoughts are allowed to gather in the mind...or we are dishonest in our dealings with others and ourselves...or we exaggerate till it means lying, and twist things till it is untruth—will it be of any use to pretend we are inwardly free? We know we are not free, and others know it.

An evangelist put his Bible on top of things in his trunk so the customs inspector might see that he was religious and would not search for undeclared, dutiable articles. Such deception betrays inward bondage. In our case, the first thing we must do is to acknowledge to ourselves just what we are. If we have been a "Bible-plus-hidden-dutiable-articles"-type of Christian, we must say so to ourselves. We must "exteriorate our rottenness," first to ourselves, and then, if necessary, to others.

O God, help us not to wriggle or excuse, but in Your sight to confess our need and have these cords of defeat cut from our inner lives. We want to be free. Amen.

TIED UP BY SELF-CONSCIOUSNESS

"Ah, Sovereign LORD," I said, "I do not know how to speak; I am only a child."

But the LORD said to me, "Do not say, 'I am only a child.' You must go to everyone I send you to and say whatever I command you. Do not be afraid of them, for I am with you and will rescue you," declares the LORD. (Jer. 1:6-8)

The spiritual life should be contagious. It should be winsome and winning. But many find it impossible to share their inner lives with others because of shyness and self-consciousness. I put these two things together, for shyness is a species of self-consciousness. When it ties up the inner life and inhibits us from being natural as Christians, it must be looked upon as bondage, as sin.

Shyness and self-consciousness mean that when an issue is raised, we refer it to ourselves—there is the constant state of self-centeredness. This is a hard statement, but it must be said. We must view shyness and self-consciousness as bondage, from which we are to find deliverance.

The speaker who becomes conscious of himself and of what he is saying will probably stumble and lose grip on the audience. Only as he forgets himself, becoming lost in his message, will his words come with power and effect. I have often said to an interpreter, "Lose yourself in the message—don't become word-conscious, or self-conscious—and the words will flow."

Self-consciousness ties up the flow of thoughts and words. I was once introduced by the principal of a Hindu college in this way: "Now, students, pay close attention to his gestures." I could have thrown a book at him! It was a full five minutes before I could forget that introduction and get lost in my message.

When the center of life is shifted from oneself to Christ, this bondage of shyness drops away. Instead of asking, "How will this affect me?" the question will be "How will this affect Christ and His kingdom?" We are then delivered from these inner cords. The taproot goes into God.

O Christ, we thank You that we can be delivered from shyness and self-consciousness. This is a deliverance we need. Amen.

TIED UP BY SHEER EMPTINESS

He told this parable: "A man had a fig tree, planted in his vineyard, and he went to look for fruit on it, but did not find any. So he said to the man who took care of the vineyard, 'For three years now I've been coming to look for fruit on this fig tree and haven't found any. Cut it down! Why should it use up the soil?' " (Luke 13:6-7)

Many of us are tied up, not so much by positive sins as by the lack of anything spiritual to give. The cords that bind the inner life are just a consciousness that we have nothing to contribute at that level.

The innate politeness of the Indian people makes them begin each letter with the assurance that everything is all right and going along beautifully. After that comes the recital of what sometimes are amazing troubles, accidents, quarrels, and deaths. So I seldom read carefully the first paragraph of a letter, but look for the words *Digar hal yih hai*—"The other condition is this." In the same way I am now spiritually habituated to say to myself and others, "After the preliminary word is over, what are the real facts? What is at the center? Stripped of all words and habitual phrases, what do we find?"

Around this emptiness we build up vast activities to atone for that central lack. As one writer puts it, "a dizzy whirl around a central emptiness." But life cannot long revolve around emptiness. No amount of mere stirring of our emotions by sermons will do. To stir emptiness is futile.

A little girl, having received her tea from her mother, began to stir it. She alternately stirred and sipped. Presently, with disappointed eyes, she said, "Mother, it won't come sweet." Her mother smilingly said, "I'm sorry, I must have forgotten the sugar."

Our lives do not need stirring—they need filling. If Christ is not in the depths of our being, no amount of stirring will make life come sweet and victorious. With Him, however, it does so naturally and inevitably.

O Christ, You have come to give us not merely life, but to give it abundantly. We need that "abundantly." For life is not enough—we want full life. Amen.

GETTING BEYOND MYSELF

Do not conform any longer to the pattern of this world, but be transformed by the renewing of your mind. Then you will be able to test and approve what God's will is—his good, pleasing and perfect will.

For by the grace given me I say to every one of you: Do not think of yourself more highly than you ought, but rather think of yourself with sober judgment, in accordance with the measure of faith God has given you. (Rom. 12:2-3)

When we find victory at the center, *the first result will be release from ourselves and our own problems.* Many never get beyond their own issues. They seem constantly tied up with them. When any occasion arises where help could be given to someone, an inhibition quickly comes from within: "But how about your own self?" That stops dead the processes of helping others.

On my way back to India, I came through Persia [Iran], on the worst roads of the world, in a sputtering, protesting, broken-down car. It would run 30 or 40 miles and then die. We would tinker with it a bit and it would start again, and the same process would be repeated. At the end of the day I was worn out.

One night after such a day, when I had to give an address, my head began to whirl and I had to stop. A badly functioning car engine had done it. How I wanted to look at the scenery as we went by, for I had never been in Persia before, and I wanted to be effective at the close of the day. I could do neither.

For many of us, our strength and attention is absorbed by badly functioning inner lives. We don't have hearts at leisure from themselves to enjoy God's world and to soothe and sympathize with others. And at the end of the day, we are worn out with ourselves. And when life presents its opportunity for service, our minds are too much in a whirl to meet it.

The victorious life would release us from our own problems and our own selves.

O Christ, Your personal problems never inhibited You from helping needy people who crowded around You. You were always free, full, and available. Make me like that. Amen.

THE LEISURED HEART

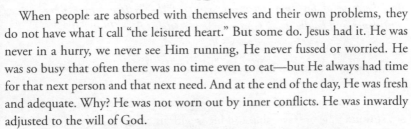

Do not worry about tomorrow, for tomorrow will worry about itself. Each day has enough trouble of its own. (Matt. 6:34)

When people are absorbed with themselves and their own problems, they do not have what I call "the leisured heart." But some do. Jesus had it. He was never in a hurry, we never see Him running, He never fussed or worried. He was so busy that often there was no time even to eat—but He always had time for that next person and that next need. And at the end of the day, He was fresh and adequate. Why? He was not worn out by inner conflicts. He was inwardly adjusted to the will of God.

Many of His followers have found the same secret. While attending college, I lived in a home in which the mother, surrounded by a dozen young people (most of them growing boys of her own), and with many interests outside the home, never seemed ruffled or angry. She always had time for your problems. She was inwardly adjusted to the will of God. That will operated as peace, power, poise, and adequacy.

When David Livingstone came back from Africa in the mid-1800s, after spending years there for his beloved Africans, someone asked him about his soul. "My soul, my soul, I almost forgot I had a soul," replied Livingstone. He was so interested in other people's souls that he had almost forgotten about his own. A healthy condition. It was much more healthy than a great deal of modern spiritual advice, which directs one to too much introspection and self-absorption. It is morbid.

Yes, we must perhaps periodically look at ourselves with one long, searching self-examination. The result should be a complete surrender, a complete adjustment—and then a dismissing of ourselves from the focus of attention in order to get on with the work.

O Christ of the adjusted will, give us that inner adjustment, that we, too, may move quietly through our tasks with our heads high, our hearts adequate, and our hands full. Amen.

ROWBOAT, SAILBOAT, OR STEAMBOAT?

I want you to know, my dear brothers and sisters, that everything that has happened to me here has helped to spread the Good News. For everyone here, including the whole palace guard, knows that I am in chains because of Christ. And because of my imprisonment, most of the believers here have gained confidence and boldly speak God's message without fear. (Phil. 1:12-14†)

The second thing that will come to us as a result of the victorious life is the power to live "in spite of."

Many of us know the power to live on account of, but not in spite of. When our surroundings are favorable and life is with us, we go on. But life is not like that always. It often turns rough. And then we are tested to the depths. If our faith is but an echo of our surroundings, it will fade out. But if it is real, it will speak from the depths.

There are three kinds of Christians: the rowboat type, the sailboat type, and the steamboat type. The rowboat type is humanistic, self-dependent, trying to get along with its own resources. But since those resources are limited, the progress is limited.

The sailboat type depends on the winds. They are the people who are dependent on circumstances—the other-dependent ones. If the winds are with them, if people are constantly complimenting and encouraging them, they make headway. But if the patting on the back stops, they stop.

Then there is the steamboat type—those who have power on the inside. They go on whether winds are favorable or unfavorable. It is true they go faster when there is a helping wind, but nevertheless they go on, wind or no wind. They have an inner adequacy. They are not self-dependent, nor circumstance-dependent, but Christ-dependent. They are dependable.

This power to go on when life is dead against us is the deepest necessity of our lives. In victorious living this becomes a working fact.

O Christ, who pushed on when life turned to such roughness that it meant a cross, help us to find that same power of going on—in spite of. Amen.

NO STRAIN

Jesus: *"Do not let your hearts be troubled. Trust in God; trust also in me."* (John 14:1)

The peace of God, which transcends all understanding, will guard your hearts and your minds in Christ Jesus. (Phil. 4:7)

The third meaning of the victorious life is that *the strain is taken out of our lives.* Many people are living strained spiritual lives. They are trying hard to be good. Their fists are clenched, their teeth set, their backs to the wall—they are fighting, fighting.

It is all very earnest, but not very inviting. A strained piety is not contagious. Furthermore, it is wearing on the person concerned. For all strain means drain. We are inwardly wound up so tightly that we snap under things.

I was once in a tin plate factory and was told that in one of the processes, the inner strain was taken out of the plates by subjecting them to the very severe heat of 1,700 degrees. By this process the molecules were so harmonized that when the tin plates were bent they would not break. Without this fiery process the bending meant a breaking.

Do we not need something like that to take place within the soul—a fiery baptism that sets every molecule of our souls in right relation to each other, so that when the strain comes we shall not break but only bend? Jesus bent in Gethsemane, for the weight upon Him was very, very heavy. But, thank God, He did not break!

Why? Because that prayer, "Not my will but your will be done," set every fiber of His spirit in right relation with the indwelling will of the Father. Thereafter, there was no inner strain.

Life is often not broken from the outside but from the inside. The victorious life takes away the inner strain and makes life so harmonized it can stand anything that outwardly happens to it.

O Christ, if You had broken, we would have broken too. Put us through Your fiery baptism till all strain is taken out! We consent to the Fire, for we know it means freedom. Amen.

E. STANLEY JONES | 95

POWER OVER EVERY SIN

Count yourselves dead to sin but alive to God in Christ Jesus. Therefore do not let sin reign in your mortal body so that you obey its evil desires. Do not offer the parts of your body to sin, as instruments of wickedness, but rather offer yourselves to God.... For sin shall not be your master, because you are not under law, but under grace. (Rom. 6:11-14)

One of the greatest difficulties in evangelism, particularly in the East, is the moral fatalism about personal sin: "What could I do? I am only human." The implication is that sin is an integral part of human nature, and as long as we remain human, we remain sinful.

The tyranny of that fatalism must be broken if we are going to live the victorious life. In the depths of our being (note: I say "the depths," for a mere surface acceptance will not do), we must get hold of the idea that sin is unnatural, an invasion, an intruder. When people sin, they are not normal humans; they are subhuman, or antihuman. Three unnatural things have invaded life: *Sin* (the unnatural evil of the soul), *error* (the unnatural evil of the mind), and *disease* (the unnatural evil of the body).

Jesus said that salvation is health. Wherever He uses the term "Be saved," it can be literally translated, "Be whole." The health of the soul is goodness, the health of the mind is truth, and the health of the body is freedom from disease.

Every sin, then, can be conquered. Hold onto that fact. Do not allow the mind to admit any exception. If you do, that exception will be the loose bolt that lets the bridge collapse. "Clothe yourselves with the Lord Jesus Christ, and do not think about how to gratify the desires of the sinful nature" (Rom. 13:14). In other words, do not provide for any failure; provide for victory.

I know the dangers of hypocrisy involved in this absoluteness. But of the two dangers, the greater is in mentally providing for sin in the life.

O Christ, we thank You for Your offer of complete release from all sin. Help us to accept that deliverance. Amen.

KEEP IT SIMPLE

Our conscience testifies that we have conducted ourselves in the world, and especially in our relations with you, in the holiness and sincerity that are from God.... For we do not write you anything you cannot read or understand. (2 Cor. 1:12-13)

During the response time at the end of one of my lectures, a Hindu sent up this comment: "I am not enamored by your dramatic gestures. If you have found Christ, tell us simply and straightforwardly."

I could only reply that my gestures were a natural part of me and that I was not conscious of them, but I was deeply impressed by his demand to be simple and straightforward. He was right. The victorious life should and does *reduce life to inward unity, and therefore to outward simplicity.*

We need to be cleansed from all double purposes in word and attitude. See what the coming of the Spirit into Peter's life did for him. At his denial he had said, "Man, I don't know what you're talking about!" (Luke 22:60). Here was Peter double-minded and double-worded. Now, in an equally frightening moment before the Sanhedrin, "Peter, filled with the Holy Spirit, replied, 'Rulers and Elders of the people,...be it known to you all, and to all the people of Israel, that through the name of Jesus Christ, the Nazarene,...this [previously lame] man stands here before you in perfect health.... And in no other [than Christ] is salvation to be found: for, indeed, there is no second name under heaven that has been given to men through which we are to be saved' " (Acts 4:8-10, 12 Weymouth).

Note the straightforwardness, the directness, the simplicity of His words. The Holy Spirit, who is the Spirit of Truth, the Spirit of Simplicity and Directness, brought this revolution into Peter's life. He will bring it into ours. Weasel-words and weasel-attitudes will give way to words that flow in simplicity out of the depths of unified life.

O Christ of the simple speech and of the direct attitude, give us Your likeness in this. For we, too, would be saved from complexities, diplomacies, and double meanings. Amen.

LIFE CREATIVE

On the last day, the climax of the festival, Jesus stood and shouted to the crowds, "Anyone who is thirsty may come to me! Anyone who believes in me may come and drink! For the Scriptures declare, 'Rivers of living water will flow from his heart.'" (When he said "living water," he was speaking of the Spirit, who would be given to everyone believing in him.) (John 7:37-39†)

Jesus: *I am the vine; you are the branches. Those who remain in me, and I in them, will produce much fruit. For apart from me you can do nothing. (John 15:5†)*

The last sign of the victorious life is the fact that *life now becomes spiritually creative*. The victorious life is life organized around love. Just as love is creative, life now becomes creative. Where there is love, there is always a plus, a margin for somebody else. We have enough, even some to spare.

A newly arrived missionary was being taken through the dirty, narrow, crowded streets of a Chinese city. Everything in her revolted against the strangeness and the dirt. "O God," she cried, "how can I live among these people without love in my heart?"

An immediate answer came in the flooding of her heart with what was nothing less than divine love. From that moment on, she forgot dirt and narrow streets and strangeness; she saw only people for whom Christ died. Instead of being driven back into herself, love drew her out of herself into amazingly creative service. She became one of the great missionaries of the world.

The victorious life means the heightening of all the powers of the personality. The mind becomes keener and more creative, the emotions become broader and more sensitive, and the will more active and decisive. The whole of life is outreaching. Lives begin to be changed, movements begin to be launched, a creative impact is made upon life.

O Christ, we thank You for the creative impact of love in our hearts. Make us creative this day as we come into contact with dull, dead life. Amen.

HOW DO I START?

If you live according to the sinful nature, you will die; but if by the Spirit you put to death the misdeeds of the body, you will live. (Rom. 8:13)

The most delicate moment for many of us now comes as we approach the question of how we may enter the victorious life. We must approach it with a prayer upon our lips and in our hearts.

First of all, there is a difference now in your coming. When you first came, you came as a stranger, a penitent rebel knocking at the door for admission. Now you are a child within that Home, but seeking a deeper and fuller alignment with the spirit of the Home. You are not asking for admission, but for adjustment. You are asking that everything be taken out of you that clashes with the spirit of the Home. You can now come with a sense of confidence and assurance, born out of contact with the Father, that if you meet the conditions, He will meet you more than halfway. The barriers are all within us, not in Him.

But the first thing we must look at is what we are not to do. *Don't undertake to gain the victorious life by fighting your individual sins.* The way into victory is not in that direction.

If you go that way, you will be compelled to center your attention on those sins. Now, it is a law of the mind that whatever gets your attention gets you. If, therefore, your sins get your attention, then your sins will get you. You will fall into the very sins you are fighting.

Many Christians are astonished to find that while praying against sins and earnestly fighting them, they succumb to them. "Why did God let me down when I was fighting so hard against my sins?" asked a perplexed soul. Later she found the way, and her perplexity vanished. She had been on the wrong track.

O Christ, take us by the hand and lead us at this hour, for without Your guidance, we stumble and lose the way. We must find the way—we can live no longer without perfect adjustment to You. Amen.

IMAGINATION: STRONGER THAN WILL POWER

Those who are dominated by the sinful nature think about sinful things, but those who are controlled by the Holy Spirit think about things that please the Spirit. So letting your sinful nature control your mind leads to death. But letting the Spirit control your mind leads to life and peace. (Rom. 8:5-6 †)

We demolish arguments and every pretension that sets itself up against the knowledge of God, and we take captive every thought to make it obedient to Christ. (2 Cor. 10:5)

Suppose you are fighting a sexual sin. In fighting that sin, you have to concentrate your attention upon it. The result is that the imagination is aroused. A battle then ensues between the imagination and the will.

Now, modern psychologists tell us that in any battle between the imagination and the will, the imagination always wins. We go where imagination goes. What should we do? The imagination must be called away from our sins and centered elsewhere—on Christ.

But the imagination cannot and will not be centered there unless we make a complete surrender to Him. The imagination goes where its supreme treasure is. As Jesus put it, "Where your treasure is, there your heart will be also" (Matt. 6:21). Your treasure must be in Christ—wholly and supremely there. If so, your imagination will be there also. So the problem is not merely shifting the imagination—it is shifting the place of your supreme treasure.

There can be no love between persons unless there is a natural inward surrender. When one withholds his inmost being from the other, there is no love. So there can be no complete love between you and Christ until there is a complete surrender to Him. When the complete surrender takes place, then love springs up and begins to burn. The imagination follows.

The problem, then, is to shift that imagination. That can only be done by shifting the center of life itself from self to Christ.

O Christ, I want You to be the home of my imagination. I want always to be centered on You. In order to do so, I will surrender to You. Amen.

FORGETTING AND REMEMBERING

Let us throw off everything that hinders and the sin that so easily entangles, and let us run with perseverance the race marked out for us. Let us fix our eyes on Jesus, the author and perfecter of our faith. (Heb. 12:1-2)

Another mistake is to try to *forget* your sins. This is to invite defeat again. The very effort made in trying to forget will call the matter back into mind.

A fakir [religious ascetic] came to an Indian village, declaring he could make gold. The villagers gathered around him as he poured water in a tub, then put some coloring matter into it, began to stir it with a stick and to repeat mantras. When their attention was diverted, he let some gold nuggets slip down the stick. He then poured off the water—and there was the gold at the bottom!

The villagers' eyes bulged. The village money-lender offered 500 rupees for the formula. The fakir explained minutely how to make it, and then added, "But you must not think of a red-faced monkey as you stir, or the gold won't come."

The money-lender promised to remember that he was to forget. But, try as hard as he would, the red-faced monkey was there before him, spoiling everything. The gold would not come!

As you try to forget your sins, they will rise before you all the more. The only way to forget your sins is to center your attention elsewhere. Of course, your attention cannot go unless you go. This, again, points to self-surrender, which produces what the Scottish preacher Thomas Chalmers called "the expulsive power of a new affection." Your sins will be fully forgotten, because Christ is fully remembered.

Perhaps one word of correction is necessary. Sometimes we do succeed by effort to get sins out of the mind, but this means they have gone into the subconscious mind, where they work havoc in the life. Whether we succeed in forgetting, or call the sin more vividly back into the mind, in either case there is defeat and disaster.

O Christ, as we clear these things from the pathway that leads to You, our hearts become the more eager to arrive at perfect victory. Lead us, we follow. Amen.

WHIPPING UP THE WILL

Now God has shown us a way to be made right with Him without keeping the requirements of the law.... We are made right with God by placing our faith in Jesus Christ.... Can we boast, then, that we have done anything to be accepted by God? No, because our acquittal is not based on obeying the law. It is based on faith. So we are made right with God through faith and not by obeying the law. (Rom. 3:21-22, 27-28†)

Many people feel they will go into victorious living if they only try a little harder. So they proceed to whip up the will. Much of our present-day Christianity is founded on this idea. Our preaching sounds this note. We lay a demand on the souls of our people. But somehow after a few days, the will relaxes, and we are back where we were. It doesn't work.

Why? The reason is that when we say, "I'll try," we are still on the basis of self. It is self-effort. But before the self can put forth any real effort, it must be released from its inner conflicting desires. On the other hand, when a person says, "I'll trust," they shift the basis from self to Christ. Their attitude is no longer self-centered, but Christ-centered.

Reinhold Niebuhr rightly says, "The moral fruits of religion are not the result of conscious effort to achieve them.... What men are able to will depends not upon the strength of their willing but upon the strength which enters their will *(An Interpretation of Christian Ethics*, p. 220).

Since the will is the self as organized at a particular moment against recalcitrant impulses, the strength of the will is in direct proportion to the strength of the self. But if the self is divided, then the will is weak.

The problem, then, is not the whipping up of the will but the unifying of the self—which cannot be unified until it comes under the complete control of the power of Christ.

O Christ, we have tried to reach our goals by urging our wills forward, but our wills are weak because we are weak. Unite and strengthen us at the center of our being. Then we shall reach our goals. Amen.

THE CRUX OF OUR PROBLEM

He said to the crowd, "If any of you wants to be my follower, you must turn from your selfish ways, take up your cross daily, and follow me. If you try to hang on to your life, you will lose it. But if you give up your life for my sake, you will save it." (Luke 9:23-24†)

Our outer sins are rooted in something deeper. Just as my fingers are rooted in the palm of my hand, so my individual sins are rooted in the unsurrendered self.

It is the thought of self-advantage in some form or other that lies at the root of our sins. Why do we lie and steal? We think the self will be protected or advantaged. Why do we quarrel with others? Because the self has been crossed. Why are we envious? Because we are afraid someone will get ahead of the self. Why do we give way to sexual passion? Because we think the self will thereby find pleasure. Alfred Adler is profoundly right when he says the ego-urge is our prime difficulty in life and is at the basis of most of our unhappiness. Victorious living centers, then, in one thing chiefly: self-surrender.

But, you ask, didn't I do that in conversion? Yes, you did, up to a point. But not wholly. Now you see deeper depths that must be surrendered. The conscious mind was given to Christ in conversion. Now the subconscious mind, the center of our divisions and inner clashes, must be laid at His feet as well. These basic instincts must come under His control, and they must be cleansed. The self we now give is a fuller self, both conscious and subconscious, for we want a fuller salvation—a complete salvation.

The difference between a quack and a real doctor is this: A quack doctor treats symptoms, a real doctor treats diseases. Christ now asks that we allow Him not merely to treat the individual sins, the symptoms of a deeper malady, but the very root, the self. His finger is on our problem.

O Christ, You have touched the seat of my disease. I know it. Help me not to wince or be afraid, or ask for halfway measures. Help me to surrender all. Amen.

LETTING THAT LAST THING GO

Large crowds were traveling with Jesus, and turning to them he said: "If anyone comes to me and does not hate his father and mother, his wife and children, his brothers and sisters—yes, even his own life—he cannot be my disciple. And anyone who does not carry his cross and follow me cannot be my disciple." (Luke 14:25-27)

The last thing we want to let go is just ourselves. It is the one and only thing we really own. And now Christ with imperious demand asks for that last one thing. It is at this place that the real battle is joined. All else have been skirmishes.

Jesus says with awful decisiveness that the family and ourselves must be placed on the altar. This does not mean we should necessarily leave the family. To "hate" means to "love less," according to the parallel passage in Matthew 10:37. A lighted candle, when it is put before a high-power electric light, casts a shadow. Thus the lesser loves, while really light, cast a shadow when this all-consuming Love makes its demand upon the human spirit. These loves are not to be abandoned. They are to be surrendered. You still live with yourself even after you surrender yourself, so you may still live with your family after you surrender them.

Now, the interesting thing to note is that the "life," or the self, is the last thing mentioned: "yes, even his own life." Why does Jesus put that last? Because it is the last thing we ever give up.

The missionary gives up his home and loved ones to come to another land; he may give up everything except self. If so, he finds his inner self touchy over position, place, and power. The minister sacrifices a great deal to go into the ministry—everything except the minister. He finds himself preaching the gospel with a great deal of vanity and personal ambition mixed up in it. The layman gives up much to follow Christ, but he finds himself easily offended. In each case, the self is still there in the very following of Christ. It must be surrendered.

O Christ, I come to You to help me in this central thing. I am hardly willing to let it go, but I am willing to be made willing. Amen.

COMPROMISES

"All these [commandments] I have kept," the young man said. "What do I still lack?"

Jesus answered, "If you want to be perfect, go, sell your possessions and give to the poor, and you will have treasure in heaven. Then come, follow me."

When the young man heard this, he went away sad, because he had great wealth. (Matt. 19:20-22)

We do not let go of ourselves without a struggle. The whole biological urge is against this, for it reverses the process of nature. It is an invasion of the rights of self-assertion.

It is true that this demand means the possibility of self-assertion on a higher level. But the lower urges do not understand this and will resist it. They will rise up like Peter and say, "Never!... This shall never happen to you!" (Matt. 16:22). Jesus turned to him and retorted, "You are seeing things merely from a human point of view, not from God's" (v. 23 †).

When you are about to take the step that will make you more than merely human, the old humanity will rise up within you and try to pull you back, pleading for the status quo. Or it will suggest compromises. If it cannot conquer by denial, it will try to conquer by dividing. Compromises ensue.

A patriot was making a speech, and glowing with passion said: "For the sake of my country I am willing to sacrifice my aged mother!—yes, I am willing to sacrifice my children!—and if necessary, I am even willing to sacrifice my own self!" But he would give up the old mother and the children first! We smile at the "patriot," but in him we see ourselves. The self presents compromises, not quite so baldly, but it is always thinking of compromises to save itself.

O Christ, I come to You. Help me not to blur this hour by compromises, by a patched-up truce between the old and the new. I want to be new, entirely new. Amen.

SMALL RESERVATIONS

Naaman after his miracle healing: *"[I] will never again make burnt offerings and sacrifices to any other god but the LORD. But may the LORD forgive [me] for this one thing: When my master enters the temple of Rimmon to bow down and he is leaning on my arm and I bow there also—when I bow down in the temple of Rimmon, may the LORD forgive [me] for this." (2 Kings 5:17-18)*

Last week I said that the self lets go reluctantly, and compromise will be asked for. This old Pharaoh, who has been used to ruling for ages, when asked to let you go into freedom, will say, "No," and then, "Yes-no." But you must insist, like Moses, that "not a hoof is to be left behind" (Exod. 10:26).

The "yes-no" attitude is subtle. During one ashram, I gave up my mattress to someone else, and felt virtuous for doing so. Then I remembered where there was another mattress, and got it for myself. I thus satisfied two things within me—one, the desire to get approval from my friends (as well as my higher life) by giving up the mattress, and the other, the desire to be comfortable!

Many Chinese offer to their gods what to them is one of the most precious things they have—a pig. It used to be that they offered the whole animal. Now they offer only the severed head with the severed tail in its mouth—keeping the body for themselves! With us Christians there is a good deal of this; we give the more or less useless remnants and keep the essential self intact. We offer our service and withhold the self. We offer Christ our talents on occasion and reserve to ourselves the right to decide the really big things of our lives.

In this way religion becomes the window-dressing that hides our essential motives. We are not necessarily hypocrites, for many of these motives are hid from us. We are just halfway givers. We pass a resolution of complete surrender, and then nullify it by adding "riders." And then we wonder why there is no liberty in our life.

O Christ, search our hearts relentlessly to find the hidden stowaway. We want everything, everything to come under Your sway. For we want everything to express Your freedom. Amen.

ONLY THE TIP?

What do righteousness and wickedness have in common? Or what fellowship can light have with darkness? What harmony is there between Christ and Belial? What does a believer have in common with an unbeliever? What agreement is there between the temple of God and idols? For we are the temple of the living God. (2 Cor. 6:14-16)

I do not want to belabor the matter of compromises, or you will become irritated with me. But this is so important that I must hold us to this point.

One can often see a Hindu swami sitting on the small raised platform, while the faithful lay their offerings at his feet. He seems to be indifferent to it all; in fact, he treats the whole ritual with contempt. After all, it belongs to the world, which he has renounced. He gets up and walks backstage with an air of utter indifference.

But as the curtains close behind him, the servants deftly gather up the rich offerings, which then go into the swami's treasury. In fact, he is wealthy beyond words.

He is probably not a conscious hypocrite, at least not now, for he has lived so long in the illusion of renunciation that he really believes he has dismissed all earthly pleasures. And others believe it—hence, their offerings. The essential self is covered so one hardly sees that it occupies the throne in the rear.

When you come to offer God your inmost self, you will be strongly drawn to do what the Hindu does when he offers a water buffalo to his god. The long knife falls toward the neck of the buffalo—but just as it is about to strike, the executioner deftly turns it, cutting off the tip of the ear instead. The sacrifice is finished, and everyone is satisfied.

When you are about to lay low your essential self, the temptation will be very strong to cut off the tip of some self-indulgence instead, and leave the matter at that. The essential self goes untouched.

O Christ, You see how we hesitate to strike the blow that would slay our most precious possession. But instill nerve into our hearts and our arms, that we may not divert the blow into irrelevancies. Amen.

TWO WELCOMES

As Jesus and his disciples were on their way, he came to a village where a woman named Martha opened her home to him. She had a sister called Mary, who sat at the Lord's feet listening to what he said. (Luke 10:38-39)

One of the Pharisees invited Jesus to have dinner with him…. When a woman who had lived a sinful life in that town learned that Jesus was eating at the Pharisee's house, she brought an alabaster jar of perfume….

When the Pharisee…saw this, he said to himself, "If this man were a prophet, he would know who is touching him and what kind of woman she is—that she is a sinner." (Luke 7:36, 37, 39)

Can you see yourself in one or the other of these welcomes?

To people like the Pharisee, someone never "*was* a sinner"—it is always a case of "*is.*" Once a sinner, always a sinner. They never forgive and forget. To Jesus, she was not one now. He said, "Simon…I came into your house. You did not give me any water for my feet…. You did not give me a kiss…. You did not put oil on my head…." (Luke 7:44-47)—all of which were common signs of hospitality in that day. In other words, "Simon, I came into your house, partway, through the door. You gave me food—but reserved your heart. You gave me a welcome—with reservations. I am in and yet not in. This woman has sinned in her flesh. You are sinning in your spirit. I can release her. But I cannot release you. For you want to retain your pride—and Me. You would like to have Me—and not have Me. You are divided—and therefore self-damned."

Mary, on the later occasion, welcomed Jesus, gave Him food—and her heart. She sat at His feet. He was at home there, for the welcome was complete.

Is your heart a Bethany to Christ, or a Pharisee's house? Self-surrender will turn that proud, barren, critical, aloof, self-righteous Pharisee's house into a Bethany.

O Christ, I fling open to You the door to my house and to my heart. I consider You no longer the threshold-Christ, but the throne-Christ. Take the very throne of my divided heart. Amen.

ALL I KNOW AND ALL I DON'T KNOW

Jesus: *"I have much more to say to you, more than you can now bear. But when he, the Spirit of truth, comes, he will guide you into all the truth. He…will tell you what is yet to come." (John 16:12-13)*

There may be the lingering fear that your giving is not complete. But if you are completely honest in giving what you know, then you can lump all the other unknown things and future contingencies into the words "I give all I know, and all I don't know."

"All I don't know" has within it the future as it unfolds. It means that your giving includes an absoluteness and yet a relativity. It is absolute in that it is once and for all, and it is also relative in that you will have to keep offering things to God as they come up day by day.

But you need not be anxious now about those things that will come up in the future; let them be met as they come. If there is no Inner Voice telling you that you are withholding, then you have a right to believe that all has been given, for if there were something left behind, the Spirit would let you know.

The absoluteness and the relativity in full self-giving can be seen in the example of marriage. There is a once-and-for-allness about self-giving in real marriage, but there is also a relativity in the continuous adjustments and unfoldings of the couple's pledge. Marriage is over in an hour, and yet it takes a lifetime to be really married.

The "all" that you use is a small word, but it has within it an amazing capacity for unfolding. It holds within it pleasure and pain, struggle and battle, joy and peace, glorious relationships and difficult adjustments. It is well that the curtain shrouds all that it holds. For we do not need to live all of life at once—that would exhaust us. We can live it a day at a time. What the future holds is not for us to ask, but whatever it may be, God has that too.

O God, I thank You that I do not need to worry about tomorrow. You have today, and You have me. Let that be enough. Amen.

ALL IN THE SUBCONSCIOUS

*Praise the LORD, O my soul; all my inmost being, praise his holy name.
(Psalm 103:1)*

*As therefore you have received the Christ, even Jesus our Lord, live and act in
vital union with Him; having the roots of your being firmly planted in Him.
(Col. 2:6-7 WEYMOUTH)*

"All I don't know" covers something else: the hidden depths of the unconscious mind. It reaches not only lengthwise into the future, but also to the
depths within us now.

The unconscious mind is a well-established fact. Long before modern psychology began describing it, sincere religious people had felt the fact within
them. It has been variously described as "another law at work in the members of
my body" (Rom. 7:23), "evil is right there with me" (Rom. 7:21), "our old self"
(Rom. 6:6), "inherited evil," "original sin," and so on.

We do not know the subconscious mind except indirectly, nor can we control
it except indirectly. That control must come from God. We can surrender to Him.
He then takes charge of the depths. They become cleansed and Christianized.

How do I know this? I do not, except indirectly. But look at the disciples
after Pentecost. They do not seem to be men sitting on the lid of an inner
volcano. They seem to be unified to the very depths of their being. The new
life comes out of them like a fragrance from a flower, the natural expression of
their unified lives.

The life controlled at the depths of the subconscious mind by the Spirit
is tensionless, not between itself and its ideals (for that tension will always
remain) but tensionless in regard to itself. The conscious and the subconscious
are both dedicated to the same purposes and working toward the same ends.

*O God, I thank You that You are about to give me healing at the very center of
my being. You will make my conscious mind and my unconscious, which are now
synchronizing, to produce music more marvelous than before. I give them both
to You. Amen*

THE ACCEPTANCE

The boy's father…answered…"If you can do anything, take pity on us and help us."

"'If you can'?" said Jesus. "Everything is possible for him who believes."

Immediately the boy's father exclaimed, "I do believe; help me overcome my unbelief!" (Mark 9:21-24)

We now come to the place where we take the step that will mean full deliverance. It is the step of faith. Faith is an adventure in acceptance. It banks on the *bona fides* of God. It believes that the character of God and the moral stability of the universe are behind this offer of full deliverance.

There is an element of quiet aggressiveness in our reaching out and taking this pearl of great price. There is inward freedom, for we have paid the ultimate price—our all—and now we have the moral right to accept all. It is a step in mutual confidence.

But some people, having paid all, stand hesitating to take all. I once saw a woman who, about to go into the Chicago Exposition, dropped her coin into the turnstile slot but then waited for it to open. It did nothing, even though she had paid the price. It needed the aggressive push of faith against it. And when she made that push, the turnstile opened.

You have paid the price. Now press, literally press against the promises held out to you, and you will walk through them into freedom.

A few days ago a doctor, who had found life turning sour, walked out into freedom through these words, "Therefore I tell you, whatever you ask for in prayer, believe that you have received it, and it will be yours" (Mark 11:24). Notice—"have received it," not "will receive it," for it is already done. It only awaits your acceptance. You cannot trust yourself, you cannot trust your own resources, but you can trust Him.

O God, my Father, I come to the moment of testing my love to You. For I know if I love You, I will trust You for this gift of full release. I do love You, and I do trust You now. Amen.

A PERSONAL WORD

Peter before the Sanhedrin: *"We cannot help speaking about what we have seen and heard."* (Acts 4:20)

Perhaps a personal word might help. I was a Christian for a year or more when one day I looked at a library shelf and was struck with the title of a book, *The Christian's Secret of a Happy Life,* by Hannah Whitall Smith.

As I read it, my heart was set on fire to find this life of freedom and fullness. I reached page 42 when the Inner Voice said very distinctly, "Now is the time to find." I pleaded that I did not yet know what I wanted, until I finished the book. But the Inner Voice was imperious: "Now is the time to seek."

I tried to read on, but the words seemed blurred. I was up against a divine insistence. So I closed the book, dropped on my knees, and asked, "What shall I do?"

The Voice replied, "Will you give me your all—your very all?"

After a moment's hesitation I replied, "I will."

"Then take my all; you are cleansed," the Voice said with a strange firmness.

"I believe it," I said and arose from my knees. I walked around the room affirming it over and over, pushing my hands away from me as if to push away my doubt. This I did for ten minutes…when suddenly I was filled with a strange refining fire that seemed to course through every portion of my being in cleansing waves. It was all very quiet, I had hold of myself—and yet the divine waves could be felt from the inmost center of my being to my fingertips. My whole being was being fused into one, and through the whole time there was a sense of sacredness and awe, along with the most exquisite joy.

Very emotional? Yes! But I knew then, and I know now, that I was not being merely emotionally stirred. The very sources of my life were being cleansed and taken over by Life itself. My will was just as much involved as my emotion. The fact is the whole of life was thereafter on a permanently higher level.

O God, I also take You in this simple way. If You are looking for a heart to refine and live in, You have mine, completely and forever. I accept the Gift. Amen.

EUREKA!

Though you have not seen him, you love him; and even though you do not see him now, you believe in him and are filled with an inexpressible and glorious joy, for you are receiving the goal of your faith, the salvation of your souls. (1 Peter 1:8-9)

I hesitated to write what I did yesterday, for some may feel they must find exactly that experience, or else they are not united and released and filled. This is a mistake. I have never known two experiences exactly alike in emotional tone. They differ widely, and yet there is the same sense of inner release and unity, followed by heightened power to live creatively. Don't seek the experience of someone else; seek Christ, and let Him give you the kind of experience suited to you, which will make you more useful.

I know the modern reaction against emotion in religion. But it often takes a real emotional upheaval to shift the center of life from self to Christ. When emotion does that, it is redemptive and releasing, not merely for selfish enjoyment.

That such a profound change could take place without emotion is unthinkable. And yet the emotion is a by-product of the facts that are taking place. We do not depend on them. We depend on Him. He comes in to abide permanently amid the flux and change of emotion.

Now if my soul takes its tambourine and dances at His coming, don't be astonished. I would be astonished at myself if I didn't do just that! Such a Guest, bearing such a Gift into such a heart—the wonder is not that we are emotional, but that we can be so restrained!

When Archimedes, after coming suddenly on a mathematical solution, ran out into the street crying, "Eureka! I've got it!" we understand him. It is just as easily understandable, and more so, if we cry out in the same way, not over a mathematical solution but over a life solution. Life is untangled, and we've found the Way!

O God, my Father, I thank You that I have put my feet upon this way of complete victory. I do not depend on anything extraneous, but I do depend on You. Amen.

WHETHER WE FEEL OR NOT

The testing of your faith develops perseverance. Perseverance must finish its work so that you may be mature and complete, not lacking anything. (James 1:3-4)

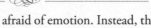

But there are many who are not afraid of emotion. Instead, they are afraid of not having any. To such people I would say that the emotion will come, if you keep your eyes on the right place. If you look inward, you will be discouraged; if you look around, you will be distracted; but if you look at Christ, you will have peace.

It may be that you will have to launch out and steer by what the mariners call "dead reckoning," a steering by instruments without any sight of the stars. You may have to act on obedience without any stars in your sky. The stars are there, but you don't see them. Still, keep affirming in your heart, "I have paid the price, and I accept the Gift—it is done."

Talk faith to God and to yourself. The answer comes back to you, "My grace is sufficient for you" (2 Cor. 12:9). That is not a promise, it is a fact. You can bank on it to cover your need and more. The Scripture says, "Thanks be to God! He gives us the victory through our Lord Jesus Christ" (1 Cor. 15:57). Victory is a gift. Empty your hands and take the gift. The emotional manifestation will follow.

A father, absent from home for a long trip, was expected by the eager family at a certain time. But he did not come. The children and the mother went to bed disappointed and dejected. The next morning, they sat at the breakfast table in sad silence—when suddenly, the father came down from upstairs! He had arrived late and had gone to bed without arousing them. But he was just as much there during the night as when he showed himself in the morning.

When you pay the price and accept the gift, God is there to protect and save you, even though the manifestation of His presence has not come. It will. And when it does, it will be morning for you!

O Christ, whether I sail by "dead reckoning" or under the clear stars, I sail with Your hand on the helm of my life. Everything is under Your control. Amen.

TALKING FAITH

I thank my God through Jesus Christ for all of you, because your faith is being reported all over the world. (Rom. 1:8)

The life appeared; we have seen it and testify to it, and we proclaim to you the eternal life, which was with the Father and has appeared to us. We proclaim to you what we have seen and heard, so that you also may have fellowship with us. (1 John 1:2-3)

We said yesterday that, in taking this step, we should talk faith to God and to ourselves. If that seems like autosuggestion, I have no apologies to make. We all practice autosuggestion in everything. It is a process of all thought. The question is, Just what do you suggest to yourself?

If it is the highest hypothesis or goal that you know, then it is legitimate autosuggestion and most necessary. You are suggesting to yourself what you honestly believe to be the highest truth, namely, that the character of God demands that if you do your part, God will do His part. You are suggesting to yourself that you launch out upon that. Therefore talk faith to yourself.

You should also probably talk faith to others. You need not tell of something that has not happened, but you can tell where you stand, and where you are going, and what your faith is on the way. This turns the whole attitude of life toward faith and affirmation. It cuts the channels through which the new life comes to you. It establishes new habits of thought. It commits you to the highest.

Accepting God's gift by faith drives in the nail. The expression of that faith to others clinches the nail on the other side. It gives the soul a push in the direction you want to go. That push may be decisive.

This is not unreality. It is a declaration of faith, not of accomplished fact. That faith will turn into fact, and the fact into feeling. In truth, the faith is a part of the fact; it is the fact begun. The redemption is now in operation in the very fact of the faith.

O God, my Father, I cannot speak of my worthiness, nor my conscious finding, but I do declare my faith in Your utter trustworthiness. You will see me through. Amen.

CLEAN THROUGH THE WORD

"Now I commit you to God and to the word of his grace, which can build you up and give you an inheritance among all those who are sanctified." (Acts 20:32)

Christ loved the church and gave himself up for her to make her holy, cleansing her by the washing with water through the word, and to present her to himself as a radiant church, without stain or wrinkle or any other blemish, but holy and blameless. (Eph. 5:25-27)

On the night of the Last Supper, Jesus uttered these remarkable words: "You are already clean because of the word I have spoken to you" (John 15:3). What was this "word" that gave them cleanness? Why did Jesus say "word" instead of "words"?

The reason seems to be that His many words had gathered themselves into such a living body of truth and insight, into such coherency and oneness, that they were no longer words, they were "the word." We see three stages: "words," "his word," "the word." Even His silences became part of "the word."

The ancient Chinese philosopher Lao-tse, founder of Taoism, believed that "the way that can be expressed is not the Eternal Way. The name that can be named is not the Eternal Name." But Lao-tse lived six centuries before Christ came. If he had seen Him, he would have seen the Eternal Way and Name walking the ways of time and speaking our names. The Word became flesh!

In naming Christ, we do not break some mystic spell or eternity; we interpret it—and more, we are cleansed by it. The alabaster box of the eternal must be broken, so that its perfume may fill our hearts and, with the filling, cleanse them.

The cleansing Jesus had been performing upon His disciples for three years was more than a personal cleansing. He was cleansing them *and their universe.* It was a cluttered-up world they faced. Jesus left them, as far as they were concerned, with a world of things and relationships cleansed.

O Christ, help us to let that Word be spoken in every part of our being as well as in all our relationships, so that they may be cleansed, and we may be cleansed. Amen.

THE WORLD-CLEANSER

Jesus answered: "Don't you know me, Philip, even after I have been among you such a long time? Anyone who has seen me has seen the Father. How can you say, 'Show us the Father'?" (John 14:9)

There is only one God and one Mediator who can reconcile God and humanity— the man Christ Jesus. (1 Tim. 2:5†)

Superstitions, magic, and wrong notions and practices filled the disciples' world. But Jesus cleansed people's ideas about God. He cleansed away the gods and half-gods, the national and local deities; He took away an autocratic, irresponsible "God" and left us with God, our Father.

He does not ask you and me to do anything that He Himself will not do. "Anything," that is, except one thing: to repent for sin committed. Beyond that, He shares everything with us. I wonder if in the cross He did not do that too. Is the cross His repenting for our sins?

Dr. Shailer Mathews, dean of the divinity school at the University of Chicago, says that the future idea of God will be the pervasive life-force within the universe, instead of God as Father. I feel he is wrong. If your eyes are on nature as the place to see God interpreted, then you will naturally think in terms of life-force. But if your eyes are on Jesus, you will interpret that life-force in terms of the Father. You have looked into the face of the Son. And that one look makes you sense that, whatever else may be said, this is the interpretation. This is what Jesus meant when He said, "No one comes to the Father except through me" (John 14:6). You cannot see the Father unless you look on the face of the Son. There you see His likeness. And what a likeness!

Jesus has forever cleansed our ideas of God through the Word He has spoken to us.

O God, how would we ever cease to love such a God. Our hearts bend in deepest gratitude that such a God fills our universe—and us. Amen.

CLEANSING THE KINGDOM

After his suffering, he showed himself to these men…over a period of forty days and spoke about the kingdom of God…. They asked him, "Lord, are you at this time going to restore the kingdom to Israel?"

He said to them: "It is not for you to know the times or dates the Father has set by his own authority." (Acts 1:3, 6-7)

But He not only cleansed our ideas of God. He went further. He cleansed our ideas of the kingdom of God.

The kingdom of God was, to the Jewish mind, a setting up of a world State, with God as ruler and the Jewish people as the vice-regent of God. Jesus took this idea and cleansed it from national elements. He universalized it, making the kingdom to be ruled by a new dynasty of vice-regents—the servant-kings. Power will now be distributed to us according to service rendered. This will be beyond all thought of race and birth and color.

All the world's dictators will ultimately break themselves upon this kingdom, for we cannot tolerate another outbreak of world-rule by a nationally messianic people. We have seen a loftier vision, the kingdom of God has been forever cleansed, and we cannot rest on this side of it.

But He also cleansed the material. Human thought has alternated between the idea of matter as God and matter as bad. The materialist takes one side, and Hinduism, on the whole, the other side. Jesus cleansed away both ideas and gave us a world of matter that God looked upon and termed "good" (Gen. 1). My body is not an enemy, but the handiwork of God. As such, it is to be kept fit and well and used in the purposes of the kingdom of God. Since I have seen the Word become "flesh" (John 1:14), I can no longer be afraid of "flesh," the material, for it has within it the possibility of expressing the Divine.

I never really saw the material until I saw Christ. Then my world was new. This amazingly worthwhile world is the scene of the coming kingdom.

O God, we thank You that we live in a world of matter. Help us not to fear it, but to use it—in Your kingdom. Amen.

STILL MORE TO CLEANSE

"It has been said, 'Anyone who divorces his wife must give her a certificate of divorce.' But I tell you that anyone who divorces his wife, except for marital unfaithfulness, causes her to become an adulteress, and anyone who marries the divorced woman commits adultery." (Matt. 5:31-32)

Religion that God our Father accepts as pure and faultless is this: to look after orphans and widows in their distress and to keep oneself from being polluted by the world. (James 1:27)

––––––––––––––––––––– ❦ –––––––––––––––––––––

Jesus went further: He cleansed the family. The home was the one and only institution He defended. But even more, He cleansed it. He cleansed it from polygamy on the one side and polyandry on the other, founding it on the life partnership of one man and one woman, a basis of an utter equality.

This is an ultimate concept. Modern looseness and promiscuity will fail, for they will break themselves upon this ultimate rock. But Jesus went further and cleansed love. He found it as lust and turned it into love—not only in the marital context, but toward all our fellow humans—orphans and widows included.

He also cleansed prayer. He found it as magic and mere petition and turned it into communion. Prayer was no longer getting something out of God, but God getting something out of us. It was a pulling of ourselves to God that, through this higher contact with higher power, higher purpose might be achieved.

He cleansed religion. He made Himself the definition of religion. To be religious is to be Christlike, and that definition forever cleanses our minds from unworthy and lesser concepts. A Hindu asked me, "But don't you shield unworthy religion behind such a definition?" No, I do not shield it; I cleanse it. We have looked into a Face, and we can no longer think of religion except in terms of this Life.

O God, our Father, thank You for the breadth and depth of this cleansing. Help us to accept both dimensions. Amen.

A RISKY STATEMENT

"Simon, Simon, Satan has asked to sift all of you as wheat. But I have prayed for you, Simon, that your faith may not fail. And when you have turned back, strengthen your brothers." (Luke 22:31-32)

Jesus' statement to His disciples in John 15:3 ("You are already clean because of the word I have spoken to you") was a bold thing to say, for He was declaring something on faith rather than on fact. Yes, they had been cleansed from many things, but it was not true just then that they were "clean." Were they not still quarreling over first places, proposing to call down fire from heaven, and asking other disciples to stop work because they did not belong to their party? This was hardly being "clean."

And yet, as far as Jesus was concerned, the power they needed for perfect cleanness was all available. It seemed to Jesus so actual that He declared it already done. This statement was the expression of His consciousness that this was all provided for in His word. He believed they would connect up with that word and take the cleanness.

It took about sixty days before it was actually accomplished at Pentecost. So this statement was made with about sixty "days of grace" attached to it. But at the first moment they were prepared to pay the price and take the cleansing, it was theirs. In other words, Jesus gave them a check they could cash at any time. All they had to do was to endorse it.

A minister living in the backwoods without many conveniences was sent a check that seemed too good to be true. He went to the city, nervously presented it to the bank, and was relieved when the teller simply told him to endorse it. On the back he wrote, "I endorse this with all my heart!"

That is what the disciples did—at Pentecost they endorsed with all their hearts the check that gave them cleanness.

O Christ. Thank You for Your adequacy and Your faith in us. We will not disappoint that faith, for we will take that adequacy. Amen.

JOINT OVERCOMERS

You, dear children, are from God and have overcome them, because the one who is in you is greater than the one who is in the world. (1 John 4:4)

Among the most penetrating and hope-bringing words Jesus ever gave us were these: "I have told you these things, so that in me you may have peace. In this world you will have trouble. But take heart! I have overcome the world" (John 16:33).

"Ah, yes," you say, "He did overcome the world, but that was 2,000 years ago—and I am living now. What does this have to do with me?"

My answer is that two ideas belong together. One is Jesus' announcement that He identified with the hunger, sickness, and imprisonment of people ("Whatever you did for one of the least of these brothers of mine, you did for me"—Matt. 25:40). The other is this verse telling us that we can have peace because He has overcome the pain-filled world. As He is identified with us in our defeats and sicknesses and hunger, so we are also identified with Him in His victory. His overcoming the world is our overcoming the world—provided, of course, that we enter into it, relate ourselves to it, and make it our very own.

This opens up to me an amazing possibility: I can make every one of His victories my very own. I can so relate my life to His in complete adjustment that when He overcomes, I overcome. I live actually by the life and victories of Another.

We sometimes smile at a married couple so deeply in love with each other that they take credit for one another's accomplishments. "We had a new baby!" "We just earned a master's degree." The individual degree of effort is submerged into their common life.

In very fact one can say to Christ, "Why, Master, did you overcome the world or did I?" We will hear Him gently answer, "We both did, for my victory is your victory."

O Christ, thank You that I, poor unworthy I, am Your partner in the most magnificent thing this planet has ever seen—Your overcoming. Help me to relate myself to it completely and make it mine. Amen.

OVERCOMING THE COMMONPLACE

Whoever can be trusted with very little can also be trusted with much, and whoever is dishonest with very little will also be dishonest with much. (Luke 16:10)

Do your best to present yourself to God as one approved, a workman who does not need to be ashamed and who correctly handles the word of truth. (2 Tim. 2:15)

Jesus overcame the boredom of the commonplace. To live in a village for 30 years amid dull humanity and work at a carpenter's bench, to support a widowed mother and the family, is not difficult if you see nothing beyond that. But if you feel the call of the living God upon you, and know in your heart of hearts you have the one thing this sad world needs…and then to be compelled to stay in cramped surroundings and to do commonplace work for 90 percent of your life in order to fulfill your real life purpose in the remaining 10 percent—if you do all this happily, then that is victory.

Jesus had one foot in the hard commonplace facts of Nazareth and another in the center of the world's needs. Two terribly conflicting worlds—was He not torn between them? And therefore unhappy?

No, for He made these worlds one. He brought the infinite into the finite and the finite into the infinite. His making of a wooden plow had within it the remaking of the world, so He would make that plow well, and worthy of a world's Redeemer. Someone has said, "If you do a small thing as though it were a great thing, God will let you do the great thing as though it were a small thing." Day by day in commonplace Nazareth, Jesus wove with infinite patience the seamless robe He would someday wear before the world.

A woman of the Balkans, working with her needle and thread, was asked if she did not tire of the awful task of sewing such tiny stitches day after day. "Oh, no," she replied; "this is my wedding dress." These stitches were no longer commonplace—they were related to something wonderful.

O Christ, You overcame dull tasks and dull hours, for You related them to the infinite. Help me to do the same. Amen.

OVERCOMING FAMILY HANDICAPS

"But Lord," Gideon asked, "how can I save Israel? My clan is the weakest in Manasseh, and I am the least in my family."

The LORD answered, "I will be with you, and you will strike down all the Midianites together." (Judg. 6:15-16)

"Nazareth! Can anything good come from there?" Nathanael asked.

"Come and see," said Philip. (John 1:46)

Jesus overcame two handicaps: He had no formal education, and He did not belong to a foremost family. That is why on one occasion "the Jews there were amazed and asked, 'How did this man get such learning without having studied?' " (John 7:15). He suffered in the eyes of the educated and cultured because He had no learning that would correspond to our college degree.

But He overcame that, and made what He had so real and worthwhile that the people who followed Him saw that He knew life and could give it.

Then, again, there was victory over a commonplace family tradition. He came from a peasant family, from a despised place. When you look at His family history as seen in the genealogy (Matt. 1), you see some streams of rather evil blood. Many of us have to gain victory here, for we come not from "the best families" but from very common stock. We must start a new tradition.

Michael Faraday, the brilliant chemist and physicist as well as committed Christian, was born in a stable, his father an invalid blacksmith, his mother a common drudge.

When people in the late 1600s objected to a noblewoman marrying the Puritan pastor Matthew Henry because of his lowly birth, she replied, "I don't care where he came from, I'm only interested in where he is going, and I want to go with him."

We too can enter into that victory Jesus gained and make people forget where we have come from as they watch us going on—with Him .

O Christ, thank You for overcoming these two things. Help us to begin a new learning and a new heredity through You. Amen.

OVERCOMING THE URGE TO SELF-PROMOTE

When the Jewish Feast of Tabernacles was near, Jesus' brothers said to him, "You ought to leave here and go to Judea, so that your disciples may see the miracles you do. No one who wants to become a public figure acts in secret. Since you are doing these things, show yourself to the world."…

Jesus told them, "The right time for me has not yet come; for you any time is right…. You go to the Feast. I am not yet going up to this Feast." (John 7:2-4, 6, 8)

<hr>

Jesus was tempted to be spectacular. He had the power—could it not be used to impress people? Of course it would all be to further the kingdom, so would it not therefore be right? But He turned down this temptation decisively. He would win by worth and service alone. Everything else was of the devil.

Had He advertised Himself, we would have forgotten Him. His reticences are more vocal than His self-display would have been. He did not go to the pinnacle of the Temple (Matt. 4:5-7), but we put Him on the throne of the universe for this very reason. He refused a do a miracle before Herod (Luke 23:8-9); we denounce the asking and remember the refusal.

Today the person who is to live victoriously must find victory at this place, for we live in an age of advertising, some of it boisterous. It is easy for the Christian to allow this psychology to ebb over into self-advertising.

I visited a beautiful "Singing Tower" dedicated to the people of a state, with charming music coming out. It was a lovely thing to do—but the donor spoiled it all by having his own grave at the foot of the tower. Had he been buried in some secluded place in the surrounding garden, we would have gone there to pay our respects. But I instinctively turned my back when I saw the grave with the great tower as its headstone. The "Singing Tower" had lost its music.

Christ kept His music, for He refused to blow His own horn. And millions now sing His praises.

O Christ of the reticent heart, teach us Your lowly ways, for we see they lead to the heights. Amen.

OVERCOMING HASTE

This is what the Sovereign LORD, the Holy One of Israel, says: "In repentance and rest is your salvation, in quietness and trust is your strength." (Isa. 30:15)

When he heard that Lazarus was sick, he stayed where he was two more days. Then he said to his disciples, "Let us go back to Judea." (John 11:6-7)

The Man who had most to do seemed never to be in a hurry. He was launching a kingdom that would turn out to be the ultimate order for all humanity, and yet He seemed to be in no feverish haste. Not that He was idle—far from it. He never wasted a moment, and yet He was never fussily busy.

The Hindus worship the great god Hari (pronounced *hurry*). The West also worships at the shrine of the great god Hurry! This is the god that dispenses fevers and strained hearts and unlovely lives, too busy to live. Jesus said to Martha, "You are worried and upset about many things" (Luke 10:41). Martha probably said beneath her breath, "Yes, but if I am not worried and upset, you'll go hungry." Martha, with all her rush and haste, fell down in her supposedly strong point.

This fussy haste of the modern day has also fallen down in its strongest point. We sped up our machines and our civilization…leaving millions upon park benches unemployed, idle, and hungry. We failed where we thought ourselves strong.

We must regain victory at the place of the unhurried heart. In our ashram, we have put up this motto, taken from a Greek writer, with our addition: "Whirl is king, having driven out Zeus—but not here!" With the decay of religion (Zeus), the ancient Greeks turned to "Whirl!" as king. In our ashram we say instead, "Calm is king, having brought in Christ." Both in our groups and in our hearts we must enthrone the unhurried Christ, that the benediction of His quiet might spread to every portion of our being.

O Christ, we thank You for Your victory over unresting haste. Give to us too that victory of the quiet, assured heart that knows God's victory is certain in the end. Amen.

OVERCOMING EXASPERATION WITH OTHERS

When Jesus' followers saw what was going to happen, they said, "Lord, should we strike with our swords?" And one of them struck the servant of the high priest, cutting off his right ear.

But Jesus answered, "No more of this!" And he touched the man's ear and healed him. (Luke 22:49-51)

The kingdom, which Jesus launched, required delicate handling. Its virtues might very easily turn into vices by the slightest twist. Its light might turn into darkness. In such circumstances He would have tremendous temptation to be impatient with the bungling instruments of His kingdom.

It is a wonder He didn't dismiss His disciples at a number of places along the way. When they twisted His highest principles into something else, why didn't He let them go and try it with another group? He didn't, for if He could salvage this group, that would be victory!

Often we face the same temptation—dismiss this group of employees and try another batch; get rid of the troublesome wife or husband and start all over; dismiss these Christian workers and try to bring in the kingdom through a fresh group; get rid of our pastor and try for a better one; change congregations, hoping the next may be more amenable—and so on. All of this is in its essence a running away from the problem. It is an attempt at escape.

After all, the next group we have to deal with will probably have the same streaky human nature. The new brooms will sweep clean for a few days—and then comes the dust! That second wife will not be an angel. Leaps from the frying pan into the fire are often very short and easy.

Jesus overcame this impatience with inept people and made them into change agents, who changed the world. That was victory. We must learn how to refashion people—the ordinary, streaky people around us, remembering that as we put up with them, Christ has to put up with us.

O Christ, thank You for Your patience and persistence with us. Help us to deal with others in the same patient, redemptive way. Amen.

OVERCOMING RESENTMENT

Therefore, as God's chosen people, holy and dearly loved, clothe yourselves with compassion, kindness, humility, gentleness and patience. Bear with each other and forgive whatever grievances you may have against one another. Forgive as the Lord forgave you. And over all these virtues put on love, which binds them all together in perfect unity. (Col. 3:12-14)

While they were stoning him, Stephen prayed, "Lord Jesus, receive my spirit." Then he fell on his knees and cried out, "Lord, do not hold this sin against them." When he had said this, he fell asleep. (Acts 7:59-60)

People of faith usually have a sensitive, eager disposition. They see beyond the status quo, want something different, and set about getting it. Almost immediately, they run into opposition, for people do not easily give up the "is" for the "ought-to-be." Christians will be tempted to resent people who do not see what they see. The person of faith must have victory over the world of resentment.

It is interesting that Jesus linked faith in God and forgiveness of others. Immediately after His inspiring teaching on mountain-moving faith (Mark 11:22-24), He continued, "When you are praying, first forgive anyone you are holding a grudge against, so that your Father in heaven will forgive your sins, too" (v. 25†).

Faith without forgiveness makes religion hard, fanatical. Forgiveness without faith makes religion soft, nonprogressive. But faith and forgiveness makes religion Christian. This forgiveness element puts love into faith, so that now faith works through love (see Gal. 5:6).

The person of faith forgives those who lash back because they do not see what we see. We follow a Man who saw His attempts at a new world end up on a cross, deserted by the multitudes whom He wanted to save, by the disciples who professed allegiance to Him, and seemingly by the Father who sent Him. Yet at the last, a prayer of forgiveness was upon His lips.

O Christ of the unresentful heart, make us like that. Make us full of faith toward God and full of tenderness toward others who do not agree with us. Amen.

OVERCOMING THE IRRELEVANT

"Woe to you, teachers of the law and Pharisees, you hypocrites! You give a tenth of your spices—mint, dill and cumin. But you have neglected the more important matters of the law—justice, mercy and faithfulness. You should have practiced the latter, without neglecting the former. You blind guides! You strain out a gnat but swallow a camel." (Matt. 23:23-24)

This is my prayer: that your love may abound more and more in knowledge and depth of insight, so that you may be able to discern what is best and may be pure and blameless until the day of Christ. (Phil. 1:9-10)

If one is to live a victorious life, he or she must live in the relevant. Many do not—they occupy their time in a lot of irrelevancies.

A friend of mine was in a terrible train wreck. Many were killed outright, and many others were groaning under the wreckage. The few unhurt were trying desperately to rescue the wounded and attend to them. In the midst of all this, a woman sat beside her suitcase, which had been torn open, and kept repeating, "Oh, my expensive pair of shoes!"

We should go over everything in our lives and ask this question: "Are you relevant to the really big issues? Do you keep me from the really worthwhile things? You may not be bad, but are you relevant?" If anything in our lives cannot answer that call, then out it should go. The Christian must have a wastebasket, not only for the bad but for the irrelevant.

Jesus had a sifted mind. He never once was led into a subordinate issue, never once missed the real point, never got into a bypath, was always on the relevant. He overcame the sinful and also the unimportant. We must cut out not only what isn't good, but also what isn't good enough. He did that, and we can share His overcoming by centering ourselves in a world of relevancies.

O Christ, You want to save us from both iniquity and irrelevancy. We now expose our minds to the searching of Your mind, and we consent to let go of the trivial. Prune us. Amen.

OVERCOMING ANXIETY

Do not be anxious about anything, but in everything, by prayer and petition, with thanksgiving, present your requests to God. And the peace of God, which transcends all understanding, will guard your hearts and your minds in Christ Jesus. (Phil. 4:6-7)

"Do not be anxious about *anything.*" Was there ever a message so deeply needed now as this one? Anxieties fill the air, and they fill us. Jesus, however, conquered the world of anxieties. Three things lie at the center of our anxieties: food, shelter, and future security. Based on this, Jesus must have been the most anxious man alive, for not one of these was assured to Him. He had no food except what was given to Him day by day. He had no assured home. Often He slept under the open heavens, huddled beneath a tree. As for future security—He knew there was none, for His road would end at a cross.

The three things we are most anxious about were utterly missing from His life. He shared our lack—but minus our anxieties. How did He do it?

His prescription was simple: Obey God, trust God. Those four words were the four cornerstones of His life. And when the storm broke, the foundation stood. Note He puts them together. You cannot really trust God unless you obey him. For if you do not obey God in your conduct, you cannot trust Him for your clothing.

A woman told me of the loss of her faith: "The Bible says, 'Ask whatever you wish.' I prayed for my father's recovery, but he died. So my faith is gone." But she did not quote the whole: "If you remain in me and my words remain in you, ask whatever you wish, and it will be given you" (John 15:7).

George MacDonald wrote to Ion Keith-Falconer, a young missionary to the Middle East: "This is a practical working faith: first, it is man's business to do the will of God; second, God takes on Himself the special care of that man; third, that man should be afraid of nothing."

O Christ, there was no corroding care in Your heart. Give me a heart like that. I will pay the price of freedom from anxiety—the price of obedience. Amen.

OVERCOMING THE URGE TO WITHDRAW

At that time some Pharisees came to Jesus and said to him, "Leave this place and go somewhere else. Herod wants to kill you."

He replied, "Go tell that fox, 'I will drive out demons and heal people today and tomorrow, and on the third day I will reach my goal.' In any case, I must keep going today and tomorrow and the next day—for surely no prophet can die outside Jerusalem!" (Luke 13:31-33)

There is a real tendency in religion to try to win victory by withdrawal. We encase ourselves with the hard shell of refusal to face the issue, withdraw into ourselves, hoping for a good result. We try to maintain peace by dodging the battle.

Jesus found His victory not by getting out but by getting in. One of the Bible's most important verses is this: "He steadfastly set His face to go to Jerusalem" (Luke 9:51 NKJV). That meant He would face issues, would precipitate crises and see the whole thing through to a bitter-glorious end. But in setting His face in that direction, He set the face of His religion in that direction too. We can never be true to Him now unless we are true to Him at this point. All withdrawal from real issues is withdrawal from Jesus.

One of the saddest verses in literature is this: "And so Pilate, willing to content the people…delivered Jesus, when he had scourged him, to be crucified" (Mark 15:15 KJV). For us, one of the saddest days in life is the day we allow group-fear to conquer the highest judgments and instincts of the soul. Sometimes we "content" the multitude when we should "contend with" the multitude.

Furthermore, "Pilate…took water and washed his hands in front of the crowd" (Matt. 27:24)—a baptism into irresponsibility. He wanted to get out from the liability of Jesus' death; meanwhile, Jesus was taking a baptism of liability for every person. One was crawling out; the other was marching in!

O Christ, I too need this power to come to grips with issues as they arise. Give me Your decisiveness. Amen.

OVERCOMING THE FEAR OF MINORITY STATUS

Paul: *At my first defense, no one came to my support, but everyone deserted me. May it not be held against them. But the Lord stood at my side and gave me strength, so that through me the message might be fully proclaimed and all the Gentiles might hear it. And I was delivered from the lion's mouth. (2 Tim. 4:16-17)*

In the beginning, truth is usually found in a minority.

A stricken boy in a faint lay on the ground before Jesus. The account says, "The more part said, He is dead" (Mark 9:26 asv). Had a majority vote been taken there, they would have decided that the boy should be buried. But the truth was in the minority of One.

' "The more part" often decides that a cause is dead. Twenty years ago in a denominational conference in India, a proposal to give India local self-government in church matters was presented. It got tabled with a bang. "The more part" decided it was dead. Twenty years later I saw that idea taken from the table and adopted by the church, not only in India, but throughout the world. "The more part" was wrong.

"The more part" decides again and again in its elections that any new order to replace the present world-order, with its injustices and wrongs, is dead. But again "the more part" is wrong. For the idea of a just social order, in which every citizen shall have an equal opportunity, is God's idea and will not go down.

We cannot get spiritual victory unless we are willing to be in "the less part," if necessary. If you look at the Gethsemane scene, you will see the relative size of the crowds: Jesus alone, then the three, then the eight, and then the Jerusalem multitude. If you want to be in the multitude, you will probably find yourself in a crowd furthest from Jesus.

The victorious life means you are released from an itching to be on the popular side. You become willing to stand alone if necessary.

O Christ, I would rather be alone with You than in a multitude without You. I want to be with You, wherever You are, with many or with few. Amen.

OVERCOMING EVERY SIN

You have been set free from sin and have become slaves to righteousness.

I put this in human terms because you are weak in your natural selves. Just as you used to offer the parts of your body in slavery to impurity and to ever-increasing wickedness, so now offer them in slavery to righteousness leading to holiness. (Rom. 6:18-19)

One of the most necessary things in living victoriously is to realize that when we are fighting evil, we are fighting a conquered foe. Jesus met every sin and conquered it. Many do not realize this, and so develop an inferiority complex before evil. They allow evil to bully them, to make them feel it is a permanent part of things and cannot be eradicated. Hence they are defeated in mind even before the battle begins.

We must get hold of the idea that sin has been conquered—*every* sin has been conquered, both within the individual and the social order. When sin begins to bully me, I quietly ask it to bend its neck and let me see. When it does, I quietly but joyfully point to the footprints of the Son of God on the neck of sin. My inferiority complex is gone. I am on the winning side. I shall meet not one single sin today that has not been defeated.

A legend runs that in an ancient battle in Central India, a leading warrior had his head cut off, but he was so determined that he fought on regardless. He killed many, in fact. However, he collapsed when a woman saw him and cried out, "But your head is off—you're dead!" At this, he fell down and succumbed!

When evil seems strong and is about to overcome, I point and say, "But look, your head is gone! Did not my Master conquer you in life? Did He not sever the head of evil by the sword of the cross? Begone!"

Evil fights on. But it is brainless. It depends on prejudice, old habits, and unreasoning emotions. We fight a fierce but brainless foe.

O Christ, I thank You that You did not succumb to a single temptation. Show me how to accept and enter into this completed victory. Amen.

THE SECRET OF OVERCOMING

All of you who were baptized into Christ have clothed yourselves with Christ.
(Gal. 3:27)

Jesus: *"I am the vine; you are the branches. Those who remain in me, and I in*
them, will produce much fruit. For apart from me you can do nothing.... But if
you remain in me and my words remain in you, you may ask for anything you
want, and it will be granted!" (John 15:5, 7†)

All this month we have been thinking together about Jesus' amazing statement about overcoming the world (John 16:33). You say, "Well and good,
wonderful. But how do I get hold of His victory and make it mine?"

The whole verse reads this way: "I have told you these things, so that in me you
may have peace. In this world you will have trouble. But take heart! I have overcome the world." Notice the contrast: "In the world...trouble." "In me...peace."

What does "in me" mean? It means being identified with Him, merged into
Him, so at one with Him that His victories become ours, and therefore His
peace becomes ours. Surrender of yourself means identification with His self.

In Isaiah 63:11-12 it says, "Where is he who...sent his glorious arm of power
to be at Moses' right hand?" God's power and Moses' efforts coincided. When
Moses raised his right hand, God's right hand went alongside of it. God's arm
didn't do everything, for that would have kept Moses from developing. Moses'
arm had to go too. But when he tried, God triumphed.

Say this to yourself today: "I am in Christ, and so His power is identified
with every single thing in my life. Today His glorious arm will go alongside my
right hand. As I take hold of my tasks, there will be a surprising strength within
me. As I face perplexities, there will be unexpected solutions. As I face relationships with others, there will be a love beyond my own, making those relations
sweet and beautiful. Nothing will meet me today that He will not be in, and
together we will go through with it. That is enough."

O Christ, I thank You that I am "in" You. Help me to accept the full meaning of
that "in-ness" and live by it, today and forever. Amen.

OLD, AND YET NEW

If any man is in Christ, he is a new creature: the old things are passed away; behold, they are become new. (2 Cor. 5:17 ASV)

For I am the least of the apostles and do not even deserve to be called an apostle, because I persecuted the church of God. But by the grace of God I am what I am, and his grace to me was not without effect. (1 Cor. 15:9-10)

Here are some of the results of being "in Christ."

In the first verse quoted above, Paul says, "Old things are passed away," and yet they have not passed away; they (the old things) "are become new." There was a sense in which old things had completely passed away, and yet there was a sense in which they had come back again completely transformed and new.

This "new creature" is much different from the old creature, and yet it is fundamentally the same, only new. The modern peach was once used in ancient Persia as a source for poison to tip arrows. The modern peach is a new creature; old things have passed away, behold, they have become new. The poison has been eliminated, but the fundamental life of the tree remains—only now, instead of being used to produce poison, it produces luscious, health-giving fruit. The term for this kind of change is *redirection*.

Paul saw that the poison of his old instincts had been eliminated, but the instincts themselves had now come back again, redirected. Whereas they had been used in purposes that ended in death, they were now being used in purposes that ended in life. He found he was the same man, with his fundamental Jewish nature intact. And yet he was so fundamentally changed that he had to change his name to express a new fact. There was discontinuity with the past, and yet a continuity. Conversion had meant a cutting and a conservation. The driving forces of his spirit were under a new control, directed toward a new end. Redirection had taken place.

O Christ, I thank You that You take this raw material of human life and cleanse and refashion it. You make it serve other ends—Your ends. I put it all at Your disposal. Make out of me what You can. Amen.

REDIRECTING THE INSTINCTS

We put no stumbling block in anyone's path, so that our ministry will not be discredited. (2 Cor. 6:3)

Christ's love compels us, because we are convinced that one died for all, and therefore all died. And he died for all, that those who live should no longer live for themselves but for him who died for them and was raised again. (2 Cor. 5:14-15)

The instincts are the driving life-forces. The stream of life energy flowing through us breaks into three instinctive channels: self, sexuality, and the group. Minor instincts can be counted, but they usually turn out to be phases of the above dominant instincts.

There are several possibilities for these instincts: straightforward expression, perversion, repression, suppression (or self-control), and redirection. The Christian way of life dismisses perversion and repression. It makes use of the other three.

The distinction between repression and suppression is this: To repress an instinct is to push it down into the subconscious and close the lid. There it works havoc. As J. A. Hadfield (University of London) says, "Repressed instincts are like bad boys who, when put out of the class, begin to throw stones at the windows." But in suppression, the instincts are kept within the conscious mind, held down at certain places in order to be redirected at others. In other words, the bad boys are kept in the class and taught to direct their energies to constructive ends. Of course, suppression without corresponding redirection may turn into repression, which is dangerous to handle.

The Christian way also uses expression, but always under the control of its ideals. That means expression at certain places and suppression at others. But the suppressed can always be redirected; the instinctive forces can be turned to higher expressions. This is what opens the door upward.

O Christ, we thank You that You have made it possible for us to be wholly dedicated to Your purposes, and that human nature is not to be eliminated, but redeemed. Redeem me. Amen.

A REDIRECTION EXAMPLE

Agrippa said to Paul, "Do you think that in such a short time you can persuade me to be a Christian?"

Paul replied, "Short time or long—I pray to God that not only you but all who are listening to me today may become what I am, except for these chains." (Acts 26:28-29)

Paul's own life is a dramatic example of his statement that "old things are passed away; behold, all things are become new." His instincts, like ours, were very old. The human tendencies stretch back to untold ages. And yet they can be abruptly changed and redeemed.

Before his conversion he was very pugnacious; he breathed out slaughter against the Christians. Then came the change on the Damascus Road. Thereafter, he was still pugnacious. But now this energy was directed against the kingdom of evil. (Sometimes it was almost unleashed against his associates!) On the whole, this pugnacious instinct was bridled and harnessed to the chariot of God's purposes, so that Paul drove it toward kingdom ends. The instinct was redirected and made constructive.

I saw a sadhu who had a tame lion, and when I asked him why he kept him, he said: "To teach the people how human nature can be changed. If this lion can become so meek, human beings can also tame their passions."

But it seemed to me that the lion had been de-lionized, becoming instead a lazy dog led about by a chain. If this lion was to be a real symbol of conversion, its magnificent energy should be tamed and harnessed to constructive tasks.

Do you have a pugnacious spirit? Don't try to get rid of it. Let Christ cleanse from it the selfish pugnacity that stands up for its own ways, and then harness it to the task of fighting disease, wrong conditions, inequalities, hate, and evil of every kind. Then you can say, "My old pugnacity has passed away; behold, it has become new."

O Christ, take this pugnacity of mine. I lay it upon Your altar. I ask You to use it. But it needs harnessing. Redirect it and use it. Amen.

REDIRECTING THE SELF INSTINCT

"I have spoken openly to the world," Jesus replied. "I always taught in synagogues or at the temple, where all the Jews come together. I said nothing in secret. Why question me? Ask those who heard me. Surely they know what I said."

When Jesus said this, one of the officials nearby struck him in the face. "Is this the way you answer the high priest?" he demanded.

"If I said something wrong," Jesus replied, "testify as to what is wrong. But if I spoke the truth, why did you strike me?" (John 18:20-23)

The ego instinct is probably the strongest of all. It is at the basis of most of our actions. We must face that fact. To talk about a person being "selfless" makes me squirm. Christ was not selfless, nor was Paul, nor should any Christian be.

It is simply hypocritical for anyone to say the self isn't there. Yes, it is, and should be. But the question is, What kind of a self is it?

The self was redirected in Jesus, the meekest of men and simultaneously the most self-assertive. He renounced power, refusing to be made a king. Yet the self gained the most amazing power ever exercised.

Paul became the servant of the churches—their troubles his troubles, their weaknesses his weaknesses. As you look at him you may say, "The man has lost his own ego." Not at all. That ego instinct was redirected, and therefore satisfied, by holding an authority over people by the very fact of his renunciation. He did not renounce the self for that purpose; had he done so, it would have spoiled it all. But the power over others was a by-product of losing himself. The self was not lost—it was loosed.

Mahatma Gandhi lost his smaller, lawyer self and found a larger servant-of-India self. With it has come an astonishing authority. He is not selfless, he is strong.

Your old ego must die, be crucified. Then it will come back, and you can say, "The old ego has passed away; behold, it has become new."

O Christ, take this ego of mine and cleanse it from all egoism. Harness it to Your purposes, so that I may be able to live with it—and perhaps even rejoice in it. Amen.

E. STANLEY JONES | 137

REDIRECTING THE SEXUAL INSTINCT

Paul: *It is fine to be zealous, provided the purpose is good, and to be so always and not just when I am with you. My dear children, for whom I am again in the pains of childbirth until Christ is formed in you, how I wish I could be with you now. (Gal. 4:18-20)*

Life is heavily weighted in the area of sex—too heavily weighted, some would say. But whether it is overemphasized or rightly emphasized in our makeup, it is an integral part of us, and as such must be dealt with frankly, sanely.

To confess sexual desire is no more shameful than to confess desire for food. Both are natural to the way we are made. Where it functions biologically for the purposes of procreation, the problem of sex is normally solved. Even there it must be under the restraint of the rest of life's ideals. For if one part of the nature demands satisfaction at the expense of the rest of oneself, the result is inner division and unhappiness.

The problem becomes more acute when the sexual instinct is denied biological expression. In that case it may be repressed, which is dangerous, setting up a complex. Or it may be redirected.

Jesus redirected his sexual instinct; He was creative in mind and spirit. He was bringing into being a new race, a higher type of humanity. He was mothering and fathering the family of God. At one point He yearned over wayward Jerusalem, "How often I have longed to gather your children together, as a hen gathers her chicks under her wings, but you were not willing" (Matt. 23:37). That is redirection.

Paul, denied a family life, was not unhappy, because he redirected his sexual instinct by being procreative in the higher reaches of life, the mind and spirit. Wherever he went, he saw the new birth take place. He was a spiritual parent.

If anyone be in Christ, he or she is a new creature; the old sex instinct has passed away; behold, it has become new.

O Christ, I thank You for release from inner bondages. Loose my soul in creative activity. Amen.

REDIRECTING CURIOSITY AND PRIDE

This is my prayer: that your love may abound more and more in knowledge and depth of insight, so that you may be able to discern what is best and may be pure and blameless until the day of Christ, filled with the fruit of righteousness that comes through Jesus Christ—to the glory and praise of God. (Phil. 1:9-11)

The instinct of curiosity shows up early in children, who ask repeatedly, "What's that?" In grown-up people it may manifest itself in ugly ways through prying into other people's affairs and meddling with their private business.

On the other hand, the instinct of curiosity may be a decided help in furthering the spiritual life, if the Christian will redirect it from lower ways to higher. Our mind and spirit should grow as we stretch to know. The instinct of curiosity can be redirected from useless, pointless prying to the purposes of infinite growth.

The instinct of pride can also be converted. I hear people say, "My pride has been killed." I hope not. Of course there is the sense in which silly pride, which thinks in terms of decorating itself to attract attention, needs to die. But pride can be harnessed to the kingdom. Paul could say, "For what is our hope or joy, or the crown of which we boast? Is it not you yourselves?… Yes, you are our glory and our joy" (1 Thessalonians 2:19 WEYMOUTH).

Here was the old Pharisaical pride turned redemptive. He was not glorying in his ancestry or learning, but in this new creation taking shape before him— proud of this new humanity that was developing in one of his churches. The instinct of pride was loosed from pettiness to glory in the worthwhile work of his own hands.

A redirected pride would save us from slovenly sermons, from unfinished work, from spiritual half-heartedness, from not being at our best for Christ. We should be able to say, "The old curiosity and pride have passed away; behold, they have become new."

O Christ, kill within me foolish pride, and raise up within me a nobler pride that will tolerate nothing less than the highest. Amen.

REDIRECTING THE DRIVE TO ACQUIRE AND TO BELONG

Do not store up for yourselves treasures on earth, where moth and rust destroy, and where thieves break in and steal. But store up for yourselves treasures in heaven. (Matt. 6:19-20)

The instinct to acquire is the driving force in many lives. It is the basis of many of our world difficulties, individual and collective. It drives people to bow at the shrine of thing-worship. It needs converting. Can it be done?

Jesus pointed the way when He spoke about acquiring treasures in heaven rather than on earth. We are still to "store up"—in other words, the instinct to get is still operative, but now toward higher values. We invest in people instead of things. We are now as eager for this new treasure of changed people and changed society as we were for the treasure through exchange.

The group (or social) instinct can be used for narrow, partisan, nationalistic ends. It can grow into a bombastic nationalism, asserting itself against its neighbors and pushing the world into war. Or it can be converted, redirected. In Christianity it must be. The group instinct can fasten upon the ultimate concept in human relationships, namely, the kingdom of God on earth. Then we can say with Jesus, "Who are my mother and my brothers?… Whoever does God's will is my brother and sister and mother" (Mark 3:33, 35).

The group instinct is not done away with; it is enlarged, enlightened, enlivened. It has now its real home. The lesser loyalties of home, country, and church take their meaning from the highest loyalty—to the Beloved Community.

Every power of our lives is to be purged and presented as instruments of the new life. "No longer lend your faculties as unrighteous weapons of wickedness for sin to use. But rather offer yourselves to God as living men risen from the dead" (Rom. 6:13 WEYMOUTH). Paul taught redirection before modern psychology named it.

O Christ, my faculties are all at Your service. Take hold of me, not at the surface but at the depths. Amen.

CHANGE BEGINS AT HOME

He said: "I tell you the truth, unless you change and become like little children, you will never enter the kingdom of heaven." (Matt. 18:3)

"Woe to you, teachers of the law and Pharisees, you hypocrites! You clean the outside of the cup and dish, but inside they are full of greed and self-indulgence." (Matt. 23:25)

So far in our quest for the victorious life we have centered upon the causes of evil within ourselves. It is well to begin there, for many people are like a person with fever, tossing on the bed to find a cool spot, when all the time the fever is inside. You cannot cure this person by giving a cool spot on new sheets as long as the germs of the fever are within.

This modern age, intent upon social change as the cure-all for human ills, must not lose sight of this fact. We have a way of brushing past our own inner problems and fastening our attention upon outer difficulties.

As theologian William Adams Brown says, "It is not so much that this modern age has lost its sense of sin as that we have developed a technique by which we are able to fasten it upon those we dislike and whom we disapprove—big businessmen, for example, wicked imperialists, or corrupt labor leaders." This transference of guilt to others is essentially dishonest.

Sincerity must begin with ourselves. Beginning any other place is insincere, an escape mentality. No one is in any fit state of mind to face the problems of the world unless they are prepared to face honestly their own life and right it. George Arliss says of fellow actor John Mason (whose work he greatly admired): "John Mason would, in my opinion, have been the greatest actor in America if his private character had been as well balanced as his public performance."

Public performance in social reconstruction is out of balance if the private character is left unattended. In this book, we have rightly begun with ourselves. But we dare not stop there.

O Christ, You have put Your hand upon our own hearts first of all. Now help us to follow You as far as You go. Amen.

ENVIRONMENT: DOES IT FEED OR POISON?

Do not be misled: "Bad company corrupts good character." (1 Cor. 15:33)

Jesus began to denounce the cities in which most of his miracles had been performed, because they did not repent. "Woe to you, Korazin! Woe to you, Bethsaida! If the miracles that were performed in you had been performed in Tyre and Sidon, they would have repented long ago." (Matt. 11:20-21)

The first emphasis in our quest for victorious living should be on ourselves—but it must not be the last. To focus on environment while passing over the personal is an escape mentality. But to stay at the personal while refusing to go to the environmental is also an escape mentality.

Many hindrances to victorious living are inside us. But many others are not; they are part of the social order. It will not do to counter this by saying that the social order is made up of individuals. It is and it isn't. The social order is not entirely the product of we who are now living. It is made up of accumulated attitudes and customs passed from generation to generation and may be only modified slightly by current individuals. The question is, Does this social order help or hinder the new life?

Life depends on two factors: an adaptive organism and a suitable environment. The organism may be very adaptive, but if there is no suitable environment, it will die. On the other hand, if the environment is suitable and the organism not healthy and adaptive, it will also die.

Does the present social order provide a good environment to which the Christian can respond? Does it feed us, or poison us? If it feeds us, it must be preserved at all costs. But if it poisons us, then we must either convert it from poison to food (as in the case of the Persian peach), or if it cannot be converted, it must be replaced by something that will feed us. For live we must, and live victoriously.

O Christ, as we move into the question of the order around us, take from our hearts the blinding prejudices that keep us from seeing things as they are. Make us open-eyed and open-hearted. Amen.

PRIVATE IS NOT ENOUGH

"This, then, is how you should pray: 'Our Father in heaven, hallowed be your name, your kingdom come, your will be done, on earth as it is in heaven.' " (Matt. 6:9-10)

Life depends on a suitable environment. No matter how healthy the palm tree may be in itself, if transferred to a northern climate, it will die. "But," the objection is made, "the analogy doesn't hold, for Christian have their own private favorable environment—the kingdom of God. As the diver down in the sea has the air-pipe leading to the surface, so the Christian has personal contact with a higher world, the kingdom of God.

But the diver cannot stay down very long and is restricted at every point by the hostility of the environment. That we can exist in this world order as Christians, I do not deny. But we are restricted at every point. It is not our native air, so that unless we periodically rise to the atmosphere of a co-operative society, a Christian church, and take off our helmets and breathe freely, we shall probably suffocate.

And what about those who live in this world order without any contacts with the kingdom? How shall they live who have to breathe one atmosphere, and one alone—the poisoned atmosphere of the modern social order?

We must have an environment that will minister to the spiritual life, one in which we can live freely and fully. Now we have to live a Christian life in spite of our environment. Is it not possible to have one in which we shall live Christianly, not in spite of the environment but on account of it?

Besides, did Jesus intend that we should have a private favorable environment and not a collective one? Did He not ask us to pray that the kingdom might come on earth as it is in heaven? Do people in heaven have only a private and personal kingdom-of-God environment, or is it built into the collective order? To ask the question is to answer it. If there, then here.

O Father, we pray again, may Your kingdom come, and may Your will be done on earth as it is in heaven. Help us to put that into our plans as well as into our prayers. Amen.

E. STANLEY JONES | 143

WHAT CAUSES SIN?

The Son of Man will send his angels, and they will remove from his Kingdom everything that causes sin and all who do evil. And the angels will throw them into the fiery furnace, where there will be weeping and gnashing of teeth. Then the righteous will shine like the sun in their Father's Kingdom. Anyone with ears to hear should listen and understand! (Matt. 13:41-43[†])

This remarkable statement comes at the end of Jesus' explanation of the Parable of the Weeds. Note the two emphases: "Everything that causes sin *and* all who do evil." The latter refers to personal, individual transgression; the former to the impersonal causes of sin. One kind of sin is in the individual will; the other is in the social order.

We have been dealing throughout our quest with sin in the individual will. We must now look at the causes of sin in the social order. For the social order may cause sin as well as good. It may push people to do evil, for they cannot otherwise survive under that order.

It is not easy for us to see the causes of evil in the society to which we belong, especially if we hold a favored position. We think emotionally more than we would like to admit; our reason tries to make our emotional attachments rational. This fact should put us on guard about the validity of our social attitudes.

A man recently died who was called "The Excise Monarch of Sind," for he controlled nearly all the liquor shops of the province of Sind. The government even gave him the title of "Rai Bahadur," because of his "cleverness in the detection of crime." But he never detected his own liquor shops as the cause of most of the crime!

He was probably not a conscious hypocrite—he didn't see it, for he thought emotionally. We all do. We shall therefore need open-eyed wisdom as we look at the causes of sin in our society.

O Christ, You pierced beneath that which was seeming to that which was real. You exposed the human hearts and put Your finger on the Temple system's festering sores. Give us Your clear-eyed vision and courage. Amen.

THE CHIEF CAUSE

Then Judas Iscariot, one of the Twelve, went to the chief priests to betray Jesus to them. They were delighted to hear this and promised to give him money. So he watched for an opportunity to hand him over. (Mark 14:10-11)

The love of money is a root of all kinds of evil. Some people, eager for money, have wandered from the faith and pierced themselves with many griefs. (1 Tim. 6:10)

In searching for causes of sin in modern society, we must brush aside the lesser causes and go straight to the central one—selfish competition. The competitively acquiring spirit in modern society is probably sin's most prolific basis. It sets the stage for evil. Under a competitive order, it is easier to be hard and ruthless than to be loving and generous. It loads the dice against goodness.

When I say that, you may quickly object, "But if competition is taken out of life, won't we lose individual initiative? Won't life sag and become stagnant?" This is a real fear to many. But note that I said *selfish* competition. There is a higher competition which is not selfish. In a cooperative order there can still be competition; we can still compete as to who can give the most to the collective good. But this friendly competition is constructive, not destructive.

As the individual self-instinct must be redeemed and turned toward constructive ends, so the collective ego-instinct must be redeemed and made to serve the public good. In either case you cannot eradicate the ego; you must harness it to the making of a better order. It must be redirected.

However, this selfish competition that holds the center of our life is a very different thing. It has been softened and civilized, but underneath is a ruthlessness, just as hidden under the soft pads of a tiger are flesh-tearing claws. If you don't believe it, ask the 10 million victims who walk our streets unemployed to show you their wounds of soul and body. They know. We all know.

Civilization is bleeding from a thousand wounds—bled white by competitive struggle. The selfish competitive order is the chief cause of sin.

O Christ, help us to face this matter calmly and courageously. Help us to correct it, in Your name. Amen.

SNATCHING AND SCRAMBLING

The buyer haggles over the price, saying, "It's worthless," then brags about getting a bargain! (Prov. 20:14[†])

Your wealth has rotted, and moths have eaten your clothes. Your gold and silver are corroded. Their corrosion will testify against you and eat your flesh like fire. You have hoarded wealth in the last days. (James 5:2-3)

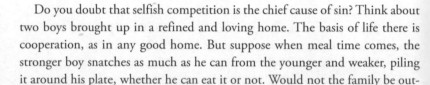

Do you doubt that selfish competition is the chief cause of sin? Think about two boys brought up in a refined and loving home. The basis of life there is cooperation, as in any good home. But suppose when meal time comes, the stronger boy snatches as much as he can from the younger and weaker, piling it around his plate, whether he can eat it or not. Would not the family be outraged? And would not such unsocial conduct be severely dealt with?

Good families are simply not built that way. Each meal is not a scramble to get all we can get. Each gets a proper share of whatever there is, and the older and stronger ones look after the younger and weaker. The whole family attitude and mind-set make it easier for the children to be cooperative and helpful. A family life is built on cooperation. So is our best education.

But the moment one of those boys steps out of that home or that school to go into the business world, most of his values are reversed. Now, in order to be successful in a competitive order, he must drive hard bargains, without too much looking into detail as to results that might ruin others in that bargain. Blinders have to be put on the eyes so that he looks straight ahead at what he wants.

He would be shocked to be told that around this table of business he is grabbing all he can from the weaker members and piling it up around his own plate regardless of whether he can eat it or not. And yet that is exactly what he is doing. The family spirit is dying in him. The competitive order is a cause of sin to him.

O Christ, who came to make us one family, forgive us that we have not put that family spirit into our total life. Help us yet to do it. Amen.

LOVE THY COMPETITOR?

We love each other because he loved us first.

If someone says, "I love God," but hates a Christian brother or sister, that person is a liar; for if we don't love people we can see, how can we love God, whom we cannot see? And he has given us this command: Those who love God must also love their Christian brothers and sisters. (1 John 4:19-21†)

When the young man introduced yesterday, who is losing his ideals and slowly becoming hardened, goes back to the family circle, he will look at his father with puzzlement and say, "Dad, this is different. I am unlearning everything you taught me at home. Why?"

His father, remembering with a sigh the reversal of his own ideals, will helplessly reply, "Son, business is business." They are both caught in a system that is a cause of sin to them.

In a meeting, I was handed a paper with this question: "Isn't the very center of Jesus' teaching that we are to love our neighbor as ourselves, and if we did that, wouldn't we have a new world?" I happened to turn the paper over and saw the printed announcement on the other side that a new printing press had been opened in that city; it asked for people to come and "give it their blessing."

Now, there were already sixty-eight printers in that small city. The oldest and best of them was going out of business due to the ruthless competition. One more participant was now entering the struggle. Could this new printer, if he were a Christian, apply the statement on the other side of the flyer—"love your neighbor as yourself"—to the field he was entering?

It isn't impossible, but it was highly improbable. The dice were loaded against him. One side of the paper said to love your neighbor, the other side said to get all the business you can, no matter if your neighbor goes bankrupt. Which side of the paper would he pursue?

O Christ, help us to make a world in which the light within us will not be snuffed out. You are calling us to build that system; we need Your help. Amen.

A "HELPFUL" FAMINE?

The wealth of the rich is their fortified city, but poverty is the ruin of the poor....
The lips of the righteous nourish many, but fools die for lack of judgment.
(Prov. 10:15, 21)

We must keep looking at selfish competition until its effects burn themselves into our souls.

India has the world's richest and the world's poorest side by side. An Indian will say to a white man, "Sahib, that wage [you are offering] means only half a stomach for me and my family." He sees wages not in terms of the possibility of the latest car, but of avoiding starvation.

In the midst of this kind of an India, I sat and talked with an able missionary, devoted and hardworking. He reviewed the economic scene and said with all sincerity: "What we need is another famine to get rid of surplus food stocks. That will raise the prices and bring back prosperity."

I felt as though I had been punched. Here was a man of most gentle, loving disposition talking about the *necessity*—mark the word—of another famine. You and I must look at "famine" until it is no longer a word but a fact—the fact of living skeletons, of thin and scrawny babies sucking in vain at the dry breasts of famished mothers…but you can't look any longer, for you're sick at the thought. And yet a missionary, a Christian, a father of little children, said we needed that!

It horrifies you? Yes. But the thing that horrifies me most is not that he said it, but that what he said was true under this system. In a selfishly competitive system you have to produce scarcity (in other words, a famine) to keep up prices, to bring back prosperity. There is something wrong here, something wrong in the system itself. It must be changed.

"Hush, don't say that," I am advised. "You'll lose some of your friends." My answer is simple and final: If I don't say it, I'll lose my own soul.

O Christ, give us a burning sense of shame that we have tolerated, and still tolerate, a system where shortage is our suggested remedy. Forgive us. Amen.

EMPLOYERS AND EMPLOYEES

Hear this, you who trample the needy and do away with the poor of the land...
skimping the measure, boosting the price and cheating with dishonest scales,
buying the poor with silver and the needy for a pair of sandals, selling even the
sweepings with the wheat. The LORD has sworn by the Pride of Jacob: "I will
never forget anything they have done." (Amos 8:4-7)

A phase of this selfishly competitive system shows up in relations between
employer and employee. It causes sin—on both sides.

Here is an employer who is a gentle, kindly man and desires to be a Christian. His Christianity tells him he should do unto others as he would like to be
done by. But he has to compete with others, so he hires workers at the lowest
wage he can get them. The competitive order loads the situation against his
being a Christian, causing him to sin.

Some of these employees may be young women, and because of their low
wages they are tempted, yes, pushed to sell their virtue to feed their bodies.
Others may not go that far, but simply take it out in resentment. To harbor
resentment, according to the gospel, is sin. The system causes that sin too.

Or because the employees feel wronged, their resentment may show up in
poor work, in loafing on the job. To skimp work is not honest; it is sin. The
system caused that sin.

Or it may be that employees are getting a decent wage but know that if they
speed up, their job will end sooner. What incentive is there to work harder if
you only work yourself into unemployment? The pressure is to string out the
tasks as long as possible. This also is not honest—hence, sin.

Then the employer finds his employees lying down on a job and reacts in
anger. He tightens the screws. More resentment bubbles up. The situation goes
from bad to worse—a strike, a lockout. Hate.

The system was a cause of sin to both.

O Christ, we have been caught in the meshes of an impossible situation. Our
souls are ground by the very machines we have produced. Help us to find a way
out. Amen.

WORSHIPING THE MACHINE

Then the LORD *said to Moses, "Go down, because your people, whom you brought up out of Egypt, have become corrupt. They have…made themselves an idol cast in the shape of a calf. They have bowed down to it and sacrificed to it and have said, 'These are your gods, O Israel, who brought you up out of Egypt.'"* (Exod. 32:7-8)

Our faulty system runs both employee and employer into a clash.

A person asks, "But what are you going to do, if you can install new 'labor-saving' machinery, which sends half the work force to the bread lines?"

"Labor-sacrificing" would be a better name." Our system causes the employer to shut his eyes, tighten his lips, and install the machinery, letting the workers go. It causes him to sin.

Once a year the Hindus worship their tools. Did they not provide them bread that year, and should they not be grateful? But I was in a great steel mill on that particular day and saw them decorating the huge machines with flowers, plantain leaves, and palms. They were celebrating as they bowed to the machines in worship.

I think I too could have been grateful to the machine if I knew it were harnessed to a cooperative order and used for the collective good. But those machines were in the hands of a competitive order, and because of the fierceness of competition many of the laborers would soon be thrown into unemployment. *Poor wretches,* I thought, *If they only knew! They are worshiping that which will send many of them to the scrap heap!*

No, I cannot worship the machine. Not now. Someday, I hope to bow to it in gratitude because it is in the hands of cooperation. For now, the spirit behind it causes people to sin.

O Christ, Your best gifts to us become a curse because we do not know how to use them. Forgive us and help us to find a new way—Your way. Amen.

ANOTHER CAUSE OF SIN: WAR

Summon your power, O God; show us your strength, O God, as you have done before…. Scatter the nations who delight in war. (Psalm 68:28, 30)

──────────────── ⤫ ────────────────

Another phase of selfish competition works out in international relationships. We call it war.

Even with the clouds of war now in the sky and the world filled with increasing armaments,[3] I am hopeful to get rid of war. Look where we have come from! The Old Testament reports from the tenth century B.C., "In the spring, at the time when kings go off to war,…David remained in Jerusalem" (2 Sam. 11:1). Kings regularly went out to battle each springtime, as routinely as farmers went to their spring plowing. It was news when David stayed at home.

We have come a long way since then. Practically every nation on earth has signed some kind of pact renouncing war. But are we ready to live up to it? No, not yet.

However, a conscience is being created. Conscience banished slavery in the 1800s, and conscience will banish war. Our world today has never been so close to war—and so close to getting rid of war. We are not more warlike than we used to be—we are far less. But science has thrown our world together by rapid communications, and it has at the same time put into our hands terrible instruments of destruction. The result? Fear. It is fear, not warlikeness, that is driving us to war.

If the very center of life could be changed from competition to cooperation, war would drop off like a dead leaf. But war is almost inevitable in a world based on competition. Selfish competition makes humanity sin the chief of collective sins—war. That is why I so badly want a cooperative world.

O Christ, we stand before this appalling fact of war. If ever we needed Your help, we need it here. And if ever we needed to follow You, it is at this place. Help us to do it. Amen.

───

3. It is important to remember that this set of devotionals was written in 1936, less than 20 years after the end of World War I, and when Nazism was rising in strength but had yet to show its full threat.

MY ATTITUDE TOWARD WAR (PART 1)

Jesus said, "My kingdom is not of this world. If it were, my servants would fight to prevent my arrest by the Jews. But now my kingdom is from another place." (John 18:36)

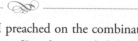

During the [First] World War, I preached on the combination of these two texts: "Herod with his soldiers set him [Jesus] at naught" (Luke 23:11 ASV) and "When the rioters saw the commander and his soldiers, they stopped beating Paul" (Acts 21:32). Militarism sets Jesus at naught, I said—but it also defends the weak and defenseless. That was my theme: German militarism was setting Jesus at naught,[4] and the Allies were on the defensive protecting the vulnerable.

How blinded I was! The distinction between an offensive and defensive war has for all practical purposes broken down. There is nothing left for us to do but to renounce all war. And that I do. I'll tell you why. Those caught in the war spirit do things they would not dream of doing otherwise. War causes people to sin in the following ways:

1. It poisons the air with lies. The first casualty in war is Truth. You cannot fight your enemy unless you make him out to be a devil.

2. It poisons the air with hate. If the first casualty is Truth, the second casualty is Love. Bitter, burning hate settles into the hearts of millions. The very air becomes toxic with it.

3. It makes us sin economically. The cost of the World War is estimated at $337 billion, so that if we had paid $20 an hour since the birth of Christ, we would not yet have finished paying for it. And yet we wonder why the world is hungry! War is economic sin—a sin against hunger.

4. It causes us to sin against human beings. The war cost directly and indirectly 40 million lives. If those dead could march past us ten abreast, it would take 184 days for them to pass. And they were the flower of our race!

O Christ, how can we stand indifferent before this collective madness? We do not. We hate it. We renounce it. Amen.

---

4. To Jones's friends and acquaintances in India, of course, Germany was viewed as "a Christian nation."

MY ATTITUDE TOWARD WAR (PART 2)

You want something but don't get it. You kill and covet, but you cannot have what you want. You quarrel and fight. You do not have, because you do not ask God. (James 4:2)

Jesus: *"You have heard that our ancestors were told, 'You must not murder. If you commit murder, you are subject to judgment.' But I say, if you are even angry with someone, you are subject to judgment!" (Matt. 5:21-22†)*

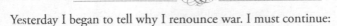

Yesterday I began to tell why I renounce war. I must continue:

5. War causes sin by killing the conscience. Here is the portion of an address delivered July 19, 1918, by a drill sergeant drilling troops in the use of the bayonet: "You've got to get down and hook them out with a bayonet; you will enjoy that, I assure you. Get sympathy out of your head. If you see a wounded German, shove him out and have no nonsense about it…. Kill them, every mother's son of them. Remember your job is to kill them, exterminate the vile creatures…." War does that to a man. That!

6. War grabs the finest virtues and prostitutes them. It grabs patriotism, heroism, self-sacrifice, idealism, and turns them toward destruction. It takes this fine gold and turns it into the very coin of hell.

7. It sins against the helpless. War protects, you say? When? Where? Did it protect millions of little children from starving? And millions of mothers and widows from weeping beside their dead? Protect the helpless? It produced them.

8. It stands against everything Christ stands for. It sins against Christ. If war is right, Christ is wrong; and if Christ is right, war is wrong. If Christ stays in this world, war must go. If war stays, Christ must go. Or if He does stay, He must be blown to pieces on a thousand battlefields.

In my opinion, Christ and war are irreconcilables. They are not combinable. If I must make my choice, I choose Him.

O Christ, help us to make the break complete. And help us to help others see the light until we have a warless world. Amen.

DROWNING THE WAR GODS

Jesus: *"You have heard the law that says, 'Love your neighbor' and hate your enemy. But I say, love your enemies! Pray for those who persecute you! In that way, you will be acting as true children of your Father in heaven. For he gives his sunlight to both the evil and the good, and he sends rain on the just and the unjust alike." (Matt. 5:43-45†)*

I once saw Hindus worshiping their two war gods. They worshiped them with the deepest reverence and most passionate loyalty…and then a strange thing happened. Immediately after the ceremony, the spirit of reverence left. They put their gods on a platform, carried them to the river, and dumped them in.

When I asked the reason, they replied, "After the worshiping has taken place, the spirit goes out of them, and they are only common clay."

We have been worshiping our war gods for centuries. Ardently we have sacrificed the finest of our youth and the noblest of our virtues upon that altar. We thought something was there—protection, chivalry, duty, love of country, perhaps even God Himself. But now we are disillusioned. The spirit has gone out of the thing for us. Nothing is there except lies and blood and mud and hate and hunger and death and desolation.

The painted mustaches of the Hindu war gods were still there, curved upward in triumph, after the departure of the spirit. But they were only painted. There was no spirit. Dictators and emperors may repaint those mustaches, but it is the painting of the dead. We may still carry these dead gods through our civilization, and we may try to make the people think they still live and can do something for them. It will not work. Our eyes are open.

I tell you: *The war gods are dead the moment you cease worshiping them.* Never, never again will I bow at their shrine. They are only clay. The next step is—to the river bank! We shall do it someday.

O Christ, Your hand, Your terrible hand, is on our consciences. Help us to put these strange gods away. They belong to our ignorant, barbarous past. Help us to begin anew without war. Amen.

ANOTHER CAUSE OF SIN: PREJUDICE

*"Are not you Israelites the same to me as the Cushites?" declares the L*ORD.
(Amos 9:7)

Peter replied, "I see very clearly that God shows no favoritism. In every nation he accepts those who fear him and do what is right." (Acts 10:34-35†)

⸻

We have looked at two causes of sin in the social order—selfish competition and war. We must now look at a third, racial prejudice. H. G. Wells says that it causes more sin than anything he knows: "I am convinced myself that there is no more evil thing in this present world than race prejudice…. It justifies and holds together more baseness, cruelty, and abomination than any other sort of error in the world." This is literally being proved true.

Race prejudice is self-starvation. An American woman, when offered the services of a physician from a different country, said, "Oh, can't we have an American doctor instead?" Why? This doctor had more than the average medical training, was an artist of rare ability, a musician of high attainment, and on top of all that, a Christian gentleman. But this woman shut herself off from all that because of one thing—racial prejudice.

I had volunteered to go to Africa as a missionary. I was in a streetcar in my home city when a black woman got into the crowded car. There was no seat for her, so I gave her mine. I heard a snicker run through the crowd behind me. "Getting up and giving a Negro woman your seat! He doesn't know what he's letting himself in for!"

But the laugh is now on the other side. I opened the door of my heart to people of another race and a different color of skin, and it has proved to be the most enriching experience of my life next to the influence of Christ. What love, what friendships, what wisdom, what Christlikeness, what nobility have come to me during these years through that open door!

The streetcar crowd closed their door with a bang of superiority. But they starved themselves.

O Christ, open my heart wide to the people of every race, and perhaps You too will come through that open door. Amen.

E. STANLEY JONES | 155

NO PLACE FOR SNOBBERY

They sang a new song with these words: "You…were slaughtered, and your blood has ransomed people for God from every tribe and language and people and nation. And you have caused them to become a Kingdom of priests for our God. And they will reign on the earth." (Rev. 5:9-10†)

If you open the door of your heart to the people of another race, you must really open it, for the people will sense the difference.

A Hindu youth told me how he rescued an outcaste boy from drowning and how his parents scolded him, saying he should have let him drown rather than touch an outcaste. But if that young man had let him die, something would have died in him. He flung away his Brahminhood and found a brotherhood.

Peter came close to keeping his Jewish "Brahminhood" when he said, "Surely not, Lord!… I have never eaten anything impure or unclean" (Acts 10:14). But soon he flung it away, went to the Gentiles, and found a brotherhood. Had he refused to open his heart, he would have shriveled and died. We would have heard little or nothing of him. You and I will shrivel and inwardly die if we refuse to open our hearts to every person, of every race, of every class.

Members of the ashram were asked to volunteer for the outcaste sweeper's work and give him a day off. It was the first time in this man's life that people of another "caste" had done such a thing! When I looked out my window that evening, I saw the sweeper back from his holiday, standing before my window with folded hands, his face wreathed in smiles! It was worth it all. Race and class prejudice would have shut me out from that joy!

O Christ, give me victory at this place—the place of my prejudices. For if I do not gain victory here, I will be poor instead of rich. Amen

ANOTHER CAUSE OF SIN: UNEQUAL WEALTH

My dear brothers and sisters, how can you claim to have faith in our glorious Lord Jesus Christ if you favor some people over others? For example, suppose someone comes into your meeting dressed in fancy clothes and expensive jewelry, and another comes in who is poor and dressed in dirty clothes. If you give special attention and a good seat to the rich person, but you say to the poor one, "You can stand over there, or else sit on the floor"—well, doesn't this discrimination show that your judgments are guided by evil motives? (James 2:1-4†)

Unequal distribution of wealth works in several directions to cause sin.

First, it harms those who have more than their legitimate share. It often produces in them the feeling that they must in some way deserve all this, and that God must be very pleased with them, when the fact of the matter is that they may have been only clever enough to choose the right parents!

Inequalities produce superiority complexes. We often think that because we have more we are worth more, which doesn't necessarily follow. It might make us decidedly worthless. Without it, we might give a great contribution to life; with it, we give only contributions. It also sets the stage for lack of ambition, parasitism, selfish heroism, and wasted time in general.

Inequality creates the mentality that tries to justify itself. Rationalization sets in, and with it an unconscious hypocrisy. Moreover, it keeps us from fellowship. How can people have fellowship across the money chasm? It sends gaps through life everywhere, separating one person from another. Meanwhile, one of the deepest needs of the world at the present time is fellowship. The Christian must question everything that makes fellowship more difficult.

I heard about a certain function in England where there were tables for "ladies" and tables for "working girls." At the one table, butter was served, and at the other, margarine. It is difficult for butter-table people to associate with margarine-table people!

O Christ, who came to break down barriers, forgive us for setting up barriers between us. And forgive us for thinking these barriers were blessings from You. Amen.

ROOTS OF BITTERNESS

Never take advantage of poor and destitute laborers, whether they are fellow Israelites or foreigners living in your towns. You must pay them their wages each day before sunset because they are poor and are counting on it. If you don't, they might cry out to the LORD against you, and it would be counted against you as sin. (Deut. 24:14-15†)

Unequal distribution of wealth also causes hurt to those who have less than their share. In an acquiring society where people's worth is judged by their wealth, the lack of wealth brands one as inferior. This is a positive sin against personality.

Moreover, from the Christian standpoint it loads the dice against inward peace and harmony. Sullenness and bitterness are stirred up. A fine lady came out of her castle to give charity to the poor. A workman saw it, spat on the ground, and said: "Let them simply be just, and we will not need their charity."

It is not enough to preach to that man that his bitterness is unchristian. We must strike at the causes that produce that bitterness.

Our preaching of contentment and cheer to the poor, while leaving untouched the causes of their gloom and discontent, is to add insult to injury. I heard an insightful saying: "An optimist is one who is hopeful about other people's troubles." No one today should address that gloom and misery unless he or she has in hand an ax to strike at the root of that misery.

And what is the root? Professor Frank A. Fetter of Princeton writes in *Facing the Facts, an Economic Diagnosis:* "We are living in a society which is financially controlled to intercept the gains of economic progress, by means of higher prices to consumers and financial rewards to insiders, thus keeping the fruits of science and technology from passing on to the people." Note the phrase "to intercept the gains." When the disadvantaged become alive to that factor, bitterness will be engendered—and will continue till the cause is removed.

O Christ, teach us to hold steady at this point and not to excuse or explain away, but in Your name to be straightforward and courageous. Amen.

ANOTHER CAUSE OF SIN: NATIONALISM

They talked together and went inside, where many others were assembled. Peter told them, "You know it is against our laws for a Jewish man to enter a Gentile home like this or to associate with you. But God has shown me that I should no longer think of anyone as impure or unclean." (Acts 10:27-28†)

One of the greatest dangers to the peace of the world is the rise of modern nationalism, as seen in the totalitarian state. It has taken that lovely sentiment called patriotism and has turned it into the deadliest enemy to our modern world. It causes people to sin where they otherwise would not.

The common people of one nation usually have no reason to hate the common people of another nation. But nationalism takes hold of these common people, subjects them to propaganda, instills fears, inspires hates, puts bayonets into their frightened hands, and flings them against the common people of another country. Why? Who knows?

This nationalism, becoming preposterous beyond words, reaches in and puts its dominating, determining hand on the one thing that is sacred between me and God—my conscience. It says it is sovereign in there.

This nationalism sees that Christianity is stretching across all barriers, and hence it looks on it as its most deadly foe. It produces a new paganism that would oust Christianity, or proceeds to render it innocuous, which amounts to the same thing. Listen to this official declaration: "The new Church leadership fully agrees that, in accordance with the fundamental principles necessary to safeguard the national existence of Germany, 'the National Socialist work of nation-building on the basis of Race, Blood, and Soil' must be recognized and supported, while at the same time the Church will preach the gospel of 'The Savior and Redeemer of all nations and races,' which bridges over all temporal and human changes."

The gospel "bridges" these gulfs, but nationalism rules at the two ends of the bridge. And Christianity is left to rule over what? The gulfs—emptiness!

O Christ, we are asked to follow another god, nationalism. How can we? We love our native land. But we love You more. Amen.

ANOTHER CAUSE OF SIN: DOMINATION

King Zedekiah had made a covenant with all the people in Jerusalem to proclaim freedom for the slaves.... So all the officials and people...set them free. But afterward they changed their minds and took back the slaves they had freed and enslaved them again.

Then the word of the LORD came to Jeremiah: "...You have not obeyed me; you have not proclaimed freedom your fellow countrymen. So I now proclaim 'freedom' for you, declares the LORD—'freedom' to fall by the sword, plague and famine. I will make you abhorrent to all the kingdoms of the earth." (Jer. 34:8, 10-12, 17)

Another cause of sin is the subjection of one group of people by another. I am persuaded that this domination over a long period of time is a cause of sin on both sides.

When Sir John Seeley said that "deterioration sets in in any subject race," he was simply recording fact. Life is weakened, loses initiative, is driven underground, loses frankness, becomes sycophantic, untruthful, and undependable. Not always, of course. But that is the tendency.

It also causes inner deterioration in the rulers. They believe in freedom for themselves, but being compelled by the system to deny it to others, an inner contradiction takes place. A defense mechanism is built up that wars against their own finest ideals.

One chairman of a public meeting of mine, a British official, said after I had spoken, "I have a quarrel with the speaker. He began his remarks by saying, 'Mr. Chairman, Brothers and Sisters'—which left me out of the brotherhood! I refuse to be left out." It was said so sincerely that the Indian crowd roared its appreciation, for he was a fine type of Christian gentleman.

But the next day when I saw him on a matter connected with India, he was a different man. He stood within the framework of the system. The system had made him not a brother, but a bureaucrat.

O God, our Father, help us to share our liberties with everyone, everywhere, for we know that if we do not share them, we cannot keep them. Amen.

ANOTHER CAUSE OF SIN: POOR SHELTER

"Woe to [Shallum king of Judah] who builds his palace by unrighteousness, his upper rooms by injustice, making his countrymen work for nothing, not paying them for their labor....

*"Does it make you a king to have more and more cedar? Did not your father have food and drink?... He defended the cause of the poor and needy, and so all went well. Is that not what it means to know me?" declares the L*ORD. (Jer. 22:13, 15-16)

We have crowded the weakest and most unfortunate members of society into that blot on human civilization called slums. Here many families are compelled to live in one room. At every moment of their lives the human personality is invaded. There is no privacy.

Now, preach to that group of human beings that modesty is a virtue, that cleanliness is a necessity, and quarrelsomeness is bad. Your words sound hollow. Why? Because the whole situation is loaded against cleanliness, modesty, and good temper. Young people growing up in such surroundings are handicapped; their very surroundings take away 50 percent of their chances for success.

Obviously, our preaching must have two sides—a demand for purity and amity, and a demand for proper housing.

A picture haunts my memory: In the Anti-Religious Museum at Leningrad, the Soviets have placed a picture of a large two-storied missionary home and beside it a tiny African grass hut. The suggestion is that religion is doing "spiritual" work for the people of that grass hut, but that the disparity between the hut and the house will remain. This indictment must be disproved.

Mission houses, on the whole, have been too large, and the huts around them are too small. There must come a closer approximation—the hut should come up a long way and the house should come down some. The ashram chambers in which most of us live are about six feet by eight. And we are happy and brotherly. But even then, our chambers give us privacy. A slum does not.

O Christ, we bring to You those who are crowded into inadequate shelter. Forgive us that these blots of our shame still exist, and help us to change them. Amen.

ANOTHER CAUSE OF SIN: INADEQUATE WORK

If there are any poor Israelites in your towns when you arrive in the land the LORD your God is giving you, do not be hard-hearted or tightfisted toward them.... If you refuse to make the loan and the needy person cries out to the LORD, you will be considered guilty of sin. Give generously to the poor, not grudgingly, for the LORD your God will bless you in everything you do. (Deut. 15:7, 9-10†)

If bad housing sets the stage for sin, so do low wages. The temptation to dishonesty becomes very great. As I sit here writing, a letter comes to my desk from one of the ablest missionaries in India telling how when she was a little girl, reared in a poor home, she went to a wealthier home where dolls were in abundance, and she had none. She felt she had a right to one, so stole one, and for many years suffered untold tortures from a sensitive conscience. Her poverty made it easier for her to take that doll. This happens on a larger scale when wages are low.

But if low wages cause sin, unemployment is worse still. It causes deterioration—to be an unwanted and unneeded person in human society is enough to take the light out of any eye and make any set of strong shoulders droop. The amazing thing to me is that, after years of fruitless knocking at doors, so often the light still shines in the eye and the shoulders are still square. I salute unconquered human nature!

But I cannot salute the system that causes these unemployed. It is all so unnecessary. In a competitive order it seems necessary and inevitable, but in a cooperative order it would not be. I therefore will give what strength and influence I have to bring it into being. Those who are jobless break my heart. Did it not strike home to me very early when I saw my own father unemployed, and I had to watch the deterioration day by day?

Unemployment causes sin in the victims, and in those who allow it to continue, because they selfishly refuse to cooperate in ending it. We are all guilty.

O God, our Father, forgive us that we have tolerated so long this inhumanity, and give us the strength, wisdom, and courage to end it. Amen.

ANOTHER CAUSE OF SIN: CLASS DISTINCTION

The Holy Spirit to Peter: *"So get up and go downstairs. Do not hesitate to go with them, for I have sent them." (Acts 10:20)*

Perhaps the reason [Onesimus] was separated from you for a little while was that you might have him back for good—no longer as a slave, but better than a slave, as a dear brother. He is very dear to me but even dearer to you, both as a man and as a brother in the Lord. So if you consider me a partner, welcome him as you would welcome me. (Philem. 15-17)

Another cause of sin in society is the existence of class. As long as society is based on class, causes of sin are in the social structure.

On board ship I saw a film that made me boil with indignation—everyone interested in bettering labor conditions was despicable, every labor leader a demagogue. On the other hand, I boil again when I hear every capitalist made out to be a bloated exploiter of the poor. It just isn't so.

These class breaches cause us to feel class-pain and class-disabilities—but not human pain and human disabilities. In this way we sin the sin of callousness to people of another class. It tends to dry up our sympathy in certain directions. Class distinctions turn the situation in an unchristian direction, making it easy for people to sin against their brothers and sisters of another class.

We must get rid of the notion that class is rooted either in nature or in the will of God. It is rooted in the human will. It is nothing less than a set of artificial barriers placed by the wrong organization of human society. Sir Algernon Sydney is right when he says, "The mass of mankind have not been born with saddles on their backs, nor a favored few booted and spurred ready to ride them legitimately by the grace of God." That attitude must die.

The roots must be cut if we are to live victoriously in the fullest sense.

O Christ, whose heart went out across these barriers and gathered people of all classes into a new living community where there was no class, give us that same spirit. Amen.

ANOTHER CAUSE OF SIN: SEXISM

So God created human beings in his own image. In the image of God he created them; male and female he created them. (Gen. 1:27[†])

Some women were watching [the Crucifixion] from a distance. Among them were Mary Magdalene, Mary the mother of James the younger and of Joses, and Salome. In Galilee these women had followed him and cared for his needs. (Mark 15:40-41)

The economic and political order is largely the result of male organizing. Women have been placed into it largely as sex-beings, and they are supposed to be treated and to act as such. Women have, in general, accepted this false mentality and have given themselves to the petty business of being attractive to the male. This has been the cause of much sin in human society.

But the position of women is changing throughout the world. Some years ago when I was about to speak to the ladies of a palace in India, I came into a large room with a screen across it. I wondered where my audience was. I soon saw the bejeweled feet of my audience under the screen. So I talked to those lotus feet!

Now, however, this is changing rapidly. A young woman of that very palace group was recently killed driving her own car. Alas, there will be many casualties in the transition from women as sex-beings to women as persons with equal rights and duties. The fact is, we are now rather appalled at the number of those casualties. Women, in driving this new force called freedom, are making a wreck of many a fine reticence, many a strong trait.

But we cannot stop until women arrive at the place where Jesus placed them as human personalities. They must be given an equal place and an equal task in the reconstruction of the world. I want this new freedom to lead women to do what one woman did when she suggested that the cannons of both Chile and Argentina be melted and cast into the "Christ of the Andes" sculpture—a symbol of perpetual peace between these two nations.

O Christ, help us to treat women as equal persons. And help women to set up a Christ of peace on every dividing line in human life. Amen.

ONE LAST CAUSE OF SIN: ECONOMIC FEAR

The word of the LORD came to me... "This is what the Sovereign Lord says about those living in Jerusalem and in the land of Israel: They will eat their food in anxiety and drink their water in despair, for their land will be stripped of everything in it because of the violence of all who live there. The inhabited towns will be laid waste and the land will be desolate." (Ezek. 12:17-20)

I mention this cause of sin last, for in many ways it is the most prolific in human society. Under the doctrine of *laissez faire,* or unrestricted competition, economic security falls to its lowest point both for the employer and the employee. In fact, it almost reaches the vanishing point.

Under unrestricted competition, three quarters of all business ventures fail. How can business owners be sure they belong to the fortunate one-fourth? And if they are sure they do, then how do they feel about their inner moral position, for in a competitive order one entrepreneur's success often causes the failure of others? If they get more than they need, somebody will have less than they need. This creates an enlightened greed that is appalling.

And the wage earners? Their economic destiny is not in their own hands, nor in the hands of fellow laborers, but in the hands of the one who owns the capital. They therefore live in constant dread of joining the ragged ranks of the unemployed. That haunting fear is one of the most desperate things in human life at the present time,[5] and it may disrupt society in an awful explosion. If it does not cause an explosion, it will drive workers to being sycophants, subservient flatterers who deny their own personhood. This will be just as disruptive of society as an explosion.

Thus economic insecurity causes the sin of fear—employers are afraid if they give better wages, their competitors will undercut them and their business will go on the rocks; meanwhile, laborers are afraid of losing their job.

O Christ, who came to take all fear from our hearts, help us to produce a system in which fear will have no place. We could do it if we knew how to love. So help us. Amen.

---

5. When this was written in 1936, U.S. unemployment was 17 percent.

WHAT CAN BE DONE ABOUT IT?

As evening approached, the disciples came to him and said, "This is a remote place, and it's already getting late. Send the crowds away, so they can go to the villages and buy themselves some food."

Jesus replied, "They do not need to go away. You give them something to eat." (Matt. 14:15-16)

If someone has enough money to live well and sees a brother or sister in need but shows no compassion—how can God's love be in that person? (1 John 3:17†)

--------------------------------- ◦◦◦ ---------------------------------

We have seen a dozen things in the social structure that set the stage for sin. These things, deeply rooted in the structure of society, hinder victorious living at every turn. They do not render it impossible, but certainly very difficult. Often under pressure, victorious life in the individual is squeezed out.

If Christianity has no response at this point, if it undertakes to live victoriously without facing these issues, it amounts to evasion. This violates two fundamental principles of victorious living, namely, mental honesty and courage to face the facts. To attempt to win by strategic retreat is to run into the pitfall of mental insincerity, without which no victorious living is possible. The process of evasion is self-defeating.

Obviously, the first thing to be done is to look at these things as causes of sin and therefore an evil in human society—something to be eradicated, not tolerated. Here is where our greatest difficulty lies. Many think these things are indelible. They accept them fatalistically. This defeatist mentality is our greatest problem. It must be broken.

Just as the individual, in order to have personal victory over personal sins, must believe it can be done, so we must gain the attitude of faith that these social sins are disease, that they are no normal part of human living and can be eradicated. The health of society demands it.

O Christ, we need to be reborn mentally and spiritually at this place. We need to come into a faith that believes that anything is possible with You. Give us this faith, for our society is very, very sick. Amen.

FACING HALF-TRUTHS

Those who passed by hurled insults at him, shaking their heads and saying, "You who are going to destroy the temple and build it in three days, save yourself! Come down from the cross, if you are the Son of God!" (Matt. 27:39-40)

In order to convince ourselves that these social evils can be overcome, we must rid our minds of certain half-truths. For if we get caught here, we will not go on to full faith.

Professor John C. Bennett, in *Social Salvation,* says there are three half-truths: (1) That individuals can rise above any combination of social circumstances; (2) That, since individuals control institutions and systems, it is enough to change individuals; (3) That you can change society without changed individuals.

To these I would add three more: (4) That society is relatively immoral but people are relatively moral. (5) That the way the kingdom of God comes is only gradual. (6) That the way the kingdom comes will be only apocalyptic.

Half-truths can become more dangerous than whole lies. There is nothing in the whole lie to hold the allegiance of good people, but a half-truth often succeeds. With their eyes fastened on that half-truth, they are oblivious of the lurking evil.

Jesus was crucified on half-truths. Religious people, seeing those half-truths, were blind to the other side and allowed themselves to commit the worst deed in human history. They did it clinging to half-truths as justification. He did say that He was a king. He did say if they destroyed this temple, He would rebuild it. He said almost everything they accused Him of, minus their twists. Half-truths.

Today Jesus and His kingdom are being crucified on half-truths. Wrong ideas are causing as much damage as wrong wills. And the wrong ideas are usually half-right ideas. Again, it is the fatal twist that sends the whole thing in a wrong direction.

O Christ, who suffered—and still suffers—from half-truths, open our eyes. We want to see whether we hold any half-truth that keeps us from seeing things as they are. Amen.

INDIVIDUALS AND THEIR CIRCUMSTANCES

Direct your children onto the right path, and when they are older, they will not leave it. (Prov. 22:6†)

Woe to the world because of the things that cause people to sin! Such things must come, but woe to the person through whom they come! (Matt. 18:7)

The first half-truth we must notice is this: That individuals can rise above any combination of social circumstances.

Sometimes they do, and this book is stressing that possibility. This was also my contention in my book *Christ and Human Suffering.*

But I was struck by a criticism from a class of Indian college girls using that book as a study text: "This is all right for the spiritually developed, for the exceptional person. But for the rank and file of ordinary Christians, it is too high. And if it is difficult for ordinary Christians, what about the great masses who have no Christian faith? Can they use pain and sorrow?"

In spite of this criticism, I still maintain that the use of suffering is the privilege of the ordinary Christian. Nevertheless, we cannot ignore the fact that the majority of people do not change their circumstances, but are changed by them. Somebody has said that if most of us had to write a letter to that most influential person called "Circumstances," we could end it with the traditional closing line, "I am, Sir, your most obedient servant." For the most of us are the obedient servants of our circumstances.

We must think in terms of the weaker members and produce a society in which it will be easier for them to grow. All of us are weak during the first 15 years of life, and during that weakest period of life we are most conditioned by environment and influenced by it. For the sake of each succeeding generation, we must produce a society that will work with and not against the total growth of youth.

O Christ, who pronounced woes on those who become causes of stumbling, especially to little ones, forgive us that we have produced a society in which this is literally a fact. Help us to correct it, for their sakes and ours. Amen.

WILL CONVERTED PEOPLE CONVERT SOCIETY?

"Woe to you Pharisees, because you give God a tenth of your mint, rue and all other kinds of garden herbs, but you neglect justice and the love of God. You should have practiced the latter without leaving the former undone." (Luke 11:42)

There is no doubt that society is made up of individuals. There is also no doubt that if you change a sufficient number of individuals, you can change society. Changed people have done it in the past.

But these are only half-truths. Society is made up of individuals, but it is also made up of inherited customs and attitudes that have become a part of the social structure. These exist apart from the will of the individual. To change the individual's will may leave this inherited social structure entirely intact.

To change individual slave owners did not get rid of the slave system. That could only be accomplished by what Bennett calls "a wide-scale frontal attack." Both in England and America, slavery was ousted by the frontal attack of legislation. It is true that the converted William Wilberforce was a big factor in the getting rid of it. But it was only after he had persuaded enough people to attack it in Parliament that it was abolished. An attack on a personal front alone would have left the slavery system to this day. Parliamentary coercion for recalcitrants had to supplement personal change.

Even where the converted will is directed toward changing the system, that change will not take place unless you have this wide-scale, concerted, frontal attack. But, suppose, instead of this will being directed toward social change, it stops at the half-way house of feeling content about its own change. In such a case, the situation is still bad. This happens often. Conversion, instead of becoming the life of social change, often becomes in lieu of social change. It often makes our attention glance away either toward ourselves or toward heaven, leaving the essential problems of life untouched. Half-conversions may become whole perversions. Conversion must be fully converted.

O Christ, I ask You to convert my conversion into the wide sweep of Your purposes for myself and all people. Put the content of social change into my individual change. Amen.

CAN SOCIETY BE CHANGED ALONE?

Make a tree good and its fruit will be good, or make a tree bad and its fruit will be bad, for a tree is recognized by its fruit. (Matt. 12:33)

"Ah, Sovereign LORD," I said, "I do not know how to speak; I am only a child."
But the LORD said to me, "Do not say, 'I am only a child.'… See, today I appoint you over nations and kingdoms to uproot and tear down, to destroy and overthrow, to build and to plant." (Jer. 1:6-7, 10)

Another half-truth is that you can change society without changed individuals. The individually-minded say that the greatest necessity is for changed individuals, and the society-minded say the greatest necessity is for a changed society. Each contains a half-truth, but only a half-truth.

For a changed society needs changed individuals to sustain it. The whole outer structure of life rests on that imponderable and subtle thing called character. If the character breaks, the confidence breaks, and if the confidence breaks, the society breaks. The best of programs need changed individuals to make them work.

"To remake this province, I need two things," said a Chinese governor to a friend of mine. "I need money, and I need men who will honestly expend that money. I can get the first, but I cannot find the second. If you can produce the men, we can remake the province."

Today I came upon a vehicle for sale belonging to a former motor syndicate. The business had broken down on account of one simple thing—a lack of character in the people who made it up. Whenever individual members saw a smaller immediate advantage in contrast to a larger long-term advantage, they didn't have enough character to resist the immediate in behalf of the more remote.

A changed society needs changed people to keep it changed.

O Christ, it is here that we need Your power. For how can we go into the new day with the old life? Cleanse us at the heart, that we may cleanse society to its utmost limits. Amen.

SOCIETY HELPS CHANGE INDIVIDUALS

Appoint judges and officials for each of your tribes in every town the LORD your God is giving you, and they shall judge the people fairly. Do not pervert justice or show partiality. Do not accept a bribe, for a bribe blinds the eyes of the wise and twists the words of the righteous. Follow justice and justice alone, so that you may live and possess the land the LORD your God is giving you. (Deut. 16:18-20)

Yesterday we insisted that you cannot change society without changed individuals to sustain those changes. But we also need to point out that a changed society tends to help change individuals. That is a point which some Christians have largely missed. They should welcome these wide-scale basic changes in the structure of society in the very interests of individual change.

We now know the power of environment in making the individual. Many things we think to be innate are in fact socially conditioned at a very early stage in life, so early that we mistake them for the innate. This can be seen in India very vividly, where caste lines are sharply drawn. Take babies out of outcaste sweeper homes at birth, and let them be subjected to a new social heredity in which they know nothing of their so-called inferior birth, and let them be given the privileges of education and culture of other children, and in nine cases out of ten you can make an almost entirely new personality out of them. Had they stayed in the sweeper home, in nine cases out of ten they would have taken on the likeness of their surroundings, catching the average outlook and conforming to it.

A competitive system works against individual change at every point; a cooperative system would work toward individual change at every point. For you cannot make a cooperative system work except by the very things that are inherent in spiritually changed character—namely, a change from the egocentric to the kingdom-centric, from self to God and others. In preaching conversion in such an environment, you would be working not against the grain of the social order as now, but with it.

O Christ, help us to have a changed society, that we may more easily have changed individuals. For we want people to be changed—and so do You. Amen.

MORAL PEOPLE, IMMORAL SOCIETY?

Do not defraud or rob your neighbor. Do not make your hired workers wait until the next day to receive their pay. Do not insult the deaf or cause the blind to stumble. You must fear your God; I am the LORD. Do not twist justice in legal matters by favoring the poor or being partial to the rich and powerful. Always judge people fairly. (Lev. 19:13-15†)

The insistence that the individual is comparatively more moral than society has a truth within it. People as individuals are not prepared to do many things that, as members of a large society, they are prepared to do: for instance, ruthlessly compete to the ruination of others, or collectively butcher in war.

But in fact, the matter might be reversed. In a cooperative system, the very opposite would be the case. Society would be comparatively moral, and the individual comparatively immoral. In our ashram this can be seen in miniature. There the organization is a sharing community. But now and again individuals break this justice and brotherhood. They are less moral than the collective order. They are then judged by the ashram.

It would be the same on a wider scale when society comes to a cooperative system. We would see more of "moral society" and "immoral people."

The insistence by Dr. Niebuhr that because society is immoral, this is all rooted in nature, and must be dealt with as such, is again only a half-truth. What seems rooted in nature may be rooted in a wrong social organization, namely, a competitive order. Change that order to a cooperative one, and many things that now appear rooted in nature will be seen not to be inherent, but collectively imposed. Much that seems to be nature is nurture under a system that produces wrong attitudes.

This gives us a basis of hope rather than pessimism, for we can change what we have made, namely, a wrong social organization.

O Christ, we come to You for strength and nerve and clear-sighted love, that we may not sink back into the pessimisms of nature, but that we may rise to the optimisms of Your redemptive grace and power. Amen.

GOD'S KINGDOM: GRADUAL OR SUDDEN? (PART 1)

"Keep watch, because you do not know on what day your Lord will come. But understand this: If the owner of the house had known at what time of night the thief was coming, he would have kept watch and would not have let his house be broken into. So you also must be ready, because the Son of Man will come at an hour when you do not expect him." (Matt. 24:42-44)

Modern liberalism has insisted that the kingdom of God will come by gradual changes. It has drawn its inspiration from two sources: modern democracy, and certain teachings of the New Testament.

Modern democracy is the process of change according to constitutions, by vote instead of by sudden, catastrophic revolution. Liberalism has assumed that the processes of the kingdom would be the same. In this they have been supported by passages in the New Testament—the yeast that works all through the batch of flour (Matt. 13:33), the grain that sprouts and grows "first the stalk, then the head, then the full kernel in the head" (Mark 4:26-29). These passages seemed to fit the spirit of evolutionary change.

But with the recent decay of faith in democratic government, much of this faith of liberalism has decayed with it. Dictatorships, veiled and overt, have arisen. Now liberalism is embracing that changed outlook. In many quarters it is saying that change can only come suddenly and in a catastrophic manner. This about-face shows how liberalism is dependent on modern culture; in fact, liberalism is modern culture turned religious. It is most unstable.

It should hold to its principle of gradualism. That lets the responsibility rest where it should rest, namely, on us, to bring in that kingdom by individual and collective endeavor cooperating with the redemptive God. This outlook holds us from flying off onto tangents or various shortcuts. Gradualism is in the New Testament as a living part of the outlook of the gospel. It is ineradicable.

But it is only a half-truth we should remember that. There is another side.

O Christ, keep us from evading responsibility by throwing it onto You or onto future circumstances. Help us to take up our tasks like adults. Amen.

GOD'S KINGDOM: GRADUAL OR SUDDEN? (PART 2)

Once, having been asked by the Pharisees when the kingdom of God would come, Jesus replied, "The kingdom of God does not come with your careful observation, nor will people say, 'Here it is,' or 'There it is,' because the kingdom of God is within you." (Luke 17:20-21)

Modern fundamentalism in many cases has rejected the principle of gradualism and has said that the kingdom will only be set up in the sudden, catastrophic Second Coming of Christ.

In this they have been supported by passages in the New Testament that teach His coming as a thief in the night (see yesterday's lead Scripture), by the parable of the nobleman who returned suddenly to set up his kingdom (Luke 19:11-27), and so on. There is no doubt that the New Testament does teach this sudden dramatic aspect.

But it is a fact that holding this view alone has produced a mentality that has diluted interest in social change by gradual processes. It has made its adherents discount those changes, and has made them look for a worsening of things in order to await a final, sudden triumph at the coming of Christ. This has been a moral and social drain.

Christian thought has moved by the dialectic from the catastrophic to the gradual and back again—thesis producing antithesis. It is now time for us to come to the synthesis. The pages of the New Testament include both gradualism and the apocalyptic. Both are integral parts of the account. They cannot be explained away. In the interests of the kingdom itself, they must not be explained away. Each is a half-truth that needs the other to complete it.

We need to understand that the task is ours and must be assumed as such. We must also see that it is God's and that He will complete it, perhaps even when we least expect it.

O Christ, thank You for teaching us that the task is ours and the consummation is Yours—but also that the task is Yours and the consummation ours. We shall work it out together, and together we shall triumph. Amen.

THE SYNTHESIS

[The kingdom of heaven] will be like a man going on a journey, who called his servants and entrusted his property to them. To one he gave five talents of money, to another two talents, and to another one talent, each according to his ability. Then he went on his journey. The man who had received the five talents went at once and put his money to work and gained five more. So also, the one with the two talents gained two more. But the man who had received the one talent went off, dug a hole in the ground and hid his master's money.

After a long time the master of those servants returned and settled accounts with them. (Matt. 25:14-19)

From many angles we have been working toward a synthesis. Modern liberal emphasis on gradualism by the endeavors of human beings has produced Barthianism, with its demand that we cease this humanism and humbly accept the kingdom as a gift of grace. We have felt the truth in each contention, but each is only a half-truth. The Christian world is working through these half-truths to a synthesis, a larger truth.

That larger truth is that the New Testament teaches both. Modern minds have hesitated to take the apocalyptic at its face value. They have thought it was something forced into the account. But extracting it has been impossible; it is an integral part. Are we not to look on every hour as the possible hour of the kingdom's dramatic unveiling? Would it not be a mistake if we failed to do so? History is not yet exhausted. Jesus was so right in everything else; will He not be right in this also?

To accept this synthesis of gradualism and apocalyptic leaves us just where we should be as Christians. We are within the stream of human history and yet above it. We live within the world process to suffer and bleed and thus remake it—and yet above the process as its judges through Him who is to be its final Judge.

O Christ, You are leading us into the larger truth of the kingdom. We accept it, for the kingdom is our one hope. Amen.

SOCIETY'S JUDGE

Christ addressing the case of a false prophet in the Thyatira congregation: *"I will strike her children dead. Then all the churches will know that I am he who searches hearts and minds, and I will repay each of you according to your deeds."* *(Rev. 2:23)*

We must look at one more partial emphasis. There are those who would tell us that the function of the church is to stand aloof from all these movements of social reconstruction, to commit to none of them, but to be the constant judge of all.

I have the feeling that this counsel is an escape-mentality. It gets out of the problem by assuming the role of a judge, instead of being in it as a participant, suffering along with it, and thus saving it from within. If we assume this in the struggle ahead of us, won't we not turn out to be the perfect Pharisee instead of the perfect Christian? Did Jesus not stand inside the society, making its sorrows, its problems, its sins His very own—the cross thus becoming inevitable?

In the early days of the Salvation Army in Britain, a young worker was placed on trial for the "sin" of seeking the lost in these scandalous ways. The judge, however, deliberately left the judgment seat and stood alongside her as the proceedings went on. He identified himself with her, as if to be tried along with her. In doing so he revealed the Christian attitude: "God did not send his Son into the world to condemn the world, but to save the world through him" (John 3:17).

Jesus rejects the role of judge. But a strange thing happens. Through this very identification with society, He surprisingly becomes its Judge. Likewise, the Christian church today can only become the judge of social reconstruction movements to the degree that it is in them and suffers vicariously. Then it gains a moral authority. To take the attitude of an aloof judge is to assume an un-Christian attitude.

O Christ, You judge us from a cross. Help us to gain our moral authority over the world from the same place—the place of our own suffering for humanity. Amen.

VISITED AND REDEEMED

"Blessed is the Lord God of Israel, for He has visited and redeemed His people." (Luke 1:68 NKJV)

Then fear came upon all, and they glorified God, saying, "A great prophet has risen up among us"; and, "God has visited His people." (Luke 7:16 NKJV)

Zechariah, father of John the Baptist, said a penetrating thing when he prophesied that the Lord, by sending the new baby, had begun to *visit* and *redeem* His people. He probably had little notion of how amazing in its sweep that redemption was, and how deep the visitation.

In redeeming the world, God might have simply issued orders from heaven. He might have incarnated Himself as a Teacher, an Example. Or He might have done just what He did, namely, become One with us, and let everything that falls on us fall on Himself—plus. This was visitation.

The church must follow in His steps at this point. It dare not merely issue condemnations of the social order from its sheltered sanctuaries; it dare not be a detached spectator of the world going through its struggles to reach a new order; it dare not merely take the role of teacher. Instead, it must visit, and that visitation must mean what it meant for Christ—a visitation that equals identification.

This identification must not be a generality. It must be specific enough to cause suffering. As Dr. Wade Crawford Barclay says, "The question is whether the Church can become specific enough to save itself." Jesus' visitation was specific—ours must be too. It must be sufficiently specific to gain a specific cross. Dealing in pious generalities is usually evasion of issues. We must find the places where the real issues are being joined and take sides.

If we refuse the visitation, we shall renounce the redemption. We cannot have one without the other.

O Christ, save us from the spirit that would save ourselves by various subterfuges. For we know if we save ourselves, we will not save others. Give us courage to be specific. Amen.

BLENDING THE TWO EMPHASES

"Here is my servant, whom I uphold, my chosen one in whom I delight; I will put my Spirit on him, and he will bring justice to the nations. He will not shout or cry out, or raise his voice in the streets. A bruised reed he will not break, and a smoldering wick he will not snuff out." (Isa. 42:1-3)

We have now come in our quest to the place where we can see the necessity of blending the individual and social emphases into a living whole. Jesus did just that. Isaiah's prophecy was applied directly to him (see Matt. 12:15-21).

Here we find this blend—a tenderness toward individuals (refusing to break the bruised reed or quench the smoking flax) and a demand for social justice. This justice was not the deciding of legal points, but the giving of a fair, equal opportunity to all.

Jesus was sensitive toward those who had been bruised by the storms of nature or by trampling feet. The gospel comes as an infinite tenderness to those hurt by the awful powers of unconscious nature, or by the conscious inhumanities of one human being to another, or bruised by their own follies and sins. To those who are smoking flax, those in whom life and hope are very dim, in whom the fires are about to go out, the gospel comes as an inspiration, hope, life. We must never fail the stricken individual by withholding this message of tender healing and life-healing hope, for this is a badly stricken world.

But we must also move along with Jesus to the injustices through which many lives are being bruised and made to burn dimly. Just as we are passionately interested in individuals, we must be passionately interested in social justice. You are really not interested in either in the fullest sense unless you are interested in both. For neither can be fully effective without the other.

O Christ, to whom these two worlds of individual and social concerns were one, help us to cease our divisions at this point and to make them one. Amen.

GOD'S ATTITUDE ON JUSTICE

How long will you defend the unjust and show partiality to the wicked? Selah. Defend the cause of the weak and fatherless; maintain the rights of the poor and oppressed. Rescue the weak and needy; deliver them from the hand of the wicked. (Psalm 82:2-4)

The blending we saw yesterday melded two integral parts of the work of Christ, so the account says. If so, then we must look more steadily at the meaning of the word *justice* (in the older translations, "judgment"). It has a history. It came down through the Hebrew tradition, where the individual and the social emphases were one. The Jewish people in their corporate life were to express the will of God. The idea of religion being a private affair between the soul and God is unthinkable to the Old Testament prophets. The nation as a nation was the chosen people of God, and as such, they were to express the mind of God in their total life. So the word *justice* came to express equality, fairness, divine law and divine love operating in the sphere of the collective life.

Jesus took this same attitude. He expected the nation to embody the kingdom. When they refused, He said, "Therefore I say to you, the kingdom of God will be taken from you and given to a *nation* bearing the fruits of it" (Matt. 21:43 NKJV). Note, it was to "a nation." His final appeal was to Jerusalem, representing the nation, "Jerusalem, Jerusalem…how often I have longed to gather your children together" to embody this divine will, "and you were not willing" (Matt. 23:37). He also demanded of the cities of Capernaum and Bethsaida a corporate repentance because He had expected a corporate obedience.

We forget this note in the gospel. And because we forget it, the world is corporately adrift, without guidance. We have allowed the corporate expression of the will of God to largely drop out of Christianity, to its own impoverishment—and to even worse impoverishment of our corporate life. We must rediscover it or allow humanity to perish through internal discord.

O Christ, who came to "lead justice to victory" (Matt. 12:20), help us to catch anew that note and fearlessly apply it to our total living. If we do not, we perish. Amen.

THE WISDOM OF BEING JUST

Endow the king with your justice, O God, the royal son with your righteousness. He will judge your people in righteousness, your afflicted ones with justice. (Psalm 72:1-2)

The angel Gabriel regarding Zechariah's future son, John: *"He will also go before Him in the spirit and power of Elijah, 'to turn the hearts of the fathers to the children,' and the disobedient to the wisdom of the just, to make ready a people prepared for the Lord." (Luke 1:17 NKJV)*

We see the deep need to set social justice into human affairs. This passage concerning John the Baptist emphasizes the same. Note that the result of his ministry, said the angel, was to be *"a people prepared"*—a nation standing ready to do the will of God.

And how were they to be prepared? By two things. One was turning the hearts of the fathers to the children—in other words, by making the generation now in power to think in terms of bettering the next generation. The second was to turn the disobedient toward "the wisdom of the just."

Note that phrase. It is a truism to say that what the poor and the dispossessed need is not charity but justice—but it needs to be said again and again. We have seen the unwisdom of injustice. We have built a society in which those in control have intercepted the gains brought by science and technology and have kept them from passing on to the people. The result—economic disaster to everybody. The unwisdom of the unjust. Each nation tried to grab all the raw materials and advantages it could for itself, regardless of what happens to others. The result? International anarchy, fear—and war! The unwisdom of the unjust.

A basic, thoroughgoing justice for everybody would be social wisdom. If we will not listen to this word from the sacred Book, then we must listen to it spoken by the fiery tongues of a world in flames. For God speaks! And the wisdom of the just is His message.

O Christ, save us from our own follies, and help us to be lovingly just in the whole of our relationships. Help us to begin now. Amen.

ON TO VICTORY

[Jesus] replied, "Every plant that my heavenly Father has not planted will be pulled up by the roots." (Matt. 15:13)

The hostile princes and rulers He stripped off from Himself, and boldly displayed them as His conquests, when by the Cross He triumphed over them. (Col. 2:15 WEYMOUTH)

God's call for us to learn the wisdom of the just makes us afraid for two reasons: It will cause loss to us, and it won't work.

I do not say that being just will cost us nothing. You have to have the selfish self knocked out before you can become fundamentally just and willing to give everybody an equal opportunity. It will mean a real renunciation.

When the master in the parable said to the grumblers at his equality, where the last hired got as much as the first, "Friend, I am doing you no wrong" (Matt. 20:13 NKJV), he spoke to a common fear. We are afraid that an equal justice will do us a wrong. To our privileged, unsocial self, it will. But a new, just, brotherly self will be born, and to that person it can be said, "Friend, I am doing you no wrong; in fact, I am doing you a supreme good."

We are also afraid that the wisdom of the just simply "won't work." However, the verse we read three days ago concerning Jesus said, "He leads justice to victory" (Matt. 12:20). Will He, can He do it? He *is* doing it! Today He is breaking down this unjust and therefore decaying social order. His hammer is striking it. It is crumbling to dust at our feet. Its injustices are breaking it down. It is the hour of judgment— judgment in the sense of condemnation, in order that the hour of judgment in the sense of social justice might come. The condemnation falls on us, that the construction might begin through us. He is leading justice to victory! The eternal God will not fail in His redemptive purpose, and His redemptive purpose includes the total life.

O Christ, we thank You that this whole redemptive process is moving ahead. It will not fail along the way. In the end there will be one word upon our lips— "Victory!" Help us to take up that word now and make it our own. Amen.

OUR ONE HOPE

Because the Sovereign LORD helps me, I will not be disgraced. Therefore, I have set my face like a stone, determined to do his will. And I know that I will not be put to shame. (Isa. 50:7†)

This age needs a renewing of hope. Cynicism and despair have bitten deep into our souls. And this is serious. Despair closes the gates against the redemptive purposes of God. But where shall we find a renewal of our hope?

The passage we have been studying says, "In his name the nations will put their hope" (Matt. 12:21). The hope lies in Him who will not break the bruised reed, and will lead justice to victory. In other words, the hope lies in One who blends in His message to us a tender redemptiveness to the individual and a stern demand for social justice. These two together will come to victory.

But one without the other will not reach the goal. Our hope does not lie in changed individuals alone. As Herbert Gray says: "Conversion has often meant going through a process of personal readjustment which has left the men and women concerned still dominated in mind by the received ideas about money, and war, and the claims of the dispossessed." The content of social justice must be put into conversion. Still, social reconstruction without individual conversion will not result in victory, either.

I have just been attending to a very sick man suffering from appendicitis, who in his agony begs me to send him back to his village, where it is warmer and all will be well. But a change of climate will not cure a festering appendix! It needs an operation. A change of the social climate will leave untouched many of our inward maladjustments, which would persist in any climate. We need a personal spiritual operation.

No, our hope lies neither in one, nor in the other, but in both. In Christ and His kingdom they are one. So in Him is our hope.

O Christ, the road of personal need and the road of a social reconstruction both lead us to Your feet. You are the one hope of our stricken world—and of us. Amen.

NO PARALYZING DIVISIONS

And HE IS before all things, and in and through Him the universe is one harmonious whole. (Col. 1:17 WEYMOUTH)

Over all these virtues put on love, which binds them all together in perfect unity. (Col. 3:14)

We have now completed half our journey in our quest for victorious living. One note running through these pages, which will continue in the pages to come, is this—if there is to be victorious living, there must be no paralyzing divisions; there must be unity. This is psychologically and spiritually sound.

But we have only begun to see how wide this demand for unity will be. It must take in everything. We saw that there must be no clashing division nor even hidden strife between the conscious and the subconscious mind.

We also saw that there must be no clashing division in the conscious mind itself. When we try to give ourselves to mutually competing ends, we find defeat. Some things are simply not "compossible"—they cannot exist side by side without causing spiritual paralysis. If we are going to have victory, we must decide between them.

Again, there must be nothing between us and God. Every barrier must go down between His will and ours.

And now we have seen the necessity of a further unity—the unity between the individual and the social. If we allow a division to grow up between these two through lack of emphasis on either side, there will be spiritual defeat. The social without the personal is a body without a soul, and the personal without the social is a soul without a body—one is a corpse and the other a ghost. But together they make a living person. This division between the individual and the social has been the root cause of the major defeats of religion in modern life. The hope of the world is in the healing of this breach.

In order to get victory, are you prepared to heal that breach as far as you are concerned?

O Christ, You are leading us to overcome our divisions. Help us to hold back at no point, but to go on to complete unity. Amen.

E. STANLEY JONES | 183

UNIFYING THE IDEAL WITH THE REAL

"The teachers of the law and the Pharisees sit in Moses' seat. So you must obey them and do everything they tell you. But do not do what they do, for they do not practice what they preach." (Matt. 23:2-3)

"Watch out for false prophets. They come to you in sheep's clothing, but inwardly they are ferocious wolves. By their fruit you will recognize them. (Matt. 7:15-16)

The demand for unity will confront us at the place of the ideal and the real, of theory and practice.

While I was in Russia, an intelligent woman said to me, "I suppose you are an idealist?" I replied that I was. She waved her hand and said, "*Au revoir,* I'm a realist." I smiled then and rather pitied her for her contempt of idealism.

But since then my smile has worn off. There has come a sense of concern that she might be right. Karl Marx, for all his other errors, propounded a worthy idea in the unity of theory and practice. He urged that you should have only one theory, and that is what you put into operation, at least in its beginnings. The only thing you really believe in is the thing you believe in enough to act upon it. This proposal searches us to the depths. It should prove a cleansing cathartic to Christendom.

Professor John Macmurray, the Scottish Quaker, says that the next great step forward for Christianity is to get rid of its idealism. As an earnest Christian he means it. His contention is that we have built up idealism as mental compensation for low practice. The very fact that we hold high ideals gives us comfort that we are lofty persons. This compensates for the real, and lets us down easy. The mind becomes a world of fantasy, while something else controls the place of action.

Is Professor Macmurray right? Must idealism go and realism take its place? Or can they be unified?

O Christ, we come needing guidance. Help us to let nothing interfere with reality. For we must be real. Amen.

LOSING OUR IDEALS TO FIND THEM AGAIN

Paul: *If others have reason for confidence in their own efforts, I have even more! I was circumcised when I was eight days old. I am a pure-blooded citizen of Israel and a member of the tribe of Benjamin—a real Hebrew if there ever was one! I was a member of the Pharisees, who demand the strictest obedience to the Jewish law. I was so zealous that I harshly persecuted the church. And as for righteousness, I obeyed the law without fault.*

I once thought these things were valuable, but now I consider them worthless because of what Christ has done. (Phil. 3:4-7†)

If we lose idealism, does it mean that we should have no ideals? On the contrary, I think we should take our idealism and sow it into the soil of the real, where it would spring up again and flower into renewed beauty. We should lose our ideals to find them again. Currently, we do not have them, for they stand apart from life. But we can have them if they are deeply rooted in life itself. Now they are castles in the air to be realized in some future age or future world. It is possible, however, for them to become houses here and now for us to live in.

In suggesting this, we find ourselves very, very close to Christ in our thought and spirit. For He had no idealism apart from realism. He told His disciples at the Last Supper, "The words I say to you are not just my own. Rather, it is the Father, living in me, who is doing his work" (John 14:10). Notice how He uses "words" and "work" synonymously—his words were works. They were one.

They must become one in your life and mine. But how?

O Christ, You are searching us with Your realism. You are calling us to overhaul and throw overboard useless thinking that we do not intend to put into operation. Help us not to ask for compromises. Help us to be true. Amen.

TAKING INVENTORY

We have renounced secret and shameful ways; we do not use deception, nor do we distort the word of God. On the contrary, by setting forth the truth plainly we commend ourselves to everyone's conscience in the sight of God. (2 Cor. 4:2)

How do we make our idealism and our realism the same? Here we have to walk softly, asking for light and a transparent honesty.

First of all, we should take an inventory of which ideals are now being used in our lives as mental compensation—things that comfort us mentally, but do not guide us morally. We may end up admitting to such contrivances as the little three-year-old girl who didn't want to go to bed. Hiding from her mother, she said to someone sitting near, "If my mother asks where I am, say I am not here—but don't tell a lie." That last phrase was idealism used as mental compensation for what she was doing. We adults may find many such things in our lives.

At the close of a question-and-answer period, someone overheard a member of my audience saying as he left, "It is our business to ask questions, and it is his business to answer them. But none of us expect to do anything about it." This was revealing. It showed that he believed religion was merely idealism, not realism.

We must end this hiatus. As we go over our lives in quietness before God, we must renounce this kind of idealism. It will hurt us to the very core, for it will mean appearing less good in our own eyes than we had led ourselves to believe. But at least we will be mentally honest. And that is the beginning of a fresh approach.

O Christ of the kindly searching eye, we open our lives to Your gaze, and we open our wills to Your full obedience. Help us to be completely honest and completely responsive. Then we can go forward. Amen.

SOCIAL APPLICATIONS

We know what real love is because Jesus gave up His life for us. So we also ought to give up our lives for our brothers and sisters. If someone has enough money to live well and sees a brother or sister in need but shows no compassion—how can God's love be in that person?

Dear children, let's not merely say that we love each other; let us show the truth by our actions. (1 John 3:16-18†)

Realizing our ideals does not depend entirely on us. Other people are involved, and social change must await their cooperation. What, then, can we do?

We can ask ourselves two questions: *First, in what direction is my face turned?* Am I convinced that the competitive order must surrender to a cooperative one? Am I really inwardly set against ghastly inequalities between person and person? Am I inwardly committed to wiping out distinctions based on class and color? Have I inwardly renounced war? Am I inwardly free from the dominance of narrow nationalism? Am I inwardly set against all exploitation of one person or group by another? Do I want to see all people free?

Second, what steps am I taking toward making these inner attitudes real in outer life? As far as it depends on me and on the circumstances I control, am I here and now taking steps to end things that are wrong? Am I going as far as I can in making things as they should be? I may not be at the goal, but am I on the way? Now?

This "now" is important. For without it, even the intention to do it some-time or other becomes a mental compensation, and therefore an opiate. A large landowner said to me in India, "Of course we've got to do away with these injustices and inequalities. But then I don't suppose, at least I hope not, that it will be in my time." There is no reality without a "now" in it. Am I prepared to put a "now" in all these intentions?

O You who are the Alpha—the Christ of the beginnings—help me to begin here and now to hold the right attitudes and take the first steps. I am used to living in two worlds. It will not be easy to begin in one. But help me to do it. Amen.

WHAT IS "SECULAR"? WHAT IS "SACRED"?

Whether you eat or drink or whatever you do, do it all for the glory of God.
(1 Cor. 10:31)

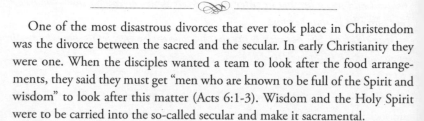

One of the most disastrous divorces that ever took place in Christendom was the divorce between the sacred and the secular. In early Christianity they were one. When the disciples wanted a team to look after the food arrangements, they said they must get "men who are known to be full of the Spirit and wisdom" to look after this matter (Acts 6:1-3). Wisdom and the Holy Spirit were to be carried into the so-called secular and make it sacramental.

Now we have divided life into the sacred and secular, sacred callings and secular callings, sacred days and secular days, sacred buildings and secular buildings, sacred books and secular books. We thought thus to preserve both. In doing so we have impoverished both. The secular has become materialized, and the sacred has become etherealized (with the emphasis on the "ether").

It has been the devil's strategy in this way to divide and rule. And he does rule where they are divided. We can never live victoriously as long as we try to live a compartmentalized life. They must be brought together.

An earnest missionary wrote to me: "When you write, show us how to live victoriously in such dull commonplaces as the keeping of books, attending to uninteresting details such as a missionary has to do. Can we not make the whole thing vicarious by the thought, that, if I do these things, someone else will be spared the drudgery of them?"

Very beautiful. And yet there was still the lurking thought that the material was less than the spiritual, and so one goes into it as one takes up a cross. Instead, it should be looked on as a part of one's spiritual life. The spiritual life cannot be manifested except in and through the material.

The word must become flesh, or die as merely a word.

O Christ, in whom everything became one, and in whom the commonplace was no longer the commonplace but glowing with meaning and purpose, help us to make them one this day. Amen.

SACRED WORK IN THE FACTORY, OFFICE, AND SCHOOL

The LORD said to Moses, "See, I have chosen Bezalel son of Uri, the son of Hur, of the tribe of Judah, and I have filled him with the Spirit of God, with skill, ability and knowledge in all kinds of crafts—to make artistic designs for work in gold, silver and bronze, to cut and set stones, to work in wood, and to engage in all kinds of craftsmanship." (Exod. 31:1-5)

We often quote approvingly the man who said he made shoes to pay expenses while he served God. But should he not have thought of serving God *through* the making of the shoes? Was not that material thing itself to become the manifestation of the spiritual? Are we not attracted to Brother Lawrence in the 1600s by the fact that he practiced the presence of God in and through the washing of his pans and the scrubbing of his floors?

The business person must be able to handle ledgers with the same sense of sacredness and mission as the minister handles the sacred Book in the pulpit. Of course that would mean the scrapping of many a business, for you cannot handle crookedness with sacredness. But it would be far better to scrap the business than to scrap one's soul.

Meanwhile, legitimate business can be made a sacrament. The attitude should be this: *Here today I stand in this business, in this workshop, in this schoolroom, to become the embodiment of Christ's spirit. I will work out His mind and spirit here in my relationship with things and persons.*

As Peter offered his boat to Jesus from which to teach the multitudes, so I offer to Him my boat, my business, my life, from which He may teach in this situation the meaning of the kingdom. I am an extension of the Incarnation.

O Christ, we thank You that You can make life glow with meaning when we take You into the whole of it. Help me this day to do that very thing. I will need power. But I know I can bank on You. Amen.

UNITING BODY AND SOUL

Physical training is of some value, but godliness has value for all things, holding promise for both the present life and the life to come. (1 Tim. 4:8)

Do not offer the parts of your body to sin, as instruments of wickedness, but rather offer yourselves to God, as those who have been brought from death to life. (Rom. 6:13)

We now come to the division between the body and the soul.

The body has too long been looked upon as the enemy of the soul. It must be suppressed, sometimes mutilated, and finally laid aside with a sigh of relief. I heard it said about one man, "He seemed to be ashamed that he inhabited his body." Religion has often intensified this war between soul and body.

But not so in Jesus. He accepted His body as He accepted His soul—gifts from God. The writer of Hebrews quoted a psalm regarding Him: "A body you prepared for me" (Heb. 10:5). His body and His soul were attuned. He did not neglect His body, nor pamper it, nor suppress it—he offered it as the vehicle of God's will and purpose. And he kept it fit for God. There is no mention of His ever being sick. Tired—yes, but never ill.

He, rather than anemic saints, must be our pattern for the way to act toward our bodies. Just enough food to keep us fit, and a little less than would keep us fat. Why carry excess luggage anyway? We may sometimes become ill, but we have no business being more ill than we should be. For many of our ills are self-induced. They come from wrong mental attitudes.

Just enough sleep to make us fresh, and a little less than that which would make us lazy. Enough exercise for fitness, with an eye on the fact that too much attention to sport may drain higher interests.

We must keep our bodies fit like a well-tuned violin. Then the music of God will come from every fiber of our being.

O Christ, we thank You that Your body and Your soul were not at cross-purposes. People throughout the ages have sought to catch the rhythm of that harmony. Help us to do the same. Amen.

"THIS IS MY BODY"

Paul: *I discipline my body like an athlete, training it to do what it should. Otherwise, I fear that after preaching to others I myself might be disqualified.* (1 Cor. 9:27†)

"Everything is permissible for me"—but not everything is beneficial. "Everything is permissible for me"—but I will not be mastered by anything. "Food for the stomach and the stomach for food"—but God will destroy them both. The body is not meant for sexual immorality, but for the Lord, and the Lord for the body. (1 Cor. 6:12-13)

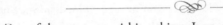

One of the most astonishing things Jesus ever said was this: "Take and eat; this is my body" (Matt. 26:26). He offered His body as food for humanity.

I would not dim the idea of the atonement in these words. That concept is certainly there, and we are grateful. But is not this idea present, too—that He offered to feed us, to enrich us through the way He treated His body, the way He made His bodily appetites subserve the purposes of the kingdom, the way He redirected His sexual impulses, and the way He kept pure in act and in thought?

Feed upon that fact, He says. And we do.

If we can say the same thing to others, then we are really coming into victory. Are we able to feed people at the place of personal victories in and through our bodies? Can we say to tempted and harassed people, "Take and eat of this victory; follow my example with regard to my bodily appetites"? If so, we are in line of the succession of Jesus' spirit. We are an extension of the Incarnation.

So when tempted today to indulge our passions in thought or in deed, we must say: "No, this cannot be. For if I do that, my lips will be silent when someone comes to observe my victory. I cannot ask Him to emulate my soul unless I can ask Him to emulate my bodily triumphs."

O Christ of the pure body, make me like that. May no impure thought or deed during this day incapacitate me for offering my victory to tempted souls at evening. Keep me pure at the place of earthly contacts. Amen.

"THIS IS MY BLOOD"

The life of every creature is its blood. (Lev. 17:14)

Then he took the cup, gave thanks and offered it to them, saying, "Drink from it, all of you. This is my blood of the covenant, which is poured out for many for the forgiveness of sins." (Matt. 26:27-28)

Jesus said another astounding thing when He invited His disciples to drink His blood. Again, we repeat that the concept and the fact of the atonement are in those words.

But is not this idea also there? He was beginning a new bloodstream, a new heredity. And now we can have the source of our blood heredity not in the tainted, contaminated past of which we are the unwilling inheritors, but in a new, pure, untainted source of inherited life.

My ancestry may be a poor, contaminated, streaky human line—whose isn't? But now I step into a new line from a new Ancestor. I am not a victim of the past; I begin a new line—in Him! "Christ is in my very blood," said a joyous Indian to me one day. Why not? When I assimilate Christ in obedience and trust, He becomes Life of my life, Blood of my blood.

And you and I must be able to say the same thing to others: "You will find coursing within my blood a new victory and a new purity. Drink from that victory and that newness."

If this is to be so, then we must let no impurity or disease get into our spiritual bloodstream. It must be kept pure and healthy, so present and future generations may receive from us a new heredity. When tempted to sin during a given day, you must say, "No, that would make me unfit at evening to say to anyone, 'Drink from my life and of my new line.' No, for their sakes I sanctify myself—yes, my very blood, so that I may be able to feed this and coming generations rather than poison them."

O Christ, I thank You that I belong to a new heredity. Help me to be worthy of such a line. And help me to preserve the dignity of the life to which I belong. May a new humble pride possess me. Amen.

GOD VS. DISEASE

He looked up to heaven and with a deep sigh said to him [a deaf mute]... *"Be opened!" (Mark 7:34)*

Regarding a crippled woman: *"Should not this woman, a daughter of Abraham, whom Satan has kept bound for eighteen long years, be set free on the Sabbath day from what bound her?" (Luke 13:16)*

To the twelve disciples: *"Heal the sick, raise the dead, cleanse those who have leprosy, drive out demons. Freely you have received, freely give." (Matt. 10:8)*

Our victory should extend to our bodies. Our bodies should be as fit as possible. I say "as possible," for some are handicapped with a poor physical frame. Even so, it can be made better, perhaps even well.

First of all, get rid of the idea that your sickness is God-sent. It isn't. God is fighting against disease. Christ never said sickness was the will of God—he cured it. The kingdom of God is an offensive against everything that cripples life, including disease.

The *British Medical Journal* says, "There is not a tissue of the human body wholly removed from the influence of spirit." If so, we must let the power of our spiritual lives pour into the physical. "The Spirit...who...is living in you... will also give life to your mortal bodies" (Rom. 8:11). All other things being equal, the Christian should be healthier than the person who is not a Christian, for the Christian has tapped a source of power for the body.

The greatest source of power for physical health is the absence of inward clash and strife in the spirit. Many people would be well physically if they were spiritually.

Hold, then, to these two things—your sickness is not the will of God, and it may depend on the state of your soul. Of course it may not. But if it does, the first step to physical health is to get rid of all inward clashes and complexes.

O Christ of the healthy soul and body, make us like that. May we pass on to our bodies no weariness of soul. May we be as healthy as You intend us to be. Amen.

ARE YOU TIRED?

"I loathe my very life; therefore I will give free rein to my complaint and speak out in the bitterness of my soul." (Job 10:1)

Those who hope in the LORD will renew their strength. They will soar on wings like eagles; they will run and not grow weary, they will walk and not be faint. (Isa. 40:31)

An African proverb says, "Don't be tired tomorrow." Many of us are, for we pass on mental states to the body. A famous physician, who has cured thousands in her sanitarium, says that nature balances up the accounts about every twenty-four hours. That is, if you are tired and will give nature twenty-four hours of rest, it will throw off the fatigue toxins within that time. She says you do not store up fatigue toxins for weeks and months—if you did, you would not be a tired person, you would be dead.

She therefore pooh-poohs the idea of lying around for weeks and months for bodily rest. Twenty-four hours will do the trick, provided the soul is adjusted and harmonious. It is amazing what the body can stand if the soul is unified. Most people do not wear out from overwork, but from under-being.

"How do you do it?" asked a colleague as we started on a group speaking tour. "Well," I replied, "there are two ways to operate. One is how the railway engines get their water in India: they stop at the station, take time off, and refill their tanks. The other is the way the engines get water in America: they scoop it up as they run."

"All right," she said, "I'll scoop it up—I'll take the power and victory of Christ as I go along." She did, and it worked.

Say to yourself, not merely as you fall asleep at night, but throughout the day, "I can do everything through him who gives me strength" (Phil. 4:13). This balm will soothe your nerves and will quicken every fiber of your being.

O Christ, who went through the strain of the day without strain, give us that inward sense of Your healing quiet upon our spirits, that we may be ready for anything. Amen.

HOW DOES GOD HEAL? (PART 1)

Worship the LORD your God, and his blessing will be on your food and water. I will take away sickness from among you. (Exod. 23:25)

Praise the LORD, O my soul, and forget not all his benefits—who forgives all your sins and heals all your diseases. (Psalm 103:2-3)

The healing of God does not flow through only one channel. He heals in many ways. He heals by physicians, by surgeons, by climate, by mental suggestion, by the direct touch of the Spirit upon our bodies, and by common sense.

By "common sense" I mean that, while God gives grace to undertake greater tasks than we are normally fitted for, nevertheless He may be saying to us through a sickness: "Lighten up. You are carrying too heavy a load." You cannot do everything, and, it may be that by doing less, you can do the worthwhile thing better. We must go to the limit of our strength, but then we must watch our margins and not go beyond them.

Common sense told me years ago that if I was to get exercise in the kind of work I was doing, I would have to get it at night just before going to bed, for it was the one time I was sure of. I found that it not only gave me exercise, but it took the blood out of my brain and distributed it through the system, so that my relaxed mind went off to sleep at once. Whereas, if I lay there with my brain congested, it continued active and sleepless.

Common sense will tell us many other things about the physical bodies we live with, and we must obey that common sense. It is one of God's methods of healing. It is not a spectacular method, but often God comes along some lowly, dusty roads to us. And we must not despise His coming because He came to us along a lowly road.

O Christ, You called Your disciples aside to rest from the many things and the many people. Help us not to despise this call of Yours as You call us to Your side for rest, and perhaps to let go of the many things in order that we may do the one thing well. Amen.

HOW DOES GOD HEAL? (PART 2)

When they [the religious authorities] *saw the courage of Peter and John and realized that they were unschooled, ordinary men, they were astonished.... Since they could see the man who had been healed standing there with them, there was nothing they could say. (Acts 4:13-14)*

Christian people have often brought discredit on Christian healing by choosing one way alone, perhaps healing by the method of prayer, while treating lightly or rejecting the other methods. This is a mistake. Doctors, on the other hand, should not despise the method of prayer, but lay hold on it and use it.

For God does sometimes touch the body directly through prayer. Once when I was asked to pray for a lady in the last stages of tuberculosis, I replied that I could not pray for her physical healing unless she were willing for Christ to heal her soul. I am not sure I was right, for Jesus did not make such a demand in His healing. Anyway, she was more than ready to meet that demand and did. So I prayed for her healing. In two months she had gained twenty pounds, and went on to become the mother of a lovely family.

A girl had a cancer on her tongue that had been cut out and burned out ten times. After she had just given herself to Christ, while we were still in prayer, I had an intuition that God would heal her. I leaned over and asked if she believed God would do this. "Why, He has!" she said in glad astonishment.

I called in a doctor who had known her case in the hospital, and without telling him anything that had happened, asked him to examine her. After examination, he turned to us and said, "She's well."

"What would you say if we told you that God had healed her?" we asked.

"Well," he said very thoughtfully, "I couldn't say anything against it."

But science should go further: It should say something *in favor of* prayer for healing, and use it. And Christians in turn should look on science's ways of healing as God's ways and use them. For God wills our health.

O Christ, whose seamless robe is alongside our beds of pain, help us to touch it in faith and rise into health. Amen.

LIVING RELAXED

Do not be anxious about anything, but in everything, by prayer and petition, with thanksgiving, present your requests to God. (Phil. 4:6)

Refrain from anger and turn from wrath; do not fret—it leads only to evil. (Psalm 37:8)

Cast all your anxiety on him because he cares for you. (1 Peter 5:7)

In our quest for victorious living, one of the most important things to learn is to live inwardly relaxed. This age seems set against it. Its whole demand is high tension, high pressure. So we do not die of the diseases our forebears died of; we go at high pressure until the boiler bursts. Nervous diseases and heart failure are the outcomes of inner tensions. And all this destroys not only the body but the mind and soul as well. For freedom and efficiency depend upon relaxation.

A bee was beating itself upon my windowpane in a frantic endeavor to get out to freedom. I tried in vain to rescue it, but the more I tried, the more it beat its head against the windowpane. Finally it fell to the windowsill exhausted.

Then as the window was raised a bit, it crawled out and immediately flew away. Until it relaxed and let go, it could find no freedom. Some of us are all inwardly tight, screwed up and frantically beating ourselves against the windowpanes of our circumstances and tasks, vainly trying to find freedom and power. We will never get it till we let go. The phrase "Let go, let God," is more than a cliché; it has sound wisdom in it.

A missionary came to our ashram with a serious countenance. He so wanted to be good and effective as a missionary, but these qualities eluded him the more earnestly he pursued them. I saw at a glance where the difficulty lay. I got him to relax and trust—which, of course, meant a self-surrender. And indeed, goodness and effectiveness are now his. He is a relaxed soul!

Relaxation means that you have ceased to worry. You are trusting, and trusting means drawing on the inexhaustible resources of God.

O Christ, amid all the strain of things, You had the relaxed spirit. Give that to us, so that we too may fully live. Amen.

TRYING TOO HARD

This is what the Sovereign LORD, the Holy One of Israel, says: "In repentance and rest is your salvation, in quietness and trust is your strength." (Isa. 30:15)

A furious squall came up, and the waves broke over the boat, so that it was nearly swamped. Jesus was in the stern, sleeping on a cushion. (Mark 4:37-38)

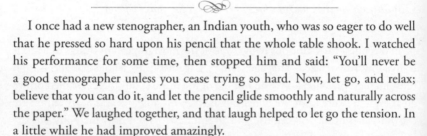

I once had a new stenographer, an Indian youth, who was so eager to do well that he pressed so hard upon his pencil that the whole table shook. I watched his performance for some time, then stopped him and said: "You'll never be a good stenographer unless you cease trying so hard. Now, let go, and relax; believe that you can do it, and let the pencil glide smoothly and naturally across the paper." We laughed together, and that laugh helped to let go the tension. In a little while he had improved amazingly.

Someone has said, "Watch a young lady trying hard not to blush, or a speaker without experience trying to address a meeting, or a novice trying to hit a golf ball, or a patient trying to go to sleep, or a person trying to remember a name. The secret of mastery is not in flogging the will."

Jesus said, "Which of you by worrying can add one cubit to his stature?" (Matt. 6:27 NKJV). He had probably seen little boys who wanted to be big, trying with bursting cheeks and bulging eyes to grow taller. So through it He talked to us grown-ups about the folly of it all. Live relaxed, He said.

A very able musician told me that her teacher insisted that every muscle be relaxed, so that her very soul could come into her fingertips. Only then was there mastery. Some live spiritually that way. They let the very power of Christ into every portion of their being—and it is all done so easily. But how effective!

Jesus was so relaxed that the power of God had an unhindered channel through Him. Spiritual relaxation meant spiritual release. The machinery of life can be oiled by the peace of God, so that it runs without friction.

O Christ, I come to You for strength to be weak, for courage to let go, and through it to find Your power in every portion of my being. Amen.

RELAXED IN OUR WORK

You are a shield around me, O LORD; you bestow glory on me and lift up my head.... I will not fear the tens of thousands drawn up against me on every side. (Psalm 3:3, 6)

I am not ashamed, because I know whom I have believed, and am convinced that he is able to guard what I have entrusted to him for that day. (2 Tim. 1:12)

I was once asked to give an address on the technique of my work among educated non-Christians. I was puzzled, for I really did not know I had a technique! But it made me think, and I suppose the center of the technique is just this relaxed spirit.

When I began my work, this word was given me: "You will be brought before governors and kings as witnesses to them.... Do not worry about what to say or how to say it. At that time you will be given what to say, for it will not be you speaking, but the Spirit of your Father speaking through you" (Matt. 10:18-20). I felt I could utterly bank on that—and have.

As I walked home from a tense meeting in which I had spoken for an hour, and very bright non-Christians, especially militant ones, had cross-examined me in no gentle way for two more hours, a lady missionary said to me: "I'm physically exhausted from that meeting tonight. I didn't know what they were going to ask next, and I didn't know what you were going to answer. So I have been sitting up in the gallery holding on to the bench with all my might for two solid hours, and I'm physically exhausted."

I replied: "Why, my sister, I was having the time of my life. I had no fears or worries whatever. I knew my verse would hold true." And it did!

In fact, my chief opponent said to the audience at the close, "You may be able to rebut his arguments, but what are you going to do with this calm confidence, this unruffled assurance and peace? Only the power of Christ can give that."

O Christ, give to me more and more this day this assurance that will take away all worry, all strain, all clash, and make me at Your best. Amen.

RELAXED AMID OPPOSITION

The chief priests accused him of many things. So again Pilate asked him, "Aren't you going to answer? See how many things they are accusing you of."
But Jesus still made no reply, and Pilate was amazed. (Mark 15:3-5)

It is comparatively easy to be relaxed in one's work. But amid opposition (especially if it is unfair), a relaxed spirit is not so easy. I have often fallen down at this place. But where I have been able to retain it, it has worked amazingly.

A missionary who always felt that he, like Uzzah in the time of King David (2 Sam. 6), must steady the ark lest the whole thing fall to pieces, said at the close of a meeting: "I do not see how Jones can stand to have the chairman summarize by picking apart everything he says and kill the whole thing. I would not tolerate it." But I could tolerate it simply because I knew the man couldn't "kill" it. My brother thought he had to defend the faith, but the fact is he didn't have faith in the faith! If he had, he would not have fretted and worried.

Across the years I have watched hostile chairmen try to take advantage of their position and spike everything I had to say, and just as often they have broken their own necks before the audience. In the very meeting mentioned above, the reaction was so strong against the college principal who took unfair advantage that the non-Christians themselves said he was no longer fit to be their college principal. There is an innate fairness in every heart, however smothered it may be, and we can depend on that to give its verdict.

I could not be relaxed amid this opposition if the message were my own. But where we are proclaiming the message of Christ, however poor and partial our interpretation may be, we know the core of that message is something eternal. It stands inside of Time and yet above Time; it does not need to be defended but rather to be proclaimed and lived; it is self-verifying. Therefore we can be relaxed even amid opposition.

O Christ, You who stood amid the crowd at the judgment hall, the only calm one amid that howling crowd, give me this day a touch of that assurance. Amen.

A PLACE FOR TENSION?

We proclaim him, admonishing and teaching everyone with all wisdom, so that we may present everyone perfect in Christ. To this end I labor, struggling with all his energy, which so powerfully works in me. (Col. 1:28-29)

See how the lilies of the field grow. They do not labor or spin. Yet I tell you that not even Solomon in all his splendor was dressed like one of these.... Will [God] not much more clothe you, O you of little faith?... But seek first his kingdom and his righteousness, and all these things will be given to you as well. (Matt. 6:28-30, 33)

But, someone objects, this talk of living relaxed is liable to let down tensions between us and our ideals. Are not the tension points the growing points? If, therefore, we let down tensions, won't we cease to grow and become flabby?

It is right to say that we must keep up places of tension in the moral life. Without them, we do not grow, and our goal is ceaseless and eternal growth. But Jesus emphasized this very thing when He advised us to notice how the lilies of the field mature. The emphasis was on the method of their growth. They do not grow by trying, by working themselves up into a frenzy of endeavor, by anxiety and worry. They grow by obeying the laws of their own nature, absorbing nutrients from the outside.

Do the same, says Jesus; obey the laws of the kingdom that is now within you; draw sustenance and calm. The fact is that you cannot draw sustenance unless there is relaxation and trust. The agitated soul is the poverty-stricken soul.

We must remember that it is the calm and relaxed people who are the strenuous people. They are strenuous but not strained. Jesus was never so powerful, never so consonant with His call, never so gripping as when He stood before Pilate calm and silent. That calmness, that silence is not flabby—it is dynamic. Out of it come the forces that reshape the world.

O Christ, I know that if I am fussy in my endeavors today, I will not reshape the world around me. Give me Your calm—and Your dynamic. I will be weak with only one of these. I must have both. Amen.

RELAXED UNDER BURDENS

Cast your cares on the LORD and he will sustain you; he will never let the righteous fall. (Psalm 55:22)

"Come to me, all you who are weary and burdened, and I will give you rest. Take my yoke upon you and learn from me, for I am gentle and humble in heart, and you will find rest for your souls. For my yoke is easy and my burden is light." (Matt. 11:28-30)

In *The Christian's Secret of a Happy Life,* Hannah Whitall Smith writes that if you go to bed and lie there with all your muscles taut and strained because you are afraid the bed will break down under you, you will get up in the morning exhausted. You have to trust to rest. Some people are still holding themselves inwardly taut, afraid that if they let go, the grace of God won't sustain them. So they live exhausted lives, worn out from the inside.

An old woman trudged along the road with a heavy pack upon her back, when a man in a wagon overtook her and offered her a lift. Grateful beyond words, she climbed in, but sat there still holding her burden on her back. When the man suggested that she put it in the back of the wagon, she replied, "Oh, but it is so kind of you to carry me, I don't want to make you carry my pack too. I'll carry that." We smile at the old lady, and yet how many of us do just as she did! We believe the grace of God can save our souls, but we do not trust that same grace to carry our daily burdens, our cares and anxieties, the worries of business and of the home—these we still continue to keep on our own backs. Exhausted souls!

From out of childhood days I can only remember this one Bible quotation spoken by my mother, "Casting all your care upon him; for he careth for you" (1 Peter 5:7 KJV). That was enough to remember, for I saw her do that very thing. She did cast all her care upon Him; otherwise how would she have gone through it all?

O Christ, You offer to carry us and our burdens. Help us to surrender our burdens as well as ourselves. For You will carry both! We thank You. Amen.

UNITED TWO DIRECTIONS

Teach me your way, O LORD, and I will walk in your truth; give me an undivided heart, that I may fear your name. (Psalm 86:11)

Jesus: *"He who is not with me is against me, and he who does not gather with me scatters." (Matt. 12:30)*

———————————————— ✐ ————————————————

Victorious living is impossible unless we are inwardly unified, no longer strained but relaxed. Matthew 9:36 (ASV) diagnoses our condition and suggests the remedy: "But when he saw the multitudes, he was moved with compassion for them, because they were distressed and scattered, as sheep not having a shepherd." They were inwardly strained—"distressed," or literally, drawn in different directions, with no inward unity. They were also "scattered"—no outer unity.

These are the two things lacking in humanity: inner and outer unity; to be at peace with oneself, and at peace with one's fellow men. And the reason for this condition then was and now is: *No shepherd*—the lack of a center around which life can find its inner and outer unity. Until we can absolutely center in some perfect life, we will lack unity. That center can only be Christ.

Even the religious world of the West is distressed and scattered because it is often missing this center. Religious leaders jump from issue to issue, from emphasis to emphasis, from doctrine to doctrine, and the whole thing lacks coherency, unity. If they would take their stand at Christ and work out from Him to these issues, emphases, and doctrines, then there would be coherency, because there would be a center.

Furthermore, life needs a personal, enduring Friendship to keep it centered. Christ offers Himself as that Friend. When our love is completely and utterly fastened on Him, we are no longer lonely, no longer drawn in different directions, no longer at war with ourselves. We have found a center—a center of unity. I see no anchor for outer unity in the world unless the sons of men find it around the Son of man.

O Christ, You are Center. Your power alone can hold the centrifugal forces of our souls from breaking our unity. Hold us, and we are held. Amen.

THE DESTROYER OF INNER UNITY

Do not call conspiracy everything that these people call conspiracy; do not fear what they fear, and do not dread it. (Isa. 8:12)

There is no fear in love. But perfect love drives out fear, because fear has to do with punishment. The one who fears is not made perfect in love. (1 John 4:18)

Of all the things that destroy inner unity, fear is perhaps the most devastating and the most prevailing. We saw earlier that there was a biological fear that produced efficiency, but there are other fears that paralyze. Victory over fear is an essential part of victorious living.

As I was speaking one day, an intelligent and beautiful Parsee [Zoroastrian] lady on the front bench fainted. I wondered what I had said to cause this. On inquiry I learned that as she sat there, the face of a woman whom she greatly feared had come before her. All her culture, intelligence, plus the spiritual atmosphere of that meeting were nothing before that fear.

A very able American doctor in Sri Lanka told me of one of his patients, a wealthy man upon whom he had operated and who was ready to be discharged from the hospital as cured. But his astrologer said a crisis would come the following week, and therefore he should not leave the hospital. The next week the man died—from no other apparent reason. Fear had snapped his will to live.

An old fable tells of someone meeting Cholera as it was returning from a devastating visit to a city. "How many died?" the man asked.

"Eighty thousand," Cholera replied, "but I touched only twenty thousand."

"And the rest?"

"Oh, they died from fear."

There is no doubt that fear is the most paralyzing thing in human life. "I was afraid and went out and hid your talent in the ground," said the nervous servant in Jesus' parable (Matt. 25:25). Fear paralyzes us and paralyzes our endeavors.

O Christ, I thank You that I do not need to be the victim of any fear. But teach me the clear road to that victory, and I will walk in it. Amen.

OVERCOMING FEAR FROM EARLY TRAUMA

I sought the LORD, and he answered me; he delivered me from all my fears.
(Psalm 34:4)

Since the children have flesh and blood, he [Jesus] too shared in their humanity
so that by his death he might destroy him who holds the power of death—that is,
the devil—and free those who all their lives were held in slavery by their fear of
death. (Heb. 2:14-15)

Some of our fears come from trauma early in our lives. The mind, always
wishing to forget the unpleasant, drops the incident that caused the shock
down into the subconscious mind and closes the door. There it works its silent
havoc, causing nervousness and general upset.

Leslie D. Weatherhead tells of an officer who during the war would stand on
the ridge of the trench rather than get down into the bottom. Some thought it
bravery, but it was really fear—fear of a closed place. Back during childhood,
he met in a narrow alleyway a fierce dog, which attacked him. That left a fear
of tight places upon him.

Now, what is to be done with a fear like that? Repress it? Try to forget it?
Nothing would be worse. It must be brought up to the surface and faced. The
incident must be gently and quietly looked at. This will of course draw its sting.
But it must be seen as a childhood incident that has no right to erect a lifelong
fear. The complex must be dissolved.

A lady missionary seeking the victorious life was found to have a dread of
deep water, and therefore never learned to swim. On inquiry I found that in
early childhood she nearly drowned, and it had left a deep fear.

Obviously, there could be no fully victorious life until that fear complex was
dissolved. And the only way was by learning to swim and then going into deep
water, which she did. She dropped her fear into the deep, deep lake! It has never
troubled her again.

O Christ, take from my inner consciousness all basis of fear, for I know I have no
business to be afraid of anything if You are my Redeemer. Amen.

OVERCOMING THE FEAR OF THE GROUP

"We know he is our son," the parents answered, "and we know he was born blind. But how he can see now, or who opened his eyes, we don't know. Ask him. He is of age; he will speak for himself." His parents said this because they were afraid of the Jews, for already the Jews had decided that anyone who acknowledged that Jesus was the Christ would be put out of the synagogue. (John 9:20-22)

But with loud shouts they insistently demanded that he be crucified, and their shouts prevailed. So Pilate decided to grant their demand. (Luke 23:23-24)

The fear of the group suppresses Christians and makes them conform to the average—which is always below Christ's way. We take on protective resemblance to our environment and fit in, become mediocre, and are slowly de-Christianized. We are afraid of being distinct. And yet it is just that distinctness that may be necessary to save us as well as the group.

Nevertheless, the group demands conformity, and it will persecute those who depart from its standards. Fall below its standards and it will punish you; rise above them, and it will persecute you. Or it may ridicule you, which is sometimes worse.

When ridiculed, simply laugh back, knowing that in the end you will laugh longest and perhaps loudest. You have a better basis for laughter. Deeper still, to get rid of the fear of the group we must surrender the group, acknowledging no dominance in our inmost spirit but that of Jesus Christ.

After I had become a Christian, I went past the crowd on the street with whom I had associated. One of them called out in derision, "Hello, Stanley, going down to see Jesus?"

"Yes, I am," I quietly replied, to their astonishment and my own. But I knew in my heart of hearts that by that defiance, the fear of the group was broken. I was free not only from them, but free to come back to them with what I now had.

O Christ, deliver me from the fear of what the group will say, and give me a deeper susceptibility to what You will say. For I must be delivered from all fear. Amen.

OVERCOMING THE FEAR OF FAILURE

"Then the man who had received the one talent came. 'Master,' he said, 'I knew that you are a hard man, harvesting where you have not sown and gathering where you have not scattered seed. So I was afraid and went out and hid your talent in the ground. See, here is what belongs to you.' " (Matt. 25:24-25)

God did not give us a spirit of timidity, but a spirit of power, of love and of self-discipline. (2 Tim. 1:7)

Like the one-talented man, many do not attempt anything with their talents because they are afraid of failing if they did. They too end in emptiness and futility—a hole in the ground. Fear produces the very failure that we fear.

Many do not start the Christian life because they are afraid they would fail if they did. So they never start. Fear feeds on failure, and failure feeds on fear.

To live victoriously, we must conquer this. But how? First of all, by looking at its worst. Suppose you fail—would you be any worse off than now? Hardly. By doing nothing you are living in a constant state of failure.

Again, suppose you did fail in obeying what you felt was the call of God. Would you really fail? Hardly, for your very obedience is success. It is not your business whether you succeed or fail—it is your business to be true to the call of God as you know it. Results are in His hands.

Besides, God has a way of turning even failure into ultimate victory. The cross is the world's supreme failure. When Jesus dropped His head onto His pulseless chest and died, everything had crashed. But had it? Ask your own heart! If it is like mine, it clings to that failure as the one hope of the race. So God has a way of turning the cross of your failure into supreme success. The seed sown fails and dies, but in its failure a new life springs up.

Therefore, away with fear, and forward with Christ! Where? Anywhere, so long as it is forward!

O You who saw Your kingdom crash about You on the cross and still held Your heart above the crash of things, give us the power this day to be unafraid of fear. Amen.

OVERCOMING THE FEAR OF OLD AGE

The LORD is my shepherd, I shall not be in want. (Psalm 23:1)

Even to your old age and gray hairs I am he, I am he who will sustain you. I have made you and I will carry you; I will sustain you and I will rescue you. (Isa. 46:4)

In a competitive system, fear of destitution in old age is real. Almost all of this fear could be cured by collective action. In a world of plenty, no one should be haunted by the fear of what will happen in old age. Someday we will banish this problem, and with it the accompanying fear. But in the meantime, what shall we do?

The world's answer is to feverishly pile up resources. Hardly the Christian answer, for by my having more than I need, someone has less than he needs. The Christian conscience can scarcely stand for that.

Jesus said, "Seek first his kingdom and his righteousness, and all these things will be given to you as well" (Matt. 6:33). What were "these things"? He had just been talking about food and clothing (see vss. 25-32). He guarantees us those two things—not motor cars and fine houses—if we put His kingdom first.

Aren't these two things enough for life? Listen to Epictetus, the Greek philosopher who was born a slave half a century after Christ: "Is it possible for a man who is unclothed and homeless, without a wife, without a country, to be happy? See, God has sent such a man to Rome to teach you that it is possible. I possess nothing but heaven and earth and this old cloak. But what do I want? Do any of you see me going about with a sad countenance?"

If a pre-Christian philosopher can say that, how much more a Christian? Away with fear! Your Father lives.

O Christ, I thank You that I can live as You did, a happy, trustful child of the Father, without fear. Help me to begin it today. Amen.

OVERCOMING THE FEAR OF BEING DEPENDENT

We who are strong ought to bear with the failings of the weak and not to please ourselves. (Rom. 15:1)

Even when I am old and gray, do not forsake me, O God, till I declare your power to the next generation, your might to all who are to come. (Psalm 71:18)

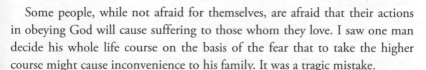

Some people, while not afraid for themselves, are afraid that their actions in obeying God will cause suffering to those whom they love. I saw one man decide his whole life course on the basis of the fear that to take the higher course might cause inconvenience to his family. It was a tragic mistake.

Our obedience to Christ may well cause suffering to those whom we love. We are all bound up in a bundle of life together, and we cannot wait to act till we can be sure that we alone will get the consequences. If we did, we would never act.

Jesus, acting on the will of God, involved His whole family in a cross—and also in a resurrection! It can work both ways.

A part of this fear of hurting others is the fear of being dependent on others in old age. Some of this springs from a false pride. We say we don't want to be dependent. Nonsense. We are all dependent, every moment of our lives, both on God and people. To act as if we weren't is silly, superficial pride.

If we honestly contribute to others during our earning period, why shouldn't others contribute to us when we need it? Besides, you took care of this younger generation when it was helpless; why shouldn't they care of you when you are old and helpless? It will probably do them good to have this responsibility; in fact, it may save them from selfish isolation. The crucifixion of your pride may turn out for their redemption.

Furthermore, if you accept the situation joyously and sweetly, you may be the kind of person they will delight to take care of.

O Christ, we thank You that You have shown us the way. You broke the heart of Your mother—and made it well again. Help us to launch out with You, no matter the cost. Amen.

OVERCOMING NEGATIVISM

"I, yes I, am the one who comforts you. So why are you afraid of mere humans, who wither like the grass and disappear? Yet you have forgotten the LORD, your Creator, the one who stretched out the sky like a canopy and laid the foundations of the earth. Will you remain in constant dread of human oppressors? Will you continue to fear the anger of your enemies? Where is their fury and anger now? It is gone!"
(Isa. 51:12-13†)

People with inner conflicts find it hard to be positive in their attitudes and decisions, so they retreat into the negative. When a proposition or opportunity is presented to them, their first impulse is to reject it. They spot the difficulties before anything else.

Such negative natures cannot lead others. It is the positive, hopeful, affirmative type who becomes a leader. Besides, to be negative is to be unchristian. The Christian is positive, affirmative, hopeful. Sometimes we do say, "No," but only to say a greater "Yes." Paul felt the sheer hopefulness, the affirmative nature of Christ when he said, "In him it has always been 'Yes' " (2 Cor. 1:19), or, as Moffatt puts it, "The divine 'yes' has at last sounded in him." To be in Him, then, is to take a positive attitude toward life.

This morning in my daily reading I read how Judas and his band showed up in the garden with torches and weapons. "Jesus fully realized all that was going to happen to him, so he stepped forward" (John 18:4†). To do what? To compromise? To escape? To soften the blow? No, he "stepped forward to meet them"! At the moment of the great "No," the betrayal, He was positive.

Be positive even in the face of impending calamity. Wring a victory out of it. Keep affirming to yourself, "I can do everything through him who gives me strength" (Phil. 4:13). Then your negative fears will drop off before the rising sap of a new, abundant life. For the Christian belongs to the great affirmation.

O Christ, I thank You that, in Your company, my negative fears are dissolved and I feel that anything is possible. Help me to catch this spirit this day—from You. Amen.

FEAR'S ROOT

I will walk about in freedom, for I have sought out your precepts.
(Psalm 119:45)

All of the fears we have been looking at are rooted in one thing—inward division. The inwardly united soul has no fears. So what is the basic remedy?

Two great modern answers are strangely similar: One comes from social commentator Walter Lippmann and the other from Mahatma Gandhi. Lippmann says, School your desires, don't expect too much, contract the area of your expectations and hopes, and then life won't hit you on too wide a front. Your fears will thus be lessened. His remedy is, Pull in.

Mahatma Gandhi, following the Gita, says, Stand inwardly aloof, without desire for the fruit of action. His remedy for fear is, Pull away.

The answer of the gospel? It is this: "Love has in it no fear; but perfect love drives away fear…and if a man fears, there is something imperfect in his love" (1 John 4:18, WEYMOUTH). The answer is not pull in, or pull away, but pull out all the stops! Expand through perfect love. That expansion drives out all fear. This answer, like the gospel itself, is positive, affirmative, expansive.

But first it contracts. It narrows its love down to one Person—God, through Christ. "The love of Christ constraineth us," says Paul (2 Cor. 5:14 KJV). We become single-pointed, with one consuming passion that eats up the lesser passions in life. This love of Christ fuses the divisions of the soul into a burning unity. There is no room for inner fear, for there is no room for inner division. Division confuses, love fuses. Fear cannot live in this fire of love that wants nothing and is therefore afraid of nothing. It wants nothing except Him.

Bowing before Him, we now bow before nothing else. We are unafraid.

O You who have conquered our inmost being, we thank You that no fear can now make us afraid. For nothing can separate us from the love of Christ—nothing. Amen.

DIVIDED LOYALTIES

Be sure that your faith is in God alone. Do not waver, for a person with divided loyalty is as unsettled as a wave of the sea that is blown and tossed by the wind. Such people should not expect to receive anything from the Lord. Their loyalty is divided between God and the world, and they are unstable in everything they do. (James 1:6-8[†])

There is no deliverance from fears unless there is an undivided loyalty to Christ. Perfect love literally does cast out fear. And, vice versa, imperfect love admits fear into the heart.

This is vividly brought home to us in the Transfiguration scene. The Jewish heart of Peter was divided in its loyalty, wanting to keep Moses (representing the Law), Elijah (representing the Prophets), and Jesus (representing the new revelation) all on the same level: "Let us put up three shelters" (Luke 9:33). This was serious, for the whole future was bound up with the question of whether Jesus was final, and whether supreme allegiance should be given to Him.

The moment division came, "a cloud...enveloped them, and they were afraid as they entered the cloud" (v. 34). Inner division brought clouds and fears.

Where there is division, there will be clouds and fears. Take the international situation today. Why are we so overshadowed with war clouds, and why do we fear? The answer is simple—division. Each nation is thinking of itself, losing a sense of the collective unity.

But out of those clouds comes a Voice. God speaks! Because we would not listen to the voice of God through intelligent reason, now we must listen as He speaks through the roaring of the cannon and the crash of our civilization. The Voice judges, but also invites us: "This is my Son, whom I have chosen; listen to him" (v. 35). Our clouds will never lift and our fears will never depart until we listen to Christ.

O God, You are speaking out of the clouds today. We shudder at Your voice of judgment. Help us not merely to shudder but to obey. Save us from our divisions. Amen.

A CLOUD OVER OUR ECONOMIC LIFE

If you do away with the yoke of oppression, with the pointing finger and malicious talk, and if you spend yourselves in behalf of the hungry and satisfy the needs of the oppressed, then your light will rise in the darkness, and your night will become like the noonday. (Isa. 58:9-10)

Today[6] clouds hang over our economy: unemployment, glutted markets, scarcity, depression, fears. Why? The reason is simple: division. Those in control of our economic structure, thinking they held the reins, intercepted too much of the gains that science and technique had brought and kept them from passing on to the people. A split went clear through society between "the haves" and "the have-nots."

And now God speaks out of this cloud of depression. Let Walter M. Horton interpret that Voice: "Is it tenable, one may ask, that God should be at once a God of wrath and a God of love? Has He two hands, one iron-gloved, the other warm and human?... Could we believe this, we might hear Him saying to this generation in tones of mingled sorrow and anger, 'You must and shall have deeper fellowship in your social order. You may take it *this* way (stretching out the right hand), or you may take it *this* way (clenching the left fist). If you will hear My word, you may make the great soulless machine of your industrial civilization an instrument for the common good and a bond of fellowship between you; but if not, then I will smash your civilization, and reduce you to a primitive level of existence, where you *must* recover the art of fellowship' " (*Realistic Theology*, p. 112).

In other words, God is speaking out of the cloud of this depression: "This is my Son...listen to him." Unless we do, that cloud will never lift, and those fears will never depart.

O God, why cannot we listen to Your still small voice? Why do we have to listen to Your voice of wrath as it speaks through our calamities? Forgive us. Amen.

---

6. Jones is here reflecting the times in which he wrote as the Great Depression wore on. But his point has relevance to our era as well.

A CLOUD OVER OUR CHURCHES (PART 1)

See to it that no one takes you captive through hollow and deceptive philosophy, which depends on human tradition and the basic principles of this world rather than on Christ…. Since you died with Christ to the basic principles of this world, why, as though you still belonged to it, do you submit to its rules? (Col. 2:8, 20)

No one has to argue that there is a cloud over the church life of Christendom. Our vague uneasiness has grown into a fear that all is not well. Why? Again, divided loyalty, inner division.

In each nation, instead of keeping the gospel of Christ in universal terms, we have more and more identified it with our various cultures. The conquest of the gospel of Christ by local cultures keeps going on, and this process means the slow de-Christianization of our churches. On the "Antioch Chalice," which is claimed by some to be the original Holy Grail, the figure of Christ is seen sitting above the Roman eagle. That was the position Christ occupied in those early centuries. He was first and the nation was second. Today the nation is using the culture for its own ends, and because the church has become so domesticated, so identified with that national culture, the nation is using the church too. As one writer observes, "A process which began with a culture molded by religious faith has ended with a religious faith molded by a national culture."

Dr. Francis Miller puts it this way: "The irony of the situation is that Protestants now find themselves in exactly the same position as the Catholics four hundred years ago. The Catholics mistook static ecclesiastic forms for the content of their faith. The Protestants are mistaking dynamic cultured forms for the content of their faith. And the triumph of cultural forms over the religious content is even more deadly than the triumph of ecclesiastic forms."

Again the clouds come over us and again the Voice speaks: "This is my Son… listen to him." Until we do the clouds will not lift and our fear will not depart. For Christ must be first.

O God, Caesar comes again, clothed in national culture, and demands our supreme allegiance. Help us not to bend the knee. Amen.

A CLOUD OVER OUR CHURCHES (PART 2)

May the God who gives endurance and encouragement give you a spirit of unity among yourselves as you follow Christ Jesus, so that with one heart and mouth you may glorify the God and Father of our Lord Jesus Christ. (Rom. 15:5-6)

But the division within Christendom is not merely between allegiance to the culture and allegiance to Christ; there is division between the churches themselves. The household of Christ is divided against itself. As a result of our family divisions, a cloud has come over us, and under that cloud we are fearful, and for good reason. For a divided church has little moral authority in a divided world. We must adjust our differences or abdicate our moral leadership.

I asked a missionary how they ever got such a lovely piece of property and received this reply: "The man who owned it built such high and expensive walls around it that he went bankrupt and had to sell the property." Bankruptcy through building walls! Is that not dangerously near the history of the Christian churches today?

We have so exhausted our resources putting up ecclesiastical walls and then keeping them in repair that we have little left to use in helping to redeem a world. If the time, intelligence, and soul-force we have expended in proving we were right compared to others had been expended in united action against the problems that now confront the world, they would not now be so far from solution. And we would be leading the procession of events instead of being led by them.

These divisions have brought a cloud over our religious life—dark, rainless clouds that presage storms of revolt, clouds that produce fear. God is today speaking out of that cloud and His voice is the same as of old: "This is my Son…listen to him." And what does that Son say to His Father? "That they may be one" (John 17:11). When we become one, the clouds will lift. But not till then.

O God, our Father, forgive us that we, Your children, have set up walls against each other. Help us to feel and act upon the solidarity of Your family. Amen.

A CLOUD OVER OUR PERSONAL LIFE

Araunah said to David, "Let my lord the king take whatever pleases him and offer it up."… But the king replied to Araunah, "No, I insist on paying you for it. I will not sacrifice to the Lord my God burnt offerings that cost me nothing." So David bought the threshing floor and the oxen and paid fifty shekels of silver for them. (2 Sam. 24:22, 24)

Now we must look within and see if there are any cloud-producing divisions left within ourselves.

It may be that you have started to pay the full price of spiritual victory and then have drawn back. That hesitation has meant a division…a cloud…a fear.

In South India the temples usually form a hollow square with high, beautiful ornate tower-gates on the four sides. In one case, I noticed that a tower-gate was closed and apparently never used. I asked why. The reason, it was explained, was that the rich man who was presenting the tower-gate to the god sat down in the midst of the building of it and began to count how much it was costing him. This offended the god—the idea that anyone should ever count the cost of a gift to him! So, they told me, the god refused to be taken out in procession through that gate. Now it stood deserted by everyone. A cloud of uselessness and decay was upon it.

Perhaps you have felt a cloud of spiritual uselessness and decay over your inner life, and perhaps you realize it is there for the same reason—you have counted the cost and have hesitated to pay the full price. You are willing to give, but not to give up.

There is one saving factor. God is speaking to you out of that cloud, and His voice is this: "This is my Son…listen to him." If we cease our hesitations and listen to that voice, we will lift up our eyes, as the three disciples did, and see "no one except Jesus" (Matt. 17:8). He will then have our complete allegiance. And there will be neither clouds nor fears.

O Christ, we know that You will only fill our horizons when You fill our hearts. Help me to let You fill my heart entirely. Amen.

SEEING WHAT MATTERS MOST

Blessed are the pure in heart, for they will see God. (Matt. 5:8)

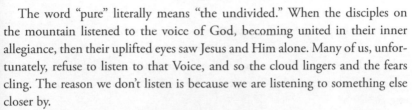

The word "pure" literally means "the undivided." When the disciples on the mountain listened to the voice of God, becoming united in their inner allegiance, then their uplifted eyes saw Jesus and Him alone. Many of us, unfortunately, refuse to listen to that Voice, and so the cloud lingers and the fears cling. The reason we don't listen is because we are listening to something else closer by.

I paused in writing the above paragraph to call down to a workman who was carrying some old tin sheets upon his head. But no matter how loudly I (and others who joined me) called, he did not hear, for the sound of the near rattling of the tin was in his ears. Some closer thing, as insignificant perhaps as old tin sheets, fills our ears with its din—some personal hurt or loss, some slight, some resentment, some clamoring habit, some foolish ambition, some infatuation, some love of money—these fill our ears, and God's voice is drowned out. And that Voice was calling us to something big.

The harbor at Galle, Sri Lanka, is beautiful. It was the original harbor of the island, but now it is comparatively deserted in favor of newer Colombo. The reason was this: When the sailing ships came, the harbor was perfect for them; but to make it fit for the big ocean liners they would have had to blast out a huge rock at the center. It would cost a great deal of money. Lesser voices of fear and hesitation prevailed, they refused to pay the price, and the city now is a dead city, a shell of its former greatness. Had they listened to the voice of faith and courage, they would now be a growing city, but the lesser voices filled their ears and prevailed.

God is speaking to each of us. Can he get a hearing?

O God, save me from these lesser things that incapacitate me from hearing Your call, and help me to pay the full price, that I may have full deliverance from fear, and the full vision of You. Amen.

CONQUERING ANGER

Better to be patient than powerful; better to have self-control than to conquer a city. (Prov. 16:32†)

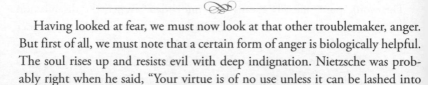

Having looked at fear, we must now look at that other troublemaker, anger. But first of all, we must note that a certain form of anger is biologically helpful. The soul rises up and resists evil with deep indignation. Nietzsche was probably right when he said, "Your virtue is of no use unless it can be lashed into a rage."

Jesus was angry: "When He had looked around at them [his legalistic critics] with anger, being grieved by the hardness of their hearts, He said to the man, 'Stretch out your hand.'" (Mark 3:5 NKJV). But note that His anger included a mix of grief. This determines the legitimate from the illegitimate type of anger. Where there is a sense of moral hurt, of moral grief, and not mere personal resentment, then the anger is right and worthy and helpful.

Note also that it was anger at something done against *someone else*. He was indignant that they had no sympathy for the stricken man. That too is a test of whether anger is legitimate. We must be suspicious of all angers that come from hurts to ourselves. They probably have in them less moral indignation than personal resentment.

Paul quotes the psalm (4:4) that says, "In your anger do not sin" (Eph. 4:26). But if we are to obey this, we must be angry at sin—and not a sin against ourselves, but others. Even this kind of anger, Paul suggests, should not be kept overnight: "Do not let the sun go down while you are still angry." If kept overnight, it might fester.

O Christ of the whip and the flashing eye, give us an inward hurt at the wrong done to others, but save us from personal resentments, for they destroy us. Amen.

ANGER'S ROOT

What causes fights and quarrels among you? Don't they come from your desires that battle within you? You want something but don't get it. You kill and covet, but you cannot have what you want. You quarrel and fight. You do not have, because you do not ask God. When you ask, you do not receive, because you ask with wrong motives, that you may spend what you get on your pleasures. (James 4:1-3)

We often dress up our personal resentments in the clothes of moral indignation and try to make them respectable and Christian. This process of rationalization allows many Christians to tolerate unchristian anger. A clergyman I know once thought he was fighting for principle. But when he honestly looked at himself, he saw that the fight had in it more personal pique than principle. He acknowledged it and got rid of it.

Those words "personal pique" point us to the root of anger. It is in the self. The self has its pride, and when that pride is wounded, it boils with anger.

It is therefore of no use to say, "I'll try not to be angry." You will almost certainly fail. You cannot kill anger in your life—but you can consent for Christ to do it. And how? By striking at the root—the self. By asking us to consent to the crucifixion of the self, in other words, its surrender. The self undergoes by that surrender its supreme mortification. It anticipates all the wounds that people can inflict upon it, then deliberately wounds itself unto death.

Having undergone that central death wound, what can marginal wounds now do? Having been torpedoed in mid-ocean and survived, are we now afraid of being drowned in a duck pond? After that central death, there is a resurrection—a new person arises. Someone who is too great and too glad to be angered by petty annoyances.

O Christ, make me too glad and too great to be angered by petty things this day. Amen.

WHEN ANGER REMAINS

Understand this, my dear brothers and sisters: You must all be quick to listen, slow to speak, and slow to get angry. Human anger does not produce the righteousness God desires. So get rid of all the filth and evil in your lives, and humbly accept the word God has planted in your hearts. (James 1:19-21†)

Often anger remains to plague us after the spiritual surrender. Why? Because of two things: Either the surrender was only partial, or the cultivation of life after the surrender has been neglected. Ninety percent of germs that fall upon a healthy skin die within minutes. Health kills them. The way to kill many of these sin germs is to strengthen the organism upon which they feed. To neglect cultivation is to let our spirits get below par. When that happens, our resistance is weakened, and the disease germs get a footing and cause havoc.

But sometimes the surrender is only partial. That sets up a dualism in the nature, and the dualism turns into a duel. There is a struggle for mastery of the spirit. We are still touchy.

The followers of Jainism, a religious minority in India, do not take life if they can help it. But dogs fill the streets in such numbers that they become an overwhelming nuisance, and then something must be done. So Jains catch them and take them out about ten miles from the city. However, they return, fighting their way through the intervening villages, where the local dogs will not allow them to stay. They arrive back in the city more bad-tempered than ever.

If we make a compromised effort to get rid of our tempers, they will come back to us again, sometimes worse than ever. We must not try to please God *and* self. If we put self out a little distance, not dealing with it decisively, the temper (which is based in the self) will, like a hungry dog, come back. We must ask God to quiet our angry temper permanently.

O Christ, in the words of the old hymn, "I lay in dust, life's glory dead," so that "from the ground there blossoms red, life that shall endless be" [7]—and angerless. Amen.

---

7. George Matheson, "O Love That Will Not Let Me Go" (1882)

MEETING CRITICISM

Why worry about a speck in your friend's eye when you have a log in your own? How can you think of saying to your friend, "Let me help you get rid of that speck in your eye," when you can't see past the log in your own eye? Hypocrite! First get rid of the log in your own eye; then you will see well enough to deal with the speck in your friend's eye. (Matt. 7:3-5†)

Yesterday I received three letters of severe criticism. One of them was very fair, and the other two were not. One of the two unjust criticisms was based on partial knowledge; the other apparently on spleen. All three of these were about different things, and yet all were in regard to what I considered my finest efforts.

What are we to do when criticism comes? First of all, I have accustomed myself to ask, "Is it true?" I had to acknowledge to myself and to the friend that the first criticism was a fair one. I would profit by it and use it. I would correct the thing I had overlooked. In this way my critics become my helpers—the unpaid watchmen of my soul. They keep me straight. I need them. If you have no friend or friends to do this for you, you are the poorer for it.

And such a helpful criticism may come from those we consider less developed than ourselves. A convert of just a few weeks, a Sikh staying at our ashram, said to me in front of the group: "Whenever we put difficult questions to you, you make us forget the question by going off the point and talking about something else that is very interesting. In this way you dodge our questions. It isn't honest."

We all laughed, but in opening my mouth to laugh I swallowed the lesson! He was right. I have never forgotten it. Now when I don't know an answer, I say so, instead of trying, perhaps unconsciously, to save face by going off to something else.

Our critics can become the very hammers of God to beat us into shape. All of us need that, for we are only Christians in the making.

O God, help me not to resent criticism, but to take it as from Your shaping hand—Your efforts to save me and make me. Amen.

MEETING UNFAIR CRITICISM

I say, love your enemies! Pray for those who persecute you! In that way, you will be acting as true children of your Father in heaven. For he gives his sunlight to both the evil and the good, and he sends rain on the just and the unjust alike. If you love only those who love you, what reward is there for that? Even corrupt tax collectors do that much. (Matt. 5:44-46†)

Other criticisms are unjust and unfair. They may come out of partial knowledge, or out of willful misrepresentation. What are we, then, to do?

First of all, quickly breathe a prayer for your critics and for yourself. It is harder to hate a person after you have prayed for them. It is harder to curse someone after you have asked God to bless them. Prayer pulls the sting of resentment. Your attitude becomes redemptive instead of resentful. You want to cure the ignorance and help get rid of the spleen. So keep your thought bathed in prayer as you think of this person. Otherwise, a prayerless thought will become a resentful thought.

Second, keep saying to yourself with Luther, "My soul is too glad and too great to be the enemy of anyone." Keep an inner spiritual dignity that will not descend to the other person's level.

Third, begin to contrive ways to do good. The person will have their armor up, awaiting your return blow. But strike where they are unguarded—at the heart. "Overcome evil with good" (Rom. 12:21). Even the Buddha said: "If a wicked man foolishly does me wrong, I will return to him the protection of my ungrudging love. The more evil comes from him, the more good shall come from me."

In loving one's enemy and turning the other cheek, as Jesus commanded and illustrated, we rise above our enemy, become superior to them—and we may win them. But if not, we have won our own souls. In either case, a victory.

O Christ of the smitten cheek and of the still-loving heart, help us to follow You at this point. These criticisms make us writhe in pain. But may that pain drive us to You. Amen.

ANSWERING CRITICS

Bless those who persecute you. Don't curse them; pray that God will bless them.... Never pay back evil with more evil. Do things in such a way that everyone can see you are honorable. (Rom. 12:14, 17†)

Sometimes we have to answer those who wrong us. We owe it to ourselves and to them to clear up things. But if you do write, then write that letter upon your knees, as it were. Don't give them a piece of your mind—you will lose your own peace of mind if you do! Don't think that Satan can cast out Satan (Mark 3:23), that by acting like the devil you can get the devil out of people. Write the kind of a letter you would like to receive.

Then after you have written it, don't send it off. Not that day. Sleep over it. Your subconscious mind may give you light. It will, if the Spirit of Christ is in that subconscious mind.

Or perhaps you shouldn't answer at all. In Luke 5:30-31 it says, "The Pharisees and the teachers of the law who belonged to their sect complained to his disciples, 'Why do you eat and drink with tax collectors and "sinners"?' Jesus answered them, 'It is not the healthy who need a doctor, but the sick.' " They criticized the disciples—and Jesus answered for them. His answer was deathless and redemptive, while the disciples' answer would probably have been evasive and unreal. Let Jesus answer for you! It is safer that way.

I once composed a devastating letter to a man who had attacked me. He deserved it. But I submitted it to the ashram group before sending it. Their verdict was, "Not sufficiently redemptive." They were right. Instead of writing, I decided to let Christ reply for me.

Some months later I got a letter from the man asking forgiveness for what he had written. My reply would never have produced that apology. Christ's did.

O Jesus, I do not know the way to people's hearts. I bungle. But You come in as softly as light, and how redemptively! Help me to win where I cannot win. Amen.

DON'T WORRY ABOUT YOUR REPUTATION

Jesus: *"Blessed are you when people insult you, persecute you and falsely say all kinds of evil against you because of me." (Matt. 5:11)*

When we are cursed, we bless; when we are persecuted, we endure it; when we are slandered, we answer kindly. Up to this moment we have become the scum of the earth, the refuse of the world. (1 Cor. 4:12-13)

"Oh," but you say, "if I don't answer, then what will become of my reputation? I must look after that." No, you don't. One who is living victoriously has gained victory over nervous concern about reputation. Look after your character, and your reputation can look after itself. Be the kind of person about whom people won't believe things.

Besides, Jesus says: "If the head of the house has been called Beelzebub, how much more the members of his household! So do not be afraid of them. There is nothing concealed that will not be disclosed, or hidden that will not be made known" (Matt. 10:25-26). In other words, don't be afraid of your reputation if they call you Beelzebub; the truth will emerge in the end. You can wait.

The most loved man America has produced was Lincoln. Most loved and most slandered. Nothing was too vile to print about him. And yet no one believes it now. His slanderers slandered themselves.

When John Wesley's wife accused him of a certain sin, he exclaimed: "There! The record is complete now; I've been accused of every sin in the catalog." But his wife only succeeded in burying herself beneath her own slanders.

When a fellow Christian who did not agree with my theology printed a pamphlet saying I was "the most dangerous devil in China," I felt rather assured that I belonged to the household of Him who was called Beelzebub. At least He seemed very near to me at that time. I was in wonderful company!

O Jesus Christ, purest of souls and yet called Beelzebub, "the lord of filth," help me not to be nervous about my reputation. Help me to have faith at this point too. Amen.

VICTORY THROUGH SUFFERING

Among God's churches we boast about your perseverance and faith in all the persecutions and trials you are enduring. All this is evidence that God's judgment is right, and as a result you will be counted worthy of the kingdom of God, for which you are suffering. (2 Thess. 1:4-5)

We come now to the question of pain and suffering. We will meet them on the pathway to victorious living; they may even be our constant companions on that way. The question is, What shall we do with them, and what will they do with us?

First of all, we must note that pain has probably saved the human race from physical extermination. Had there been no such thing as pain, we would probably have thrust our fingers into fire and let them be withered. If disease did not cause us pain, we would probably think little about it. Pain says, "Something is wrong—attend to it." This pain is a form of God's preventive grace, built into the structure of our physical life, to keep us from committing individual and collective suicide.

Nevertheless, there is much needless pain in the world—far beyond its biological uses in survival. We inflict it on ourselves and others needlessly. Much of this pain is curable and should be relieved by individual and collective action.

"Suffering" is a wider term. It may be caused by pain, but it has other and deeper causes. Suffering may be intensely mental and spiritual. Suffering too may be a part of God's preventive grace. It may be God's danger signal that something is wrong.

Our first step, then, is to look on pain and suffering not entirely as enemies. They may become our allies in gaining fuller life.

O Christ, we thank You that here at this place of pain and suffering You have an authentic word to speak to us. For You know. Amen.

ARE CHRISTIANS EXEMPT?

Dear friends, do not be surprised at the painful trial you are suffering, as though something strange were happening to you. But rejoice that you participate in the sufferings of Christ, so that you may be overjoyed when his glory is revealed…. If you suffer, it should not be as a murderer or thief or any other kind of criminal, or even as a meddler. However, if you suffer as a Christian, do not be ashamed, but praise God that you bear that name. (1 Peter 4:12-13, 15-16)

Pain and suffering are the common lot of all. That is the result of being surrounded by nature, by other human beings, and by our own physical bodies. The fact of our being Christians does not exempt us.

A young man was stunned by failing a major examination. "I cannot understand!" he cried. "I prayed very hard before the examination, and I lived a very good life. Then why did I not pass? My faith in God is gone." Well, if it could be proved that living a good life and praying hard would get us through examinations, our classrooms would be deserted the week before tests are given, and students would flock to the hillsides for prayer and meditation. In the process their minds would dry up. Mental suffering that comes from slovenliness in studying is one of God's methods of keeping the human race mentally alive. It is a hard spur, but it is redemptive.

I grant you that real Christians are exempt from sufferings that come from within, from their own wrong moral choices. This does save them from an enormous amount of suffering. But it does not save them from sufferings that come through nature, through other human beings, and through their physical bodies. Nor does it exempt them from the suffering that comes from the very fact that they are a new moral and spiritual alternative to the world. This itself brings suffering.

O Christ, You are our way out. Help us to learn Your secrets. Amen.

A QUESTION OF ATTITUDE

I consider that our present sufferings are not worth comparing with the glory that will be revealed in us. (Rom. 8:18)

The apostles left the Sanhedrin, rejoicing because they had been counted worthy of suffering disgrace for the Name. (Acts 5:41)

While suffering happens to us all, it does not have the same effect upon us all. It all depends upon inner attitudes. As someone has said, "What life does to us in the long run depends upon what life finds in us." Sorrow and suffering makes some people querulous and bitter; others it sweetens and refines. Same event, but with opposite effects.

There were three crosses that day on a Judean hill. The same event was happening to three people. But it had three different effects upon them. One thief complained and railed at Jesus for not saving them. Another saw this tragedy as a result of his sins, repented, and through it found an open door into paradise. The third, through that cross, redeemed a race. The same event, but with three entirely different results.

So what matters is not what happens to you, but what you do with it after it does happen to you. Your cross can become the bitterest of unrelieved agonies, or it may become to you the most blessed of unlimited opportunities. The same sunshine falling on two branches of a tree causes decay in one, growth in the other. It all depends on the responses the branches give. One meets the sunshine with inner life, and more life results. The other meets it with inner death, and more death results.

Suffering leaves some people writhing in helpless agony; others it leaves stronger and more capable of meeting more suffering, capable of meeting anything. It depends on inward response.

O Christ, give us such inner attitudes this day that we transmute the base metal of ordinary happenings into the gold of victorious living. Amen.

DO YOU KNOW WHAT TO DO WITH SUFFERING?

Saul began to destroy the church. Going from house to house, he dragged off men and women and put them in prison.

Those who had been scattered preached the word wherever they went. Philip went down to a city in Samaria and proclaimed the Christ there. When the crowds heard Philip and saw the miraculous signs he did, they all paid close attention.... So there was great joy in that city. (Acts 8:3-6, 8)

In my book *Christ and Human Suffering* I took the position that we are not to escape suffering, nor merely to bear it, but to use it. We can take it up into the purpose of our lives and make it contribute to the ends for which we really live. The raw materials of human life, the things that come on us day by day, can be woven into garments of character.

All of this depends on what inner attitudes we take. Two women in a certain city in India, both intelligent and refined, are suffering from practically the same illness. One is becoming bitter and querulous and hopeless, the other is becoming radiant. She will emerge from it pure gold. Her very attitudes are helping her, for nothing tones up the body as a peaceful, hopeful, victorious spirit. The other woman may not emerge, for she is handicapping herself by dragging her body down with her despairing spirit. One inner life is adjusted to the will of God, and the other is not. Same circumstances, two results.

Two families each lost an only son, one the family of a minister and the other an unbelieving family. A boy of twelve years said, "Mother, it isn't so hard on the minister and his wife, for they know what to do. But these other people don't know what to do." He had put his finger on the crux of the matter.

What are suffering Christians to do? They can say to themselves: "I cannot determine what happens to me, but I can determine what it will do to me after it does happen. It will make me a better person and more useful." That is victory.

O Christ, help me this day not to be determined by my circumstances, but to use them. Amen.

LETTING GOD GUIDE OUR PAIN

We are hard pressed on every side, but not crushed; perplexed, but not in despair; persecuted, but not abandoned; struck down, but not destroyed. We always carry around in our body the death of Jesus, so that the life of Jesus may also be revealed in our body. For we who are alive are always being given over to death for Jesus' sake, so that his life may be revealed in our mortal body. (2 Cor. 4:8-11)

The pain God is allowed to guide ends in a saving repentance never to be regretted, whereas the world's pain ends in death. (2 Cor. 7:10 MOFFATT)

The above translation by Moffatt shows that some pain leads to life and some leads to death. The difference is this: In one case a person keeps their pains in their own hands and deals with them on an entirely human level. This makes for bitterness, cynicism and complaints. On the other hand, a person takes God into the pains and allows Him to guide them. God then turns what would have been senseless suffering into a spiritual discipline. A better person emerges.

In every happening that comes to you, there is the potential for life or death. The common places of life make us common—or Christian! The wife of a rather imperious man called his attention to a wonderful sunset, where the sky was streaked with fleecy clouds. "Yes," he said. "It reminds me—I'd like to see my bacon streaked with more lean meat." He turned a radiant sunset into a reminder of bacon! That is how some people make the glorious into the commonplace, while other make the commonplace glorious.

Our pain may have come from some evil source, but the question is not where it came from, but where it is going! The future is determined by whether we allow it to be guided to life or guided to death—and that depends on whether we put God into the pain, offering it to Him as we offer everything else, and making it a part of His redemptive purpose for us. The cross of Jesus is an example of God-guided pain. It resulted in salvation. So may our crosses do the same.

O Christ, who turned Your cross into a throne, help me this day to wear my sorrows and sufferings with regal dignity. Amen.

LIFE ISN'T FAIR

"I have become a laughingstock to my friends, though I called upon God and he answered—a mere laughingstock, though righteous and blameless!" (Job 12:4)

Peter addressing a Jerusalem crowd: *"You disowned the Holy and Righteous One and asked that a murderer be released to you. You killed the author of life, but God raised him from the dead. We are witnesses of this." (Acts 3:14-15)*

--------------------------------- ✧ ---------------------------------

When our sufferings come from an evil source outside our own will, we reply, "This is unjust." Yes, it is. But you must not expect life to be fair. It isn't. Christianity never taught that it would be. On the contrary, it has a cross at its heart—and that is the world's supreme injustice. Don't ask for justice from life; ask for power to turn injustice into fuller life. Then you have life itself.

Life wasn't just to Paul. He found life coming to him in the form of imprisonments, beatings, desertions, anxiety, and care. But he made his life into something better than justice. "In all things God works for the good to those who love him," he declared (Rom. 8:28). The thing itself may not be good; it may have come from the very devil himself, but God throws in enough good to make it result in good. Like two cogwheels that work together, God actually uses evil for the destruction of evil. He uses devil-sourced evil for the making of God-inspired people. If you work together with God, you can turn your very defeats into victories. That is what the cross itself is.

I know an Indian Christian lady who has served others for many years, with a beautiful character—but now she is blind. Life wasn't fair to her. But she made it more than fair, she made it beautiful. "It's all dark," she said to me, "but then it's all very lovely," she added, thoughtfully, with a quiet smile. Don't offer that woman justice; she has grace, which is far more.

O Christ, to whom life was supremely unjust, make me to know Your secret this day so that I shall not whine for justice, but boldly turn the worst into the best. Amen.

SEIZING FATE BY THE THROAT

The crowd joined in the attack against Paul and Silas, and the magistrates ordered them to be stripped and beaten. After they had been severely flogged, they were thrown into prison, and the jailer was commanded to guard them carefully. Upon receiving such orders, he put them in the inner cell and fastened their feet in the stocks.

About midnight Paul and Silas were praying and singing hymns to God, and the other prisoners were listening to them. Suddenly there was such a violent earthquake that the foundations of the prison were shaken. At once all the prison doors flew open, and everybody's chains came loose. (Acts 16:22-26)

A certain doctor named Vail was performing more operations, I suppose, than any other man in India, among them thousands of cancer operations. And yet he himself developed cancer. Unfair! He flew to Germany for treatment. While not cured himself, he came back to India with a new treatment for cancer that will relieve thousands. He has now died, but we will always remember him for seizing fate by the throat!

So did Beethoven. He began going deaf in his late twenties and had lost everything by his late forties. "Oh, if I were only rid of this affliction, I could embrace the world." But says a biographer, "We are eternal debtors to his deafness. It is doubtful if such lofty music could have been created except as self-compensation for some affliction, and in the utter isolation which the affliction brought about."

The first Sunday school pupil I ever had became an engineer. An explosion left him totally deaf and totally blind. There is now no way to communicate with him, except to spell out the letters with your finger on the back of his hand. He is shut off from the world—but not at all! He has gained more information and knowledge through other people's fingertips and through his own inner meditations than 99 percent of those who have eyes and ears. Moreover, he has established a far-flung business for the blind.

O Christ, help me this day to seize fate by the throat and make it serve Your purposes and mine. Amen.

LIGHT FOR THE DARKEST PROBLEM

As he went along, he saw a man blind from birth. His disciples asked him, "Rabbi, who sinned, this man or his parents, that he was born blind?"

"Neither this man nor his parents sinned," said Jesus, "but this happened so that the work of God might be displayed in his life. As long as it is day, we must do the work of him who sent me. Night is coming, when no one can work. While I am in the world, I am the light of the world." (John 9:1-5)

Jesus said He was "the light of the world" on two different occasions. One was at the center of Jerusalem's power and influence (see John 7:12)—but the other was in connection with a destitute man born blind whom he met along the road. In response to the disciples' question, Jesus said this was clearly a case of unmerited suffering. In no way was it the man's fault.

The more I have listened to various proposals of philosophy and religion about this problem of unmerited suffering, the more I am convinced that Jesus is the light of the world at the place of the world's darkest problem. Marx said concerning the world as a whole, "Philosophers have explained the world; we must now change it." Christ, in substance, said that very thing, only in expanded terms: That philosophers have tried to explain it, or explain it away, but we must now change it into something else. We must use suffering for the very purpose of the kingdom of God. He then showed us what He meant by restoring the man's sight.

He turned every single adverse circumstance, every single injustice, every single disappointment, every single betrayal and desertion, every single cross into a contribution for the ends He had in view. To be able to use pain and sorrow—this is light. And the Man who can give us power to do this very thing is the light of the world.

O Christ, who spoke the word of light when life seemed dark and mysterious, help me this day to take that light and live by it, becoming light to others at this place of suffering. Amen.

WHEN LIFE SNUBS US

Now one of the Pharisees invited Jesus to have dinner with him, so he went to the Pharisee's house and reclined at the table. When a woman who had lived a sinful life in that town learned that Jesus was eating at the Pharisee's house, she brought an alabaster jar of perfume....

When the Pharisee who had invited him saw this, he said to himself, "If this man were a prophet, he would know who is touching him and what kind of woman she is—that she is a sinner."

Jesus answered him, "Simon, I have something to tell you."
(Luke 7:36-37, 39-40)

The world needs nothing so deeply as it needs two things: light on the mystery of life, and life for the mastery of life. Jesus gives both, for He was both.

A Pharisee had asked Him to dine with him, and then to show his own superiority and semi-contempt for this Man, he omitted all of the courtesies he would customarily give to a guest. He gave Him no kiss of greeting, no water for His feet, and no oil for His hair. It was a social snub.

Instead of resenting the man, something else happened. A poor, stricken sinful woman came to make up what the host had left undone. And never was there such courtesy—tears to wash His feet, her hair instead of a towel, and ointment for His head. All this came from the depths of the heart and not from mere custom.

The Pharisee hardened and inwardly criticized Him. Then Jesus assumed moral control of the situation. He pointed out the Pharisee's discourtesy, and then proceeded to bracket both him and the woman in the same category of needy sinners. Jesus, without the gifts that courtesy should have brought, turned and gave the gift of forgiveness. Instead of being a snubbed guest, He became the dispenser of a bounty. He did not endure that snub, He used it. No wonder the world sits at the feet of such moral mastery and learns how to live.

O Christ, when I am socially hurt and snubbed, help me not to be resentful and bitter, but big and forgiving, and through it to be masterful. Amen.

LET THE GLORY OUT!

Therefore we do not lose heart. Though outwardly we are wasting away, yet inwardly we are being renewed day by day. For our light and momentary troubles are achieving for us an eternal glory that far outweighs them all. (2 Cor. 4:16-17)

Hard circumstances often make people. Who has not seen a frail, clinging-vine type of woman, who upon the death of her husband straightens up and becomes oak, around which the growing children twine their lives, and are forever grateful for such a mother? But this strength would never have come out and developed had it not been for the tears that watered the vine and made it into an oak.

Says the famous poet Edwin Markham:

> *Defeat may serve as well as victory*
> *To shake the soul and let the glory out.*
> *When the great oak is straining in the wind,*
> *The boughs drink in new beauty, and the trunk*
> *Sends down a deeper root on the windward side.*
> *Only the soul that knows the mighty grief*
> *Can know the mighty rapture. Sorrows come*
> *To stretch our spaces in the heart of joy.*

Hudson Taylor was seated in a Chinese inn with a new missionary. He filled a glass full of water, then struck the table with his fist. As the water splashed out, he said, "You will be struck by the blows of many sorrows and troubles in China. But remember, they will only splash out of you what is in you." Out of some people come complaint and bitterness, but out of others joy and victory. Life brings out what is in you.

Will trouble in your life serve to shake the glory out? Then you have victory.

O Christ, I thank You that this is what trouble did to You. It shook You to death and scattered grace across the world. Help me this day to have such victory that trouble will only scatter peace and joy to those around me. Amen.

IS TROUBLE A PUNISHMENT FROM GOD?

Now there were some present at that time who told Jesus about the Galileans whose blood Pilate had mixed with their sacrifices. Jesus answered, "Do you think that these Galileans were worse sinners than all the other Galileans because they suffered this way? I tell you, no!" (Luke 13:1-3)

Though the fig tree does not bud and there are no grapes on the vines, though the olive crop fails and the fields produce no food, though there are no sheep in the pen and no cattle in the stalls, yet I will rejoice in the LORD, I will be joyful in God my Savior. (Hab. 3:17-18)

Many feel that when trouble comes, it is God's punishment upon them for some sin. This attitude makes victory impossible.

We must admit that this is a world of moral consequence, and that sin does bring trouble. But Jesus repudiated the idea that calamity and sin were always connected. In his comment on Pilate's atrocity against the worshipers who brought sacrifices, the victims were not worse than the rest, He said.

No, look upon trouble as opportunity for you to show what stuff is in you. An Indian proverb says, "The bursting of the petals says the flowers are coming." So when your heart bursts with pain and grief, it only means the flowers are about to come out. The heartbreak of Gethsemane was the bursting of the sheath that let the Passion Flower out. And the world is filled with its perfume.

As someone has said, "It is wonderful what God can do with a broken heart if He can get all the pieces." Let Him put your broken life together again, perhaps in a new glorious pattern. He had to break it to make it.

In the Mission Agricultural Farm at Allahabad they discovered that when the tops of the eggplants were frostbitten, the plants gave a second crop. Now, after the plants have given one crop, the workers cut them back so that they give a second. The cuts you receive from life may not be God's punishments, but instead God's prunings toward greater fruitfulness.

O Christ, we know that every branch in You that bears fruit receives a pruning in order to bear more fruit. Prune me this day, for I would be fruitful. Amen.

WHEN LIFE KNOCKS AWAY OUR CRUTCHES

Jesus to the disciples at the Last Supper: *"I tell you the truth: It is for your good that I am going away. Unless I go away, the Counselor will not come to you; but if I go, I will send him to you. When he comes, he will convict the world of guilt in regard to sin and righteousness and judgment." (John 16:7-8)*

A Christian lady who lives near where I am writing was afflicted for some years with spinal trouble and could not walk without crutches. One day as she was coming down the stairs, she slipped and fell to the bottom, her crutches being lost on the way. She lay there calling for help, but no one was near. With a great effort she pulled herself up by the banister, began to walk, and has been walking ever since—without the crutches! The fall was the best thing that ever happened to her.

There are many things in your life and mine upon which we lean heavily—family relationships, money, position. They may not be wrong, but they become crutches that weaken our moral fiber. We depend on them too much. Then calamity knocks them away. At first we are stunned and crushed. Our crutches are gone—what is left? Why, our feet, our own backbone, and the grace of God! That is enough upon which to begin life anew.

A famous physician lost everything in the San Francisco earthquake of 1906—his home, his hospital, his medical records, the very tools of his trade. He was left practically penniless. When a friend began to console him, he said: "Ah! It will be good fun to start all over again. I feel younger already, and now people will need a physician for their souls." The old routine was broken up; he started a new, wider one.

Do not weep over lost crutches. God wishes to make you strong. Your backbone has been weakened by too much dependence on the things of a material civilization. Stand up!

O God, help me not to whimper and whine, but to stand on my feet when You take away my crutches. Amen.

GOD'S INSULATIONS

We...rejoice in our sufferings, because we know that suffering produces perseverance; perseverance, character; and character, hope. And hope does not disappoint us, because God has poured out his love into our hearts by the Holy Spirit, whom he has given us. (Rom. 5:3-5)

Many of us try to meet pain and calamity in one of two ways: either by isolation, or by insulation.

Some try to win by flight. They lose their nerve and want to run away. A man said to me, "I am praying that either I shall die or my wife shall die." (I am not sure that he put himself first! Perhaps not.) "What else can I do?" he added. "For we cannot get along together." I told him I thought he was a moral coward, and that a Christian had another way out. I suggested that he might do what an oyster does when it gets an irritating grain of sand inside its shell—it grows a pearl around it. The oyster turns irritations into iridescence.

There are many people who turn their daily naggings into character, patience, and beauty. Having withstood that lesser thing in the home, they are ready for bigger troubles on the outside. They are insulated. Troubles become the process by which we put on insulations against greater troubles. It is nature hardening us for bigger strains.

Milo of Croton, the ancient Greek wrestler, is said to have wagered that he could lift a bull into the air. He bought a calf and lifted that, and each day as the calf grew bigger he lifted it, so that when it became a full-grown bull he could lift it even then. God increases our strength by helping us conquer our daily trials, until one day we shall lift more than a human load.

At one place in the process of making tin plates, the thin steel is put through a pickling bath to corrode it with acid, so it will take and retain the insulating tin bath that comes next. Without the corroding acid, the tin would not stick to the steel, and rust would set in. So God lets us go through acid sorrows, that we may hold the insulations of His grace, lest life rust and destroy us.

O God, if today some acid sorrow eats into me, help me to remember Your insulations and rejoice! Amen.

E. STANLEY JONES | 237

CHOOSE YOUR COLOR

Christ, to the church at Smyrna: *"I know your afflictions and your poverty—yet you are rich! I know the slander of those who say they are Jews and are not, but are a synagogue of Satan. Do not be afraid of what you are about to suffer. I tell you, the devil will put some of you in prison to test you, and you will suffer persecution for ten days. Be faithful, even to the point of death, and I will give you the crown of life." (Rev. 2:9-10)*

The God of all grace, who called you to his eternal glory in Christ, after you have suffered a little while, will himself restore you and make you strong, firm and steadfast. (1 Peter 5:10)

"Affliction does so color life," said a sympathizing friend. "Yes," said the sufferer, "and I propose to choose the color."

I once went to see an invalid who had been on her bed for 50 straight years. Struck by a lightning flash during young womanhood, she was left paralyzed. No, she wasn't paralyzed—only her body was. That room had become the center of spiritual power in that city. I had never seen a more beautiful face chiseled into beauty and dignity. She was choosing the color.

Father Damien de Veuster, living among his lepers in Hawaii, stood up one day to address them and began, "We lepers." This was his announcement that he too had contracted leprosy. But it made no difference. He went straight on and went deeper. He too was choosing the colors!

A Muslim teacher wrote me of the loss of his son, and also of his decision to become a Christian. "I was standing at the door, and God pushed me in." Affliction might have pushed him in or out. He decided to go in. He chose the color.

O God, we will fight alongside of You to take away suffering, for it is not Your will; but where we cannot banish it, help us to use it. Amen.

TIME OUT

Paul: *It pleased [God] to reveal his Son to me so that I would proclaim the Good News about Jesus to the Gentiles. When this happened, I did not rush out to consult with any human being. Nor did I go up to Jerusalem to consult with those who were apostles before I was. Instead, I went away into Arabia, and later I returned to the city of Damascus.*

Then three years later I went to Jerusalem to get to know Peter, and I stayed with him for fifteen days. (Gal. 1:15-18†)

Beyond our discussion of pain and suffering, there are other troubles that arise out of being laid aside, rendered inactive, shelved. Some of these come from temporary indispositions, some through unemployment, and some through approaching old age. In all of these, our tasks are suspended, and we have to face life inactive. This is sometimes harder to handle than positive suffering.

Someone has said that in the field of music, "pauses are music in the making." There is a momentary suspense only to produce music more lovely than before. The pause prepares everyone for the finer music.

Is it possible that these pauses in our lives—these suspensions from activity—may become music in the making? I grant that continued unemployment of healthy, active persons may and does cause deterioration. The only remedy for them is employment, and society must provide it, or it isn't worthy of the name "society." But apart from this extreme case, cannot the temporary periods of being laid aside, or of being blocked from our real lifework, be made into periods that bear future benefit?

It was so in the life of Jesus. The call to give His message must have burned in His soul like fire during those silent years at Nazareth, making oxen yokes as a carpenter when He was commissioned to strike off the yoke of sin and misery from the world's neck! But He did not chafe. He could wait—yes, for thirty long years. So it may be in your life and mine.

O Christ, make me patient under restriction, that I may be richer under release. Help me not to chafe, but trust. Amen.

INTERRUPTIONS FOR GOOD

Because so many people were coming and going that they did not even have a chance to eat, he said to them, "Come with me by yourselves to a quiet place and get some rest."

So they went away by themselves in a boat to a solitary place. But many who saw them leaving recognized them and ran on foot from all the towns and got there ahead of them. When Jesus landed and saw a large crowd, he had compassion on them, because they were like sheep without a shepherd. So he began teaching them many things. (Mark 6:31-34)

Young people often chafe under the years of disciplined schooling. Many throw away the opportunity for study, and it never returns. They wear a lifelong regret within the heart.

Perhaps one of the most distressing pauses we have to meet are interruptions during the day. We plan our work, and then people upset those plans—and us. We say our work is spoiled.

But it may be that those very interruptions *are* our work. Jesus made them so. Some of His finest teaching, His finest deeds, the revelation of His finest spirit came out of some person or some circumstance upsetting His plans. These interruptions did not upset His plans, they only sent His grace off at new angles. He looked upon them as God thrusting human need across His path.

When the crowd followed Jesus and His disciples to a desert place, "he welcomed them and spoke to them about the kingdom of God, and healed those who needed healing" (Luke 9:11). After that, He fed the multitude. He taught, healed, and fed the breakers of His plans and interrupters of His quiet!

Those three words, "He welcomed them," are worth to us more than multitudes of books on patience and love. They throw open a window into the heart of goodness.

O Christ, this day I will meet with many interruptions, sometimes by very trying people. Help me to make those very interruptions into a revelation of Your Spirit within me. Amen.

THE FINAL PAUSE

Paul: *For to me, to live is Christ and to die is gain. If I am to go on living in the body, this will mean fruitful labor for me. Yet what shall I choose? I do not know! I am torn between the two: I desire to depart and be with Christ, which is better by far; but it is more necessary for you that I remain in the body. (Phil. 1:21-24)*

None of these pauses we have mentioned can be compared with the solemn pause of death. Our work is stopped, our plans are broken off, our ties with others are snapped. This is the most devastating pause of all.

But is it? It may be the pause that turns out to be only life's gladdest music in the making.

It was so with Alice Means, one of the rarest missionaries we have ever had in India. What an amazing life she was living—building, teaching, making leaders! And then cancer struck her. She thought she might get to America before she died, but was stopped in Bombay by the doctors, knowing she would never complete the voyage. She wrote me a letter from the Bombay hospital: "Use me as an illustration in your book. I haven't suffered much yet, and when I do, I may not be able to tell you how it goes. How thankful I am for all these years of perfect, abounding health! What a happy life I have had!"

She then went on to tell of a vision she had received. She was working in a large field with her head down and didn't notice she had reached the edge. Then a Voice said, "'Alice, that's enough; come over here and sit down a bit.' I looked up and there stood Jesus smiling at me. I went over and sat down on the grass by Him. He said, 'You have been busy working and have not had time for all those intimacies that go with a great friendship, such as I want with you. Come along and let us walk together here.' "

Who can say that this pause of death to her was not music in the making?

O Christ, we know that even death is but a transition to greater music. Help us to welcome it with joy. Amen.

THE MOST FRUITFUL PAUSE

*I call to God, and the L*ORD *saves me. Evening, morning and noon I cry out in distress, and he hears my voice. (Psalm 55:16-17)*

Jesus told his disciples a parable to show them that they should always pray and not give up. (Luke 18:1)

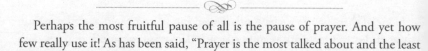

Perhaps the most fruitful pause of all is the pause of prayer. And yet how few really use it! As has been said, "Prayer is the most talked about and the least used force in the world."

By using prayer, I do not mean gaining a benefit from the reflex influence of quiet thought and meditation. I mean something more. I mean that my lesser spirit can come into intimate, personal contact with the Spirit called God, that I can come to a common understanding with Him, can adjust my will to His will, and through the contact can find my personality heightened, enlightened, reinforced, used. Is this only a reflex influence? Humbly I say it, I know better! Experience shows that those who think of prayer as only a reflex influence soon give it up.

Is it possible for God to respond by putting a thought into the heart of one who prays? Of course; He has instilled His very life! He can reinforce the very foundations of a person's being in that way. Life flows into life, Will into will, Love into love—that is what prayer means. It all comes when we are attuned, and prayer attunes us to the Eternal God.

I have gone to my knees broken, all in, defeated, and have arisen reinforced, new, and victorious. Everything within me said I had met God. And I had.

O Christ, use this pause of prayer today as a working way for me to live. Amen.

WHAT PRAYER IS NOT

Delight yourself in the LORD and he will give you the desires of your heart. Commit your way to the LORD; trust in him and he will do this. (Psalm 37:4-5)

This is the confidence we have in approaching God: that if we ask anything according to his will, he hears us. And if we know that he hears us—whatever we ask—we know that we have what we asked of him. (1 John 5:14-15)

Let us get rid of certain notions about prayer. Prayer is not a lightning rod to save us from the lightnings of God's wrath. Many think if they don't pray, something bad will happen to them. "We don't have prayer or grace in our house, and nothing has happened yet," said a little girl in awed tones. No, dear, nothing has happened yet—except deterioration. But that's enough. Prayerlessness means slow rot, not sudden calamity.

Again, prayer is not bending God to our wills. It is bringing our wills to God's. When we throw out a boat hook and catch hold of the shore, do we pull the shore to ourselves? No, we pull ourselves to the shore. Prayer does not pull God to us, it pulls us to God. It aligns our wills with His will, so that He can do things through us that He would not otherwise have been able to do. An almighty Will works through our weak wills, and we can do things all out of proportion to our ability.

Prayer is, therefore, not overcoming God's reluctance; it is laying hold of His highest willingness. Those who pray link up with that willingness. If God has left certain things open in the universe around us, waiting on the contingency of our human will—i.e., things that will not be done unless we act—is it strange that He has left certain things contingent upon prayer—things that will never be done unless we pray about them?

In real prayer our will coincides with His. That is what we mean when we pray "in Jesus' name"—that is, we pray the kind of prayer He would pray. If we pray outside of His will, we have basically used His name in a forgery.

O God, help me this day to make my will coincide with Yours, so that Your power may coincide with mine. Amen.

MORE THAN PENNIES FROM HEAVEN

Be always on the watch, and pray that you may be able to escape all that is about to happen, and that you may be able to stand before the Son of Man. (Luke 21:36)

Pray in the Spirit on all occasions with all kinds of prayers and requests. With this in mind, be alert and always keep on praying for all the saints.

Pray also for me, that whenever I open my mouth, words may be given me so that I will fearlessly make known the mystery of the gospel, for which I am an ambassador in chains. Pray that I may declare it fearlessly, as I should. (Eph. 6:18-20)

When praying, I seldom ask for things; more and more I ask God for Himself, for the assurance that my will and His are not at cross-purposes, that we are agreed on all major and minor matters. If this is so, then I shall get all the things I need. If I seek first the kingdom of God, then all these things will be added unto me, as Matthew 6:33 says.

God is interested in things. But I do not want the reality of prayer to depend on whether I get this thing or that thing. If I get Him in loving communion, then the prayer is answered and is effective. Things are a side issue.

With many Christians, however, they are central, like the little boy who said to me: "I love my daddy. He gives me pennies every day." Penny-praying, like penny-loving, belongs to immature childhood.

Prayer is the power to get through difficulties, to be at your best, to become effective. Through prayer one can cross uncrossable rivers, scale impassable mountains, and do impossible things. God the Eternal works with us and in us. To those who think prayer is a religious obligation, I say prayer is the kind of burden that sails are to a ship, and wings to a bird. If you want to live victoriously, you will run in the direction of prayer.

O Christ, when You prayed, powerful things ensued. Let the same be true for me this day. Amen.

MAKING PRAYER TIME EFFECTIVE

Who may ascend the hill of the Lord? Who may stand in his holy place? He who has clean hands and a pure heart, who does not lift up his soul to an idol or swear by what is false. He will receive blessing from the Lord and vindication from God his Savior. (Psalm 24:3-5)

To make the time of prayer effective:

First of all, sacredly keep it. Build the habits of your life around that hour. Make things fit into it, not it into things. Anyone who, neglecting the fixed hour of prayer, says they can pray all the time will probably end in praying none of the time. But if you do keep the fixed hour, it will probably project its spirit through the whole day.

In the beginning of the prayer hour, be silent. Let your mind relax, and let it roam across your life to see whether it stops at anything wrong. If so, tell God you will correct it. Let the first moment be a sincere moral search. If nothing is shown to be wrong, then you are ready for bold praying.

Immerse your thought in His Word. It will wash the dust from your eyes, so you can see with insight. You will get right attitudes through the Word, so you will pray right prayers. You are pulling your thought up alongside His thought, your purposes up to His purposes.

Take a pen or pencil and write down what comes to you as you pore over His Word. That pen is the sign of your faith that something will come. And it will. Don't hurry. Every word is precious. Pause, assimilate. When a person hurries through a forest, they see few birds or animals. But if the person sits down and waits, the animals come out of hiding. It will be so with you. "Prayer is a time exposure photo of the soul to God." Expose your inmost being to His Word.

Take obedience with you into this hour, for you will know only as much of God as you are willing to put into practice. In fact, God will answer many of your prayers *through you.*

O Christ, help me make this hour of prayer effective, that I may make the whole of today effective. Amen.

THE TWO SIDES OF PRAYER

As [the two disciples] talked and discussed these things with each other, Jesus himself came up and walked along with them....

[Later:] *They asked each other, "Were not our hearts burning within us while he talked with us on the road and opened the Scriptures to us?" (Luke 24:15, 32)*

Prayer seems many-sided, but really there are only two sides—communion and commission. The rest are phases of these two. These are the two heartbeats of the prayer life, and a heart has to keep beating in two directions, or death ensues.

First, there is communion. As I have looked at freshly tapped rubber trees, with the cup nestling up against the wound and taking the sap from the heart of the tree, I have thought of prayer. We press our empty lives up against the wounds of the Eternal God and take from Him life and power. Every day, let me nestle up against His wounded side, for I am empty without it.

Then comes commission. Every day, let my cup be emptied in loving help to others.

In the call of the disciples there were three things: "He appointed twelve... (1) that they might be with him (2) and that he might send them out to preach (3) and to have authority to drive out demons" (Mark 3:14-15). First was the call to be with Him—hold that intact, and everything else follows. Anyone who neglects communion will find the last two fading out.

But also, if you neglect commission, the first and the last will die. And moral authority—the third part—depends upon the other two. Dim either the communion or the commission, and moral authority will dim.

Empty prayer closet, empty heart, empty hands—this is the spiritual history of many. In contrast, Jesus "often withdrew to lonely places and prayed.... And the power of the Lord was present for him to heal the sick" (Luke 5:16-17). Cause and effect.

O Christ, who by Your example showed us the Source of power, give to us the will to tap that power and to channel it to other lives. Amen.

DOES GOD GUIDE OUR LIVES?

Since you are my rock and my fortress, for the sake of your name lead and guide me. (Psalm 31:3)

You guide me with your counsel, and afterward you will take me into glory. (Psalm 73:24)

The LORD will guide you always; he will satisfy your needs in a sun-scorched land and will strengthen your frame. You will be like a well-watered garden, like a spring whose waters never fail. (Isa. 58:11)

Out of communion, commission follows. In communion, you feel the hand of God upon your life guiding you to do certain things.

We have organized our religious lives around certain services in the church, one on Sunday, one on Wednesday, and so on. If we attend these services, we think we are very good, faithful Christians.

But between these services are great gaps where God functions very feebly or not at all. Guidance fills up these gaps, making us responsible to God every moment. He is no longer in the crevasses of life. He is in the very fiber of the whole structure.

Guidance, therefore, brings God in from the occasional to the continuous. Every Christian should live a God-guided life. For if God is, He should be in everything that concerns us—directing, controlling, inspiring. The Christian who doesn't know this sense of guidance is missing something vital.

Mind you, if you are not guided by God, you are guided by something else. Perhaps yourself. But we all know that to be self-managed is to be self-damaged. We are not good enough and we don't know enough to guide our lives. God must guide us.

O God, help me to discern Your touch upon my life and to obey it. Amen.

HOW DOES GOD GUIDE US?

I want you to know, my dear brothers and sisters, that everything that has happened to me here has helped to spread the Good News. For everyone here, including the whole palace guard, knows that I am in chains because of Christ. (Phil. 1:12-13†)

God guides us in not just one way, but many. We shall consider them one by one.

Sometimes He guides by circumstances—or shall we call them providences? Just when we are in perplexity, something opens before us, perhaps unexpectedly. We walk through that open door and find it to be God's way. Or He may close something before us, and that proves to be God's preventive guidance.

Many a time God lets us fail in a secondary thing in order that we may succeed in a primary thing. For many people are ruined by secondary successes. They get tangled up in them and never get to the really worthwhile things. I am sure God prevented me from becoming fond of game-hunting in India. As a young missionary, I found my area filled with blackbuck, the Indian antelope with long spiral horns. What's more natural than to take a gun along while visiting villages for evangelistic purposes? I shot eighteen times at them and never hit one!

Did that mean I was a bad marksman? No, as a young man I was the best marksman in our crowd. But I had the feeling that God was making me miss. So I took the gun home and sold it, concluding that God had not called me to be a hunter, but an evangelist.

Many a woman, finding she has beauty, soon finds she has nothing else. The secondary success of beauty makes her neglect the primary assets of intelligence, soul, and usefulness. God's preventive grace can save us at such points. He shuts lesser doors to open bigger ones.

O God, sometimes You send hard refusals and sometimes You open doors. Help us to see You in both—to accept the first without murmuring, the second without hesitation. Amen.

GUIDANCE THROUGH ENLIGHTENED INTELLIGENCE

Reflect on what I am saying, for the Lord will give you insight into all this. (2 Tim. 2:7)

--------------------------------- ⨋ ---------------------------------

The development of Christian discernment is a necessary part of Christian development. Hebrews 5:14 says, "But solid food is for adults—that is, for those who through constant practice have their spiritual faculties carefully trained to distinguish good from evil" (WEYMOUTH).

God wants you to "love the Lord your God with...all your mind" (Matt. 22:37). Any guidance method that neglects the mind is, to that degree, not Christian. For the whole person is to be perfected. God's problem is how to guide us but not override us. In guidance He must not merely make us do certain things; He must also make us free, upstanding, and discerning. I question any approach to guidance that insists only or largely on the blank-sheet method, where God is to write down, as it were, what He wants us to do.

Now, I believe God does guide us by the Inner Voice. But to make that practically the only method, depending on that Inner Voice to dictate the minute details of our lives, would be to weaken us. Suppose a father or mother should undertake to dictate the smallest things in a child's life, asking only for implicit obedience, leaving little room for intelligent weighing of moral issues and free decision. Would that be guiding or overriding? Wouldn't the child's personality remain undeveloped?

Furthermore, if we ask for dictated guidance in every little thing, we shall be tempted to manufacture it if we don't get it. This makes for unreality.

No, we must not take one method alone and exclude others. God will guide our mental processes if we are inwardly honest with ourselves and all the facts.

O Christ, we need the impact of Your mind upon our minds, for without it our minds are confused and perplexed. Help us to obey our highest light. Amen.

GUIDANCE THROUGH OTHER PEOPLE

The LORD called Samuel a third time, and Samuel got up and went to Eli and said, "Here I am; you called me." Then Eli realized that the LORD was calling the boy. So Eli told Samuel, "Go and lie down, and if he calls you, say, 'Speak, LORD, for your servant is listening.' " (1 Sam. 3:8-9)

Sometimes God guides us through the written or spoken word of others. Some passage in a book becomes luminous, speaking directly to our need. It is the very voice of God to us. Some word in a sermon seems to be more than the word of the speaker—it is God speaking. Or it may be a quiet word with a friend that opens the door to the solution of the problem, or relief from a grief.

Everyone should have such a friend, a confidant—someone to whom you can open your heart to the depths, so that he or she really knows you for all you are; someone with whom you can share your deepest perplexity. As the old saying goes, "a grief shared is a grief halved."

What is a friend for except to share our problems and our sins as well as our joy and our goodness? The friend, detached from your inner emotions, may see the thing in just the way necessary to give needed light.

But even your friend's word must be tested by the other tests of guidance. Don't depend on it too implicitly. A student once asked me if I thought she should marry either of two men. I told her I didn't think she should. "Thank you," she said, "that settles it. I told God last night that I would take your voice for His voice." I was right in my advice to her, for both men were questionable, but she was wrong in taking my word too implicitly and blindly.

Take the word of the friend, but make your decision in quietness before God.

O Christ, who yearned for a human friend in the hour of Gethsemane's darkness but did not find one, help me to find such a friend. For I shall need it. Amen.

GUIDANCE THROUGH A GROUP

In the church at Antioch there were prophets and teachers.... While they were worshiping the Lord and fasting, the Holy Spirit said, "Set apart for me Barnabas and Saul for the work to which I have called them." So after they had fasted and prayed, they placed their hands on them and sent them off. (Acts 13:1-3)

Many small-group movements with varying emphases have sprung up throughout the world, including the Christian ashram movement in India. I cannot help but feel that God's Spirit has been raising up these groups to meet particular needs. Not that I think any one of them has the complete truth, but each does seem to have some particular phase of truth partly neglected by others. The difficulty comes if a group becomes exclusive and self-righteous.

God is speaking to this generation through groups. He spoke to the first generation this way. The fact is that Jesus formed a group movement when He and His disciples fellowshiped and worked together. It was out of that fellowship that the New Testament came. The play of mind upon mind, of attitude upon attitude, of method upon method, of life upon life brought out a body of common ideas and attitudes. These became the New Testament. Individual writers wrote them down, but the Christian groups produced them in their interaction with the Spirit of God and with each other.

When the apostles and elders wrote, "It seemed good to the Holy Spirit and to us" (Acts 15:28), they could have said it not merely about that particular decision, but in reference to the whole body of truth and attitude that was growing up. The group had become not merely a collection of people, but an organism of the Holy Spirit. He was expressing His mind and redemptive purposes through that group.

Today God still guides the individual through such closely-knit fellowships. Each individual needs the correction and sustenance of some such group. The group checks up and tends to keep individual guidance from going astray.

O Christ, touch me through my fellow believers, and help me to discern Your voice when You speak through their voice. Amen.

GUIDANCE THROUGH THE INNER VOICE

When he, the Spirit of truth, comes, he will guide you into all truth. He will not speak on his own; he will speak only what he hears, and he will tell you what is yet to come. (John 16:13)

When they [Paul and his group] came to the border of Mysia, they tried to enter Bithynia, but the Spirit of Jesus would not allow them to. So they passed by Mysia and went down to Troas. (Acts 16:7-8)

By the "Inner Voice" I do not mean the voice of conscience, for the Inner Voice gives guidance beyond matters of right and wrong. It speaks where one is making life directions, deciding perplexities, and evaluating the call to take up tasks and responsibilities. The Inner Voice is not contradictory to an enlightened conscience, but is in addition to it and beyond it. It is the Spirit of God speaking to a person directly and authentically.

When we turn to the early records of the Christian movement (the New Testament), we find guidance moving gradually from the external to the internal. The Gospels open with dreams and visions and the voices of angels, as in the cases of Zechariah and Joseph. With Jesus it was different: He got His guidance through prayer and the direct voice of the Spirit within. In the beginning of the Acts of the Apostles we find the disciples fumbling badly, casting lots as to which one would become a disciple in place of Judas, and giving God the choice between only two at that! How often we narrow God's choices for Him. God didn't want either of them—He wanted Paul.

But they did not repeat this initial mistake of depending on outer signs. The guidance became more and more inward. Not entirely, but the tendency was distinctly there. This led toward deeper Christianizing, for the gospel produces a person who is not compelled by an external sign, but impelled by an internal Spirit. The Holy Spirit and our spirit work harmoniously and therefore effectively.

O Christ, who so lived that the Father's gentlest whisper was like thunder to You, help us to have that same responsiveness this day, and all the days. Amen.

GUIDANCE THEN AND NOW

If you are pleased with me, teach me your ways so I may know you and continue to find favor with you. Remember that this nation is your people." The LORD replied, "My Presence will go with you, and I will give you rest." Then Moses said to him, "If your Presence does not go with us, do not send us up from here." (Exod. 33:13-15)

Whether you turn to the right or to the left, your ears will hear a voice behind you, saying, "This is the way; walk in it." (Isa. 30:21)

It is good, as in Acts, to become less dependent on outer signs and more upon the gentle pressures of the Spirit within. A personality should be produced that naturally and normally takes the Christian attitude from within, just as a well-trained horse doesn't need flogging; the slightest nudge will do.

The Book of Acts shows us methods of guidance other than the direct voice of the Spirit. There was the *exercise of Christian common sense:* "It does not seem fitting…" (6:2 WEYMOUTH). They were led by *facts:* "When they heard this…" (11:18). They came to *group conclusions by vote:* "In every Church, after prayer and fasting, they selected Elders by a show of hands" (14:23 WEYMOUTH). They employed the *exercise of thought:* "While Peter was still thinking about the vision, the Spirit said to him…" (10:19). God guide us in many ways, not one way only.

In the passage quoted yesterday about Paul and his group, the Holy Spirit was called "the Spirit of Jesus." Apparently, the universalized Jesus and the Holy Spirit were one; the accents of the mind of Jesus were heard in the voice of the Holy Spirit; the Holy Spirit was acting as Jesus would act.

This gives a key by which we can discern the Voice of the Spirit: Does that Voice sound like what we have seen in Christ? If so, I accept it. If not, I question it.

O Christ, we thank You that we can belong to the sheep that hear Your voice and know it and follow it. Help us to be quick to catch Your accents this day. Amen.

TWO NECESSARY RAILS

Jesus replied, "Are you not in error because you do not know the Scriptures or the power of God?" (Mark 12:24)

The Counselor, the Holy Spirit, whom the Father will send in my name, will teach you all things and will remind you of everything I have said to you. (John 14:26)

The key to discerning the Voice of the Spirit is this: Does that Voice match the revelation in Jesus? If so, it is authentic; if not, we should question it.

For instance, when Peter said in telling about the messengers from Cornelius, a Gentile, "The Spirit bade me go with them, making no distinction" (Acts 11:12 ASV), I feel this was an authentic voice of the Spirit, for this is just what we see revealed in Christ—a mind that made no distinction between one group and another. But if Peter, when he pulled back in Antioch and refused to eat with Gentiles (see Gal. 2:11-21), had said, "The Spirit bade me make that distinction," we would have said: "Peter, you are wrong. That was not the voice of the Spirit. It was the voice of prejudice. Your wires are crossed."

Jesus gave a penetrating word to a group of Sadducees trying to trick him; he said they were in double error—ignorance of the Scriptures, and also of the power of God. The way for us to keep from erring is to know those two things: the Scriptures (the past revelations) and the power of God (His present continuous activity). Some people know only the Scriptures—they do not link themselves with the creative activity of God here and now. Others know only the power of God now—they do not know in any real sense the Scriptures.

No one will go astray who is in constant fellowship with the power of God now working, and who constantly tests that working against the revelation through the historic Jesus. Revelation producing experience, and experience inspired and checked by revelation—these are the two rails that keep life on track. Take off one rail or the other, and we land in the ditch.

O Christ, help us to know You in history and in ourselves, and help us to find no difference. Amen.

GUIDANCE OUTSIDE THE LINES

I will lead the blind by ways they have not known, along unfamiliar paths I will guide them; I will turn the darkness into light before them and make the rough places smooth. These are the things I will do; I will not forsake them. (Isa. 42:16)

The LORD had said to Abram, "Leave your country, your people and your father's household and go to the land I will show you." (Gen. 12:1)

We also need to remind ourselves that guidance may be narrowed, or even controlled, by the framework of society in which we find ourselves. The guidance often seems to conform to our established order.

One of the things that makes me feel the guidance in the Book of Acts was authentic is that it did *not* conform to the established order. In a framework of Jewish exclusiveness, they broke out and founded a fellowship beyond race and class. In a competitive order they founded a society based on cooperation, economic sharing, and equality. They broke the patterns of their society and formed new ones.

Now, much of our guidance today doesn't do that. It conforms to the pattern of society in which we live. Why aren't more people now guided not merely to modify the present order but to change its very foundations? One would think that would be the normal Christian happening.

A lady, with fingers full of sparkling diamonds, told how she was guided to pay back two-penny worth of stuff that did not belong to her. The reason she was sensitive at that point was that she belonged to a society built around the sacredness of property; therefore, stealing was very wrong. But she apparently had no guidance about sharing the worth of her useless diamonds with the poor and underfed around her. For she belonged to a class that tacitly approved of these economic disparities. She got her guidance within the framework of her class. It, therefore, was only faintly Christian. It was not insincere—but it was limited.

O Christ, open my eyes to my narrowing framework, and help me to catch the breadth of Your mind. Amen.

THE INNER VOICE IS DEPENDABLE

The man who enters by the gate is the shepherd of his sheep. The watchman opens the gate for him, and the sheep listen to his voice. He calls his own sheep by name and leads them out. When he has brought out all his own, he goes on ahead of them, and his sheep follow him because they know his voice. (John 10:2-4)

Sometimes our guidance will be like the voice to Philip, "Go south to the road—the desert road—that goes down from Jerusalem to Gaza" (Acts 8:26). God often sends us seemingly into a desert. But if He guides us there, He works at the other end so that we meet someone there who needs us.

As I look back across the years, I am impressed that whenever I have sincerely listened to and followed that Voice, it has never let me down. It has always proved right. Whenever I have doubted it and followed the voice of my own desires, my choice has always proved wrong. Not that the Voice is always against my desires—God's will is not always unpleasant. But whether across the desires or with them, the Voice has always proven right.

Take one instance out of many: I lost my only pair of glasses on a mountainside in India. I tried to find them that night but couldn't. The Voice was unmistakable: "It's all right. Don't worry, you will find them." I arose at dawn to search before anyone else came out. No glasses. The search went on till well into the day. I was helpless without my glasses. I said, "Well, I must be mistaken about the Voice." So I started toward the city to order another pair.

Noticing my shoestring untied, I put my foot on the railing of a fence to tie it. Looking past my foot and down into the gully ten feet below—there were my glasses! Coincidence? Perhaps. But you cannot convince me that my Father, seeing I needed the glasses, did not help me find them.

If His care extends to the little, why not to the big? Both the sparrow and the star are in His care—and so am I, and you.

O Father, I thank You that You have never let me down. Help me not to let You down. Amen.

You found my contact lens in the grass and umbrella tree!

GUIDANCE IN SPARE MOMENTS

Who among you fears the LORD and obeys the word of his servant? Let him who walks in the dark, who has no light, trust in the name of the LORD and rely on his God. (Isa. 50:10)

Several times the Scriptures tells about Abraham "standing before the LORD" (Gen. 18:22, among others). This models for us the need for prayer, standing at attention before God to get His orders for the day. You may not get any suggestions then. If you don't, that means you should carry on as you have been.

But in regard to an important decision, if you are uncertain—don't. Wait till the guidance is clear. Don't act on half-light.

Have particular times to wait for guidance, and fill in the gaps of life with spare-moment praying. Peter got the vision that changed his whole life while he was waiting for lunch to be prepared (Acts 10). There on a rooftop he saw the essential unity of the human race, acted on it, and was forever changed. The difference in the spiritual lives of many people is what they do with the spare moment. Some waste it—and themselves with it. Others gather it up and make it contribute.

It was through a spare-moment prayer that I became a missionary. In college I had to give a talk on missions. I became burdened for something to actually happen that night; this should be more than just a speech. I had a few moments before the meeting began, so I stepped into a side room and prayed, "O God, give me a missionary as a result of this meeting. I'll not go in until I am assured that someone will actually respond." The answer came, "According to your faith be it unto you."

I went into that room with an inner assurance. I gave my remarks. It turned out that I was the one gripped; I myself was the missionary! I had prayed myself into it.

Pray, and then put yourself in place to be guided to answer that prayer.

O Christ, help me to have my heart open every moment, for I must be Your minuteman, ready at any time to do Your bidding. Amen.

A STAINLESS COMMISSION

In the presence of God who is the Life of all, and of Christ Jesus who testified to the good confession before Pontius Pilate, I charge you to keep your commission free from stain, free from reproach, till the appearance of our Lord Jesus Christ. (1 Tim. 6:13-14 MOFFATT)

As you listen during prayer, you will get your commission. And when you get that commission, keep it free from stain. In the above Scripture, Paul was writing to a young man; what stain did he have in mind? The stain of emptiness.

Here, he says, is this Life of God throbbing in every fiber of the universe. In light of that fact, keep from staining what He asks you to do. If God commissions you, if He guides you to take up a task however small or large, He will provide resources. Commission and equipment go together. If God commissions you to speak to a person, or to fight for social justice, He will equip you for that work.

Don't be like this nearby bird that is now calling out in wild notes, so the Indians say, *"Pilao, pilao"* ("Give me a drink"), when water is right here in Sat Tal (Seven Lakes), and the bird could have all it wants! Don't cry to God for spiritual equipment. Take it. Emptiness is now sin, for fullness is now your privilege.

Keep saying to yourself, "I can do anything I ought to do through Him who strengthens me." You will be astonished at your ability. Nothing can make you afraid—nothing. God is your life, and God is your life-equipment.

O God, who is the life of my very life, help me to keep the channels open, that this Life may not only be present but operative. Amen.

THE STAIN OF PARTIAL COMPLETION

My righteous one will live by faith. And if he shrinks back, I will not be pleased with him. (Heb. 10:38)

We…[keep] our eyes on Jesus, the champion who initiates and perfects our faith. Because of the joy awaiting him, he endured the cross, disregarding its shame. Now he is seated in the place of honor beside God's throne. Think of all the hostility he endured from sinful people; then you won't become weary and give up. (Heb. 12:2-3†)

Jesus witnessed His conviction before Pontius Pilate, though witnessing meant a cross. His commission included orders to push all the way through, and that is what He did. These were no half-way completions, no feints at doing it and then pulling back. He put His commission into the concrete.

Carrying out the will of God is not always a pleasant thing in a tangled world like this. Our friends will misunderstand us and pull away, and we shall be left to witness our confession alone. So be it. We must ask for strong inner fiber to be able to endure and to see the thing through.

During the French Revolution, one prominent man wrote to another: "There is a terrific struggle going on here. Our heads are in danger. Come and offer yours." The man did. If people can do that when a friend and a cause call, why cannot we do it for a Friend and a Cause?

We will be tempted to compromise and call it a day just short of putting our commission into operation. That would make us compromised Christians—refusers of the cross.

To try to put justice at the heart of human society will cause a cross. So we may decide that our commission reads only to change *individuals*, and leave it at that, side-stepping our witness before Pontius Pilate. Jesus did not. He declared His kingship to His individual disciples; He also declared it before the Roman Empire's governor and said He was King there too, in the corporate relationships of society. That cost Him a cross. But He still said it.

O Christ, I thank You that nowhere did You pull back. Help me to imitate You. Amen.

FREE TO FOLLOW THROUGH

Stephen, a man full of God's grace and power, did great wonders and miraculous signs among the people. Opposition arose, however, from members of the Synagogue of the Freedmen (as it was called)—Jews of Cyrene and Alexandria as well as the provinces of Cilicia and Asia. These men began to argue with Stephen, but they could not stand up against his wisdom or the Spirit by whom he spoke. (Acts 6:8-10)

It is for freedom that Christ has set us free. Stand firm, then, and do not let yourselves be burdened again by a yoke of slavery. (Gal. 5:1)

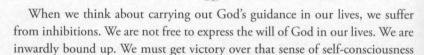

When we think about carrying out God's guidance in our lives, we suffer from inhibitions. We are not free to express the will of God in our lives. We are inwardly bound up. We must get victory over that sense of self-consciousness and shyness, or we will never be useful for the kingdom of God.

Psychologists often find themselves dealing with an inverted self, a tendency to close in and become wrapped up with oneself. Obviously, this inhibited self must be loosed and freed. It is unnatural and therefore unchristian. When Peter and John were before the Sanhedrin, it was said, "As they looked on Peter and John so fearlessly outspoken—and also discovered that they were illiterate persons, untrained in the schools—they were surprised; and now they recognized them as having been with Jesus" (Acts 4:13 WEYMOUTH). Their fearlessness was a sign of Jesus' impact on their lives. It was so then—it is so now.

A person who is in company with Jesus is freed from cramping inhibitions and self-consciousness. The Son of God has power to impart. "I will give you words and wisdom that none of your adversaries will be able to resist or contradict," said Jesus (Luke 21:15). Some have many words and no wisdom, while others have wisdom and no words. Jesus said he would give us both—something to talk about, and help to open our mouths.

Tied-up lives can be loosed and made victorious.

O Christ, I thank You that no cramping fears or inhibitions crippled You. Freely You received, and freely You gave. Help me to be like that. Amen.

THROWING OFF ALL RESERVE

Seeing the crowds, the Jews, filled with angry jealousy, opposed Paul's statements and abused him. Then, throwing off all reserve, Paul and Barnabas said, "We were bound to proclaim the word of God to you first. But since you spurn it and judge yourselves to be unworthy of eternal Life—well, we turn to the Gentiles. For such is the Lord's command to us." (Acts 13:45-47 WEYMOUTH)

A crisis had come in early Christianity. The apostles kept going to the Jews alone, acting as though this were a Jewish gospel, from Jews to Jews. But God's larger agenda had to be served. In the end, they threw off all reserve and saved themselves as well as their gospel.

They had a larger gospel in their hearts than they were actually proclaiming. They were proclaiming a gospel for Jews when it was a gospel for all people.

Today a similar crisis has arisen in Christianity. We have a larger gospel in our hearts than we are actually proclaiming. This gospel will cure our individual sickness *and* our social sickness. We have had our reserves about one or the other. We have acted on less than the whole. Now, a world-shaking crisis is forcing us to throw off all reserve.

We must act upon the larger implications of our gospel. It is always safe to do so. It is always dangerous to minimize Christ, for there we are always wrong. It is always safe to act upon the larger Christ, for there we are always right. The smaller view of Christ has always proven wrong, the larger always right.

Now, some of us have reservations about giving this gospel to the individual—we are tongue-tied. We cannot impart the vital spark. We are not spiritually contagious. We either haven't anything to give, or we can't give what we have.

Others are tied up at the place of giving this gospel to the collective order. They either haven't anything to give, or else they fear to give it.

O Christ, deliver us from both paralyses, and help us to throw off all our reserves and be out and out for You and Your kingdom. Amen.

A MAGNIFICENT OBSESSION

The kingdom of heaven is like treasure hidden in a field. When a man found it, he hid it again, and then in his joy went and sold all he had and bought that field.

Again, the kingdom of heaven is like a merchant looking for fine pearls. When he found one of great value, he went away and sold everything he had and bought it. (Matt. 13:44-46)

A world crisis is upon us. Life is running into new molds. Shall we allow greed to set those molds as in the past, or shall we set the kingdom of God on earth as the mold for the future? I choose the kingdom.

A bishop, criticizing my last book, said I seemed to be "obsessed with the idea of the kingdom of God on earth." I do confess to a passion (I only wish it more ablaze) for a new order on earth, the kingdom of God.

I *am* obsessed with the idea that poverty could end for all, for we have both the knowledge and the instruments of science to do it. We have everything to do it except the collective will. The kingdom of God would mean that that collective will would be turned toward abolishing that poverty. I am therefore obsessed with that kingdom.

I *am* obsessed with the idea that race hatred and social clashes could cease and that humanity could be formed into a fellowship. The kingdom of God would mean just that. So I am obsessed with that kingdom.

I *am* obsessed with the thought that these preparations for war are so stupid, so thoroughly devilish, so unnecessary, and so futile. The kingdom of God would mean an end of war. Therefore I am obsessed with that kingdom.

I *am* obsessed with the idea that the kingdom of God is the only workable order, and that this kingdom is at our doors. I shall therefore throw off all reserve and say so. I read recently about certain Christians who "fairly shouted their answer to the world." I wish we could do that! What a magnificent obsession!

O Christ, help us fairly to shout our answer to the world's need. For we know it is an answer—and the only one. Amen.

REDUCING THE KINGDOM

When they met together, they asked him, "Lord, are you at this time going to restore the kingdom to Israel?" (Acts 1:6)

Many people spread their cloaks on the road, while others spread branches they had cut in the fields. Those who went ahead and those who followed shouted, "Hosanna!… Blessed is the coming kingdom of our father David!" (Mark 11:8-10)

Note two attempts to reduce the kingdom. After the resurrection of Jesus, his disciples wanted to know if Israel would now get its kingdom back. After three years of teaching, they did not reject the kingdom of God, but they reduced it. They made it into something less than it really was.

Earlier, when Jesus came into Jerusalem in triumphal entry, the multitudes cried their praise for "the coming kingdom of our father David." The kingdom of God was shriveled down to the kingdom of one who ruled a thousand years back.

This has been the bane of the gospel of Christ: He inaugurates something big and challenging, and we interpret it in terms of "our father David." Denominationalism is taking the kingdom of God—a worldwide, universal kingdom—and turning it into the Church of England, the Wesleyans, the Lutherans, the Baptists, the Presbyterians, the Pentecostals…as if the kingdom of God weren't larger than England, than John Wesley, than Martin Luther, than a mode of baptism, an emphasis on presbyters, or on Pentecost! All of these, and others, are narrowing a universal concept into a local one. Luther announces the kingdom of God; his followers announce the kingdom of our father Luther!

And when I make the kingdom of God, which is to take in the whole of life, into a means of my individual salvation alone, leaving the social order untouched, am I not making the kingdom of God into the kingdom of self?

I repeat, a crisis is on us. We Christians must throw off all reserve and give our answer to the world's need without hesitation, without compromise.

O Christ, forgive us that we have made Your kingdom into the small and irrelevant. Help us now to make it into the big and adequate. Amen.

STRONG AT THE WEAKEST PLACE

"Ah, Sovereign LORD," I said, "I do not know how to speak; I am only a child."
(Jer. 1:6)

[Later:] *But if I say, "I will not mention him or speak any more in his name," his*
word is in my heart like a fire, a fire shut up in my bones. I am weary of holding
it in; indeed, I cannot. (Jer. 20:9)

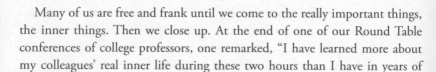

Many of us are free and frank until we come to the really important things, the inner things. Then we close up. At the end of one of our Round Table conferences of college professors, one remarked, "I have learned more about my colleagues' real inner life during these two hours than I have in years of working together."

We need to be freed from binding reservations. You say, "I am shy and self-conscious; I cannot do it." True, but you can overcome that. YMCA president John R. Mott says that the phrase he has repeated most in his life is "You can become strongest in your weakest place."

When the call of God came to Jeremiah, he pleaded that he could not speak well. But he offered that trembling hesitation to God, and when he did open his mouth, how mightily he spoke! When the call of God came to Moses, he pleaded much the same thing. But God loosed him, and when he did get started, he made a speech that covered the whole book of Deuteronomy!

Some people look on faith as something so sacred that it becomes secret. Suppose a mother said to her children, "Now, children, food is such a sacred thing I cannot talk to you about, nor can I invite you to partake of it." Absurd! But not more absurd than the unnatural attitudes we assume about the deepest thing we have—the good news about the power of Christ. There we should be natural and contagious.

Someone has defined a Christian as one who says by word and by life, "I commend my Savior to you." No better definition. No greater need.

O Christ, loose me from these inhibiting shackles, and help me to be free to
impart. Amen.

THE POWER THAT GIVES RELEASE

"You will receive power when the Holy Spirit comes on you; and you will be my witnesses in Jerusalem, and in all Judea and Samaria, and to the ends of the earth." (Acts 1:8)

The only way to get rid of self-consciousness is through God-consciousness. We can become so conscious of another Self within us that we lose sight of our self. "Where the Spirit of the Lord is, there is freedom" (2 Cor. 3:17)—freedom from cramping bondages and inhibitions and paralyzing sins.

But this age has lost its grip upon the Holy Spirit. We have taught this age to follow Jesus as an example, and it has produced a pale, colorless Christianity. The gospel does not ask you to only follow Jesus as an example—it also offers you the resources of the Holy Spirit in the inner life, and then you follow Jesus because of an impulsion. This kind of Christianity becomes colorful and red-blooded. It has resources, and therefore power.

One modern translation of the Gospels spells the "holy spirit" thus, without capitals. That is symbolic of what has happened to this age. It has turned the Holy Spirit into a "holy spirit," a vague, impersonal influence, which impoverishes us. That is not the Holy Spirit of the Acts of the Apostles. There the Holy Spirit was God meeting them inwardly, reinforcing, cleansing, fusing the soul forces into a loving unity, and setting them ablaze with God.

Weymouth was right when he translated the passage about Stephen, "They were quite unable, however, to resist the wisdom and the Spirit with which he spoke" (Acts 6:10). Note the capital S. You couldn't tell where Stephen's spirit ended and the Holy Spirit began. When the disciples got hold of that secret at Pentecost, they were decisively freed from cramping inhibitions and spiritual bondages to become flaming evangels of the Good News.

We need to rediscover the actual resources of the Holy Spirit. Otherwise, we live in bondage.

O Christ, help us to rediscover Your offer to us and to live by its resources, rejoice in its liberties, and become effective by its power. Amen.

BREAKING DOWN THE INNER DAM

On the last and greatest day of the Feast, Jesus stood and said in a loud voice, "If anyone is thirsty, let him come to me and drink. Whoever believes in me, as the Scripture has said, streams of living water will flow from within him." By this he meant the Spirit, whom those who believed in him were later to receive. (John 7:37-39)

The King James Version of this Scripture reads, "…out of his belly shall flow rivers of living water." We have shied away from such visceral language—to our loss. For the "belly" was considered the seat of life, the deepest portion of one's nature.

We might say today, "From the depths of the subconscious shall flow rivers of living waters," in other words, the Spirit in the depths of the subconscious, cleansing, controlling, empowering. This brings the whole of life into a living unity. In the flood of this new Life, all compartmentalizing, inhibiting dams are broken down. This is not mere doctrine, but a fact. The disciples knew it; it turned timid believers into irresistible apostles.

A highly cultured lady said with beaming joy, "I have just stumbled across the meaning of the Holy Ghost. All my life I have tried to find out His meaning. Now I know." And the "rivers" from her life attested to the fact.

Nine "rivers" flow out of a Spirit-controlled life: "love, joy, peace; patience toward others, kindness, benevolence; good faith, meekness, self-restraint" (Gal. 5:22, 23 WEYMOUTH). The next sentence adds, "Against such things there is no law." Have those things at the center of your life, and you can act as you please, for you are not constrained by a law to do them, but impelled by an inner Life. You can act naturally because you act supernaturally.

But note that the first one is "love" and the last "self-restraint." You restrain your lower self because you love the higher Self. Also note that each one of these fruits of the Spirit is valid and vital today.

O Spirit of the Living God, break down the dams in our lives and make us free. Take over the depths, and we shall not worry about the surface. Amen.

INTERPRETERS OR INTERFERERS?

"Build up, build up, prepare the road! Remove the obstacles out of the way of my people." (Isa. 57:14)

Do not cause anyone to stumble, whether Jews, Greeks or the church of God—even as I try to please everybody in every way. For I am not seeking my own good but the good of many, so that they may be saved. (1 Cor. 10:32-33)

Through our lives, we are to extend the Incarnation. As a missionary spoke about Christ, a Persian interrupted. "I know who you are talking about: Dr. ----------. He comes to our village." The doctor had interpreted Christ to them. In fact, once while on an errand of mercy, bandits had stripped him of everything, even his clothes. But strange to say, they left him with his camera. So he took their picture. Later, one of these bandits showed up at his hospital for an operation. They recognized each other. The man was now in the doctor's power, and helpless. The doctor used that power to forgive him and heal him. While doing so, he interpreted the meaning of Christ.

Some of us, on the other hand, interfere with that meaning, like the Twelve did with the children who came to Jesus. "But the disciples interfered" (Mark 10:13 WEYMOUTH). In doing so, they blocked the spirit and purpose of Christ. You and I are *interpreters* of Christ or *interferers* with Christ. We represent either the cure or the disease.

Jesus interpreted the Father. John 1:18 says, "The One and Only, who is at the Father's side, has made him known," literally, "has interpreted him." And what an interpretation! As I listen to Jesus' words, watch His acts, and see His spirit, God grows tenderly beautiful before me. I fall in love with such a God.

Once it was said, "Then Jesus went through the towns and villages, teaching as he made his way to Jerusalem" (Luke 13:22), where the cross awaited Him. Many of us would have nursed our coming pain. But He had an inward leisure to teach the love of God to others, while on the way to die! What an interpreter He was!

O Christ, as You interpreted the Father, help me this day to interpret You. Amen.

ENHANCING THE MESSAGE

Paul: *For Christ did not send me to baptize, but to preach the gospel—not with words of human wisdom, lest the cross of Christ be emptied of its power. (1 Cor. 1:17)*

I have used many interpreters through the years, and some have enhanced my message, while others, unfortunately, have subtracted from it. Once they said to me in China, "This man is such a wonderful interpreter that no matter what you say, he will make a good address out of it." He did! He would take a commonplace statement and make it live.

But some have used the opportunity for self-display. I once had to stop an interpreter who was doing this so obviously that he was spoiling everything. When I did so, I felt I was rebuking myself, for often I have used the opportunity to interpret Christ as a chance to display myself. I thus became an interferer instead of an interpreter. Much of modern preaching is interfering with Christ instead of interpreting Him. It is self-display instead of Christ-interpretation.

Sometimes we block the message because we are in it too much, and other times because we are not in it at all. We are perfunctory. It doesn't consume us. We do not burn with it. We take the affairs of the kingdom into our hands but will not let them reach our heart. We are dead channels of a living Christ.

"When I came to this ashram I was a flickering torch," said a radiant young man to me. "Now I have become a flaming torch." And he had! If Christ doesn't get into your blood and raise your temperature, I wonder why? Such a Christ, such a message, such a need! By our inner deadness we flatten out what should live and challenge and redeem.

Do we interfere with the message because the self is too much in it, or because we are not in it at all? Or do we truly interpret Him?

O Christ, forgive me that I have again and again become like static on the radio breaking up clear reception. Help me to become an enhancer of Your redemptive message. Amen.

GETTING THE MESSAGE THROUGH TO OTHERS

God's word is not chained. (2 Tim. 2:9)

Now he had to go through Samaria. So he came to a town in Samaria called Sychar…and Jesus, tired as he was from the journey, sat down by the well. It was about the sixth hour…. A Samaritan woman came to draw water. (John 4:4-7)

We must now study how to get the message through to human need, for it is not enough for us to live victoriously—we must help others to do so. Nothing is really ours until we can pass it on. One definition of a Christian is a person "who makes it easy for others to believe in God." Jesus did that. He did not prove God. He brought Him.

In Korea they do not baptize a new convert until he has brought another to Christ. Then they know he is Christian, for he is Christianizing.

In the exceedingly difficult case of the Samaritan woman, Jesus gives us a vivid example in helping other people to live. We shall take His delicate dealings with her step by step, learning as we go.

First, the account says, "He had to go through Samaria." It was an inevitable thing, so He "evangelized the inevitable." Certain things in your life and mine are inevitable—we have to go to the office, to school, to the workplace, to home duties, or we may be compelled by circumstance to sit unemployed. Evangelize that inevitable thing—find your opportunity in the ordinary contacts of the day.

Then that day will no longer be ordinary, for the contacts are redemptive. You are turning the commonplace into the consequential. The little things of life become the big things—big with destiny. Life-contacts become life-changing. Nothing under heaven is bigger than that.

O Christ, help us to gather up these contacts so drab and commonplace and make them live with meaning and destiny, as You did. Amen.

THE FIRST APPROACH

When a Samaritan woman came to draw water, Jesus said to her, "Will you give me a drink?" (John 4:7)

The first step in opening the conversation is the most difficult. Many hesitate to take it for fear of being snubbed. But truthfully, I cannot remember through the years when I have had a real snub in approaching people about Christ. Even if they should snub you, what of it? Be so spiritually cheerful that you don't know when you are snubbed!

There were a great many reasons why He should not have spoken to this woman. (1) He was tired and hungry. (2) To talk to a woman in public was to risk His reputation. (3) She was a woman of loose character. (4) The town name "Sychar" means "drunken," probably taken from the character of the inhabitants; nothing could be done with such a group. (5) It was noontime, the hour in hot countries when everyone rests.

But there was one reason in favor of approaching her: She needed it! That one reason outweighed all the others. You will find many reasons why you should not share what you have found. I never speak to a person without having to fight past those reasons. But the one reason always persists—people need it as they need absolutely nothing else. Let that be the determining factor.

Jesus began at the place of her dominant interest—water. From there He went to living water, and then to fountains of living water in the heart. Try to find out the dominant interest in people, and lead them along the line of that dominant interest. Is a young person's interest in athletics? Talk about a strong body, and the necessity of purity if that body is to stay strong, and the dynamic in Christ to keep one pure. Is a parent wrapped up in his or her children? Then suggest that they no doubt want to give the child the best—but they cannot do it unless they have it themselves.

O Christ, help me this day to find someone's dominant interest and to lead them through that interest to You. For all real roads run to You. Amen.

SIDE-STEPPING THE BARRIERS

The Samaritan woman said to him, "You are a Jew and I am a Samaritan woman. How can you ask me for a drink?" (For Jews do not associate with Samaritans.)

Jesus answered her, "If you knew the gift of God and who it is that asks you for a drink, you would have asked him and he would have given you living water." (John 4:9-10)

The first tendency of the human heart is to close up at the approach of an intruder, as this woman did. It is the instinct of self-preservation. We do not easily let people into our lives. So many Christian workers stop right here and say it is of no use. The casualties are very great at this point. They stop before they begin—discouraged. For there are many counterparts today to the Jew-Samaritan barrier.

But if the first instinct is to close, the second is to reveal. Everyone wants to share their inmost self, provided they can find someone in whom to have confidence. So do not be abashed at the first barrier; wait for the working of that deeper instinct, self-revelation.

How did Jesus get rid of the issue between Jew and Samaritan? He might have been drawn off into that controversy. Instead, He dismissed the lesser issue by raising a higher one. He talked about "living water," and as He did so she forgot about the issue she had raised. That is the principle: *When people raise lesser issues, get rid of them by turning their attention to higher issues.* Don't get tangled up in irrelevancies; drive toward the main business at hand.

Jesus showed an amazing confidence in the woman when he said, "If you knew the gift of God and who it is that asks you for a drink, you would have asked him and he would have given you living water." In other words, if you see the good, you will want it! That was an amazing assumption to make about such a woman. Everybody else had probably suggested the opposite.

To influence people you must believe in them despite what they are.

O Christ, great believer in humanity, You who believe in me when I cannot believe in myself, help me this day to believe in people, so that they may believe in You. Amen.

OUR BEST FOR THE WORST

"Sir," the woman said, "you have nothing to draw with and the well is deep. Where can you get this living water? Are you greater than our father Jacob, who gave us the well and drank from it himself, as did also his sons and his flocks and herds?"

Jesus answered, "Everyone who drinks this water will be thirsty again, but whoever drinks the water I give him will never thirst. Indeed, the water I give him will become in him a spring of water welling up to eternal life." (John 4:11-14)

The people who influence you for good are not the people who tell you how bad you are, but who tell you how good you may become. Nag people, and they sag; believe in people, and they bloom.

But the woman was not yet through with barriers. She said, "Are you greater than our father Jacob?" She wanted a comparison.

Now, Jesus might have said, "Woman, your father Jacob was a scheming liar who stole his brother's birthright." And it would have been perfectly true! She would have gone away angry and hurt. You and I must not strive to win arguments, but to win people. To win the argument you need only to be clever; to win the person you need to be Christian.

But Jesus did get beyond Jacob. He slid him out of the picture so gently that we scarcely notice he is gone. How? Again, by raising a higher issue. Jesus replied with his most wonderful offer of water that would satisfy forever. As the woman's thought became fastened on that fountain of water in the heart, she forgot Jacob and the controversy. The higher issue pushed out the lower.

This verse, one of the most beautiful in Scripture, was given to a disreputable woman. He did not hesitate to give His best to the worst. Your best is none too good for the worst. So lavish it, as He did. And the worst will become the best, as she did.

O Christ, Your best is offered at the shrine of my worst. Help me to exchange my worst for Your best. And help me to help others to do the same. Amen.

THE DELICATE MOMENT

The woman said to him, "Sir, give me this water so that I won't get thirsty and have to keep coming here to draw water."
   He told her, "Go, call your husband and come back."
   "I have no husband," she replied. (John 4:15-17)

The woman said she wanted the water Jesus offered, because for one thing it would save her a long trip to the village well each day. Her motives were mixed. People not only have mixed minds but also mixed motives. Many of us would have dismissed the woman right there. Why bother with her? But Jesus was infinite patience.

A young man told me he went to take Communion as a semi-joke. But having done so, he suddenly felt he should stand by what he had professed—and did. He became a wonderful Christian. Christ took the hand held out in jest, and forever gripped it.

But, in order to purify the Samaritan woman's motive, He needed to purify her. He had to get to her moral problem. Take it as an axiom: *There is a moral problem in every life.* Get to that problem, or you will miss the point on which everything else hinges.

How did He get to her sin? He might have said, "Woman, I happen to know that you are living a bad, adulterous life." But had He done so, she would have recoiled at the shock. It is not enough to point out other people's sins; they must be led to point them out themselves. Then, and then only, are they on the road to get rid of them. So He led the woman to acknowledge her sin by making a delicate request, "Go, call your husband and come back."

At the word "husband" her eyes dropped; a guilty flush went across the soul. "I have no husband," she said simply, and the words meant more than they seem. The moral problem was exposed. She inwardly crumpled before her newly exposed self—and Him.

O Christ, when we get people to that awful point of sin exposure, give us the sure word to offer, that we may point to a sin exit through You. Amen.

FACING UP

"Sir," the woman said, "I can see that you are a prophet. Our fathers worshiped on this mountain, but you Jews claim that the place where we must worship is in Jerusalem."

Jesus declared, "Believe me, woman, a time is coming when you will worship the Father neither on this mountain nor in Jerusalem." (John 4:19-21)

Yesterday we left the woman face to face with her sins. We must get people to this place, for no matter what this sophisticated age may say, this is our personal problem: How can I get rid of sin? The first step is to expose it. Sin is like a seed: Cover it, and you cultivate it.

But you ask, "How can I get people to uncover their moral need?" First, be free to talk about your own moral needs and your victory over them. Second, don't be shocked at disclosures. Third, establish confidence that you are a doctor who knows the way through.

To get people to face up to their moral need, I find it effective to mention my friend who examines his life in the light of the five tests: "Am I truthful? Am I honest? Am I pure? Am I loving? Am I consecrated?" Repeat them, very slowly, and ask the person where they come out. Many will tell you where they break down, glad to get out the whole wretched business. Others, to save face, will wriggle and excuse. Or they may try to go off on another subject.

The woman did this. She quickly brought out a question about where people should worship. Why did she ask this question just now? Because she found the conversation very uncomfortable, and preferred to draw it off to a more abstract religious debate. It is easier to discuss abstract religious questions than to face one's own sin—easier, and more deadly. Beware of people's attempt to pull you off the real thing by drawing the red herring of abstract religious questions across the path. Stick to the moral problem. For life and death lie in this issue. They do not lie in the question of where to worship.

O Christ, we often want to go off on tangents from salvation. Save us from ourselves. Amen.

RELIGIOUS BUT ROTTEN

"A time is coming and has now come when the true worshipers will worship the Father in spirit and truth, for they are the kind of worshipers the Father seeks. God is spirit, and his worshipers must worship in spirit and in truth."

The woman said, "I know that Messiah" (called Christ) "is coming. When he comes, he will explain everything to us." (John 4:23-25)

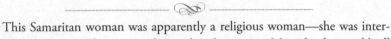

This Samaritan woman was apparently a religious woman—she was interested in the proper place to worship and in the coming Messiah who would tell them everything. Don't be put off the track when people talk religion to you, for we all may be very religious—and very rotten.

Or we may be religious in spots and rotten in spots. As an author named Streeter puts it: "Some people are only half-awake. They feel paroxysms of contrition because [they are] haunted by impure dreams, and yet are perfectly unconscious that their lives are one long expression of envy, malice, hatred, and uncharitableness. Others are sexually impure and yet haunted with remorse for an unkind word."

Or as Niebuhr says, "We have two motives: the one we publish and the real one. Good people want to do the selfish thing, but they don't until they [can] find an unselfish reason for doing it."

We insist then: Take nothing and nobody for granted.

Did Jesus answer this abstract religious question about the proper place to worship? Yes, but note how He did it. "God is spirit"—that rendered both Jerusalem and the Samaritan mountain irrelevant. God desires people to "worship in spirit and in truth"—that rendered the moral life relevant to worship. The moral problem was still central.

No matter how far you go off the point momentarily, bring the conversation back to the central issue. You yourself must guide the conversation—not the other person, nor circumstances. As you lead toward liberty and release, stay in moral control of the situation, as Jesus did.

O Christ, You point us to the wicket gate that leads to release. Help us to do that same thing with someone today. Amen.

THE GOAL

Jesus declared, "I who speak to you am he."…

Then, leaving her water jar, the woman went back to the town and said to the people, "Come, see a man who told me everything I ever did. Could this be the Christ?" They came out of the town and made their way toward him. (John 4:26, 28-30)

What was the goal of the conversation, the end toward which everything was being led? It was the revelation of who Jesus actually was. He got her to see herself, in order that she might then see Him as the source of salvation.

The end of our work and conversation is just one simple thing—to get people to see Jesus. If we have failed in that, we have failed in our task. Our business is not to be clever, but to be Christian, and we can only be Christian as we show people Christ.

But it must not be an intellectual apprehension of Him. It must be a moral apprehension, a taking hold of Christ as the power that changes and transforms life. The person must not merely survey Christ, but surrender to Him. That is what we mean by seeing Christ. Then the person has "root in himself" (Matt. 13:21 KJV), and that root is Christ.

Actually, there is one step further. The woman, having seen Christ, emerged so full of that vision that she went off to give it to somebody else. The end of evangelism is to produce an evangelist. We must not be satisfied to get somebody "in"—we must only be satisfied when they are getting someone else "in." Then we have really started something that knows no end. For I cannot repeat often enough: You belong either to the cure or to the disease. If you are not curing, you are causing disease. But as you cure, you will be more deeply cured.

The Easter account says that as the women "went to tell his disciples, behold, Jesus met them" (Matt. 28:9 KJV). On the way to tell others, Jesus met them—He always does. On the way to tell others, you will sense a warm, living Presence.

O Christ, help us not to feel that we are changed till we are changing, and help us to begin today. Amen.

CHANGE WE CAN BELIEVE IN

Meanwhile his disciples urged him, "Rabbi, eat something." But he said to them, "I have food to eat that you know nothing about."

Then his disciples said to each other, "Could someone have brought him food?"

"My food," said Jesus, "is to do the will of him who sent me and to finish his work." (John 4:31-34)

When the disciples returned, they found Jesus in an exalted state. He did not care to eat. When they urged Him, He said He had food they didn't know, food that consisted of doing God's work. Why should Jesus be so carried away over such a small incident?

In the simple changing of an individual He saw the biggest thing on earth, something He identified with the will of God. That will, He said, fed Him.

If Jesus felt that way about changing the individual, why should it be sneered at, as some religious people of a social bent are now doing? Are we too small to hold *two* great emphases? Must we swing back from one to the other? The kingdom of God does mean the changing of the social order, but it also means just what happened to this woman—a changed individual life.

Here in our mountain garden some grafted peach trees were planted ten years ago, but today they are not over two feet high. The reason is that deer came in from the forest at night and ate off the growing tips as fast as they came out. The trees have life, but growth has been impossible.

Now that we have surrounded the garden with a barbed-wire fence, the trees are growing. A barbed-wire fence (a social restraint) and a good quality of grafted life (an individual change) are necessary for fruitfulness. But a barbed-wire fence around ungrafted wild peach trees will not bring fruitfulness. Nor will a grafted tree without that fence be fruitful. Individual change without social restraint won't do. Both are needed.

Jesus rejoiced that day in Samaria that He had put the graft of a higher life into a human soul. That was the will of God for Him. It must be for us.

O Christ, keep me mindful of this central necessity, and give me power to put the graft of Your life into other lives. Amen.

HIS WILL, MY FOOD

I desire to do your will, O my God; your law is within my heart." (Psalm 40:8)

I delight in your decrees; I will not neglect your word. (Psalm 119:16)

Nothing exalts the soul or gives it a sheer sense of buoyancy and victory so much as our being used to change the lives of other people. This is a necessary and integral part of victorious living. Without it, life remains an unfulfilled dream. The battle of life is won not by the defensive, but by the offensive. The will of God is redemptive, and when we feed upon that will, we too shall become redemptive.

Jesus said that, to Him, the will of God was food; it was something that sustained Him, something He lived by. Now, to some of us the will of God is medicine. It is something to be taken now and again to straighten us out. It is bitter, but it is needed to get rid of our ills. This view of the will of God is very common—it is something to be accepted, with a sigh. The will of God is a trial to be borne. When death and calamity visit us, we say, "Thy will be done."

To others the will of God is more like dessert at the end of a meal—something to round off life and give it taste. But you don't live by desserts. Nor do such people live by the will of God if they view it as the occasional treat that gives life its flavor but not its nutrition.

To Jesus, the will of God was neither medicine nor dessert; it was the thing that sustained Him. This implies that we are made for the will of God as the body is made for food. It fits our moral and spiritual make-up. Everything else is poison—this is food. I live as I live by the will of God. I wither and die as I live by some other will, particularly my own.

Help me, O Christ, to feed upon the will of God as my very food. May that will within me turn to moral strength and spiritual victory. May it be life to me. Amen.

MY WILL, MY POISON

If men comply with their lower nature, their thoughts are shaped by the lower nature; if with their spiritual nature, by the spiritual. Thoughts shaped by the lower nature mean death; thoughts shaped by the spiritual mean life and peace. For thoughts shaped by the lower nature mean a state of enmity to God. (Rom. 8:5-7 WEYMOUTH)

If we are made for the will of God as the body is made for food, then the will of God feeds us, while everything else outside will poison us.

The British science fiction author H. G. Wells has fed upon as fine a thing as his *Utopias,* and yet it has left him dissatisfied, unfed. He confesses: "I cannot adjust myself to secure any fruitful peace. Here I am at 65 still seeking for peace." Brilliant, modern, and far-seeing, but agnostic, and therefore feeding on some will other than that of God. And still hungry!

If Wells cannot not find sustenance in his *Utopias,* how about some of us who try to live by the will of the flesh? Paul says it leads to death; it is poison to us. Everyone who has tried it knows it to be true. We are not made to live by our lower nature, but by our higher, as that higher is led by the will of God.

In South America there are leaves of a tree that, if eaten, take away all appetite; one no longer cares for food. The leaves are a drug and not a food. Anything that apparently satisfies you, outside the will of God, is a drug.

But the will of God is food—real food. When people feed on that, they are adequate for anything, afraid of nothing. They feel that at the center of their being they have resources, sustenance, a reinforcement, Life not their own, and they live by that very Life. Victorious living is the natural, normal outcome of that fact. A person is immovably fixed in God, and immeasurably fed by God.

Nothing quite sustains us like the fact that we know the universe backs our will when we act. Is it any wonder that we share the same sense of exalted joy Jesus had on this occasion?

O Father, I come to You to put my life alongside Yours, to be guided and fed by You this day. Amen.

MAKING THE VITAL CONNECTION

Then one of the crowd answered and said, "Teacher, I brought You my son, who has a mute spirit. And wherever it seizes him, it throws him down; he foams at the mouth, gnashes his teeth, and becomes rigid. So I spoke to Your disciples, that they should cast it out, but they could not."

He answered him and said, "O faithless generation, how long shall…I bear with you? Bring him to Me." Then they brought him to Him. (Mark 9:17-20 NKJV)

In this account of the desperate father with the convulsing son, the sentence reads, "They brought him to Him." At one end was the "him" of human need, at the other end the "Him" who could meet that need.

Never was this "him" more needy than at the present time. Torn from old moorings, adrift, distracted, and desperately wanting something. Going—but he doesn't know where! Feeling—but for what? Thinking—but with no great certainties. This modern "him" is in critical need.

The "Him" who can meet that need stands ready, available, adequate. But He cannot reach that human need without a human connection. That is the "unto," and the "unto" is the Christian. He touches the "him" of human need on one side and the "Him," the Savior, on the other, bringing them together. To do so, the Christian has to be in living touch with both.

But some are in touch with "him" while out of touch with "Him"—the humanists. Others are in touch with "Him" while out of touch with "him"— the isolated religionists.

The king of England was making a speech over the radio to the whole empire when a connection broke. An attendant grabbed the two broken ends of the wire and held them together throughout the speech, so that the message got across. He was the vital link between king and people. You and I are to be in such close touch with Christ and human need that we mediate His very life to that need. What a place to occupy!

O Christ, we know that if we fail, the message will not get across. Help us not to fail You or them today. Amen.

VICTORY OVER TEMPTATION

If your hand causes you to sin, cut it off. It is better for you to enter life maimed than with two hands to go into hell, where the fire never goes out. And if your foot causes you to sin, cut it off. It is better for you to enter life crippled than to have two feet and be thrown into hell. And if your eye causes you to sin, pluck it out. It is better for you to enter the kingdom of God with one eye than to have two eyes and be thrown into hell. (Mark 9:43-47)

Victorious living means saying "Yes" to something—the will of God. But that implies saying "No" to something else—temptation. Christianity is not a prohibition, it is a privilege—but it does have a prohibition in it.

Jesus said if your hand, foot, or eye causes you to stumble, get rid of it. In other words, do not tolerate anything from head to foot that cuts across the central purpose of your life. From head to foot you are to belong to Christ.

Now, note the order of these three: hand, foot, eye. The hand represents the doing of evil; the foot is the approach toward evil, going up to it but not actually doing it; the eye is the seeing of evil with desire from afar. Cut evil out in any stage. The place to cut it out most effectively, of course, is at the place of the eye, the thought.

But some live a great deal in that intermediate stage between eye and hand; they dally with sin at the foot stage. They go beyond thinking about it. They actually approach it, come to the brink of it, and expect to pull back before the deed. In this way they get the partial pleasure of getting up close to evil, feeling its burning warmth, but also the partial pleasure of being good enough finally to restrain. It is an attempt to get the best out of both worlds.

A foolish attempt, for it leaves you homeless. You are not at home in Christ and not at home in evil. So watch your feet. Don't let them take you to any brink.

O Christ, thank You for being decisive. Save us from all double-mindedness; help us to be decisive. Amen.

EYE-SIN

Again, the devil took him to a very high mountain and showed him all the kingdoms of the world and their splendor. "All this I will give you," he said, "if you will bow down and worship me."

Jesus said to him, "Away from me, Satan! For it is written: 'Worship the Lord your God, and serve him only.'" (Matt. 4:8-10)

The most effective place to kill sin is in the eye stage. That may mean actually seeing evil with the physical eye, or imagining it with the mental eye. Either way, the best place to kill a cobra is in its egg.

I pass on a little plan of my own: When an evil thought comes, I find that by batting my eyes very rapidly, the thought is broken up. It is a voluntary act demanding voluntary attention, and it draws the attention away from the thought. I catch my equilibrium enough to pray, "O Christ, save me."

But we might offer other suggestions:

1. Change what you are doing at once in order to put your attention elsewhere. Once, while going through a forest, I was troubled with an evil thought. I deliberately picked up a very heavy log and carried it back to the ashram. The attention necessary to carry such a load made me forget the thought. So take on yourself such a heavy task that it demands your whole attention. I find that the greatest battles take place not when one is absorbed in a task, but when one is on a vacation, where you let down and have nothing particular to absorb you.

2. If you are alone when an evil thought assails you, deliberately go, if possible, to a group of people. We sometimes talk of the temptation of crowds. On the other hand, they often save us from ourselves and our evil thoughts. We are ashamed to harbor them when we are in the company of others.

3. Change the mental picture to a spiritual one. Train your mind to run at once to the thought of the Crucified. It is hard to think of evil and of Him at the same time. They are incompatible.

O Christ, give me purity in mind, for I want the kind of mind in which You can be at home. Amen.

MORE WAYS TO OVERCOME

We demolish arguments and every pretension that sets itself up against the knowledge of God, and we take captive every thought to make it obedient to Christ. (2 Cor. 10:5)

May the words of my mouth and the meditation of my heart be pleasing in your sight, O LORD, my Rock and my Redeemer. (Psalm 19:14)

———— ✥ ————

We continue to look at the way evil thoughts may be overcome:

4. Put your mind under a rigid discipline. The mind is the servant of the personality and can be made to obey. You can turn off your thoughts as you turn off a radio. The mind soon begins to understand who is master. But the mind will play tricks on you if it knows that in the end you give in. So be unbending in your discipline of yourself.

5. In order to determine your waking thoughts, think of the purest, finest thoughts just before going to sleep. Those last thoughts before dropping into unconsciousness are very determinative, for the door into the subconscious is opening, and they drop into it to work good or ill. The dream life can be largely controlled by your waking life. Psychologists tell us that you dream only of things that have occupied your consciousness in the last three or four days. Of course these things may touch off older memories by association, but the dream life of the next three or four days can be controlled in great measure by the waking life of today. Do not let your last waking thought be an impure thought, for it will fasten itself upon the mind like a burr. Crowd it out by making your last thought the horizon-filling Christ.

6. Get plenty of exercise. Take up sports and become interested in them.

7. Undertake to help someone else in the battle. The very sense of your responsibility for the other person will help you in yours, for the thought will persist, "I must not let them down."

8. Breathe an impromptu prayer the moment an impure thought arises.

O Christ of the pure mind, make me pure in mind this day—and always. Amen.

HEARING IS ABSORBING

We must pay more careful attention, therefore, to what we have heard, so that we do not drift away. (Heb. 2:1)

"Consider carefully what you hear," he continued. "With the measure you use, it will be measured to you—and even more." (Mark 4:24)

In our study of the control of the mind, it will help us to look at a most important verse printed just above. Jesus is saying to be careful of what we hear, for the measure of attention we give to anything will come back to us in impression.

After taking a course in memory training, the only thing I remember (!) from the course is this: It is not a matter of memory, it is a matter of attention. A bad memory is the result of bad attention. So one should not really say, "I have a bad memory;" one should say, "I have bad attention."

Someone has said there are just three laws of learning: concentrate, concentrate, concentrate. Be careful, Jesus said, of the things you concentrate on. That part of your environment on which you concentrate influences you.

This age is thinking about sex—which is to the good. But it is thinking too much about sex—which is to the bad. If you concentrate your attention upon sex, don't be surprised if it comes back to you in sex-impression. And then don't be surprised if you lose your sex battle. Be frank about sex, by all means, but after taking a frank view of the fact of sex, dismiss it from the center of consciousness. If you are constantly wading through books on sex in the name of frankness, you will soon be wading through filth, at least in your mind. For you follow your attention.

Glance at the fact of sex, but gaze at the fact of Christ. Some people gaze at sex, and then wonder why sex, not Christ, has such a hold on them. Attention determines your spiritual destiny.

O Christ, thank You for speaking this law so plainly. Help us to obey it just as plainly. Amen.

TEMPTED TO FOCUS ON OTHERS

Therefore, dear friends, since you already know this, be on your guard so that you may not be carried away by the error of lawless men and fall from your secure position. (2 Peter 3:17)

Peter turned and saw that the disciple whom Jesus loved was following them.... When Peter saw him, he asked, "Lord, what about him?"
Jesus answered, "If I want him to remain alive until I return, what is that to you? You must follow me." (John 21:20-22)

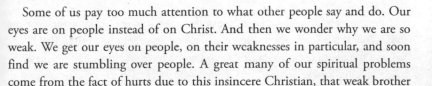

Some of us pay too much attention to what other people say and do. Our eyes are on people instead of on Christ. And then we wonder why we are so weak. We get our eyes on people, on their weaknesses in particular, and soon find we are stumbling over people. A great many of our spiritual problems come from the fact of hurts due to this insincere Christian, that weak brother or sister.

One of the outstanding Christians of the world became bitter and soured. As he recounted his grievances against this one and that one, I quietly quoted this saying from Jesus to Peter: "What is that to thee? Follow thou me" (KJV). He was startled, but resumed his criticisms. In one of the pauses I again quoted this passage, "What is that to thee? Follow thou me." He was then honest enough to say, "Good, you've got me." He was on the wrong track and knew it. He had starved himself gnawing on these bones.

One of the most pathetic sights in India is a skinny dog gnawing on a dry bone. But not more pathetic than a Christian gnawing on some dry bone of grievance against others. It is a poor diet, and the soul grows thin on it.

You are not following that person—you are following Christ. "To his own master he stands or falls" (Rom. 14:4). Christ is the only one who is always the same, dependable, sure, adequate. Follow Him! He will never let you down, though people do.

O Christ, help me get my eyes on You and You alone, so that no matter what people may do or not do, I may be focused. Amen.

TEMPTED TO FOCUS ON FEELINGS

In this you greatly rejoice, though now for a little while you may have had to suffer grief in all kinds of trials. These have come so that your faith—of greater worth than gold, which perishes even though refined by fire—may be proved genuine and may result in praise, glory and honor when Jesus Christ is revealed. (1 Peter 1:6-7)

While many stumble by getting their eyes on people, others stumble by getting their eyes on their emotional states. They go up or down with their feelings.

I do not minimize the place of emotion, for it is the driving force of the soul. Only those ideals that have an emotional tone get our loyalty. But if you pay too much attention to emotion, you won't have any ideals. Emotion is the by-product of a great driving conviction—the waves that are cast up as the ship pushes forward. Think about your directions, your power to go ahead, and your emotions will take care of themselves.

Besides, our feelings are often largely determined by our physical condition. It is hard to feel spiritual with a toothache!

The moon sails sublimely in the sky. Your feelings are like the moon's reflection on the water. You throw a stone into the water and destroy the moon reflected there. But do you really destroy it? No. Your faith in Christ is like the moon in the sky, unchanged by what happens to the reflections in the water.

The Italian patriot Giuseppe Mazzini once said, "Whether the sun shines with the serene splendor of an Italian noon, or [whether] the leaden corpselike hue of the northern mist be above us, I cannot see that this changes our duty." Great words, and applicable to every Christian!

O Christ, save me when I, like Peter, get my eyes on myself and the waves around me instead of on You. For amid the flux of things, You remain the same. Amen.

OUTGROWING CERTAIN TEMPTATIONS

Jesus to the Philadelphia church: *Since you have kept my command to endure patiently, I will also keep you from the hour of trial that is going to come upon the whole world to test those who live on the earth. (Rev. 3:10)*

The Lord knows how to rescue godly people from their trials. (2 Peter 2:9†)

Temptation has its uses. As we grapple, we grow. Goethe said, "Difficulties prove men." When Jesus entered the wilderness, He went in "full of the Holy Spirit," but He came out "in the power of the Spirit" (Luke 4:1, 14). Mere fullness had turned to power under temptation. His spiritual tissues had been hardened in the struggle. So it is with us. Two things happen as we grow spiritually: (1) Our temptations move up to a higher plane, and (2) we outgrow many of them.

The temptations of Jesus were on a very high plane indeed. In the wilderness He did not struggle with lust and passion, but with subtle questions of how to bring in the kingdom. Here, light could very easily become darkness.

It is a compliment to be tempted on that plane. As you grow spiritually, you find your temptations less gross and more subtle. The battle with things like spiritual pride takes the place of the battle with dishonesty and lies.

And then there comes the time when you outgrow some temptations entirely. This is the highest state of all—to be on a spiritual level where these things no longer incite you. You have gone beyond them.

The last petition in the Lord's Prayer is "And lead us not into temptation." I used to think it was an anticlimax. But I now see that it was the highest petition of all: *Lead me to the place where temptation has lost its grip.* We do that in many things. We say of someone, "He can't be tempted by bribery." His character now automatically spurns it. It can be the same with us in thing after thing. We will get the habit of victory. The unconscious effort will more and more take over the functions of the conscious effort. We will become fixed in goodness. Habit will work with us now instead of against us.

O Christ, I thank You that every battle now makes the next one easier. Help me to win every one today. Amen.

E. STANLEY JONES | 287

PART OF SOMETHING BIGGER

All the believers were one in heart and mind. No one claimed that any of his possessions was his own, but they shared everything they had. With great power the apostles continued to testify to the resurrection of the Lord Jesus, and much grace was upon them all. There were no needy persons among them. (Acts 4:32-34)

We have been studying the difficulties that come out of temptations from within ourselves. But many of our spiritual problems arise from our relations with others. It is not an easy thing to adjust oneself to other people and their wills.

Christianity should teach us that very thing, for Christianity is the science of living well with others according to Jesus Christ. Many of our attempts to live together with others are haphazard; they do not obey the underlying principles of corporate living. We must attempt to discover them and live by them. All of us have to live in relationship with others but too often end in disaster with its resultant bitterness and strife. If we depend too much on emotion, and not enough on intelligent planning, the result will be disaster.

John Wesley said he was "a man sent from God to persuade people to put Christ at the center of their relationships." It would be difficult to give a better definition of what our Christian task is than just those words.

What are some of the principles we should embody if we are to live together well?

1. *Life is corporate.* Many do not recognize this. They still look on life as an individual thing. The consequence is that they are continually in trouble with other people. They want to turn whole situations to themselves, instead of relating themselves to the whole. A cancer cell is one that demands that it be served instead of serving the rest of the body. It is therefore cancerous instead of contributive. There are many who are cancerous in society. They look at what they can get from the whole instead of what they can give it.

O Christ, teach me how to live well with others, for I want others to live well with me. Amen.

THE IMPORTANCE OF LOYALTY

Those who convict the innocent by their false testimony will disappear. A similar fate awaits those who use trickery to pervert justice and who tell lies to destroy the innocent. (Isa. 29:21 †)

After we recognize that we are corporate, we must proceed to….

2. *Fix our loyalty to the group in which we are in immediate contact.* There are degrees of loyalty, of course. There is the loyalty to oneself, to one's family, to one's group, to one's nation, to the kingdom of God. Our final loyalty should be to the kingdom of God. Where loyalty to that kingdom conflicts with any of the lesser loyalties, then the lesser must give way. However, there must also be a loyalty to a group in which we work out the principles of that kingdom and make them operative. If we do not work them out in the smaller arena, we shall never work them out in the larger.

3. *Loyalty to that group should mean that we never criticize any member behind his or her back.* There is bound to be criticism, for this is an imperfect world of imperfect persons. But the criticism should always be open, frank, and redemptive. One of the mottoes on our ashram walls is this: "Fellowship is based on confidence; secret criticism undermines that confidence; therefore we renounce all secret criticism." You cannot have fellowship if you know or suspect that secret criticism is taking place. But when you know that since there is no open criticism, there is no secret criticism, the situation can be filled with confidence and freedom—and therefore with fellowship.

Another motto on our ashram walls is this: "When about to criticize another, ask three questions: (1) Is it true? (2) Is it necessary? (3) Is it kind?" If it can pass these three tests, then the criticism should be given openly and frankly.

Religious people are in the business of endeavoring to be good. They are therefore tempted to point out the faults of others, so that by implication they themselves may appear better. It is a miserable business.

O Christ, save me this day and every day from the disloyalty of secret criticism. May the words die upon my lips and in my heart because of Your love. Amen.

A TWO-WAY STREET

As you endure this divine discipline, remember that God is treating you as his own children. Who ever heard of a child who is never disciplined by its father?… No discipline is enjoyable while it is happening—it's painful! But afterward there will be a peaceful harvest of right living for those who are trained in this way. (Heb. 12:7, 11 †)

In corporate living, the fourth principle is this:

4. *We should not only be willing to criticize another for his or her good, but we should also be willing to take it for ourselves—and rejoice in it.* No one has earned the right to criticize someone else unless they welcome the lessons to be learned from others. The principle of give-and-take must be in operation within the group.

5. *But we should be on our guard that we do not thus become petty, always looking for something to correct in the other person.* We should perhaps be more inclined to compliment and encourage than to correct. We do not need to be afraid that we will make people proud, for sincere souls are often more humbled by compliments than by criticism. If we are always looking for things to correct, we become dangerously near to the speck-picking that Jesus talked about.

Two prominent Indians went to England. One came back enthused with ideas, which he put into practice, and is now a great spiritual leader. The other came back and could scarcely talk of anything except the signs he saw in public places, "Beware of pickpockets." The idea of such a sign being necessary in a Christian country! He fed his soul on speck-picking and withered into insignificance.

Our attitude should be to find excellent things, stopping to point out weakness only occasionally. The emphasis should be on the search for the good. For people are made more by compliments than by corrections.

O Christ, You who find fine things in me when I cannot find them in myself, help me this day to find the good in those around me, and to say so. Amen.

SMALL MATTERS FOR SMALL PEOPLE

Let your gentleness be evident to all. The Lord is near. (Phil. 4:5)

Love…is not unmannerly, nor selfish, nor irritable, nor mindful of wrongs. (1 Cor. 13:4-5 WEYMOUTH)

Going on from where we stopped yesterday….

6. *Be willing to give way in small things that do not involve principles.* Many tiny things can become mountains because we insist on making them so. It is far better to step aside in small matters, so that we might stand on the big ones. The bigness of a person can be judged by the size of the thing upon which they take a stand. One of the great things in life is to learn to keep small things small and great things great. We often reverse these things in our relationship to each other.

7. *Refuse to look for slights and offenses.* No one is more difficult than the touchy person who is always getting feelings hurt. If we look for slights, we shall find them. But it shows we are on the defensive, which means we are dominated by fear. The defensive attitude shows that either the inferiority complex or the fear complex is at work.

8. *Pay more attention to our duties than to our rights.* If we are always looking after our rights, we throw the emphasis on the wrong side of things. Think about the privileges of service and you will have more rights than you will know what to do with.

9. *Deal with issues before they get cold.* If you harbor a thing in the heart, it will fester. Get it up and out at once. Don't put it off through cowardice. Jesus said, "Settle matters *quickly* with your adversary…*while you are still with him on the way*" (Matt. 5:25). Don't let the matter get cold. Cultivate the habit of spiritual decisiveness.

O Christ, thank You that in facing issues You did not hesitate. Give me that same nerve. Amen.

SIDING AGAINST YOURSELF

Live in harmony with one another. Do not be proud, but be willing to associate with people of low position. Do not be conceited. (Rom. 12:16)

Do not be overrighteous, neither be overwise—why destroy yourself? (Eccl. 7:16)

Corporate life in the Christian way means that....

10. *We shall often have to side with the group against ourselves and our own interests.* A mother was teaching her little boy to get guidance in life. He had taken the scissors, cut off one side of his hair, and left the pillowcase in shreds. When his mother returned, instead of losing her temper, she suggested a "quiet time" in which they could seek guidance as to what should be done.

His answer after the "quiet time" was this: "I think we had better not let me have the scissors again." Sound guidance! He had sided with his mother against himself. This is something you and I have to do very often. We have to admit that the group-claim is stronger than our personal claim.

11. *Be willing to laugh at yourself.* It will keep you from taking yourself too seriously. The capacity of a person to laugh at himself determines how high he or she has risen. In fact, there are these stages: the lowest person, who doesn't laugh at all; then the person who laughs only at their own jokes; then the one who laughs at the jokes of others; and highest of all, the person who can laugh at himself. This shows the power to look at oneself objectively.

12. *If you find a basic inequality or injustice at the heart of your relationship with anyone in the group, don't call for patience unless and until you are doing your best to correct that basic injustice or inequality.* Otherwise, it will poison relationships, breaking out again and again until righted. No surface kindness can atone for that central wrong. Build your fundamental relationships on justice and equality, and everything else becomes easier.

O Christ, help us to put Your mind into all our relationships, and then we shall know how to live together. Amen.

STRENGTHS FOR ONE ANOTHER

The body is a unit, though it is made up of many parts; and though all its parts are many, they form one body. So it is with Christ. For we were all baptized by one Spirit into one body—whether Jews or Greeks, slave or free—and we were all given the one Spirit to drink. (1 Cor. 12:12-13)

We come to an important principle in corporate living:

13. *Recognize the group achievement.* Remember what Paul says: "Individually we serve as organs for one another" (Rom. 12:6 WEYMOUTH). This thought should keep us from jealousy. If a member of your group excels in singing, that person becomes your organ of song. You should therefore rejoice that your organ is so beautiful! Another may exceed you in executive ability. You should rejoice that your organ of executive power is functioning.

For the point is, you are striving to get a corporate job done, and the strength of any is the strength of all. You will have something that will be the organ of someone else, something in which you are strong and they are weak. None of us has everything, but we all have something.

14. *Keep up the prayer life, and underneath that prayer life keep a surrendered heart.* When we are inwardly surrendered, we don't expect anything—and if anything comes our way, it is sheer gain. Furthermore, when we are inwardly surrendered, we become immune to many of the slights and clashes of ordinary contact. So let your thought of each other turn to prayer for each other.

A woman rather dreaded the arrival of a critical person who was coming to stay a week at her house. She felt a night of prayer alone would fortify her against the trial. No sooner had she knelt than the promise came, "God will meet all your needs" (Phil. 4:19). Her fears vanished. She jumped into bed and slept the night through.

The guest came the next day, and her hostess quite enjoyed the visit. Prayer had tapped the power of Christ. It will do it for you as well.

O Christ, Your power alone can sweeten relationships and make impossible situations glorious. Give me that power this day. Amen.

SEVEN COLORS OF LIGHT

Awe came upon everyone.... And all the believers kept together, and had everything in common. They sold their lands and other property, and distributed the proceeds among all, according to everyone's necessities.... They took their meals with great happiness and single-heartedness, praising God and being regarded with favour by all the people. Also day by day the Lord added to their number those whom He was saving. (Acts 2:43-47 WEYMOUTH)

Here is a cross-section of corporate Christianity in the first century:

1. *Awe.* The supernatural was working down through human relationships and was being embodied in a new society. God became an incarnate fact.

2. *Unity.* Many shades of belief and class and color were present, but they had a living unity that transcended differences.

3. *That unity included the social and economic life.* These Christians were not merely one in spirit, apart from matters of money and status. The whole of life was one. They held no difference between the sacred and the secular.

4. *Need was abolished.* Good news to the poor (the first item in Christ's agenda, according to Luke 4:18) was fulfilled.

5. *Community, family, and individual life were preserved.* Verse 46 tells us they were "in the Temple with one accord," the place of community; they ate bread "at home," the place of family life; and they experienced "great happiness" on the individual level.

6. *Single-heartedness.* The divisions were gone both on the inside and on the outside, in their relationships with each other. Life was reduced to simplicity.

7. *Life became winsome and contagious.* They were "regarded with favor," and so, "day by day the Lord added."

These are the seven colors into which the white light of God's society breaks up. We must rediscover this light for a darkened age, putting it not merely into the small group but into society as a whole. For God wills it!

O God, we cannot be fully victorious until everyone shares that victory. Help us to embody that victory in our total life. Amen.

TWO DANGERS

Then Judas Iscariot, one of the Twelve, went to the chief priests to betray Jesus to them. They were delighted to hear this and promised to give him money. So he watched for an opportunity to hand him over. (Mark 14:10-11)

The love of money is a root of all kinds of evil. Some people, eager for money, have wandered from the faith and pierced themselves with many griefs. (1 Tim. 6:10)

The greatest dangers to this new emerging society, the kingdom of God, came from two directions: money and power.

The new society was threatened when Judas gave in to the love of money. It was also threatened from within when the disciples began to quarrel over the places of power. It was more than threatened from the outside when the Jewish religious authorities and the Roman secular power came into conflict with the authority of God's kingdom, as represented in Jesus. They saw their power challenged, and they struck back with a cross. Money and power crucified Christ.

It is strange that sex apparently had nothing to do with it, though we usually think of sex as the greatest moral danger. In hunting for causes of the crucifixion of Jesus, there is no need to look for a woman in the case. Money and power held the field of causes. They did then, and they do today.

It is said that "Jesus sat down opposite the place where the offerings were put and watched the crowd" (Mark 12:41). It is a serious and awful moment when Jesus surveys the money side of our religion and our civilization. He sees how we make money, how we keep it, how we spend it, and the hypocrisies and strife that have grown up around it all. He is searching that side of our civilization as never before. He is probing to the roots. His awful eye of judgment is upon that central moral fact.

We will not be able to get complete victory in human living, individually and collectively, until we get it at the place of money.

O Christ, become the Conscience of our conscience at this point, for here we need light to show us the way out, and we need power that will deliver us from the love of money. Amen.

VICTORIOUS OVER MONEY

I have learned to be content whatever the circumstances. I know what it is to be in need, and I know what it is to have plenty. I have learned the secret of being content in any and every situation, whether well fed or hungry, whether living in plenty or in want. (Phil. 4:11-12)

When we think about victory in the financial area, there are individual and social aspects. We must apply self-surrender to both of these.

Money must be individually surrendered. That is, we will say something like this: "I know I need money in a world of this kind, but I don't need more than I need. I will draw a line at the place where my needs end, for at that place other people's needs begin. To go beyond that line is to steal from them, and I cannot do that and be Christian. In prayer and counsel with others I will find that line, and put the surplus toward other people's needs."

In other words, I master money by making it serve my need and the needs of others. So long as money makes me more mentally, morally, physically, and spiritually fit for the purposes of the kingdom of God, it is legitimate and right—a servant of the kingdom.

On the social side, we should inwardly renounce (and get as many other people as possible to renounce) a system of money use based on competition that turns society into "a scramble of pursuers and pursued." We should renounce this order based on the unchristian principle of selfish competition and give ourselves to producing an order based on the Christian principle of cooperation.

We will not be able to accomplish this fully at once. Society is not prepared for it. Society must blunder on and suffer more until it is beaten to its knees by the chastening rod of God, and then we try God's way. But in the meantime, we can renounce the old order and work for a new one. On that basis we can live victoriously both individually and collectively, because we are acting as though the victory were already here. It is, as far as we are concerned.

O Christ, help me this day to renounce money as master and to realize it as servant by Your power. Amen.

VICTORIOUS OVER POWER

Jesus called them together and said, "You know that the rulers of the Gentiles lord it over them, and their high officials exercise authority over them. Not so with you. Instead, whoever wants to become great among you must be your servant, and whoever wants to be first must be your slave—just as the Son of Man did not come to be served, but to serve, and to give his life as a ransom for many." (Matt. 20:25-28)

We must now see how power, which usually corrupts people, may serve people. Power is the expression or projection of personality. When the personality is converted, power must be converted along with it. But the matter of power has its individual and its social aspects. So it must be doubly converted.

"As Jesus was sitting on the Mount of Olives opposite the temple" (Mark 13:3), He surveyed it and judged it. The power represented in that temple had turned from service to exploitation. Given to serve the people, it now made the people serve it. It must therefore be cleansed, and if it did not respond, then it had to come down. Jesus is surveying the power side of our civilization today. His searching eye rests on the exploitations taking place through power. And we feel His burning condemnations.

Again, we must get the victory by surrender. Jesus told us that the road to greatness lay through servanthood. I must therefore renounce all power over others in my life that is not gained by service to others. All power based on money, prestige, class, race, or gender must go. This is personal.

In regard to the social, we must do the same. We must inwardly renounce all power in the social and political order that does not serve the people in their total needs, and we must influence as many others as possible to do the same. Now, society is not ready to make this the criterion of power. Here too, society must blunder on and suffer more before it is beaten to its knees under God's chastening rod. Meanwhile we renounce all exploiting power and are willing to suffer because of that renunciation.

O God, help me not to bend the knee to insolent might. May I know no sovereignty but Yours. Amen.

AN INEVITABLE CROSS

Anyone who does not carry his cross and follow me cannot be my disciple.
(Luke 14:27)

Then Thomas (called Didymus) said to the rest of the disciples, "Let us also go, that we may die with him." (John 11:16)

If we are in sympathetic contact with people and situations around us, we react in sorrow to what is happening. The effect of the gospel is to deepen and widen one's sensitivities. Your sympathies will be so widened that life will touch you on a wider front. The process of your Christianization is the deepening of your capacity for suffering. Each new friendship you form, each new convert you win, each new injustice you see in the social order, each new sin in others that you notice, each new task you take on yourself, will become a possible suffering point. The cross thus becomes inevitable.

In the case of Jesus, His sensitivities were universal in range and infinite in depth. He was the Son of man, and the cross that came as a result of that fact was universal and infinite. It had cosmic significance. He touched all life in love, and out of that love contact, all His being reacted in suffering. The cross is the focal point of that suffering.

The actors in that terrible drama unwittingly bore witness to this universal cross when they put up His inscription in Latin, Greek, and Hebrew. That was unusual. Did they dimly sense that here was suffering breaking out into all languages? Or was it that they expressed His guilt in all these languages? It doesn't matter, for it was the same—His guilt was His love—the guilt of loving universally, and therefore suffering universally.

As you become personally and socially Christianized, a cross awaits you. It is inevitable.

O Christ, we see Your cross was not an isolated thing; it continues in us. May I this day be in the succession of Your cross-bearers. Amen.

THE CROSS IN ACTION

I speak the truth in Christ—I am not lying, my conscience confirms it in the Holy Spirit—I have great sorrow and unceasing anguish in my heart. For I could wish that I myself were cursed and cut off from Christ for the sake of my brothers, those of my own race. (Rom. 9:1-3)

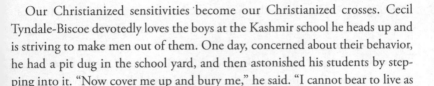

Our Christianized sensitivities become our Christianized crosses. Cecil Tyndale-Biscoe devotedly loves the boys at the Kashmir school he heads up and is striving to make men out of them. One day, concerned about their behavior, he had a pit dug in the school yard, and then astonished his students by stepping into it. "Now cover me up and bury me," he said. "I cannot bear to live as long as you do these things. I would rather die. You must bury me, or you must bury your sins." The boys decided to bury their sins.

Going out into life as a Christian, you may not confront evil so dramatically as that, but your contact will turn into a cross for you. I heard about a man who wanted to build a house with no windows and no doors except the slits of a cross as the single opening, so he could look out upon the world through a cross alone. Beautiful. But we must do more than that; we must *touch* life through a cross. Our very contacts must become vicarious.

We must deliberately take on ourselves what really doesn't belong to us, except as Christ makes us belong to everybody, and, therefore, everyone's sorrows belong to us. When anyone is called an ethnic slur, we wince; when one is an outsider, we are lonely and degraded alongside them; when one is hungry, we suffer their pangs; when children are exploited, they become our own children; when a black person suffers discrimination on account of color, we become whiter—with pain; when war takes a young man and binds him to its nefarious purposes, how can we be free unless we are bound with him—perhaps in prison, as a result of our protest? Our love bleeds into sacrifice as it meets the world's sin. In a world of this kind, a crossless Christian is a Christless Christian.

O Christ, make me willing to open my heart deeply to the world's anguish and woe, and may my heart become a place of healing. Amen.

WHEN TRAGEDY STRIKES

I have been crucified with Christ and I no longer live, but Christ lives in me. The life I live in the body, I live by faith in the Son of God, who loved me and gave himself for me. (Gal. 2:20)

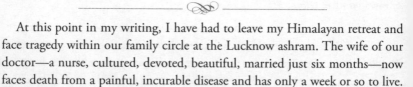

At this point in my writing, I have had to leave my Himalayan retreat and face tragedy within our family circle at the Lucknow ashram. The wife of our doctor—a nurse, cultured, devoted, beautiful, married just six months—now faces death from a painful, incurable disease and has only a week or so to live. She will not be able to get back to her home in Holland to die there among her loved ones. Cut off at the end of five months of devoted service in India! My God, why?

No one can look into the face of this kind of a tragedy without raising ultimate questions about the universe. Is there any meaning and purpose? If there is a God, does He care? I have no answer, except as I look at life through the cross. There I see a God who comes into the very struggle and suffers all I suffer, and more. I can love a God like that.

When I stand beside the bedside of Sister Winnie—who would have stood in tender ministry at the bedside of thousands had she lived—I see light only in a cross. In this way my universe holds steady. Said a Christian Indian professor, "The cross saves me from pessimism and saves the truth at the heart of pessimism." The truth in pessimism is: This is indeed a world of pain, sorrow, and tragedy. But the cross saves us from pessimism by using that pain, sorrow, and tragedy for redemptive purposes. Through it all, it shows the very love of God seeking, redeeming, healing, saving. The cross is light—the only light.

Christ, we come thanking You that we can see life through Your wound-prints, and that through them we can see light—the very light of life. Amen.

THE FOUR WHO CARRIED CROSSES

God is pleased with you when you do what you know is right and patiently endure unfair treatment…. [Jesus] did not retaliate when he was insulted, nor threaten revenge when he suffered. He left his case in the hands of God, who always judges fairly. (1 Peter 2:19, 23†)

That awful day at Golgotha, four different men carried crosses. They represent four attitudes.

The first was the unrepentant thief—it was a cross of unrelieved gloom. He blamed Christ for not saving Himself and them. He died blaming everybody but himself, and therefore bore a cross that had no light in it. Some people carry that kind of a cross to the very end of their lives. No repentance, no reconciliation, no release.

The other thief looked through and beyond the shame of it all to see that Jesus really was a King. He asked to be remembered when He came in His kingdom. That was the cross that had light in it. It had thrown him into contact with Jesus. That cross lifted up his head, and he saw the gates of forgiveness open to him. It had started in gloom but ended in gladness.

The third cross was laid upon the shoulders of Simon, a foreigner from Cyrene in North Africa. They laid on him an undeserved cross; in fact, "they forced him to carry" it (Mark 14:21). Life does that with us sometimes; it grabs us and puts a cross on our unwilling shoulders. But this incident changed the whole course of life for Simon and his family. His wife and his son Rufus became well-known Christians (see Rom. 16:13). Simon did not endure his cross—he used it. When life lays its cross on us, we can make that cross throw us in company with Christ, a contact that will forever change us.

The last cross-bearer was Jesus Himself. The others were involuntary—this cross was chosen. He put Himself in such deep contact with humanity that the cross became inevitable. Since life is bound to give you a cross, it is better to anticipate it, to accept it, and through it to lift others.

O Christ, help me to take that chosen cross and to make it redemptive for myself and others. Amen.

E. STANLEY JONES | 301

SONGS OF JOY

You will go out in joy and be led forth in peace; the mountains and hills will burst into song before you, and all the trees of the field will clap their hands! (Isa. 55:12)

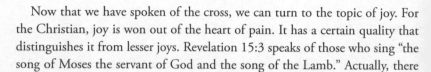

Now that we have spoken of the cross, we can turn to the topic of joy. For the Christian, joy is won out of the heart of pain. It has a certain quality that distinguishes it from lesser joys. Revelation 15:3 speaks of those who sing "the song of Moses the servant of God and the song of the Lamb." Actually, there are three notable songs: the song of Nature, the song of Moses, and the song of the Lamb.

The song of Nature is the song of the strong triumphing over the weak. I heard a bird singing happily with a quivering dragonfly in its mouth. It beat the insect from one side to another and interspersed the ghastly killing with cheerful singing. Such a song comes out of the lower nature—it is a song mingled with the pains of others. Hunger and power are satisfied, even though it costs lives.

Many sing that song. Their joy comes from personal advantage, no matter what it may cost others. They rejoice that they have gained in the stock market, even though their gain was somebody's loss. They rejoice in business success, even though they may have pushed somebody else to the wall. It is the joy of knowing that the head of John the Baptist is off, even though they do not like the sight of it on a platter in front of them. They have won. That is enough.

There is a slightly higher joy in the song of Moses (see Deut. 32). It is the song of limited rights, an eye for an eye, and a tooth for a tooth. We rejoice that we got even with someone. Our sense of rough justice is satisfied. We often sing the song of Moses. We go through life getting satisfactions out of strict justice. That too is superficial and precarious.

O Christ, save us from the satisfactions of the lesser joys that leave their sting, and help us to know Your joy because we know Your cross. Amen.

THE SONG OF THE LAMB

What blessings await you when people hate you and exclude you and mock you and curse you as evil because you follow the Son of Man. When that happens, be happy! Yes, leap for joy! For a great reward awaits you in heaven. (Luke 6:22-23†)

We must now look at the song of the Lamb—the song of unlimited love, the song of doing good to those who despitefully use you, the song of One who dies for His crucifiers. This is life's deepest song. Those who can sing this song are in the highest stage of spiritual evolution. They really have victory.

A widow of a murdered prime minister had this song when she gathered her children around the coffin of her husband and prayed for his murderer's forgiveness. Our young ashram doctor has this song when cruel nature snatches his young wife away and he carries on helping to save others, rejoicing in the opportunity.

I had a canary that would not sing until after it had taken its bath. Then it would sing deliriously. My heart is like that, and so is yours. It will not sing until it is washed from all bitterness, all revenge, all hate. Only then can it really sing with all the stops out.

A Brahmin convert suffered because of his stand for Christ, but this is what he writes: "I am always bubbling over with joy to the bursting point. My Lord is always with me to save, to comfort, to guide and to cheer. May He be with you similarly." That is the Christian note.

Don't downplay this joy in the name of modern sophistication. It is the most cleansing, most energizing, most service-inspiring, most rhythm-producing fact on earth. It is salvation by joy. One drop of that puts more oil into the machinery of life than anything else.

O Christ, we thank You for this exquisite joy. When we have tasted it, we know we have tasted life itself. Help us to share it. Amen.

RESURRECTION POWER

He will swallow up death forever. The Sovereign Lord will wipe away the tears from all faces; he will remove the disgrace of his people from all the earth. The Lord has spoken. (Isa. 25:8)

Since, then, you have been raised with Christ, set your hearts on things above, where Christ is seated at the right hand of God. (Col. 3:1)

The song of the Lamb leads us a step further. We find joy in realizing "the power of his resurrection" (Phil. 3:10).

The resurrection of Jesus means that the worst has been met and conquered. This puts an ultimate optimism at the heart of things. The resurrection says that no matter how life may seem to go to pieces around you, the last word is still with love—on the physical plane, in the here and now.

This sweeps the whole horizon and says that here and now we can meet and conquer anything. No wonder Christians in the midst of a decaying order are no pessimists. They have solid grounds for optimism.

When Paul came to the Athenians "preaching the good news about Jesus and the resurrection," they said, "He seems to be advocating foreign gods" (Acts 17:18). They apparently thought the resurrection was a separate god because of Paul's emphasis. In our age, there is no danger of that happening, for the resurrection has been dimmed—and with it an infinite sadness has come over us.

We Christians do not deify the resurrection, but neither shall we dim it; we shall declare it as the most amazing and transforming fact of human history. Nothing really matters now except this one thing: He is alive forevermore! Related to Him, realizing Him, drawing life from Him, we are fellowshiping with ultimate Life, and nothing again can dismay us or make us afraid. If in the end everything will come out all right, then what does it matter what happens to us on the way? He is risen!

O Christ, I thank You for the joy of knowing that nothing need now defeat me, since nothing defeated You. Help me to take hold of that fact and live by it. Amen.

THE JOY OF HIS PRESENCE

You have made known to me the path of life; you will fill me with joy in your presence, with eternal pleasures at your right hand. (Psalm 16:11)

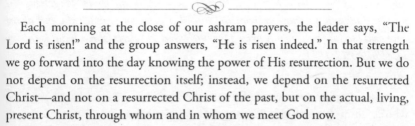

Each morning at the close of our ashram prayers, the leader says, "The Lord is risen!" and the group answers, "He is risen indeed." In that strength we go forward into the day knowing the power of His resurrection. But we do not depend on the resurrection itself; instead, we depend on the resurrected Christ—and not on a resurrected Christ of the past, but on the actual, living, present Christ, through whom and in whom we meet God now.

The deepest joy is the communion of Person with person. Sometimes our earthly vessels can scarcely contain this exquisite joy. We are almost tempted to ask Him to withhold His hand. But we wouldn't have Him actually do it for the world, for this is Life, Life. "I feel so sacred within," wrote a very modern girl after tasting this new Life.

And no wonder! In the center of our being we commune with Life—our thoughts are washed in His thoughts, our wills are strengthened by His will, our affections are bathed in His. The German theologian Adolf von Harnack, speaking of the mystics, says, "Some perceive the presence of the Spirit with every sense: they see the brilliant light, they hear its voice, they smell the fragrance of immortality, and taste its sweetness." Yes, indeed—one moment of that, and it is worth the world. Life can never be the same.

To us it is not strange that God spoke to Moses out of a burning bush, for have not our hearts become in living fact a burning bush, out of which God speaks to us in tenderest tones as well as directive? Out of this fellowship with the fire comes the call to redeem, to bid my people go. So this communion ends in a commission. And that commission in turn feeds upon the communion.

The wonder is not that we should speak of it, but the wonder is that we should speak of anything else.

O God, my Father, I enter the shrine of my heart and commune with You there, and one minute of that is an eternity. For there we become eternal. Amen.

CERTAINTY AND OPENNESS

I don't mean to say that I have…already reached perfection. But I press on to possess that perfection for which Christ Jesus first possessed me. No, dear brothers and sisters, I have not achieved it, but I focus on this one thing: Forgetting the past and looking forward to what lies ahead, I press on to reach the end of the race and receive the heavenly prize for which God, through Christ Jesus, is calling us. (Phil. 3:12-14†)

Is there any joy more wonderful than the joy of being in touch with the One who is ultimate Fact? Life becomes immovably centered and fixed. It is not subject to the changes around it. A certainty that is open-eyed and still remains certain is certainty indeed.

A very intelligent woman wrote: "I had spiritual certainty, but it was without an open road. I was afraid of open roads. So I clung to my spiritual certainty, and became blind to everything else. Then I went to a university and took postgraduate work, and there I got the open road, but I lost my certainty. I groped along for some time. Now I have both certainty and the open road."

Some people's ideas, minds, and theological systems are fixed. It is a certainty gained at the expense of sight! Others have the open road, but no certainties. They know the quest, but no rest. They journey and journey and never arrive. And they call this emptiness a virtue. They want no certainties, they say.

But the heart knows better. It journeys with a new buoyancy when there is certainty within. It is not a dead certainty, but a certainty that sets us on fire to know more. We know we cannot live on an afterglow of some past experience, just as the French philosopher Ernest Renan says, "We cannot go on living on the perfume of a broken vase." There must be fresh discovery every day.

And there is! The deepest sign of life is that we want more life. The surest sign that we are on the right road is that we feel it is an open road. The joy of growth is one of the deepest joys of life.

O Christ, You have touched us, and our hearts are afire to know more. Feed us the "more," and we will be satisfied. Amen.

THE SPIRIT'S LAW

There is therefore now no condemnation for those who are in Christ Jesus; for the Spirit's law—life in Christ Jesus—has set me free from the law of sin and death. (Rom. 8:1 WEYMOUTH)

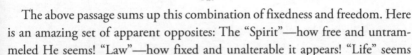

The above passage sums up this combination of fixedness and freedom. Here is an amazing set of apparent opposites: The "Spirit"—how free and untrammeled He seems! "Law"—how fixed and unalterable it appears! "Life" seems free and unfixed, while "Christ Jesus" is fixed in the historic facts. Yet Paul puts them together and says the Spirit's law is life in Christ Jesus.

A scholar named Sabatier divides religions into "religions of the Spirit" and "religions of authority." One is directed from within, and the other from without; one depends on inner life, the other on outer law. Paul here puts them together.

Life in Christ Jesus is the fixed norm. We are not now adrift—we know what life is, for we know what God is. We had to have God transformed so He could become available. As Bernard Bell puts it: "Over a wire comes a mighty electric current. I cannot use it. It is too powerful for my motor. It would melt the thing, ruin it. I shunt off the current into a resistance box and transform it into voltage which is usable. My motor is no longer destroyed, but empowered. So Jesus thus transforms God" (*Beyond Agnosticism,* p. 72).

The awful God becomes the accessible God. We now see what He is like and what we can be like. We have a fixed point in our universe. No one knows the worth and significance of that until seeing it in contrast with systems where there is no norm, no fixed point. Whole systems adrift! But God has met us in history, and that meeting is Christ. "Life in Christ Jesus"—that gives us a starting point.

O God, we thank You that we have seen You in a face. Now we can never be satisfied until we are like that. Our hearts glow with gratitude. Amen.

THE SPIRIT'S UNFOLDING

When he, the Spirit of truth, comes, he will guide you into all truth. He will not speak on his own; he will speak only what he hears, and he will tell you what is yet to come. He will bring glory to me by taking from what is mine and making it known to you. (John 16:13-14)

The Spirit *unfolds* what is *infolded* in Christ. The Spirit will not guide us contrary to what we find in the life and teaching of Christ. This is as fixed as a law. But the range of unfolding is infinite.

In John 14:26 we see again the combination: "But the Counselor, the Holy Spirit…will teach you all things and will remind you of everything I have said to you." The reminding part is the turning back to fixed facts. The teaching part is the Spirit's direct, immediate voice to each age and to each individual.

And what is the Spirit's voice for this troubled and distracted age, searching for a way of life and plans for the future? The kingdom of God on earth! The Spirit is unfolding the possibility of a new world according to God's Plan. This Plan haunts the political councils, where all plans are being examined. Our world is not ready to take the Plan yet, for we are not ready for salvation. We will stumble along until one day we shall fall on our knees and take God's Plan—and then! A new age, a new world, a new community, new men and women!

I refuse to take my eyes off that possibility and listen to the cynics, inside and outside the Christian church, who tell me it is but a dream, and the only reality is force and compulsion. Force and compulsion are what have healed one while wounding ten! No, I hear the Spirit's voice amid the clamor, reminding us that our Master proclaimed the kingdom as His message, and He does not change. The kingdom is still at our doors—our one open road, our one hope. "Anyone with ears to hear must listen to the Spirit and understand what he is saying" (Rev. 2:7 †).

O Spirit of the Living God, You are speaking to dulled ears. Your voice calls us anew to the kingdom. Help us to listen, or we perish. Amen.

PRACTICAL WAYS TO GROW

Speaking the truth in love, we will in all things grow up into him who is the Head, that is, Christ. From him the whole body, joined and held together by every supporting ligament, grows and builds itself up in love, as each part does its work. (Eph. 4:15-16)

If we have been put under a Living Mind, under a Law that is an unfolding Life, we must therefore grow in order to remain Christian.

Grow by your mistakes, even by your sins. Many people collapse under a fall and stay down. But losing a skirmish does not necessarily mean losing the battle. We can win if it makes us more watchful, more humble, and more determined in the future.

There is an old saying: "When a good man falls, he falls on his knees." A good place to fall! Get up at once, and say: "Well, that was a jolt, but I've learned my lesson. I shall ask for reinforcements and get them for that weakness." You can become strongest at your weakest places. Both the apostle Paul and John Wesley were converted Pharisees who became strongest where they were weakest—they became men of humility, depending on grace. If you fall, don't give up—get up.

Grow by taking on a task beyond your powers. That will throw you back on God's grace. Don't limit yourself to things you can do that won't stretch you. Do something you *can't* do, and that will make you grow in the doing.

All my life I've done things I couldn't do. I undertake them at His bidding, and somehow there is divine reinforcement. Phillips Brooks has memorably said, "Do not pray for tasks equal to your powers, but for powers equal to your tasks." We need big and demanding tasks in order to grow.

When God called the young Mary, she did not shrink, nor did she become proud. She simply said, "I am the Lord's servant…. May it be to me as you have said" (Luke 1:38). In other words, I am ready for anything. And she was.

O God, my Father, give me this day spiritual tasks that are beyond me, so I may draw heavily upon Your resources. Amen.

GROWING FARTHER, DEEPER

These are the words of him who is holy and true, who holds the key of David. What he opens no one can shut, and what he shuts no one can open. I know your deeds. See, I have placed before you an open door that no one can shut. (Rev. 3:7-8)

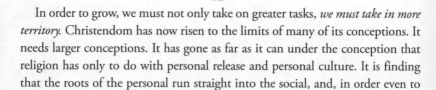

In order to grow, we must not only take on greater tasks, *we must take in more territory.* Christendom has now risen to the limits of many of its conceptions. It needs larger conceptions. It has gone as far as it can under the conception that religion has only to do with personal release and personal culture. It is finding that the roots of the personal run straight into the social, and, in order even to develop the personal, we must Christianize the social.

This is the area of future growth for many of us, for we have been like potted plants, confined to the cramping conceptions of a personal gospel. We must be transplanted to the garden of larger social conceptions and endeavors. Then we will grow.

An expert told me that in planting trees at the ashram, we should dig a very deep pit, put in a layer of manure, then one of ordinary earth, then another layer of manure followed again by a layer of earth, and so on up to the top. This, he said, gives the growing tree something to reach for. Its roots get to one level and then feel the call of the deeper level of richness.

Christianity must put its roots into the total life of humanity, or else it will die, pot-bound. Or it will remain a dwarfed, pathetic thing in this modern world. But we must not talk about Christianity in general; we must talk about ourselves. We cannot wait till everybody else is ready to act. It is said in the parable of the mustard seed that the man cast the seed "in his garden" (Luke 13:19)—we must begin there. Jesus announced His own program at Nazareth first before He announced the program for the disciples in the Sermon on the Mount. We must do the same.

O Christ, help us today to set forth the stakes of Your kingdom and claim new territory for Your redemptive purposes. Help us to fear not, but begin. Amen.

DELIBERATELY PLANNING TO GROW

Enlarge the place of your tent, stretch your tent curtains wide, do not hold back; lengthen your cords, strengthen your stakes. For you will spread out to the right and to the left; your descendants will dispossess nations and settle in their desolate cities. (Isa. 54:2-3)

Taking in more territory on the social plane in order to further our own growth should not be our motive, however. We should save the total life of humanity simply because it is right. Nothing less than all belongs to Christ. But if we do so, it will result in our own enlargement.

How shall we claim more territory?

1. Do it mentally. Renounce in the depths of your heart a system based on the unchristian principle of selfish competition. Give yourself inwardly to the principle of cooperation.

2. Go out today and see how you can apply that inward renunciation in positive action. If you are a businessperson, begin to build a cooperative order within your area of influence. If you are a laborer, organize a cooperative alliance no matter how small a scale. It will train you and others in cooperative thinking and endeavor.

3. See where your vote can be cast on behalf of more justice. For this new day must come down through the political, as well as up through cooperative organizations. They must be supplemented by political action.

4. Break down some race or class barrier today. Invite to your home someone not of your race or class. Do not patronize them—they will sense it at once. The will to be a friend is as important as the will to believe. In the beginning you may have to act friendly before you feel friendly.

5. Get as many others to come with you as possible. Win converts, unashamedly, unblushingly.

6. Become saturated with the kingdom idea, the rule of Sovereign Love.

O God, my Father, help me this day to begin the kingdom program and to know the kingdom power in every single one of my relationships. Amen.

BEWARE OF THE DEVIL'S ATONEMENT

Jesus said to the crowds and to his disciples, "The teachers of religious law and the Pharisees…don't practice what they teach. They crush people with unbearable religious demands and never lift a finger to ease the burden. (Matt. 23:1-4†)

To act as though the kingdom were already in operation, anticipating its full coming, may cost you. It will likely mean a cross. You will find your cross at the point of tension between the new and the old.

But here a temptation will set in: You will be tempted to plan other people's sacrifices rather than your own. That is the devil's atonement. When Caiaphas the high priest "advised the Jews that it would be good if one man died for the people" (John 18:14), he was practicing the devil's atonement, for he was not preparing to sacrifice himself but someone else. When patrioteers call young people to sacrifice for the sake of the country while they sit safe and sound behind their counters and desks—it is the devil's atonement. When agitators get people to sacrifice for a cause but they will not sacrifice themselves—again, it is the devil's atonement. When ministers bind burdens of moral responsibility upon others and feel their duty is thereby discharged, not touching the burden with their little finger—is this not the devil's atonement? When we talk about a day of social justice and thus get the prestige that comes from renouncing this present system while at the same time gladly taking the comforts and privileges that belong to it—it is the devil's atonement.

If, therefore, we take our cross in order to bring in God's order, let us be sure we do take it and not put it on someone else instead.

O Christ, we want to fulfill Your word this day, that each shall take their own cross and come and follow You. Show me my cross, and help me take it. Amen.

UNIFYING THE MIND

You were taught, with regard to your former way of life, to put off your old self, which is being corrupted by its deceitful desires; to be made new in the attitude of your minds; and to put on the new self, created to be like God in true righteousness and holiness. (Eph. 4:22-24)

For real spiritual growth, there must be unity between the conscious and the subconscious minds. The subconscious can be taught the purposes of the conscious mind. It is educable. But it will not listen to what you say—only to what you do.

In his book *Reality,* Canon Burnett H. Streeter says: "The subconscious is always learning from the conscious, but it both learns and forgets more slowly. And the lessons it takes to heart most deeply are not the purely intellectual notions of the conscious mind, but the values and emotions associated with them. A man, for instance, may believe with his conscious mind that God is good and that all men are brothers, but only if he plans and acts…as if these things were true will his subconscious mind believe them also."

You cannot therefore teach the subconscious mind any unreality. It will not learn it. Jesus put His finger on this when He sent out the Twelve saying, "And do not…put on an extra inner garment" (Mark 6:9 WEYMOUTH). Think about the person who takes only one cloak—as if traveling humbly—but then puts on an extra, secret, inner garment. The subconscious mind will learn from the secret inner garment of comfort rather than from the one outer garment of ostensible renunciation.

St. Francis, when induced to wear an inner garment of wool for warmth, insisted on pinning a piece of wool to the outside, so no one would take him for more sacrificial than what he was.

Go over your life and ask whether there are any extra inner garments being held—special privileges, special securities. Growth is growth in reality.

O Christ, help me this day to tolerate no unreality, no make-believe. Help me to be real. Amen.

LIVE TODAY!

Do not be anxious, therefore, about to-morrow, for to-morrow will bring its own anxieties. Enough for each day is its own trouble. (Matt. 6:34 WEYMOUTH)

Give us today our daily bread. (Matt. 6:11)

In your spiritual growth, you must learn to live today. Many of us spoil today by bringing the troubles of tomorrow into it. Worry is the advance interest we pay on tomorrow's troubles. Many of us go bankrupt paying interest on troubles that never come. Worry becomes sin against the goodness and love of God.

Dr. Elwood Worcester says, "You could pack all the actual misfortunes of your life into a moderate-sized closet, while your whole house, no matter how big it is, would scarcely hold all the unrealized evils and misfortunes you have feared and looked forward to."

While writing on this book, a telegram was handed to me. A series of possible calamities flashed through my mind—things such as "Eunice" [my daughter] "is ill, come home at once." I jumped to all the implications of what that would mean—plans tumbling to pieces. Then I opened the telegram, and it read, "Jacob fully reconciled"—the good news of a healed misunderstanding! Life is like that. Nine-tenths of our troubles never come, and we can stand the one-tenth.

The English novelist Charles Kingsley said, "Do today's duty, fight today's temptation, and do not weaken and distract yourself by looking forward to things which you cannot see and could not understand if you saw them." In other words, live today! You do not have to win tomorrow's battles just now. Win the ones you face today, and tomorrow will take care of itself. God's power keeps you in this present moment; that keeping will extend to the next, and to the next, and at the end of the day you will find yourself victorious.

O Christ, thank You for calling us to the adventure of today. Help me to make today eternal because I have put eternal worth into it. Amen.

GROW THROUGH OBSTACLES

Among God's churches we boast about your perseverance and faith in all the persecutions and trials you are enduring. All this is evidence that God's judgment is right, and as a result you will be counted worthy of the kingdom of God, for which you are suffering. (2 Thess. 1:4-5)

When the Samaritans refused to receive Jesus and His disciples, the account says that after He rebuked the disciples for wanting to retaliate, "they went to another village" (Luke 9:56). Life always has "another village." If you are blocked in this one, pass on to the next. And that next village was nearer Jesus' final goal. He didn't have so far to go the next day. He advanced toward His goal by the snobbery of that first village.

Were you disappointed in searching for the life-mate you had hoped to find? Then pass on to another village. The early impact of Christianity produced the household of Philip, who "had four unmarried daughters who prophesied" (Acts 21:9). Singleness thus emerged to a new level seldom seen in the non-Christian faiths. Many unmarried people feel the call to relieve the sorrows, sufferings, and ignorance of the world. Like the daughters of Philip, their singleness becomes prophetic.

Have you been disappointed in your lifework? Grow by that disappointment. Henry Martyn, after years of patient toil, finished his Persian translation of the Bible and journeyed to present it to the Shah. He went into the court. As he placed it before them, they began to realize what book it was, and one by one they walked out, including the Shah himself. Henry Martyn was left alone with his new translation, rejected.

His comment was "I refuse to be disappointed." And he passed on to another village. Disappointment can be a spiritual growing place. It may make us start new endeavors, jolt us out of old ruts, deepen our sympathy, and altogether make us better persons.

O Christ, I thank You that You made Your frustrations into fruitfulness. Help me to do that this day. Amen.

FACING OBSTACLES WITH PRAYER

In the congregation was a man whose right hand was withered. The Scribes and the Pharisees were on the watch to see whether He would cure him on the Sabbath.... The hand was restored. But they were filled with madness, and began to discuss what they should do to Jesus.

It was at about that time that He went into the hill country to pray; and He remained all night in prayer to God. (Luke 6:6-7, 11-12 WEYMOUTH)

These illuminating verses tell of a unique obstacle: the madness of Jesus' opponents, which drove them to plot what they would do to Jesus. They felt they had the final say. Over against that, Jesus matched prayer. They counseled together as to what they should do to Him, and He counseled as to what the Father should do through Him.

What will my circumstances do to me today? Rather I should ask, what shall I do today through my circumstances by prayer? Again, here are my limitations, and they conspire to cramp me, to keep me from being effective. Is the last word with them? Not at all. I decide through prayer.

Many a person spurred on by a limitation has become great through that very limitation. Alfred Adler says, "This feeling that the individual has of his own inferiority furnishes the inward impulse to advance"—and much more if coupled with prayer, which gives power to advance.

What shall my enemies do with me? Rather I will ask, what shall I do with my enemies through prayer? I shall have power to forgive them. I can meet them from above. Said a Roman judge to a defendant, "I have power to kill you." The Christian replied, "But I have power to be killed." And that was the greater and final power.

We grow by meeting an obstacle—not merely through the obstacle, but through prayer induced by that very obstacle.

O Christ, I thank You that the last word, even upon the cross, was not with Your enemies but with You. Help me this day to turn every obstacle into opportunity through prayer. Amen.

DISMISS YOUR FEARS AND SINS

Since we are surrounded by so great a cloud of witnesses, let us lay aside every weight, and the sin which so easily ensnares us, and let us run with endurance the race that is set before us. (Heb. 12:1 NKJV)

Watch your life and doctrine closely. Persevere in them, because if you do, you will save both yourself and your hearers. (1 Tim. 4:16)

————————————— ⨯⨯⨯ —————————————

Our circumstances do not decide our destiny, but prayer does. Our spiritual lives are determined by the power we take into them through prayer. So when the calamity of blindness struck John Milton, the English poet who gave us *Paradise Lost,* he could say, "I argue not against Heaven's hand or will, nor bate [restrain] a jot of heart or hope; but still bear up and steer right onward." He was not the victim of circumstances, but the victor over circumstances.

God said to Paul at a treacherous juncture, "Dismiss your fears: go on speaking, and do not be silent. I am with you, and no one shall attack you to injure you" (Acts 18:10, WEYMOUTH). Note that God doesn't say that there shall be no attacks, but there shall be no attacks *to injure you.* Outside attacks cannot truly injure you—only those from within, by your own wrong choices. You are absolutely safe as long as you are right with God.

Grow in victory over half-sins—things that may be lawful to you but are not expedient. Paul calls us to lay aside "every weight, and the sin" that besets. Every weight! Things that bring no condemnation, but also no contribution. Do not ask, "Is it wrong?" Instead, ask, "Does it contribute?" Away with every noncontributing thing!

Jesus said to His disciples, "Take heed to yourselves" (Mark 13:9 KJV). Why? So that you might escape coming calamity? No. But so you will be prepared to give your witness (see vss. 9-11). Be spiritually fit, He says, so you may not be unprepared when called on to give your witness before high and low. For that hour depends not on your circumstances but upon you. Therefore let everything go that will not help you in that hour.

O Christ, help me this day to let go off every weight that might slow my pace. I want to be spiritually fit. Amen.

E. STANLEY JONES | 317

GROW YOUR FAITH IN HUMANITY

Take heed to yourselves. If your brother sins against you…seven times in a day, and seven times in a day returns to you, saying, 'I repent,' you shall forgive him."

And the apostles said to the Lord, "Increase our faith."

So the Lord said, "If you have faith as a mustard seed, you can say to this mulberry tree, 'Be pulled up by the roots and be planted in the sea,' and it would obey you." (Luke 17:3-6 NKJV)

Jesus used that phrase, "Take heed to yourselves," in another connection. He tied it to having an undiscouraged, creative faith in people. When the disciples asked that their faith be increased, it wasn't so much faith in God as faith in people—in wobbly people—that needed to be increased.

Such faith, He said, could transplant a mulberry tree into the most unstable soil in the world—the sea! You and I can make souls stable by a creative faith. Never did the world need people of creative faith so much as now, for a vast cynicism has crept across our spirits. We are falling to pieces for lack of them. The *Epistle to Diognetus* (second century) says of the Christians, "They hold the world together." This was written at a time when the social order was falling to pieces around them. The Christians did not belong to that decaying order— they belonged to the undecaying kingdom of God. Therefore they held the world together by their faith.

They did then, they must now. We must, by our creative faith, hold society and individuals from falling to pieces. So grow in your belief in people, in their possibilities, in the fact that the worst can become the best. Take heed to yourself, and let nothing hurt your faith in the weakest.

O Christ, help me this day to believe in people as You did. And help me to remake them by that very faith. Amen.

A PEOPLE PREPARED

The angel Gabriel: *"[John the Baptizer] will be great in the sight of the Lord. He is never to take wine or other fermented drink, and he will be filled with the Holy Spirit even from birth. Many of the people of Israel will he bring back to the Lord their God. And he will go on before the Lord, in the spirit and power of Elijah, to turn the hearts of the fathers to their children and the disobedient to the wisdom of the righteous—to make ready a people prepared for the Lord."* (Luke 1:15-17)

"A people prepared"! Did we ever need that so much as we need it now, in the midst of a world in change, a world seeking new moorings, a world feeling after a new order?

What kind of people can be said to be "prepared"? The account tells us that John was sound in three directions—toward God, toward himself, and toward others. (1) He was "great in the sight of the Lord." We need people such as that, who care not a rap if they are great or small on the human plane. (2) He was able to deny himself all alcoholic drink—while on the positive side, he was "filled with the Holy Spirit." We very much need people who can give up things for a great cause and who are filled with God's Spirit. (3) He was prepared in relation to others. He summed up the best and finest of the past—he came "in the spirit and power of Elijah." We need people who do not lose sight of God's dealings in history and who will hold to every fine gain from years gone by. They must be conservative.

But they must also be radical: John would "turn the hearts of the fathers to their children." We might have thought it would have been stated the other way round. But no, this older generation must turn its heart to the children, must think in terms of making the world safe and just for them. We must therefore be radical.

Let us be sound in these three ways, with these emphases. If so, we shall be a people prepared.

O Christ, make me this day a person prepared, that I may help to produce "a people prepared." Amen.

E. STANLEY JONES | 319

FORCED TO THINK

Jesus replied: " 'Love the Lord your God with all your heart and with all your soul and with all your mind.' This is the first and greatest commandment." (Matt. 22:37-38)

Therefore, prepare your minds for action; be self-controlled; set your hope fully on the grace to be given you when Jesus Christ is revealed. (1 Peter 1:13)

No people can be prepared unless they are growing mentally. Religion today is up against the most complex problems, both within ourselves and within society, for our faith is being challenged from the side of psychology and of economics. It will not do to say with social reformer Charles H. Parkhurst that "skepticism is the friction caused by a small brain trying to absorb a great idea." We must be able to show how the "great idea"—God—is great and dynamic enough to meet a world need.

Today, Christians are being forced to think because they have come to grips with making a new world. Our faith must function there, or it will be discarded as irrelevant. The kingdom concept demands it. We are grateful for what uneducated Christians have done, but this is no time for ignorant piety. The world suffers almost as much from wrong ideas as from wrong wills. Wrong ideas in history have produced as much havoc as wrong intentions. Christians, therefore, must think straight as well as act straight.

Therefore, grow in mind. Try to read at least fifty pages of some book each day. If your mind ceases to grow, your soul will cease to grow. You will become the victim of set phrases and stereotyped ideas caught in mental ruts. A new book will help jolt you out. The seventeenth-century philosopher Spinoza spoke of "an intellectual love of God," and Jesus spoke of loving God "with all your mind"—a phrase He added to the Old Testament quotation (see Deut. 6:5). It must have been important. It is.

O Christ, help us this day to conquer some new worthy idea and harness it to the purposes of Your kingdom. Save our minds from ruts. Amen.

GROW IN LOVE

Jesus knew that the time had come for him to leave this world and go to the Father. Having loved his own who were in the world, he now showed them the full extent of his love. (John 13:1)

This is my prayer: that your love may abound more and more in knowledge and depth of insight, so that you may be able to discern what is best and may be pure and blameless until the day of Christ. (Phil. 1:9-10)

In all our growth, we must grow in love. Unless we are growing in love we are not growing at all.

Jesus' love for his own was the greatest thing He had done in life, and it would be the last thing He would do in death. There is nothing greater in life or death, either for Him or for us. Therefore, make love your quest.

But let it be an intelligent quest. Go over your life and see if there are unloving and, therefore, unlovely spots. Perhaps you will find some tinge of jealousy toward someone. Set yourself to say something nice about that person today.

Or perhaps you will find that your service of Christ is becoming mixed with motives other than pure love. A quaint little story: One morning, Bradley put beside his mother's plate a small piece of paper: "Mother owes Bradley: For running errands, $0.25. For being good, $0.10. For taking music lessons, $0.15. Extras, $0.05. Total, $0.55."

His mother smiled but did not say anything, and when lunch time came she placed the bill on Bradley's plate with the fifty-five cents. Bradley's eyes danced.

But there was another little bill, which read: "Bradley owes Mother: For being good, $0.00. For nursing him through a long illness, $0.00. For shoes, clothes, gloves, and toys, $0.00. For all his meals and beautiful room, $0.00. Total: Bradley owes Mother $0.00."

Tears came into Bradley's eyes, he put his arms around his mother's neck, thrust his little hand with the fifty-five cents into hers, and said: "Take this money all back, Mamma, and let me love you and do things for nothing!"

O Christ, cleanse from my heart this day all bargaining and help me to serve You and others for love alone. Amen.

E. STANLEY JONES | 321

LOVE'S WIDER APPLICATION

If someone has enough money to live well and sees a brother or sister in need but shows no compassion—how can God's love be in that person? Dear children, let's not merely say that we love each other; let us show the truth by our actions. Our actions will show that we belong to the truth, so we will be confident when we stand before God. (1 John 3:17-19†)

The real test of spiritual growth is the test of whether we are growing in love. But this test applies to society as well as to individuals. The test of how much a society is civilized is to what degree love is being built into the social structure.

Two great forces are driving human life—hunger and love. The first is the struggle for life, the second is the struggle for the life of others. We have organized our collective life largely around the hunger drive, with love coming only here and there at the edges to soften the grim struggle. This puts disruption and clash at the very center.

If we would change the center from hunger to love, then we would organize life cooperatively. In that case, hunger would be at the edges and love at the center as the driving force. This would not only be good Christianity but good economics, for we have now discovered the means of supplying all the economic needs of every last man, woman, and child—provided we can cooperate to do it. To get cooperation, life must be organized on the basis of love.

When hunger is at the center, we live a cow's existence, nine-tenths of whose time is taken up with eating or re-chewing what it has eaten. The supplying of economic needs should be an incident in human life instead of its absorbing passion. During the agony of the crucifixion, "knowing that all was now completed…Jesus said, 'I am thirsty'" (John 19:28). After He had done all He could for others, He thought of His own needs.

We have put our thirsts first. This is not civilization—it is chaos. If we are to be Christian, love must be dominant and individual thirsts subordinate.

O Christ, help us grow in Your way—the way of love. For only as we love do we live. Amen.

A CORPORATE QUEST

There was a man in Jerusalem called Simeon, who was righteous and devout. He was waiting for the consolation of Israel, and the Holy Spirit was upon him. It had been revealed to him by the Holy Spirit that he would not die before he had seen the Lord's Christ. Moved by the Spirit, he went into the temple courts. (Luke 2:25-27)

We cannot grow unless we fellowship with other questing lives. Hence the church. How can we get most out of that corporate fellowship? Simeon came into the Temple and saw the Lord's Christ. How did it happen? He brought something to that hour, and seeing the Lord's Christ was the result.

If you come to church like Simeon, "moved by the Spirit," you will see something. But many go to church "moved by the flesh." It is all to display clothes or oratory. Or it is all "moved by the mind," to hear some new or attractive thing. Or it is "moved by the emotions," to let our aesthetic natures relish the music and the stately ritual. But the Lord's Christ does not appear. We do not come in the Spirit.

Simeon, on the other hand, came with a foundation of four things: (1) He "was righteous" in relation to the people around him; (2) he was "devout" toward God; (3) he was loyal to his nation, "waiting for the consolation of Israel"; and (4) he was yielded in himself—"the Holy Spirit was upon him."

But his attention to his own people did not keep him from seeing the possibilities in other groups. His prophecy about the Christ Child included this descriptor: "a light for revelation to the Gentiles" (v. 32). He saw that Christ would not only bring consolation to Israel but would also reveal good things for others. This is Christianity—narrow nationalism is not.

Bring with you these four basic things, and you will come into God's house "in the Spirit." Then you will see amazing possibilities in yourself, in your nation, in other nations. All through Christ.

O Christ, as we prepare to go into Your temple, help us to take this fourfold rightness with us. Then we shall see You so that when we return, we can stand foursquare to life. Amen.

A UNIFIED QUEST

There is one body and one Spirit—just as you were called to one hope when you were called—one Lord, one faith, one baptism; one God and Father of all, who is over all and through all and in all…so that the body of Christ may be built up until we all reach unity in the faith and in the knowledge of the Son of God and become mature, attaining to the whole measure of the fullness of Christ. (Eph. 4:4-6, 12-13)

In a world seeking unity, Christians have little moral authority unless they can demonstrate unity. Currently we demonstrate *dis*unity.

I believe we have gone as far as we can in spiritual development under separate denominationalism. We may advance here and there, but there will be no great burst of collective spirituality until we come together.

But you ask, "How can we come together unless we agree in everything?" Notice that we do not make that a prerequisite of fellowship in the home. The one thing that binds us together is that all are children of the same parents. So in the family of God, the thing that binds us together is not that we all have the same spiritual temperament, nor the same shades of belief, but the fact that we are all children of the same Father. Let that suffice.

We need our differences as possible growing points. The music of the Hindus is based on melody and not on harmony, as is Western music. A Hindu heard a black ensemble singing the spirituals in parts, bringing out marvelous harmony. But his comment was, "What a pity they can't all sing the same tune!"

Had they done so, it wouldn't have been harmony! The very differences made for richness. We shall never get melody-unity in the church, for we cannot all sing the same part. But we can have harmony-unity, which will be far richer. Each denomination will sing its part, and out of it will come the full richness of our gospel.

O Christ, we thank You that You are bringing together many differing parts to make one great harmony. Help us to sing our part while we appreciate and appropriate the parts of others. Amen.

THE GIFT THAT STRENGTHENS

The path of the righteous is like the first gleam of dawn, shining ever brighter till the full light of day. (Prov. 4:18)

Grow in the grace and knowledge of our Lord and Savior Jesus Christ. To him be glory both now and forever! Amen. (2 Peter 3:18)

Perhaps the most distinctive thing in the gospel is grace. So the most distinctive thing in our growth must be growth in grace. The grace of God is love judging our sins, suffering for our sins, forgiving our sins, removing our sins, and then abiding in unworthy hearts. That is grace.

Living by that very grace is to grow in the deepest thing in our gospel. But the modern mind is afraid of the doctrine of grace, however much the deepest instincts long for it. We are afraid that to depend on someone else will destroy initiative, weaken our fiber, and turn the upstanding person into the clinging person. If this were the result of grace, I would reject it too.

But a strange paradox is found in the gospel at this place. God's gifts do not weaken personality, they strengthen it. Jesus says, "Those who drink the water I give will never be thirsty again. It becomes a fresh, bubbling spring within them, giving them eternal life." (John 4:13-14†). Note: The gift of water becomes a well of water springing up. The gift produces spontaneity!

Now, many gifts do not. They weaken. It is hard to give to people and not weaken them. But here is a gift that strengthens in the very act of giving.

It is not the kind of gift that demands nothing on our part. It is, in fact, the most expensive gift we shall ever receive. For when we take it, our very *all* goes out in exchange. Now, having given to God, there is a mutuality. We are no longer worms of the dust; we are cooperating persons. At the very moment we bend lowest, we stand straightest. Those who depend most on the grace of God develop the strongest personalities. So when we grow in grace, we grow in personal initiative and energy.

O Christ, may this well of spontaneous life always spring up within us, since we depend so much upon Your life. Amen.

SMALL AND LARGE

Jesus knew that the Father had put all things under his power, and that he had come from God and was returning to God; so he got up from the meal, took off his outer clothing, and wrapped a towel around his waist. After that, he poured water into a basin and began to wash his disciples' feet, drying them with the towel that was wrapped around him. (John 13:3-5)

Yesterday we saw that grace strengthens personality. But the very strengthening of the personality will bring a hazard. As you grow, spiritual pride becomes a real danger. Many fall because of it.

Yesterday I went out after a storm and found a beautiful branch of a tree broken off and lying on the pathway. Parasites had done it. When the test of the storm came, it broke and fell. The most dangerous parasite is spiritual pride. Many are weakened by it and fall in the times of testing.

The Boston clergyman Phillips Brooks said, "The true way to be humble is not to stoop until you are smaller than yourself, but to stand at your real height against some higher nature that will show you what the real smallness of your greatness is." Stand at your very highest, then look at Christ—and go away forever humble!

When we lose sight of Christ, we ourselves begin to loom large. A Hindu said to me: "I used to believe in idols. Now I don't believe in God at all. But I am coming 'round to believe that I myself am God." He gave up his idols and made one of himself! When we lose God, we lose our source of humility.

The account of the Last Supper says that Jesus, knowing full well who he was in the eternal sense, was quite comfortable taking a towel and washing His disciples' feet. The consciousness of greatness was the secret of humility.

Remember, only the humble can lead. There is a saying that "People who parade their virtues seldom lead the procession." They cannot lead, for we simply cannot respond to the proud, however "spiritual" they may seem.

O Christ, give me Your mind, for You are meek and lowly in heart. I want to be like You. Amen.

THE WORD THAT ENERGIZES

When He had stopped speaking, He said to Simon, "Launch out into the deep and let down your nets for a catch." But Simon answered and said to Him, "Master, we have toiled all night and caught nothing; nevertheless at Your word I will let down the net." And when they had done this, they caught a great number of fish, and their net was breaking. (Luke 5:4-6 NKJV)

Simon Peter's statement is half-doubt, half-faith. He is tired; he is reluctant; but he is also willing to do what Jesus has directed.

"At Your word I will"—could fewer words sum up the Christian attitude? That *word,* speaking to us all through the ages, has never let us down. Whenever people have obeyed it, they have found an open road; where they have disobeyed it, they have found themselves running into dead ends.

That *word* has been energy to the living and grace to the dying. Other words let me down—this *word* does not. Nothing has been so utterly tested in history as Jesus' rightness, and nothing has proven itself so utterly.

So there is only one thing left for us to say: "At Your word I will!" But many of us do not say that. We say, "At Your word I think." We are intellectually aroused by Him, but not controlled by Him at the place of volition. We are mere intellectualists in religion. Or some of us say, "At Your word I feel." We are moved with strong emotional responses to Him; sermons stir us, the reading of the gospel brings a thrill, but it does not get beyond that, it does not work itself into our wills. We are emotionalists in religion.

But there are those who say, "At Your word I will." They are the Christians. This is the test of whether the gospel is functioning on the inside.

Many of us are willing to do God's work, but not God's will. If so, the center remains unchristianized. I am Christian to the degree that Christ has my will. When you can say, "At Your word I will," then you are really growing.

O Christ, I can bank on You. Help me to do it this day, and may I show that I do by the way I will. Amen.

ULTIMATE COURAGE

The wicked run away when no one is chasing them, but the godly are as bold as lions. (Prov. 28:1†)

"I will make you as unyielding and hardened as they are. I will make your forehead like the hardest stone, harder than flint. Do not be afraid of them or terrified by them, though they are a rebellious house." (Ezek. 3:8-9)

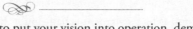

To break with the present order, to put your vision into operation, demands courage. But that is what the Christian is here to do—the impossible. When a thing becomes merely possible, the politicians take it over!

Two incidents of courage spring to my mind. An Afghan convert felt the call of Christ to witness for Him in the closed country of Afghanistan. He no sooner began in Kandahar than he was captured and driven to Kabul at the command of the Emir. Literally "driven," for they put a bridle in his mouth and drove him like a donkey the 200 miles, and along the way men were invited to pluck his beard and spit in his face. Arriving at Kabul, he was asked by the Emir if he would renounce his faith. He refused. One arm was then cut off. He was offered everything to recant, but again he refused. The other arm went off. When he refused even then to deny his Master, his head went off. Courage!

A lamp burns perpetually before the Martyr's Shrine at Peshawar [now Pakistan], and high up on the list is this man's name.

The British commissioner of Peshawar, a Christian, was asked if mission work could be started on that wild frontier. His reply: "What, do you want us all to be killed in our beds?" He wasn't killed in his bed, but a Muslim fanatic did stab him to death on the veranda. What he feared came on him.

Mr. Edwards, the next commissioner, when asked the same question, replied, "It is not a matter of our safety, it is a matter of the will of God. Of course we will do it, for we Christians have no other choice." He called his staff people together, took a collection of 3,000 rupees on the spot, and invited the missionaries in. His name is loved and revered by Christian and non-Christian alike.

O Christ, give me this gift of courage, for You have it, and I need it today. Amen.

RECONCILIATION FOR US, TOO

We are therefore Christ's ambassadors, as though God were making his appeal through us. We implore you on Christ's behalf: Be reconciled to God.... As God's fellow workers we urge you not to receive God's grace in vain. (2 Cor. 5:20; 6:1)

How familiar this Scripture sounds as a text for the unconverted! But Paul wrote it for the converted, for "fellow workers" who had received the grace of God. He pled not for initial reconciliation but for a continuous reconciliation. Otherwise the grace of God would be received in vain.

Christ is calling to the church today to be reconciled to God in at least three ways:

1. In regard to our message. We have not preached the kingdom of God as a head-on sweeping answer to the world's needs. We have preached a doctrine here and a doctrine there for individuals; however, this full answer to humanity's total needs, individual and social, has not been pointedly proclaimed. We need to be reconciled to God with regard to our message.

2. We need to be reconciled to God in making human interactions vicarious. We have made them antagonistic, or legal, but not vicarious. We need to suffer in the sufferings of those who suffer, to be hungry in the hunger of the hungry, and to be guilty in the guilt of every person.

3. We need to go over our lives and see where there are any points not reconciled to God. Has self-will crept in and taken the place of God's will?

Hardly anything is needed in the world today so much as for the church to genuinely reconcile its total life to the total will of God.

O God, show me any point of difference between Your mind and mine, so I can be reconciled to You this day. Amen.

MAKING THE HOME CHRISTIAN

[Following the birth of John the Baptist:] *The neighbors were all filled with awe, and throughout the hill country of Judea people were talking about all these things. Everyone who heard this wondered about it, asking, "What then is this child going to be?" For the Lord's hand was with him. (Luke 1:65-66)*

We win our families not merely by a once-and-for-all spectacular sacrifice, but by the constancy of a Christian example. Early on, the neighbors could tell that the hand of the Lord was with young John. This led them to speculate, "What then is this child going to be?"

The question could be asked many ways. What will a child be if the hand of narrow aggressive propaganda is upon him? To ask it is to answer it: a narrow, partisan hater prepared to fight! What will a child be if the hand of a ruthlessly competitive system is upon him? Either a hard-tempered crusher of others, or one who grows up to become a beaten soul. What will a child be if the hand of sex-saturated movies is upon him? A modern libertine!

But what will a child be if the hand of a consistent and contagious Christian example is upon him? The possibilities are infinite. Is that your goal as a father or mother?

Jesus finally won His whole family to His cause. There had been a time when "his own brothers did not believe in him" (John 7:5). But by the time of Pentecost, they were all there, waiting for the gift of the Spirit (see Acts 1:14). Apparently, they had all been won.

But Jesus did not win His family by compromising with them. He made sacrifices that cost both Himself and them. Some people are willing to sacrifice for the kingdom of God, but not if it costs disruption to their loved ones. This is a mistake. Our decisions will involve our loved ones in common suffering with us. It is a part of the price.

It works both ways, however. As sacrifice lifts us, so it will lift them. We separate from them on a lower level in order to meet them on a higher level.

O Christ, You won Your family; help me to do the same. Amen.

DO YOU APPRECIATE?

Now about brotherly love we do not need to write to you, for you yourselves have been taught by God to love each other. And in fact, you do love all the brothers throughout Macedonia. Yet we urge you, brothers, to do so more and more. (1 Thess. 4:9-10)

Fathers, do not embitter your children, or they will become discouraged. (Col. 3:21)

Love is patient, love is kind. It does not envy, it does not boast, it is not proud. It is not rude, it is not self-seeking, it is not easily angered, it keeps no record of wrongs. Love does not delight in evil but rejoices with the truth. It always protects, always trusts, always hopes, always perseveres. (1 Cor. 13:4-7)

We cannot change our loved ones, or anyone else, by nagging complaints. The Pharisees thought the only way to change people was by disapproval. They tried it and only ended in being themselves disapproved.

Once, they journeyed all the way from Jerusalem to Galilee, and what did they see? The glorious coming of the long-awaited kingdom? The wonder of the Man with the healing hands? The gates of life being opened to stricken souls? Oh, no! They saw only the fact that the disciples ate with unwashed hands (see Mark 7:1-5). They passed by the great and saw only the trivial. They became small by what they saw.

I once met a little boy who honestly thought his name was "Johnny Don't," for that was what he was always called at home. The parent who is hypercritical is usually hypocritical. On the other hand, bring into the home a whole lot of appreciation, and you will find that the little flowers will open to its genial warmth. Otherwise, they close up.

A Hindu student came to a college principal to tell him of his decision to follow Christ. But he forgot to take off his cap, was rebuked for it by the principal, was chilled—and never told his heart's decision. He never became a Christian.

O Christ, help me to appreciate people not only for what they are, but for what they may be in You. Amen.

WHAT GENERATIONS GENERATE

On Herod's birthday the daughter of Herodias danced for them and pleased Herod so much that he promised with an oath to give her whatever she asked. Prompted by her mother, she said, "Give me here on a platter the head of John the Baptist." (Matt. 14:6-8)

It is a solemn fact that children in the home catch their parents' attitudes rather than their words. The child is much like the subconscious mind—it learns by what it sees people doing rather than by what they say.

In the regrettable story of Herodias and her daughter, what did the daughter desire? Well, that depended on what the mother desired. She wanted what her mother wanted.

We wonder at today's undisciplined young people. Do we not need to look back to the previous generation? Our youth have been "prompted" by the parents of today. They are astonished at their offspring, for did not the parents repeat the claims of morality and religion? Why didn't their children listen?

Well, because the words were repeated with less and less conviction and certainty. The generation before these parents, having undergone conversion in the evangelical revivals of the past, had some personal living convictions. The next generation lived on that afterglow but with little personal experience. This generation of youth learned not what their parents said, which was too remote and faint, but what they did, which was neither remote nor faint. The actions of the generation of parents now living "prompted" this newest generation— and this is the result.

The story of the young dancer in Herod's court is the story of "the prodigal daughter," the counterpart of "the prodigal son." They both said, "Give me"— which is always the first step down. The prodigal son eventually came back, because he had a good father. The prodigal daughter never came back, because she had a bad mother.

O God, our Father, help us this day to so live that we will "prompt" the next generation to desire the noblest and highest, because they see it in us. Amen.

A LAMP FOR THE DARK PATH

These commandments that I give you today are to be upon your hearts. Impress them on your children. Talk about them when you sit at home and when you walk along the road, when you lie down and when you get up. (Deut. 6:6-7)

In an ancient Syrian church of Travancore, India, is a wonderful old brass lamp with about a hundred arms hanging from the ceiling. At the end of each is a cup with oil and a wick. At the close of the service, the young people come up and take one of the lights to guide them home through the night. Standing on a hill, you can see the points of light here and there moving amid the darkness.

That is what a Christian home should be—a place where young people receive into their hands a light to guide them as they go out into the gloom. There are many such lights: the torch of basic honesty, of good will, of cooperative living, of respect for all races and classes, of hatred for war, of the spirit of self-giving service, of a rich personal experience of Christ.

Once my mother put a torch in my hands though she did not know it. The shadow of financial and other calamities was upon our home; it was one of those periods when pain and trouble seem to saturate the very atmosphere. Going upstairs at midnight, I heard a muffled voice. I stopped, and heard my mother praying—a heart-breaking prayer. The little crack of the door, the little peek into her heart—for at midnight the reserve she had kept up so bravely during the day was all down now, and I saw into the depths. What a flame of suffering love was there! I took a light from that lamp of devotion that night, and it has lighted me down the years.

The saddest thing on earth is a home of spiritual poverty, where there is no central lamp from which young people can get a torch. Be victorious in the home, and you will be victorious everywhere.

O Christ, help me this day to bring into the home such a flame of pure living that the next generation will get a torch that will never go out. Amen.

A MODEL TO EMULATE

"Whoever welcomes a little child like this in my name welcomes me. But if anyone causes one of these little ones who believe in me to sin, it would be better for him to have a large millstone hung around his neck and to be drowned in the depths of the sea." (Matt. 18:5-6)

Many a young person, when smitten by modern doubt, holds steady because of the clean living faith of a father, a mother. But some are wrecked when the parent lets down. Hear the cry of this disillusioned soul:

Because I believed God brought him to me,
And because I believed him gifted of God
With honor, truth, and love of the Right
I believed in God and worshiped God;
Then when I found he was just a thief of love,
When I found he was full of treason and prejudices,
All for money and worldly pride,
The wreck of him was the wreck of God;
So I fainted amid the ruin
Of plaster and sticks and sat in the stillness
That followed the fallen bust of God.

If a child looks on you as the sculpture of God, do not let him down. If you are in danger of slipping, remember that victorious living is possible, even in the modern city and home.

We blame the wicked city for many ills—and yet the Master asked His followers to "stay in the city until you have been clothed with power from on high" (Luke 24:49). Despite the urban temptations, strains, greed, and injustices, he said to wait right there to be made adequate and victorious. And it happened.

Pentecost took place in an upper room of a common home, not in a church or temple. Don't run away; wait right where you are for adequate power.

O Christ, who gave them power in the very place where they had failed, give me the power this day, in this city, in this home. Amen.

HOLDING THE HOME TOGETHER

You are the salt of the earth. But what good is salt if it has lost its flavor? Can you make it salty again? It will be thrown out and trampled underfoot as worthless. (Matt. 5:13†)

Salt is good, but if it loses its saltiness, how can you make it salty again? Have salt in yourselves, and be at peace with each other. (Mark 9:50)

Earlier we saw that the *Epistle of Diognetus* says, "The Christians hold the world together." They do, and they also hold the home together. A homeless unmarried Man became the power that sanctifies marriage and anchors the home! His power was never more needed than in this realm, for the home is being assailed from many directions. If it survives—and it will—the Christians must save it.

Christians do not fly to pieces under trouble and misunderstanding. They know how to give forgiveness when wronged, and they know how to make an apology when they wrong another. An apology often saves a situation.

When Jesus says to have salt in ourselves and be at peace with one another, He means that we should not be dependent on our environment for life's taste. Instead, have springs from within. Then the ups and downs of the home will not mean going up and down. You are fed from inside. That very self-contained sense of taste will help you to be at peace with one another, for the greatest cause of breaking peace with others is the sense of tastelessness within ourselves. We feel out of sorts with ourselves and take it out on others.

Christians hold the world together and the home as well, for they hold themselves together by the fact that life has inward taste, no matter what happens on the outside.

O Christ, give us that inward salt that we may give outward peace. Hold us together, that we may hold the home and all situations together. Amen.

A NEW KIND OF PEOPLE

You were cleansed from your sins when you obeyed the truth, so now you must show sincere love to each other as brothers and sisters. Love each other deeply with all your heart. (1 Peter 1:22†)

The Christian is the emergence of a new type of person, as different from ordinary humanity as ordinary humanity is different from the animal. This may be seen from the statement of the Athenian orator, Aristides, who wrote to the Emperor Hadrian (A.D. 117-138) as follows:

"The Christians know and trust God…. They placate those who oppress them and make them their friends; they do good to their enemies. Their wives are absolutely pure, and their daughters modest. Their men abstain from unlawful marriage and from all impurity….

"They love one another. They do not refuse to help the widows. They rescue the orphan from him who does him violence. He who has gives ungrudgingly to him who has not. If they see a stranger, they take him to their dwellings and rejoice over him as over a real brother; for they do not call themselves brothers after the flesh, but after the Spirit and in God…. If anyone among them is poor and needy, and they do not have food to spare, they fast for two or three days, so that they may supply him with necessary food.

"They scrupulously obey the commands of their Messiah. Every morning and every hour they thank and praise God for His loving-kindness toward them…. Because of them there flows forth all the beauty that there is in the world. But the good deeds they do they do not proclaim in the ears of the multitude, but they take care that no one shall perceive them. Thus they labor to become righteous…. Truly, this is a new people, and there is something divine in them."

This is the spirit that will create a new world. We must rediscover it and embody it.

O Christ, make us worthy of this inheritance, and help us worthily give it to this age, which is so desperately in need of just this. Amen.

COSMIC OPTIMISM

God did this so that…we who have fled to take hold of the hope offered to us may be greatly encouraged. We have this hope as an anchor for the soul, firm and secure. (Heb. 6:18-19)

We began this study and quest for victorious living by asking whether life is an empty bubble or an egg. We have now come out, I trust, firmly believing that life is an egg, with infinite possibilities if we can get hold of the redemptive energies in Jesus Christ.

Leo Tolstoy, in his book *My Confessions and My Religion*, says in substance: There are those who say (1) Life is all bad, so get drunk to evade it. (2) Life is bad, but struggle against it anyway (the stoical attitude). (3) Life is bad, so do the logical thing—commit suicide. (4) Life is bad, but live on like myself, illogically accepting life as it comes.

Obviously, this is not the full Christian statement, for in Christ we do not merely accept life as it comes. We make life what it ought to be. Redemptive energy is available to change the quality of life itself and to turn its course toward moral mastery. It is true that this new life has its present limitations, for there are other human wills that thwart, and there is recalcitrant nature. Though Jesus "returned to Galilee in the power of the Spirit" (Luke 4:14), He soon had to confess that "no prophet is accepted in his hometown" (v. 24). He was thwarted. The seed may be sound, but a lot depends on the soil and other conditions if it is to be fruitful.

So there are limitations. But we are not limited in the end by them. We can turn those very limitations into contributions. When the invited people in the parable refused the invitation to the feast, the servant was told to go out into the highways and hedges and get everybody he could to come in. Thwarted at first, the invitation became universal.

So Christianity has been described as "cosmic optimism." It is—but an optimism with scars on it.

O Christ, I thank You that I can now face life with a solid foundation for hope—for You are my hope. Amen.

E. STANLEY JONES | 337

WHY CHRISTIANS FAIL

Once you were alienated from God and were enemies in your minds because of your evil behavior. But now he has reconciled you…if you continue in your faith, established and firm, not moved from the hope held out in the gospel. This is the gospel that you heard and that has been proclaimed to every creature under heaven. (Col. 1:21-23)

In spite of the great foundation for hope that we have in Christ, it is true that there are occasional failures among Christians, even sincere ones. The reason? I think I saw it one morning after a storm as I sat on our prayer knoll at Sat Tal. A vine had reached its delicate fingers up and across the void until it had grasped the branch of a pine tree. It had arrived! But the morning after the storm it was drooping with its head hanging to the earth—the branch had broken in the storm. The vine had fastened itself upon a rotten branch instead of the strong, central healthy trunk.

Many Christians are like that—they attach themselves to some dead branch of Christianity, a special rite or doctrine or custom or person, but do not get to the central trunk, Christ. The storm comes, and they go down along with the dead branch. This has happened during these years of economic depression; people have gone down because they were attached to the culture surrounding the Christian church but had no living contact with Christ, the central trunk.

Where people grasp the central reality, Christ, they stand up against things victoriously and toughen under adversity. In Acts 13:17, Paul says that God "made the people prosper during their stay in Egypt." In more ways than one did they prosper. Adversity can make us excel provided we have hold of the central trunk, Christ. Our Christianity is a cosmic optimism only if it is Christ-optimism.

Christ, my Lord, You have become my one steady place amid a world of flux. Help me to catch Your dependableness so that people depending on me may not be let down. Amen.

UP FROM THE TOMBS

When Jesus got out of the boat, a man with an evil spirit came from the tombs to meet him. This man lived in the tombs, and no one could bind him any more, not even with a chain. For he had often been chained hand and foot, but he tore the chains apart and broke the irons on his feet. No one was strong enough to subdue him. Night and day among the tombs and in the hills he would cry out and cut himself with stones. (Mark 5:1-5)

Why are you downcast, O my soul? Why so disturbed within me? Put your hope in God, for I will yet praise him, my Savior and my God. (Psalm 43:5)

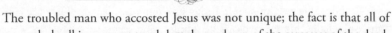

The troubled man who accosted Jesus was not unique; the fact is that all of us on earth dwell in one vast tomb largely made up of the carcasses of the dead. We are on our way to becoming part of that cosmic dust. That is the truth in pessimism.

This particular man raved and cut himself. On his way to death, he dealt death to himself. He was also a "man from the city who…wore no clothes, nor did he live in a house" (Luke 8:27 NKJV). The city with its problems and oppressions had driven him mad. The city is doing that to many people today, for it is the focal point of human problems. It gets on our nerves and defeats us. So we retreat to tombs and live there, tormented by devils of depression, gloom, and fear.

But as we pointed out last week, Jesus told His disciples, "Stay in the city until you have been clothed with power from on high" (Luke 24:49). This man had stayed in the city until he was clothed with fears from below. The city can become the place of torment or the place of triumph. It all depends what occupies the inside—demonic fears or the Holy Spirit.

When we have learned the secret of the Holy Spirit's indwelling, we have found the secret of cosmic optimism amid cosmic death, for in Christ we are eternal.

I thank You, O Christ, that Your tomb was but the gateway to fuller life. Help me this day to break the seals in this cosmic tomb that keep me from abundant living. Amen.

SAYING NO TO "NO!"

Then Paul, knowing that some of them were Sadducees and the others Pharisees, called out in the Sanhedrin, "My brothers, I am a Pharisee, the son of a Pharisee. I stand on trial because of my hope in the resurrection of the dead." When he said this, a dispute broke out between the Pharisees and the Sadducees, and the assembly was divided. (The Sadducees say that there is no resurrection, and that there are neither angels nor spirits, but the Pharisees acknowledge them all.) (Acts 23:6-8)

The best the Sadducees could say was, "There is no…." They lived on negation—a poor diet. Many people today are living on denials. They are getting more spiritually thin every day. The whole thing seems so anomalous—denying the fact of God and the fact of meaning in the universe by using the very powers God has given them.

I once found myself looking for my glasses with the aid of the very glasses I was looking for! I had them on! This is like those who deny reason in the universe with the very reason God has given them.

Christians do not deny death. They say rather: "There is a resurrection, because I am resurrected. I live now in victory over all negation, all denials." For, as Macmurray says, "This is the first and supreme lie of the devil, 'Ye shall not surely die' " (Gen. 3:4). Many try to get rid of death by denying it. We do not. We acknowledge death and then proceed to overcome it and use it.

A friend of mine, while journeying from the warmer climate of Persia to the colder climate of Russia and Finland, experienced five successive springtimes along the way. Christians do even better—they live in perpetual spring. A renewal is taking place every moment.

But you say, "Hopes may be dupes." Our reply is, "Yes, and fears may be liars." I know them to be. For when I look at Christ, I realize that nothing He says is too big to be believed or too great to be true.

O Christ, You save me and my universe—and You put a "yes" at the heart of both. I thank You. Amen.

RELIABLY SOLID

Nevertheless, God's solid foundation stands firm, sealed with this inscription: "The Lord knows those who are his," and, "Everyone who confesses the name of the Lord must turn away from wickedness." (2 Tim. 2:19)

A member of our ashram, a cultured Indian woman of deep spirituality, lost her husband. She went on with her work, undismayed and radiant. Some Sikh village women came to her and said: "You astonish us. We go to pieces under sorrow. You do not. Are all Christians like you? Your religion is very *puckha*, while ours is very *kuchha*."

Kuchha means unbaked, *puckha* means well-done. The two words are used in various ways. For example, a dirt road is *kuchha*, a paved road is *puckha*. A mud house is *kuchha*, a brick house is *puckha*. Green fruit is *kuchha*, ripe fruit is *puckha*.

These simple women put their finger on the central distinction—the Christian way is *puckha*, solid, adequate. All other ways of life are *kuchha*—flimsy, liable to crumbling. The Christian way stands up under life. It has wearing qualities. It will outlast all other ways.

In Persia I saw hills with a central ridge of igneous rock. All the others had been flattened out by the rains and the gnawing tooth of time, becoming part of the plains. I find people everywhere who are being flattened out by the wear and tear of life. Life becomes too much for them. But Christians have a central Rock beneath them, and that Rock is Christ. Fused in the fires of the cross, it is igneous, the ultimate granite upon which the universe is built.

One philosopher said that "all philosophers are sad." Why? Well, they deal in ideas—which is all very *kuchha*. The Christian deals in ideas that have become facts—the Word made flesh. It is all very *puckha*.

O Christ, the Rock beneath my feet, help me this day to help someone on sinking sand to get their feet on this. Amen.

THE OPTIMISTIC CHRIST

The high priest arose and said to Him, "Do You answer nothing? What is it these men testify against You?" But Jesus kept silent. And the high priest answered and said to Him, "I put You under oath by the living God: Tell us if You are the Christ, the Son of God!"

Jesus said to him, "It is as you said. Nevertheless, I say to you, hereafter you will see the Son of Man sitting at the right hand of the Power, and coming on the clouds of heaven." (Matt. 26:62-64 NKJV)

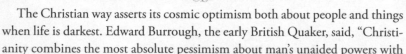

The Christian way asserts its cosmic optimism both about people and things when life is darkest. Edward Burrough, the early British Quaker, said, "Christianity combines the most absolute pessimism about man's unaided powers with an unquenchable optimism as to what in God's hands he may become."

If there was ever a moment when Jesus should have been pessimistic, it was when standing before the Council. They had struck Him in the face, blindfolded Him, spat upon Him—and yet in the midst of it all He stood and spoke about His ultimate ascension to a heavenly throne. What a victorious soul! With both His hands bound, He talked about sitting at the right hand of power. With swollen lips and bloody face, He said, "Final power is mine!" And it is! The ages have confirmed it.

The amazing thing is that He asserted it while in abject subjection to brutal authority. This is an important element in victorious living. He did not say, "I hope victory will be mine someday." He proclaimed, "Hereafter." He brought His future into the here and now. That is a part of the victory, a very large part.

When the shadow of the cross fell upon Jesus, He saw in it His Father's face, and amid it all said, "Hereafter…." We too must catch and assert the immediacy of victory. Our song must ring out with confidence about what God has planned ahead.

O Christ, You have put a song within me. Help me to sing it this day with immediacy. Amen.

AN INNER CORRECTIVE

Christ loved the church and gave himself up for her to make her holy, cleansing her by the washing with water through the word, and to present her to himself as a radiant church, without stain or wrinkle or any other blemish, but holy and blameless. (Eph. 5:25-27)

It is time for judgment to begin with the family of God. (1 Peter 4:17)

As we talk about holding a cosmic optimism, the many, many futilities and immaturities within the Christian church itself rise up before us. These things dampen, if not destroy, that optimism. They stand out especially now against the background of world need. We have built up things about Christ that embarrass Him—and us.

A pious monk found that a little mouse disturbed his devotions, so he tied a cat to a nearby post in order to frighten away the mouse. After his death his followers wanted to do everything just as the master did, so they tied cats to the posts in rooms where they meditated. Over the course of time, the original reason for tying the cat was forgotten, but they had long discussions on what kind and color of cat should be used, how far from the worshiper, and so on.

Many things that occupy our attention in Christendom today are as meaningless as tying cats in devotional hours. This tendency drives one almost to despair—except for one fact. The Christian system has a built-in corrective in the person of Christ. He has an antiseptic influence upon our irrelevancies. He exerts a constant cleansing impact from within. This inner corrective is our hope.

He is today confronting us with the same question He asked His disciples, "What were you arguing about on the road?" (Mark 9:33). And we are silent, as they were, for we too have debated about our own greatness, our denominationalisms and petty irrelevancies. But as He corrected them, so He shall correct us. His Spirit is pleading strongly through voices both inside and outside the Christian church. Above all, it is pleading through the world need itself. Those who hear that voice will live; those who do not will perish.

O Christ, may Your call to us lead us to repentance and obedience, fully following You. Amen.

E. STANLEY JONES | 343

A CORNERSTONE IGNORED

You are coming to Christ, who is the living cornerstone of God's temple. He was rejected by people, but he was chosen by God for great honor.

And you are living stones that God is building into his spiritual temple. What's more, you are his holy priests. Through the mediation of Jesus Christ, you offer spiritual sacrifices that please God. As the Scriptures say, "I am placing a cornerstone in Jerusalem, chosen for great honor, and anyone who trusts in him will never be disgraced." (1 Peter 2:4-6†)

As we look at the world situation, we are struck with the fact that the mind of Christ is not only relevant but imperative to every part of world need. An erratic genius like George Bernard Shaw occasionally flashes out a truth such as this one: "The only man who came out of the World War with an enhanced reputation for common sense was Jesus Christ. Though we crucified Christ on a stick, yet He somehow managed to get hold of the right end of that stick... and if we were better men, we might try His plan."

Never have so many people come to this realization as now. And yet never have we seemed so desperately near to abandoning His plan altogether. We were never nearer war and yet never nearer getting rid of war than now. The world situation may go one way or the other.

The builders of our civilization have tried to build it without Christ. True, we thought we could put Him in as a decoration, to make the building religiously respectable. But now the structure of civilization is crumbling around us. The foundations are wrong—they are Christless, hence crumbling. "The builders"—the experts—have failed us, because they ignored Christ. All their attempts at diplomacy, balances of power, security through armaments, and selfish nationalism have broken down.

We must begin again. This time Jesus must be not merely decorative but in the foundation itself. It is our one hope.

Your patience, O Christ, astounds us. You have waited for this hour. We have messed up the world with our Christless planning. Save us. Amen.

SUBSTITUTE STONES

You have been called to live in freedom, my brothers and sisters. But don't use your freedom to satisfy your sinful nature. Instead, use your freedom to serve one another in love. For the whole law can be summed up in this one command: "Love your neighbor as yourself." But if you are always biting and devouring one another, watch out! Beware of destroying one another. (Gal. 5:13-15†)

If Christ is to be put into the foundation of civilization, He must become the cornerstone of collective living. We have not put Him there. The builders rejected Him. Instead they put something that was anti-Christ, namely, ruthless selfish competition. I cannot see how these two things can be made compatible. Either Christ or ruthless selfish competition must go.

Capitalism has been captured by this competitive outlook. We need capital, to be sure—but not as we now have it. If labor had hired capital toward the goal of the collective good, instead of capital hiring labor for the benefit of the few, our world situation would have been different. Such a mild critic as University of Wales Professor J. Morgan Rees makes these charges against the present order: "Without in the least subscribing to the view that this capitalistic order is being attacked, we must face the facts: (1) That it does not secure the maximum production of goods and services for our people; (2) That it does not attain justice in its distribution of wealth; (3) That it has failed to provide a tolerable existence for its producers when there are millions of unemployed and many more millions needy in a world of plenty; (4) That it fails to give the greatest possible freedom and stimulus to personalities and to social progress."

Those words may not be an "attack" upon capitalism, but it is an indictment that no system can survive for long without fundamental change. That change must be from competition to cooperation. If so, Christ would be in the foundation. His principles would permeate the whole of society with a regulating love.

O Christ, this stone of love, rejected by the builders, is now so desperately needed that we will perish without it. Give it to us, lest we destroy ourselves. Amen.

A REJECTED STONE: LOVE

Dear friends, since God so loved us, we also ought to love one another. No one has ever seen God; but if we love one another, God lives in us and his love is made complete in us. (1 John 4:11-12)

Religion that God our Father accepts as pure and faultless is this: to look after orphans and widows in their distress and to keep oneself from being polluted by the world. (James 1:17)

Love must be built into the social structure. Not practical? Then living is not practicable, for living demands love. We suggested last month that society must organize itself around one of two motives—the hunger motive or the love motive. We have organized life around the hunger motive, largely for the benefit of the few to the exploitation of the many. This has brought us discontent, disruption, disaster.

Communism has organized life in Russia on the hunger motive, not on behalf of the few, but on behalf of all, it says. But note that it is the hunger motive still. This means that ultimately there will be disruption in Communism, for the hunger motive is disruptive. Says Macmurray, "In practice, a dominant hunger may maintain cooperation with the help of the love-principle which is subordinated to it, but only at the expense of a mutual tension, breaking out inevitably in the long run into open struggle between individuals and groups" (*Creative Society*, p. 116). Only love can provide the ultimate motive for society, for it includes the satisfaction of hunger. People who love one another will, if their love is real, cooperate in satisfying one another's distinct and individual needs.

This love motive—rejected by the builders—has now become essential. We perish without it.

We come to You, O living Christ, to give us courage to believe that the love-motive is the only way to live. Help us to act on it. Amen.

ANOTHER REJECTED STONE: THE KINGDOM

"I tell you, the Kingdom of God will be taken away from you and given to a nation that will produce the proper fruit. Anyone who stumbles over that stone will be broken to pieces, and it will crush anyone it falls on." (Matt. 21:43-44†)

Clearly, the message of Jesus was the kingdom of God. But when we study "church history" (a significant phrase; the history of the Christian centuries is commonly called "church history" rather than "kingdom history"), we find that the main topic is the church. Why this replacement? Jesus intended the church to be subordinated to the kingdom. But we have reversed that.

Jesus said to the Pharisees, "The kingdom of God does not come with your careful observation" (Luke 17:20). Instead, it permeates silently like leaven from the inside. But we embraced the external church, observing its statistics, buildings, and outer forms. The kingdom, on the other hand, obeys the fundamental Christian law of losing oneself and finding it again. Hence the kingdom has gone further than the church.

If you doubt this, ask yourself this question: Is the church a sufficient foundation upon which to build a new world society? It was tried during the medieval age and failed. So then we must ask: Is the kingdom of God a sufficient basis for the new society? The answer is that it is the only foundation. This stone, which the builders (both secular and religious) rejected, has now become essential. It is emerging as the only solid foundation for human society. It is the kingdom—or chaos.

The kingdom of God is emerging as the only solid foundation for human society. We have hid this kingdom light under the bushel basket of church forms and structures. We must now put it on top of the bushel as a shining beacon. If we do, we will save both. The church can only be revived as it becomes no longer an end in itself, but the servant of the kingdom, which is far larger than the church. What the world cries out for is the kingdom.

O God, our Father, in rejecting the kingdom we have rejected You. But Your patience has worn us down. We now see Your kingdom as our only light. Help us to take it. Amen.

THE KINGDOM IS NEAR

"When these things begin to take place, stand up and lift up your heads, because your redemption is drawing near."

He told them this parable: "Look at the fig tree and all the trees. When they sprout leaves, you can see for yourselves and know that summer is near. Even so, when you see these things happening, you know that the kingdom of God is near." (Luke 21:28-30)

In the parallel passage to this Scripture, Mark records Jesus' statement in this way: "Now learn a lesson from the fig tree: As soon as its twigs get tender and its leaves come out, you know that summer is near" (13:28). When life becomes sensitive and tender, when it has an urge for fuller life, when it is ready to branch out, then we know that the kingdom of God is close by.

Was ever a world situation more tender and sensitive, tired of the old and yearning for a greater fullness of life, than just now? We have wanted fuller life for individuals, but we have never yearned like this for a fuller life for everybody, in everything. Does this not mean that the kingdom is at our door?

In the Luke passage (above), the kingdom is linked with redemption; they are both said to be "near." The kingdom is life, but it is the redemption of life as well. Many modernists who preach the kingdom of God as "life" fail to emphasize the fact that it is redemption. We need nothing so much as we need a concept that is synonymous with life—and at the same time looses a power for the redemption of life, to make life what it ought to be. The kingdom covers both.

The kingdom, therefore, is the one open door before a confused and morally collapsed world. It is the stone the builders have rejected, but is now becoming absolutely mandatory.

O Father God, Your kingdom is near. It is now within us, and yet we yearn for it to burst upon the world with redemptive power. Help us to bring it close this day. Amen.

ANOTHER REJECTED STONE: REDEMPTION

He has rescued us from the dominion of darkness and brought us into the kingdom of the Son he loves, in whom we have redemption, the forgiveness of sins. (Col. 1:13-14)

O Israel, put your hope in the LORD, for with the LORD is unfailing love and with him is full redemption. He himself will redeem Israel from all their sins. (Psalm 130:7-8)

Of all the stones the builders of civilization have rejected, none has been more tragic in its effects than the absence of redemption. Of course individuals here and there have been redeemed, but we have not called on these resources for remaking the world. We thought we could make a changed world without changed persons, and we have found it will not work. For as the saying goes, "You cannot make the golden age out of leaden instincts." Human sin is the real barrier to the new world.

But the church must also take its share of responsibility for rejecting this stone of redemption by confining it to a restricted sphere. We reduced it. We entered into a compromise with the world in which we said we would confine ourselves to saving souls, while turning over the economic and social life to other forces to manage. In this we have betrayed Christ.

I have seen the idols of Chinese temples bricked up and entombed when the temples were turned into schools. They were not thrown out—that would be sacrilege; they were lovingly preserved and confined! We have done that with Christ—we have bricked Him up, confined Him to the personal, while turning over the rest of life to other lords and masters.

Now we see where the issues must be joined. The economic realm belongs to Christ, too. If we do not master economics, then economics will master us. Christ must master and redeem both.

This stone of redemption of the whole of life is now becoming vital. We perish without it.

Redeemer of the whole of life, redeem us wholly. And help us not to fear to claim all life for You. Amen.

E. STANLEY JONES | 349

ANOTHER REJECTED STONE: THE REALISM OF JESUS

Jesus told them, "Go back to John and tell him what you have heard and seen— the blind see, the lame walk, the lepers are cured, the deaf hear, the dead are raised to life, and the Good News is being preached to the poor. And tell him, 'God blesses those who do not turn away because of me.' " (Matt. 11:4-6†)

Of all the strange anomalies in history, the strangest is this: The Man who was the greatest realist in history has been turned into the greatest idealist. Jesus' realism was so astonishing, so different that people did not know what to do with it. They had to act on it or reject it. But they couldn't bring themselves to do either, so they found a way to hold onto Jesus and also hold onto the old order of life—they made Him into an ideal. That ideal would be practiced some day, they said—but not now. They thus satisfied their wish to be loyal to the high while practicing the low.

Our age has adopted Christianity as an idealism, lifted up high above life, inoperative except here and there in small things. Because we could hold high ideals, we thought we were thereby spiritual. But idealism makes a divorce between body and spirit, referring religion to the Spirit while other ways of life control the material.

Jesus was astonishingly realistic. When He said we must love our neighbor as ourselves, He was being realistic—and we are discovering that it is the only realism, for nothing else will work. Unless you give an equal and fair chance to everybody, you will have none for yourself. Selfishness is suicide.

When Jesus said we must lose ourselves to find ourselves, this is realism. It is obeying a fundamental law of life. Nothing else will finally work. The world is demanding that religion be realistic; in fact, it is perishing for the need of just this thing. So the realism of Jesus, rejected by the builders, is becoming essential.

O realistic Christ, make us realistic. Save us from ideals that become opium to us. Amen.

THE ANSWER TO OUR TWO CENTRAL NEEDS

The gospel of God...regarding his Son, who as to his human nature was a descendant of David, and who through the Spirit of holiness was declared with power to be the Son of God by his resurrection from the dead: Jesus Christ our Lord. (Rom. 1:1-4)

Then Jesus came to them and said, "All authority in heaven and on earth has been given to me." (Matt. 28:18)

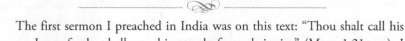

The first sermon I preached in India was on this text: "Thou shalt call his name Jesus; for he shall save his people from their sins" (Matt. 1:21 KJV). I would be happy if it were my last text as well. In these words, our greatest needs are met.

Humanity needs two things: light on the mystery of life, and power for the mastery of life. Jesus gives light on the mystery of life by the way He Himself lived. His life becomes a focal point of life's problems—all of them find their solution. But He is more—He is power to master life, to save us from its crookedness. He saves His people from their sins.

A university woman of keen mind was telling me how she had discovered Christ as a human being. His humanity brought Him so near to us, she said; He was no longer in the heavens but alongside of us, struggling with our struggles. This left her mentally satisfied...but morally defeated.

I told her that in Jesus we have two things: One who is like us, meeting life as we meet it, not as God, but as a man. Therefore He is my example. But I find something else in Him. He confronts me on the Godward side with an offer of redemption. He is thus unlike me, therefore my Redeemer. Had He been only like me, He could have been only my example; had He been only unlike me, He could have been only my Redeemer. But He was both, and therefore meets my dual need, for I need light and I need power.

"Say that in every sermon, won't you?" the woman said, as this truth dawned on her and made her utterly new. She had found Jesus as power.

O Christ, help me not to stop halfway, but to enter my full inheritance of victory. Amen.

WHY THE MOOD OF DESPAIR?

If you do not obey the LORD *your God…you will find no repose, no resting place for the sole of your foot. There the* LORD *will give you an anxious mind, eyes weary with longing, and a despairing heart. You will live in constant suspense, filled with dread both night and day, never sure of your life. (Deut. 28:15, 65-66)*

H. S. Wood says that if anyone wants to summarize modern scientific humanism in a sentence, these words would suffice: "Put your trust in science and have confidence in yourselves." This is supposed to be the faith of all educated persons under 40. And the scientific humanists have been very sure about it all.

This modern gospel, however, has turned out to have no music at its heart. It doesn't sing. The fact is that scientific humanism has grown very weary, its feet are leaden, and its soul is confused and dismayed. It has lost nerve, because it has lost meaning from its universe. Bertrand Russell says evolution is a long, wearisome story with a poor point, like a tedious anecdote related by a doddering old gentleman. "I think the external world may be an illusion; but if it exists, it consists of events [that are] short, small, and haphazard."

Scientific humanism, thinking it needed no Savior except itself, has found itself disillusioned and full of despair. Wood comments, "Scientific humanism is fundamentally bankrupt. It can sustain neither faith in science, nor our hopes for mankind." If you want to see the necessity of our having a Savior, do not look at the down-and-outs in the gutter, but look at the finest intellectual flower of our race who are at the end of their resources, sad and dismayed. Christ is necessary for us all, not merely for the degraded.

Jesus Christ saves His people from the sins of despair and gloom because He saves us from ourselves. We know nothing of gloom, or dismay, or discouragement, and if you ask us why, we point to Christ. That is all. But that is enough.

O Christ, You are my cure for gloom. For in You I find a central gladness. I thank You. Amen.

WIDE AND NARROW

Enter through the narrow gate. For wide is the gate and broad is the road that leads to destruction, and many enter through it. But small is the gate and narrow the road that leads to life, and only a few find it. (Matt. 7:13-14)

A great fear in the minds of many is to be considered "narrow." This holds them back from a complete freedom in Christ.

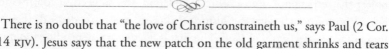

There is no doubt that "the love of Christ constraineth us," says Paul (2 Cor. 5:14 KJV). Jesus says that the new patch on the old garment shrinks and tears the old. There is a sense in which the Christian does pull and tear relationships and situations with a very definite shrinking tendency. Christ keeps us from doing many things we otherwise would do.

But that is only one phase of the truth. Jesus, at the very time He mentions the shrinking, also says the new life within you will be like expanding wine, which will constantly need new wineskins.

Christian are at once the narrowest and broadest of people. They become people of one Book and one Person. And yet "all things are yours"(1 Cor. 3:21), so they break all bonds and barriers. One compass point is on Christ while the other sweeps the horizon. To sweep the horizon without having an anchor on Christ turns out to be Theosophy. To hold one point on Christ without sweeping the horizon turns out to be narrow conservatism. To have both an anchor point and an all-inclusiveness is to be a Christian. If you belong to Christ, then all things are yours—you are at once the narrowest and the broadest person in the world!

O Christ, I cling to You, and now I am free to walk the earth. I thank You for this bondage-freedom. Amen.

EXPERIENCE AND REVELATION

We proclaim to you what we have seen and heard, so that you also may have fellowship with us. And our fellowship is with the Father and with his Son, Jesus Christ. We write this to make our joy complete. (1 John 1:3-4)

As we have talked about experience during our pilgrimage, some would object that experience is an unsure foundation, too subjective, too mystical, bound up too much with the historical process. We must depend, they say, upon the objective Word of God. The first is fluctuating, depending too much on emotional states; the latter is abiding and sure.

There is something in this objection and we must listen to it. But it is only a corrective, not the full truth. It seems that the full truth lies in both experience and revelation. The passage about the Emmaus disciples puts them together: "Then the two told what had happened on the way"—experience— "and how Jesus was recognized by them when he broke the bread"—revelation (Luke 24:35).

They told how the living Christ was with them and how their hearts burned within them as He spoke to them on the road. To discount that is to discount an authentic meeting with Christ that is individual, personal, intimate, life-changing. We therefore make no apology for experience. Christ is in that experience just as definitely as He is in the objective revelation. To repudiate experience, or to minimize it, is to repudiate this living Christ of experience.

At the same time we must not minimize the objective revelation. Jesus does speak through the Word, and that revelation is redemptive. Experience needs constantly to be corrected by this objective revelation. To take one or the other is to impoverish each. We need both. When we take both, we become people of the burning heart *and* of the constantly illuminated soul. Then we are safe— and saved!

O living God, live within me day by day in intimate experience, and then may I listen to Your voice through Your Word in humble obedience. Amen.

JESUS SAVES FROM LAZINESS

As a door swings back and forth on its hinges, so the lazy person turns over in bed. Lazy people take food in their hand but don't even lift it to their mouth. Lazy people consider themselves smarter than seven wise counselors. (Prov. 26:14-16†)

Even while we were with you, we gave you this command: "Those unwilling to work will not get to eat." (2 Thess. 3:10†)

We need to be saved from inertia, lack of ambition, and noncreativeness. The soul must be re-energized, enkindled, made alive and fruitful.

Christ does that very thing. Said some Hindus in regard to a certain Christian, "By his energy and happiness we know he has found God." The soul has now "a clean joy"—a joy that does not produce counter-currents of disquiet as some joys do; instead, there is a sense of rhythm and harmony and therefore of fruitful energy. The soul is not wasted on the lesser issues of life. It is focused.

When the disciples said to Jesus, "But Rabbi, a short while ago the Jews tried to stone you, and yet you are going back there?" Jesus answered, "Are there not twelve hours of daylight?" (John 11:8-9). It was not a question of what the Jewish leaders would do or not do; He must complete His task.

What a sense of inward drive is found in these words! The redemptive life within Him must give vent to itself in spite of threats or obstacles. The life of Christ within us breaks up inertia. "Jesus disturbs my complacency," said a sincere Indian youth. "He becomes the Conscience of my conscience," said another. And because of this there can be no wasting of time.

A sixty-year-old society lady complained of lack of ambition, staleness, and inertia. Christ came into her life, and immediately her soul was energized, so much so that she wrote a book—her first—which went into a number of editions and met the spiritual need of many. Christ gave her a second wind.

When we are in fellowship with this renewing, life-giving Christ, we gain a sense of abounding energy.

O Christ, I ask You that today I may be saved from all lethargy, all dodging of responsibility; may I be really alive—and alive in worthwhile things. Amen.

SALVATION TO THE EXTREME

You have been given fullness in Christ, who is the head over every power and authority. (Col. 2:10)

Therefore He is also able to save to the uttermost those who come to God through Him, since He always lives to make intercession for them. (Heb. 7:25 NKJV)

I can never again be a pessimist. Yes, there are enough hard, brutal facts to warrant pessimism if you take your eyes off Christ. But with my eyes on Him, my pessimism is cured. Here is adequacy—here is power. Of course that power can only be released if we activate it by a complete abandon to His will. But given that, anything can happen.

I have social hope amid the hopelessness around me. For as we discover the larger meaning of sin—as we discover that the central social sin is organizing our life on the unchristian principle of selfish competition even though cooperation is open to us, then we shall turn to Him for a larger salvation. There will be a larger release of larger power in larger realms. Wishful thinking? So be it! I would rather wishfully think toward faith than toward collapse.

The Scripture assures us that "He is also able to save to the uttermost." In that word I see provision for every one of my personal sins and for every one of the social sins of this and succeeding ages. We have seen Christ in the cramping, imprisoning framework of an order based on ruthless competition, and we have wondered why His power is limited. It is bound to be. But put Him in the framework of a cooperative order, and His full power can be loosed. He will then save us to the uttermost because we will allow Him to the uttermost. He will indeed do what the angel said before His birth, which was to save us from our sins.

Christ of the Almighty Arm, work today in my life in saving me from my sins, and in helping me to save society from our sins. Amen.

"YOUR HOUR"..."MY TIME"

Then Jesus said to the chief priests, the officers of the temple guard, and the elders, who had come for him.... "Every day I was with you in the temple courts, and you did not lay a hand on me. But this is your hour—when darkness reigns." (Luke 22:52-53)

But when the right time came, God sent his Son, born of a woman, subject to the law. God sent him to buy freedom for us who were slaves to the law, so that he could adopt us as his very own children. (Gal. 4:4-5†)

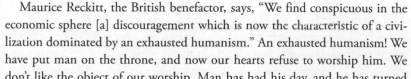

Maurice Reckitt, the British benefactor, says, "We find conspicuous in the economic sphere [a] discouragement which is now the characteristic of a civilization dominated by an exhausted humanism." An exhausted humanism! We have put man on the throne, and now our hearts refuse to worship him. We don't like the object of our worship. Man has had his day, and he has turned it to darkness. As Jesus said to the mob in the Garden, the best they could do with their hour was to turn it into midnight. These words can be used of this day of humanism.

Meanwhile, Jesus used another phrase about His mission to earth: "My time" (see John 2:4; 7:6-8). While His enemies' "hour" brought darkness, His "time" revealed light, love, and healing. He sacrificed Himself, and thereby universalized His impact. Through the death they inflicted upon Him, He brought life to all. He was master even when most passive. He conquered even when He was most conquered. He saved even when He could not save Himself.

Then and now, He is the vibrant Christ. His "time" will yet come. The "hour" of exhausted humanity is drawing to a close; the "time" of the inexhaustible God-Man will dawn. It is here at our door. Some have already taken Him and know His power.

The "hour" of deified, defeated man is brief. The "time" of the undefeated God-Man is eternal. We belong to that eternal, and we will not be dismayed at this "hour." We rejoice in a victory that now is, and is to come.

O Christ, we thank You that we belong to the inexhaustible. Help us to draw heavily upon it today. Amen.

E. STANLEY JONES | 357

"AMID ALL THESE THINGS"

Who shall separate us from Christ's love? Shall affliction or distress, persecution or hunger, nakedness or danger or the sword? As it is written, 'FOR THY SAKE WE ARE BEING KILLED ALL DAY LONG. WE ARE COUNTED AS SHEEP FOR SLAUGHTER.' Yet in all this we are more than conquerors through Him who has loved us. (Rom. 8:35-37 WEYMOUTH)

If I were to choose a Scripture to sum up what I have been trying to say during this year's quest, it would be this one. It combines an intense realism with an amazing assertion of victorious optimism. There is no ignoring of the difficulties that confront us. The writer is open-eyed and frank to say, "Yes, I see the difficulties that come from distress, persecution, hunger, nakedness, danger of the sword, from death, from life, from things present, from the future—and yet, amid all these things we are more than conquerors." He takes in all the facts and yet asserts the central fact of victory.

Note that word "amid." The test of any system is not what it does with the spiritual life, but with the material—"all these things." What is its relationship with things? Does its spirituality include the material?

The Vedantist [Hindu] philosopher's phrase is, "Beyond all these things." The Muslim says, "Accommodation to all things." The Buddhist says, "Disillusionment with all these things." The ordinary Hindu phrase is, "*Maya* [illusion] of all these things." The Communist says, "Through all these things." The materialist says, "By all these things." But the Christian's phrase is, "Amid all these things." That word depicts relationship to, and yet not identification with, all these things. It shows realistic contact, and yet inward transcendence.

And that is exactly the relationship we need. We must not ignore "these things," nor must we be blinded by them. For while we are dependent every moment on matter, nevertheless as Jesus taught us, "Is not life more important than food?" (Matt. 6:25).

O Christ, make me more than a conqueror amid all these things. May I know how to be at home in the world and yet not at home—as You were. Amen.

COUNTERING EVIL WITH GOOD

Therefore put on the full armor of God, so that when the day of evil comes, you may be able to stand your ground, and after you have done everything, to stand. (Eph. 6:13)

Our battle is an embodied battle, so the victory must be an embodied victory. Our spirituality must be shown in relationship to material things, or it is not spirituality. A person is more spiritual who is spiritual through matter than the one who tries to be spiritual apart from matter. So "amid all these things" we must be conquerors.

But how can we do so when so many of our social problems have not yet been solved and we cannot solve them personally? We can acknowledge that the full victory is not here, but our faces and our powers are set in the right direction and dedicated to that end.

In the meantime we can start a counter-good against every evil. When evils came upon Jesus, He did not dodge them, nor bear them, but He started an opposite impulse. Through His crucifixion He started the counter-good of redemption. When evil came upon Him, He loosed forces for the very destruction of that evil. When hate becomes bitter against us, we can start the counter-good of reconciling love. If poverty is our lot, we can start the counter-good of a regal spirit amid rags. If death takes our loved ones, we can start the counter-good of a living hope amid it all.

If we live amid turmoil and clash, we can start the counter-good of a peaceful mind, an unperturbed calm. If we live in an unfriendly world, we can start the counter-good of a charitable spirit.

"Why, these Christians love each other even before they are acquainted," complained an early enemy of Christianity. They had started the counter-good of reconciling love that transcended class. Every evil that comes upon Christians can make us produce a counter-offensive of victorious love.

O Christ, You turn our hearts to the mighty offensive. Help us this day in every situation to whisper to ourselves and You, "More than conquerors." Amen.

THE SIGN IS A BABY

The angel said to them... "This will be a sign to you: You will find a baby wrapped in cloths and lying in a manger." (Luke 2:10, 12)

The Word became flesh and made his dwelling among us. We have seen his glory, the glory of the One and Only, who came from the Father, full of grace and truth. (John 1:14)

On the first Christmas morning, a sign was announced. The Baby was a fact, an embodied fact. This is the key to the whole of Christianity.

India would have said, "You will find a mystic light that will be the sign." China would have said, "You will find a correct code of morality." Greece would have said, "You will find a philosophical concept." But the gospel said, "You will find a baby." The mystic light, the correct code, the philosophical conception, and much, much more came together in an embodied Person.

He became the reconciling place where opposites met. He was the meeting place of God and people. We the aspiring and God the inspiring meet in Him. Heaven and earth came together and are forever reconciled. The material and the spiritual, after their long divorce, have in Him found their reconciliation. The natural and the supernatural blend into one in His life—you cannot tell where one ends and the other begins. The passive and the militant are so united in Him that He is militantly passive and passively militant. The gentle qualities of womanhood and the sterner qualities of manhood so mingle that both men and women see Him as their ideal. The activism of the West and the meditative passivism of the East come together in Him and are forever reconciled. The new individual, born from above, and the new society—the kingdom of God on earth—are both offered to us in Him. The sign is a fact. And so it had to be.

A weeping child would not be satisfied with the mere idea of motherhood— it wants a mother! We cannot be satisfied with the idea of salvation—we need a Savior!

O Christ, since the sign must be an embodied fact, help me this day to embody victorious living, and may this be true in my total life. Amen.

THE FACTOR OF *MORE*

If you love only those who love you, what reward is there for that? Even corrupt tax collectors do that much. If you are kind only to your friends, how are you different from anyone else? Even pagans do that. (Matt. 5:46-47†)

When Romans 8:37 declares that "we are more than conquerors through him who loved us," the word *more* stands out with peculiar force. It is a window-word that lets us see into the inexhaustible nature of our resources and the unlimited development before us. This "plus" is characteristic of the gospel. It allows us to emerge beyond the ordinary level in goodness, in achievement, in joy, in radiant living. It is what gives survival value to the Christian.

This extra power that Christians have at their disposal keeps them from breaking when everything is breaking around them. It keeps them hopeful amid hopelessness, radiant amid the shadows, morally able amid surrounding moral collapse. In the race of life, the extra resources we find in Christ make us a moral winner. Since these extra resources were at the disciples' disposal, Jesus expected them to excel, to surpass the rest of society. He expected them to do more because they had more.

The first testimony I ever gave in public after conversion was this: "There is only one thing better than faith, and that is more faith—and I want more." One touch, and my soul was afire for more. Such inward passion should be an eternal thing. Not dissatisfied, but forever unsatisfied!

This inward cry for more is met by God's offer of a perpetual more. Thus there is no limit to what the Christian might be and do. Professor William James says, "The potentialities of the human soul for development are unfathomable." They are if one is in contact with unfathomable Resources.

O Christ of the limitless love, take away the limitations from my love. Put me under the spell of the "more." Amen.

FAITH'S OFFSPRING

This is my prayer: that your love may abound more and more in knowledge and depth of insight, so that you may be able to discern what is best and may be pure and blameless until the day of Christ, filled with the fruit of righteousness that comes through Jesus Christ—to the glory and praise of God. (Phil. 1:9-11)

One professor states that the Christian faith has had an ongoing role in various arts of everyday life, contributing vitality and richness. American academic Henry P. Van Dusen says: "Christianity has borne one after another of the arts—not only music and painting and sculpture and drama and architecture, but also dancing, legislation, science, philosophy, moral control; has given them birth and matured them through their critical infancy.... Hospitals, schools, colleges, institutions for the unfortunate and the outcast, general philanthropy all had their birth within the life of the Church" (*God in These Times,* p. 145). These and many other things, such as prison reforms, the abolition of slavery, improved conditions of labor, and movements for world peace were the result of Christian parentage. A spiritual fertility is within the gospel of Christ.

And now victorious living is under a new test. Does it have enough power to give birth to a new social order? This is the demand now laid on us. If it can show spiritual productivity here, it will become the mother of a new world.

We who are launching out into victorious living must be so alive that new movements, new initiatives, new impulses, and new lives follow as a manifestation of the creative spirit within us. We are more than conquerors because we not only conquer in our own battle, but we bring forth movements that help other people to conquer.

O Christ, may Your power produce in me today some life-giving movement, however small. Amen.

STRETCHING THE VOCABULARY

Thanks be to God for his indescribable gift! (2 Cor. 9:15)

All who are victorious will inherit all these blessings, and I will be their God, and they will be my children. (Rev. 21:7†)

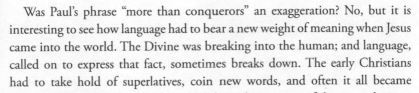

Was Paul's phrase "more than conquerors" an exaggeration? No, but it is interesting to see how language had to bear a new weight of meaning when Jesus came into the world. The Divine was breaking into the human; and language, called on to express that fact, sometimes breaks down. The early Christians had to take hold of superlatives, coin new words, and often it all became overwhelming. The dictionary couldn't bear the pressure of this new, glorious, effervescent life. The new wine had to be put not only into the new wineskins of new organizations and institutions, but also into the new wineskins of a new vocabulary. For here was a fresh, new set of facts.

"More than conquerors"—what does it mean? Some of the African tribes believe that when one man conquers another, the strength of the conquered passes into the conqueror. That is what happens spiritually. When you conquer an evil through the power of Christ, new strength passes into you in two ways. First, it establishes the habit of victory within you and makes the next battle easier. This means that the more you conquer, the more you can conquer. Goodness becomes a habit and hence the normal attitude toward life. The grooves are cut within our nerve tissues so that life flows naturally in the direction of victory.

Second, by conquering you are able to pass on to others that victory. But in passing it on, it becomes more fixed within yourself. So in a double way you are more than a conqueror.

O Christ, we thank You that we are bursting into freedom—freedom from fear of failure and from the fear of future contingencies. For You are getting into our blood and nerve tissue. Amen.

OUR BASIS FOR CONQUEST

You have been given fullness in Christ, who is the head over every power and authority. (Col. 2:10)

The spirit which God has given us is not a spirit of cowardice, but one of power and of love and of sound judgment. (2 Tim. 1:7 WEYMOUTH)

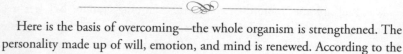

Here is the basis of overcoming—the whole organism is strengthened. The personality made up of will, emotion, and mind is renewed. According to the 2 Timothy verse, there is "power" for the will, "love" for the emotion, and "sound judgment" for the mind. By renewing the total life, the spirit of fear is cast out.

You cannot get rid of fear by telling the fears to depart. They will not. They will depart only as they are cast out by some positive influence that possesses you, thereby making these fears absurd. This positive influence is the spirit of power, of love, and of sound judgment—in other words, the Spirit of Christ working in the depths of your being.

The reasons for fear are rooted in one or more of these: (1) A sense of being weak in the will, a feeling that we are morally inadequate for life. Life is too much for us. It demands more than we have to give. (2) A lack of love. We do not love people, so we are afraid of them; we do not love God supremely, so we are uncomfortable at the thought of Him; we do not love His will, so are afraid of what He will ask us to do; we do not love life, so we are afraid of it. (3) We feel helpless and confused, for our minds lack a sound, unified judgment. We have no key in our hands that fits the problem of human living, so we fear because of intellectual inadequacy.

But now the whole being is brought under a unified control—the Spirit of Christ. That means power for the will, love for the emotions, and sound judgment for the mind. It is Life's answer to inadequate life.

O Christ, I can overcome anything outside of me if You possess everything inside of me. Take it all. Amen.

THE BASIS OF OUR CERTAINTY

"Surely God is my salvation; I will trust and not be afraid. The LORD, the LORD, is my strength and my song; he has become my salvation." With joy you will draw water from the wells of salvation. (Isa. 12:2-3)

I hope a deep spiritual certainty has grown up during our quest this year. We must now say a final word about that certainty and its basis.

In Hebrews 2:3-4 we read, "This, after having first of all been announced by the Lord Himself, had its truth made sure to us by those who heard Him, while God corroborated their testimony by…gifts of the Holy Spirit distributed in accordance with His own will" (WEYMOUTH).

There are three things in this passage: (1) the historic—"announced by the Lord Himself"; (2) the experimental—"corroborated by the gifts of the Holy Spirit"; (3) the collective witness—"made sure to us by those who heard." It is interesting that the Christian church has often fastened on one or another of these factors as the basis of certainty and place of authority in Christianity. Many Protestants have said the place of authority is the infallible Bible—the historical. Other Protestants have made the basis of authority an infallible Christian experience—the experimental. Roman Catholics have made the infallible Church the basis of authority—the collective witness.

The true basis of authority is at the junction of the three. (1) The historical—in Jesus a norm has been established in history that becomes the touchstone of all life. (2) But that Life passes from the historical into the experimental as the Jesus of history becomes the Christ of experience. We do not only remember Christ, we realize Him. (3) But that personal experience may be a hallucination if we remain alone. It must be tried on a widespread scale and corroborated.

In fact, it is. People of all ages and all parts of the globe give a unanimous witness that it works. The merger of the historical, the experimental, and the collective witness, all saying the same thing, gives a certainty far beyond any one taken alone.

O Christ, I rejoice in this certainty. Help me to live worthy of it. Amen.

THE FIXED ABODE

In whom, you also are being built up together to become a fixed abode for God through the Spirit. (Eph. 2:22 WEYMOUTH)

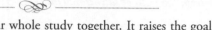

This last passage sums up our whole study together. It raises the goal of a fixed abode for God, who is not the dim, fugitive unknown, but God the real, the intimate, the permanent. And how will this goal be reached? By being "built up together."

Finding God, the Spirit, is an individual thing, but it is also deeply collective. We cannot expect the permanent residence of God unless we are built up together. Only a fellowship that transcends race and class and color can be the fixed abode of God. Up to now we have asked Him to abide in a compartmentalized society and in a divided heart. It cannot be.

When Moses was about to build the Tabernacle, he was given a vision, and the Voice said, "Make this tabernacle and all its furnishings exactly like the pattern I will show you" (Exod. 25:9). He did. Then the account says, "So Moses finished the work. Then…the glory of the LORD filled the tabernacle" (Exod. 40:33-34). When? When he had made all things according to the pattern.

We have seen the pattern—the kingdom of God on earth. It has spoiled us for any other pattern. This is it. We will live and bleed for it, and if necessary die. We will go out and make all things according to that pattern, both within ourselves and in society. And God will take up His fixed abode with us.

We cannot ask Him again to abide in this ramshackle thing we call society, where some children are pinched and starved while others have an unused surplus, where the weaker are exploited by the stronger, and injustice is deeply imbedded. No, we will be built together, where the sufferings of one are the sufferings of all, and where the gifts of God are shared with all the children. Into that holy tabernacle of humanity we can ask Him to come—and He will!

O God, our Father, we cease our divisions within ourselves and in society, asking You to take up Your fixed abode with us. We will do our part. Amen.

NOTES

NOTES